ECHOES OF JESUS
IN THE FIRST EPISTLE OF PETER

Echoes of Jesus
in the First Epistle of Peter

TIMOTHY E. MILLER

◆PICKWICK *Publications* · Eugene, Oregon

ECHOES OF JESUS IN THE FIRST EPISTLE OF PETER

Copyright © 2022 Timothy E. Miller. All rights reserved. Except for brief quotations in critical publications or reviews, no part of this book may be reproduced in any manner without prior written permission from the publisher. Write: Permissions, Wipf and Stock Publishers, 199 W. 8th Ave., Suite 3, Eugene, OR 97401.

Pickwick Publications
An Imprint of Wipf and Stock Publishers
199 W. 8th Ave., Suite 3
Eugene, OR 97401

www.wipfandstock.com

PAPERBACK ISBN: 978-1-6667-3337-2
HARDCOVER ISBN: 978-1-6667-2796-8
EBOOK ISBN: 978-1-6667-2797-5

Cataloguing-in-Publication data:

Names: Miller, Timothy E., author.
Title: Echoes of Jesus in the First Epistle of Peter / by Timothy E. Miller.
Description: Eugene, OR: Pickwick Publications, 2022 | Includes bibliographical references.
Identifiers: ISBN 978-1-6667-3337-2 (paperback) | ISBN 978-1-6667-2796-8 (hardcover) | ISBN 978-1-6667-2797-5 (ebook)
Subjects: LCSH: Bible. Peter, 1st—Criticism, interpretation, etc. | Jesus Christ. | Bible. Gospels—Criticism, interpretation, etc.
Classification: BS2795 M55 2022 (paperback) | BS2795 (ebook)

VERSION NUMBER 030222

All Scripture quotations are from the New Revised Standard Version Bible, copyright © 1989 National Council of the Churches of Christ in the United States of America. Used by permission. All rights reserved worldwide.

For David and Deborah Miller,
Faithful Parents

Contents

List of Tables | xi
Acknowledgments | xiii

1 Introduction | 1

2 History of Scholarship | 4
    E. G. Selwyn | 4
    Ceslas Spicq | 6
    Robert H. Gundry and Ernest Best | 7
    John H. Elliott | 12
    Gerhard Maier | 13
    Rainer Metzner | 15
    Theron K. Wong | 16
    Summary of the State of the Research | 18

3 Assumptions, Criteria, and Method | 24
    Availability and Authenticity of the Jesus Tradition | 24
        Availability of the Jesus Tradition | 25
        Authenticity of the Jesus Tradition | 28
    Intertextuality: Location, Definition, and Criteria | 31
        Intertextuality: Location | 32
        Intertextuality: Definitions | 35
        Intertextuality: Criteria | 44
        Intertextuality: Frustration and Opportunity | 55
        Intertextuality: Expectations | 56
    Method for Interpreting Jesus' Words in 1 Peter | 60

4 First Peter 1:1–2 | 62
    Exegetical Considerations | 63
        The Audience | 63
        The Third Preposition | 64

The Words of Jesus and 1 Peter 1:1–2 | 66
　　　　　1 Peter 1:2 and Mark 14:23; Matthew 26:28; Luke 22:20b | 66
　　　　　1 Peter 1:2 and Matthew 28:18–20 | 69
　　　Conclusion to 1 Peter 1:1–2 | 71

5 First Peter 1:3–12 | 73
　　1 Peter 1:3–5 | 74
　　　　1 Peter 1:3 and John 3:3–7 | 75
　　　　1 Peter 1:4 and Luke 12:33; Matthew 6:20 | 80
　　1 Peter 1:6–9 | 84
　　　　1 Peter 1:6 and Matthew 5:10–12; Luke 6:22–23 | 85
　　　　1 Peter 1:8 and John 20:29 | 88
　　1 Peter 1:10–12 | 90
　　　　1 Peter 1:10 and Matthew 13:16–17; Luke 10:23–24 | 91
　　　　1 Peter 1:11 and Luke 24:25–27 | 95
　　Conclusion to 1 Peter 1:3–12 | 97

6 First Peter 1:13—2:10 | 100
　　1 Peter 1:13–16 | 102
　　1 Peter 1:17–21 | 106
　　　　1 Peter 1:17 and Matthew 6:9; Luke 11:2 | 108
　　　　1 Peter 1:18 and Mark 10:45; Matthew 20:28 | 110
　　1 Peter 1:22–25 | 113
　　　　1 Peter 1:22 and John 13:34–35; 15:12 | 115
　　　　1 Peter 1:23–25 and the Parable of the Sower (Mark 4:3–20; Matt 13:1–23; Luke 8:4–15) | 119
　　1 Peter 2:1–3 | 121
　　1 Peter 2:4–10 | 124
　　Conclusion to 1 Peter 1:13—2:10 | 133

7 First Peter 2:11—3:7 | 135
　　1 Peter 2:11–12 | 136
　　1 Peter 2:13–17 | 140
　　1 Peter 2:18–25 | 146
　　　　1 Peter 2:18–21 and Luke 6:32–35 | 147
　　　　1 Peter 2:25 and John 10:11–18 | 153
　　1 Peter 3:1–7 | 157
　　Conclusion to 1 Peter 2:11—3:7 | 158

8 First Peter 3:8—4:11 | 161
　　1 Peter 3:8–12 | 162
　　1 Peter 3:13–17 | 169

  1 Peter 3:14 and Matthew 5:10; Luke 6:22 | 171
  1 Peter 3:14 and Matthew 10:26-28 | 174
  1 Peter 3:16 and Luke 6:28 | 176
  1 Peter 3:13-17 and Luke 21:12-19 | 177
 1 Peter 3:18-22 | 181
 1 Peter 4:1-6 | 186
 1 Peter 4:7-11 | 188
  1 Peter 4:7-8 and Jesus' Eschatological Teaching | 189
  1 Peter 4:10 and Luke 12:42-48 | 191
 Conclusion to 1 Peter 3:8—4:11 | 194

9 First Peter 4:12—5:14 | 196
 1 Peter 4:12-19 | 196
  1 Peter 4:13-14 and Matthew 5:10-12; Luke 6:22-23 | 197
  1 Peter 4:14 and Luke 12:10-12; Mark 13:11; Matthew 10:20 | 201
 1 Peter 5:1-5 | 203
  1 Peter 5:2-4 and John 21:15-17 | 205
  1 Peter 5:2-4 and Luke 22:25-30; Mark 10:42-45; Matthew 20:25-28 | 207
  1 Peter 5:5 and John 13:1-17 | 211
 1 Peter 5:6-11 | 213
  1 Peter 5:6 and Matthew 23:12; Luke 14:11 (cf. Lk 18:14) | 215
  1 Peter 5:7 and Matthew 6:25-34; Luke 12:22-31 | 217
  1 Peter 5:8-9a and Luke 22:31-32 | 220
 1 Peter 5:12-14 | 224
 Conclusion to 1 Peter 4:12—5:14 | 224

10 Summary and Conclusions | 226
 Tables of Research | 226
 Implications of the Research | 234
  Authorship | 235
  Gospel Affinity | 235
  Peter's Rhetorical Use of Jesus' Words | 237
 Suggestions for Future Research | 240

Appendix: Proposed Parallels | 243
 Parallels Organized by Author | 247

Bibliography | 259

Tables

Figure 3.1: Measures for Intertextual References | 37

Table 4.1: 1 Peter 1:2 and Mark 14:23; Matthew 26:28; Luke 22:20b | 67

Table 4.2: 1 Peter 1:2 and Matthew 28:19–20 | 69

Table 5.1: 1 Peter 1:3 and John 3:3 | 75

Table 5.2: 1 Peter 1:4 and Luke 12:33b; Matthew 6:20 | 81

Table 5.3: 1 Peter 1:6 and Matthew 5:10–12; Luke 6:22–23 | 85

Table 5.4: 1 Peter 1:8 and John 20:29 | 88

Table 5.5: 1 Peter 1:10 and Matthew 13:16–17; Luke 10:23–24 | 91

Table 5.6: 1 Peter 1:11 and Luke 24:25–27 | 95

Table 5.7: Intertextual Resonances to *Dominical Logia* in 1 Peter 1:3–12 | 98

Table 6.1: 1 Peter 1:13 and Luke 12:35, 45 | 102

Table 6.2: 1 Peter 1:17 and Matthew 6:9; Luke 11:2 | 108

Table 6.3: 1 Peter 1:18 and Mark 10:45; Matthew 20:28 | 110

Table 6.4: 1 Peter 1:22 and John 13:34–35; 15:12 | 115

Table 6.5: 1 Peter 2:3 and Luke 6:35 | 122

Table 6.6: 1 Peter 2:7–8 and Mark 12:10, 11; Matthew 21:42, 43; Luke 20:17, 18 | 127

Table 6.7: Intertextual Resonances to *Dominical Logia* in 1 Peter 1:13–2:10 | 133

Table 7.1: 1 Peter 2:12 and Matthew 5:16 | 137

Table 7.2: 1 Peter 2:13–17 and Matthew 17:25–27 (cf. Matt 22:21) | 141

Table 7.3: 1 Peter 2:18–21 and Luke 6:32–35 | 146

Table 7.4: Common Themes between 1 Peter 2:19–21 and Luke 6:32–35 | 151

Table 7.5: 1 Peter 2:25 and John 10:11–18 | 155

Table 7.6: 1 Peter 3:4 and Matthew 5:5 | 157

Table 7.7: Intertextual Resonances to *Dominical Logia* in 1 Peter 2:11—3:7 | 158

Table 8.1: 1 Peter 3:9a and Luke 6:27–30; Matthew 5:39–44 | 163

Table 8.2: 1 Peter 3:14 and Matthew 5:10; Luke 6:22 | 171

Table 8.3: 1 Peter 3:14 and Matthew 10:26–28 | 174

Table 8.4: 1 Peter 3:16 and Luke 6:28 | 176

Table 8.5: 1 Peter 3:13–15 and Luke 21:12–19 | 178

Table 8.6: 1 Peter 3:22 and Mark 14:62; Matthew 26:64; Luke 22:69 | 184

Table 8.7: 1 Peter 4:10 and Luke 12:42–48 | 192

Table 8.8: Intertextual Resonances to *Dominical Logia* in 1 Peter 3:8—4:11 | 194

Table 9.1: 1 Peter 4:13–14 and Matthew 5:10–12; Luke 6:22–23 | 198

Table 9.2: 1 Peter 4:14 and Luke 12:11–12; Mark 13:11; Matthew 10:20 | 201

Table 9.3: 1 Peter 5:2–4 and John 21:15–17 | 205

Table 9.4: 1 Peter 5:2–4 and Luke 22:25–30; Mark 10:42–45; Matthew 20:25–28 | 208

Table 9.5: 1 Peter 5:6 and Matthew 23:12; Luke 14:11 (cf. 18:14) | 215

Table 9.6: 1 Peter 5:7 and Matthew 6:31–33; Luke 12:22, 29–31 | 217

Table 9.7: 1 Peter 5:8–9a and Luke 22:31–32 | 221

Table 9.8: Intertextual Resonances to *Dominical Logia* in 1 Peter 4:12–5:14 | 224

Table 10.2: Distribution of References to Gospel Traditions in 1 Peter | 234

Table 10.3: Themes of Peter's Dominical Reflections | 237

Table A.1 All Proposed Gospel Parallels | 244

Table A.2: Parallels Proposed by more than One Scholar | 254

Table A.3: Distribution of the Multiple Proposed Parallels within the Gospels | 256

Acknowledgments

THE COMPLETION OF A project like this is never the work of one person. Many hands have made this book possible. I am grateful for my wife, Hannah, who has supported me with love, grace, and companionship. All who know her recognize that she is elegantly adorned with the imperishable beauty of a gentle and quiet spirit, which is in God's sight (as well as her husband's) very precious (1P 3:4). My children, though still young, are a motivation to pursue truth. I desire to be an obedient child of my heavenly Father (1:14), so that they may obey Him as well.

Others more directly influenced this work. Ryan Myer edited the document, not only providing helpful content suggestions, but also helping me avoid grammatical and format issues. Radu Gheorghita and Todd Chipman, were helpful in directing my path, not only through comments on the book, but also by their example of scholarship and excellence. Peter Davids worked tirelessly, providing copious review notes, which challenged me to think harder about my conclusions. Cynthia Long Westfall immensely helped me reshape this work from a dissertation to a stand-alone volume. These servants used their Spirit-given gifts to serve me, as they strove to be good stewards of God's varied grace (4:10). May God receive from their labor glory through Jesus Christ, for "To him belong glory and dominion forever and ever. Amen" (4:11).

1

Introduction

"THE ECHOES OF JESUS," in the title of this work alludes to the groundbreaking scholarship of Richard Hays in mining out the echoes of the Old Testament (OT)[1] in the New Testament (NT).[2] Hays work is largely responsible for the significant uptick in scholarly interest in the function of source texts in biblical studies, referred to by Hays as intertextuality.[3] While Hays was focused primarily on the relation of OT texts to NT texts, Michael Fishbane has spearheaded interest in the use of the OT within the OT, often referred

---

1. While "Old Testament" is not a neutral term, few others are helpful. For instance, the title, Hebrew Scriptures, masks the existence of Aramaic in the text and overlooks the fact that the New Testament (NT) authors frequently use the Septuagint (LXX), the Greek translation of the Hebrew and Aramaic. "Israel's Scriptures" is also a possibility (and it is the title taken by Hays), but the title is unwieldy and may suggest that the scriptures are not the church's scriptures. Thus, I maintain the classic designation, Old Testament, while recognizing its shortcomings. Similarly, I maintain the title New Testament.

2. Hays, *Echoes of Scripture in the Letters of Paul.* More recently Hays has written about echoes of the OT in the Gospels (Hays, *Echoes of Scripture in the Gospels*).

3. Hays defines it as "the imbedding of fragments of an earlier text within a later one" (Hays, *Echoes: Paul,* 14). Significant debate surrounds the term intertextuality, with some claiming that the term cannot be used in the general sense implied by Hays and others. One might think it wise to avoid the term altogether, but Kynes is right in noting that the use of the term is nearly unavoidable (Kynes, *My Psalm Has Turned into Weeping*). This thesis will follow Hays in a general use of the term, while acknowledging that the term is defined in various ways, especially outside biblical studies where it was originally coined by Julia Kristeva. For the original definition of the term, see Kristeva, "Word," 34–61. For a survey of how the term has developed over time, see Alfaro, "Intertextuality," 268–85.

to as inner-biblical exegesis.[4] An area less explored, though rich in potential, is the relation between NT texts and the tradition of Jesus' words in the early church.[5] Hay has rightly noted that "wherever there is a community of readers who hearken to earlier texts as powerful and evocative voices with a claim to be heard in the present, intertextual writing and reading will take place."[6] Accordingly, since this was certainly the case with the early church, there is reason to engage in this study.[7]

A thesis on the use of Jesus Tradition (JT) in the First Epistle of Peter (1P) exists at the crossroads of two areas of scholarship historically overlooked. John Elliott's now famous description of 1P as the "exegetical step-child" of NT scholarship highlights how 1P was historically treated by scholars.[8] Thankfully, due in part to Elliott's own efforts, scholarship on 1P has taken significant steps since the publication of that article.[9] As for the use of JT outside the Gospels, Bauckham has referred to it as "the Cinderella of scholarship," because it has generated relatively few book-length studies. Indeed, Batten and Kloppenborg describe the study of JT in 1P (along with James and 2 Peter) as being "on the periphery of New Testament scholarship."[10]

Like the interest in 1P more broadly, interest in JT in 1P has improved in recent years. This is in part due to the work of Duane Watson and Peter Davids in organizing a *Society of Biblical Literature* program unit dedicated to the use of JT in the letters of James, Peter, and Jude. This unit ran from 2009–14 and resulted in a book on the same topic.[11] Much of the recent research has demonstrated that Bauckham was right when he suggested that epistles like 1P "provide much important evidence about the extent to which Gospel traditions were known and the ways in which they were used

---

4. Fishbane, *Biblical Interpretation in Ancient Israel*.

5. One notable exception is the study by Thompson, titled *Clothed with Christ*. The oral nature of JT in the early church will be considered below, for the influence of a written text on a new text may be different than the influence of an oral tradition on a new text.

6. Hays, *Echoes: Paul*, 15.

7. While "text" primarily references a written document, it can also be used more generally to speak of a body of verbal material. In this sense, a particular oral tradition of Jesus may be called a "text" (see, e.g., Derico, *Oral Tradition and Synoptic Verbal Agreement*, 1–16).

8. Elliott, "Rehabilitation," 243–54.

9. While the following bibliography is now dated, it reveals the significant uptick of interest in 1P: Casurella, *Bibliography of Literature on First Peter*.

10. Batten and Kloppenborg, *James*, 13.

11. Batten and Kloppenborg, *James*.

in the early church before and during the time of writing of the canonical Gospels."[12]

Despite the increased attention of scholarship on 1P and on the JT in epistolary literature, one area at that intersection remains relatively unexplored. Previous studies have not attempted to demonstrate how the JT, particularly the words of Jesus, are used by the author of 1P in the development of the epistle. This is the focus of the present study, which seeks to show how 1P uses the words of Jesus to instruct, encourage, warn, and strengthen the readers.

In order to answer this question, it is necessary to survey the work that has been done on the topic. This will be the purpose of chapter two. The third chapter will address the assumptions made in this study, develop criteria to determine the presence of the JT, and formulate a method to accomplish the stated goal. Once the criteria have been established in the third chapter, chapters four through nine work through 1P according to contextual divisions (1:1–2; 1:3–12; 1:13—2:10; 2:11—3:12; 3:13—4:11; 4:12—5:14), evaluating places where *dominical logia* have been suggested in previous scholarship. Each chapter will end with a summary of how the words of Jesus function within the considered text. Chapter ten, the conclusion, will make comprehensive observations concerning Peter's use of his dominical source throughout the epistle. Following the conclusion, an appendix is included that reveals where scholars have proposed *verba Christi*.

---

12. Bauckham, "Study of Gospel Traditions," 371.

2

History of Scholarship

A FEW NOTABLE WORKS have attempted to identify the use of the JT in 1P, usually in an attempt to establish various historical, theological, and literary conclusions. The following chronological survey of research will highlight the major articles, books, monographs, and dissertations which have contributed to the question of JT in 1P.[1] After this consideration of the state of scholarship, a summary of the trends within scholarship is presented, which will reveal that the present thesis can contribute meaningfully within this scholarly space.

A quick note concerning terminology is necessary. Frequent use of the word "parallel" will be made throughout the literature review. Later in the study, we will make more explicit definitions, but for now *parallel* is used to refer to an unclassified intertextual reference.[2]

E. G. SELWYN

In the *Expository Times* series, *Unsolved New Testament Problems*, E. G. Selwyn addressed the use of JT in 1P in order to answer the question of

---

1. Space prohibits a more extensive consideration of the history of research. Other titles that may have been included here include: Scharfe, *Die petrinische Strömung*; Chase, "Peter"; Foster, *Literary Relations*; Schattenmann, "Little Apocalypse of the Synoptics," 193–98; Brown, "Synoptic Parallels in the Epistles," 27–48; Tenney, "Some Possible Parallels," 370–77; Brox, "Erste Petrusbrief," 183–92; Wilkes, "The Synoptic Tradition in 1 Peter"; Horrell, "Jesus Remembered in 1 Peter?," 151–65; Watson, "Early Jesus Tradition," 123–50.

2. Later classifications include quotation, allusion, echo, or trace (see chapter three).

authorship.³ While others thought the question unimportant to interpretation, Selwyn suggests that several passages "take on a new and more vivid meaning if St. Peter were the author."⁴ These passages concern events of significance in the life of Peter (e.g., the Passion, the Transfiguration). And while Selwyn does not make a list of parallels to the words of Christ in 1P in this article (presumably because he has identified them in his commentary),⁵ he states that there are a "large number of *verba Christi* which can be traced below the surface of the Epistle."⁶

Selwyn offers a series of conclusions about the *verba Christi* in 1P. First, the parallels are mainly Matthean, though many are likely derived from Q (or QQ).⁷ Second, some of the *verba* do not match known Gospel sayings, but instead point to "what one may call 'ear-witness.'"⁸ Finally, Selwyn suggests that the *verba Christi* is a relatively unexplored field, which is wide open to future scholarly consideration.⁹

The core of Selwyn's article derives from his prior commentary on 1P, which contains a protracted attempt to unearth the *verba Christi* in 1P, "which lie below the surface of the epistle, and usually not far below it."¹⁰ Selwyn made the title, *verba Christi*, popular within Petrine scholarship, and he labeled it as such because he believed that Peter was reflecting a collection of the words of Jesus that had achieved ecclesiastical status.¹¹ These collections were, according to Selwyn, numerous, both oral and written, and composed in Greek.¹²

Of significant importance is Selwyn's division of the Synoptic Gospels into two types: *halakhah* and *haggadic*. The former indicate how one ought to live, and would be mainly composed of Jesus' sayings. Matthew's Gospel

---

3. Selwyn, "Unsolved New Testament Problems," 256–58.
4. Selwyn, "Unsolved New Testament Problems," 258.
5. Selwyn, *The First Epistle of St. Peter*.
6. Selwyn, "Unsolved New Testament Problems," 258.
7. Selwyn, "Unsolved New Testament Problems," 258.
8. Selwyn, "Unsolved New Testament Problems," 258. Selwyn may be echoing Fronmüller, who likewise spoke of 1P as containing "references to the sayings of our Lord, which . . . prove him to have been the ear-witness of the words of Jesus" (Fronmüller, *The Epistles General of Peter*, 6).
9. More specifically, he notes that in regard to the verba, "A wide field of study lies open here to scholars, and one which in its early stages requires no great supply of books" (Selwyn, "Unsolved New Testament Problems," 258).
10. Selwyn, *The First Epistle of St. Peter*, 23.
11. Selwyn, *The First Epistle of St. Peter*, 23–24.
12. He also suggests that Antioch would have been the most likely place of origin (Selwyn, *The First Epistle of St. Peter*, 23–24).

and Luke's Gospel follow this tradition, being based on Q, which Selwyn defines as "a collection of Christ's sayings compiled for hortatory purposes."[13] On the other hand, Mark's Gospel was *haggadic* in form, stressing the narrative of Jesus' life. As noted above, Selwyn believes that Peter's epistle agrees with Matthew's Gospel most often, though he suggests this is because it is in Matthew's Gospel "that we find the hortatory material in Q aggregated most markedly into 'blocs' of sermon or discourse."[14] In light of his two-fold categorization, one would expect little similarity between Peter's epistle and Mark's Gospel in reference to Jesus' words, for the *verba Christi* belong to the *halakhah* tradition.[15]

Selwyn's commentary provides abundant parallels between Gospel accounts and the epistle of Peter.[16] But Selwyn is convinced that such relationships are not indicative of the canonical Gospel's priority. Instead, Peter's text concerns sayings which are "not the filiation of materials which ended in the Gospels as the ripe fruit of the genealogical tree, but rather in a number of collateral relationships which present themselves to view before—or largely before—that point is reached."[17] It is for this reason that some have sought to show the reliance of 1P on other NT epistles. But no such relationship has been established, for the answer is more complex, with shared tradition likely. In a lengthy essay following the commentary proper,[18] Selwyn compares the shared tradition between 1P and other epistolary NT literature, often pointing to their shared reliance on prior *verba Christi*.

CESLAS SPICQ

Spicq argues that even though ancient interpreters have recognized the voice of Jesus in 1P, the use of Jesus' words had not been sufficiently analyzed.[19] This article, a companion to his commentary published the same

---

13. Selwyn, *The First Epistle of St. Peter*, 24.

14. Selwyn, *The First Epistle of St. Peter*, 24.

15. Selwyn argues that his two-fold distinction accounts "for the much greater frequency with which we hear echoes of St. Matthew or Q in this Epistle than of St. Mark; for Q and St. Matthew had the same practical interest as our author in *halakhah*, the tradition of how Christ's disciples should behave, whereas St. Mark is concerned rather with *haggada*, the tradition of what happened" (Selwyn, *The First Epistle of St. Peter*, 366–67).

16. See the appendix for a full list.

17. Selwyn, *The First Epistle of St. Peter*, 367–68.

18. Selwyn, *The First Epistle of St. Peter*, 363–488.

19. Spicq, "Ia Petri," 38–39.

year,[20] was written to fill this gap. Spicq's conclusion is stated at the outset of the article: the citations of Jesus' words in 1P reveal that the author was Peter the Apostle, whose recollections are eyewitness testimony. Further, Peter felt the same freedom as the Gospel writers to apply the words of Jesus to various settings.[21] In light of this, 1P is significant among the NT, being the "richest source" of JT in the epistolary literature.[22]

In the article, Spicq presents his argument in three points. First, he offers textual parallels between the epistle and the Gospels, both by referring to specific passages[23] as well as by tracing major themes (e.g., the role of good works, Jesus as Messiah). Second, he highlights the historical parallels between the content of the epistle and the life of the apostle Peter, arguing that such analogies make the apostle the likely author of the work. The final section aligns the speeches in Acts with 1P in order to highlight the similarities and thereby support Peter the Apostle as the author. In sum, Spicq argues that there is a distinct voice of Peter that pervades the epistle. This voice is also heard in the speeches of Acts, and often echoes remembrances of historical events connected to Peter the Apostle.

ROBERT H. GUNDRY AND ERNEST BEST

A significant mountain peak in the history of scholarship on the present issue concerns the debate between Robert Gundry and Ernest Best concerning the significance, scope, and meaning of the JT in 1 Peter. The debate was expressed in three articles, which will be considered chronologically.

In the first article, Gundry follows the steps of Selwyn as he attempts to trace the influence of the *verba Christi* on 1P.[24] He notes that while some have argued that there is little internal evidence for Petrine authorship, he desires to show that the *verba Christi* provide substantial evidence to the contrary. Gundry recognizes that all scholars see extensive use of the *verba*, but he contends that the evidence is more substantial than sometimes assumed. While some references are clear, "others are not so easily detected

---

20. Some of the article is nearly a word for word representation of the commentary. Thus, the article can be viewed as Spicq's attempt to put in one place the theme which he presented in pieces throughout the commentary (Spicq, *Les Épîtres de Saint Pierre*).

21. Spicq, "Ia Petri," 39.

22. Spicq, *Les Épîtres de Saint Pierre*, 17.

23. See the appendix for a full list of his proposed parallels.

24. In this first article, Gundry appears unaware of Ceslas Spicq's work on the issue (Gundry, "'Verba Christi' in I Peter").

when considered in isolation."[25] These can be discerned, however, because Peter often references Jesus' words according to distinct patterns and in line with certain text-blocks from the tradition.[26]

The purpose of Gundry's article is to "ferret out the certain and the probable *verba Christi* in I Peter and then to draw inferences concerning the epistle and concerning the gospel tradition from which the quotations were drawn."[27] Consequently, Gundry provides a substantial amount of parallels between Gospel traditions and 1P.[28] After working through the details of the parallels, Gundry offers a remarkable conclusion:

> The most striking feature about the *verba Christi* in I Peter, however, is that they refer to contexts in the gospels which are specially associated with the Apostle Peter or treat topics that would especially interest the Apostle Peter according to the gospel tradition concerning him. There is, so to speak, a "Petrine pattern" in the *verba Christi* reflected in I Peter.[29]

This pattern, Gundry argues, suggests the authorial authenticity of the letter. Indeed, the results go a step farther, for "Only Petrine authorship of the epistle and authenticity of the gospel-passages adequately account for the Petrine pattern of the *verba Christi*. The evidence works both ways, in favour of the Petrine claim of the epistle and in favour of the gospel tradition."[30]

Ernest Best wrote a response article in the same journal a few years later.[31] Despite his clear concern to respond to Gundry's analysis, Best seeks to cast his net wider, responding to what he calls "renewed attempts" to argue for the authorship of the Apostle Peter on the basis of parallels with the Gospel tradition.[32] Due to this broader scope, he brings in many other conversation partners: Scharfe, Chase, Selwyn, Spicq, and Gundry. Best's stated purpose is not to disprove the authorial thesis; instead, he desires to work through the connections between the Gospels and the material in 1P, drawing conclusions only after such an analysis has been made.

---

25. Gundry, "'Verba Christi' in I Peter," 337.

26. Gundry, "'Verba Christi' in I Peter," 337. Unfrotunately, Gundry does not make explicit the criteria by which he judges the presence of JT.

27. Gundry, "'Verba Christi' in I Peter," 337.

28. See the appendix for a full list of his proposed parallels.

29. Gundry, "'Verba Christi' in I Peter," 345.

30. Gundry recognizes that some may claim he has made a circular argument. He responds, "This is not reasoning in a circle. It is the self-consistency we expect from historically reliable material" (Gundry, "'Verba Christi' in I Peter," 350).

31. Best, "I Peter and the Gospel Tradition."

32. Best, "I Peter and the Gospel Tradition," 95.

Before walking through each Gospel, Best offers a few preliminary ideas that guide the work. First, he asserts that if 1P is from Peter the Apostle, one should not expect close verbal similarity between the Gospels and the epistle, for Peter would have presumably made his own translation from Jesus' Aramaic teaching.[33] If there are close verbal similarities, this would suggest dependence on Gospel traditions. Second, if Peter is responsible for the information contained in Mark's Gospel, "we should expect a link between the Epistle and that Gospel."[34] Third, if the epistle reveals dependence on a Lukan form, this would suggest the author knew redacted tradition and would favor non-Petrine authorship.[35] Finally, Best suggests that Peter's use of Jesus' words may be similar to his use of the OT, and since Peter often uses OT passages without clear reference that he is doing so, the same likely applies to his use of JT.[36]

The main body of Best's article considers each of the Gospels individually, seeking to align 1P with each Gospel. His starting point for each text is the parallels argued for by prior commentators. Best concludes that there is no evidence Peter knew the traditions retained in John's Gospel[37] or Mark's Gospel.[38] On the other hand, there is evidence the author knew and used limited traditions from Luke's Gospel[39] and Matthew's Gospel.[40]

Best draws a number of conclusions from his analysis, many of which are of interest in the present study:[41]

---

33. Best, "I Peter and the Gospel Tradition," 95.

34. Best, "I Peter and the Gospel Tradition," 95.

35. Best, "I Peter and the Gospel Tradition," 95–96.

36. "We may expect that if he has access to gospel traditions he will normally introduce them without explicit indication that he is so doing" (Best, "I Peter and the Gospel Tradition," 96).

37. "We see no reason . . . to conclude that the author of 1 Peter knew the tradition of the Gospel of John; this Gospel therefore provides no evidence that Peter wrote 1 Peter" (Best, "I Peter and the Gospel Tradition," 99).

38. "There is consequently no connection between 1 Peter and the gospel tradition enshrined in Mark nor any reason to see the author of 1 Peter as one who was present at the sayings or events recorded in Mark" (Best, "I Peter and the Gospel Tradition," 102).

39. 1:4 (Luke 12:33); 1:13 (Luke 12:35); 2:19–21 (Luke 6:32–36); 3:16 (Luke 6:28); 4:10–11 (Luke 12:42); 4:14 (Luke 6:22); 5:2–4 (Luke 12:32); Best, "I Peter and the Gospel Tradition," 105–6.

40. "Matt. 5:10 and 1 Pet. 3:14; Matt. 5:16 and 1 Pet. 2:12 are the only possible parallels and the case for the latter is relatively strong" (Best, "I Peter and the Gospel Tradition," 111).

41. Best, "I Peter and the Gospel Tradition," 111–12.

1. The tradition used in 1P occurs in blocks, but if Peter the Apostle wrote the text, one would assume a greater diversity of reference.[42]
2. The parallels refer only to Jesus' sayings, not to miracles or parables.
3. There is no special relationship between Mark's Gospel and 1P.
4. The parallels are to developed tradition, not eyewitness remembrance.
5. First Peter uses OT references where sayings of Jesus could have been used.
6. In a few places, a Gospel tradition could have been used but was not.
7. Some parallels indicate 1P's knowledge of the tradition *in Greek*.
8. "There are no necessary references to events or incidents in which Peter was involved."[43]
9. First Peter uses Gospel traditions just as it uses the OT and catechetical material.
10. In light of the above, "There is no reason to conclude that the Apostle Peter wrote 1 Peter."[44]

Four years after Best's article and seven years after Gundry's initial article, Gundry published a response to Best's critique.[45] Gundry argues that while Best's article was "in large measure" devoted to critiquing Gundry's work, the inclusion of others purported parallels (e.g., Scharfe, Spicq, Chase) resulted in a "commendable comprehensiveness of treatment and an unfortunate blurring of the picture so far as the more probable allusions are concerned."[46]

Gundry begins the article by challenging Best's assumptions. Would Peter have made his own translation from the Aramaic as Best suggests? Four points are given in response.[47] First, Peter could have used a translation that had gained traction in the church. Second, an amanuensis may have aligned Peter's remembrances with the tradition current in the church. Third, Jesus may have sometimes spoken in Greek. Finally, the form of the Gospel tradition may have been influenced by Peter, and thus similarity is

---

42. "If the author of 1Peter had been the Apostle Peter we should have expected a more haphazard distribution of the contacts" (Best, "I Peter and the Gospel Tradition," 111).
43. Best, "I Peter and the Gospel Tradition," 112.
44. Best, "I Peter and the Gospel Tradition," 112.
45. Gundry, "Further Verba," 211–32.
46. Gundry, "Further Verba," 211–12.
47. Gundry, "Further Verba," 212.

due to the tradition having been formed initially by Peter's remembrances. The second assumption Gundry questions concerns the relation between Mark's Gospel and 1P. Gundry believes Best has not taken into account "the notable fact that by comparison with other gospels Mark contains little of Jesus' teaching. Allusions to dominical teaching in a Petrine epistle would therefore bear more similarities to the gospels with larger amounts of that teaching."[48]

Gundry highlights what he believes is an inconsistency in Best's argument. Best suggested that if the Apostle was the author, one should not expect verbal similarity, for the apostle would have had to translate from the Aramaic. Nevertheless, throughout the article, Best only allows parallels for passages that show verbal similarity. Gundry indicates that Best's method is better than his theory, for verbal similarity should be evident, even if there exist parallel translations, as the various, independent translations of the Hebrew OT into Greek attest.[49]

The core of the article engages Best's critiques of the proposed parallels. Gundry often returns to a few key themes: Best has mixed probable and improbable parallels, resulting in a negative view of all; Best uses a different, looser standard in allowing parallels in 1 Clement than he does for 1P; and apostles, including Peter, may have been willing to use developed tradition, or may have been the source of the developing tradition.

Having responded to Best's critiques of the proposed parallels, Gundry concludes by reassessing Best's points of conclusion. Most of Best's conclusions are denied by Gundry. For instance, since Gundry recognizes more parallels than Best, he does not agree that the parallels fall only within very limited sections of Matthew's and Luke's Gospel. Further, Best's argument that Peter would have used JT in certain places is countered by Gundry's observation that in "the specific places where Best thinks 1 Pt might have used a dominical saying, every one already does contain such allusions (though they are not all acceptable to Best)!"[50] Other of Best's conclusions are not denied, but are explained. For example, Gundry recognizes that there are fewer obvious connection points between Mark's Gospel and 1P, but he suggests that this is due to the nature of Mark's Gospel, which includes minimal teaching.[51]

---

48. Gundry, "Further Verba," 212.
49. Gundry, "Further Verba," 213.
50. Gundry, "Further Verba," 231.
51. Gundry, "Further Verba," 230.

JOHN H. ELLIOTT

The same year Best published the article considered above,[52] John Elliott wrote about the place of 1P 5:1–5 in the development of church order in the NT.[53] Elliott argues that the language of the passage indicates the use and combination of prior traditions which had not yet been fixed in written form.[54] He highlights seven "points of contact" between the Synoptic Gospels and this passage from Peter,[55] emphasizing the parallels with the "rank dispute" tradition (Mark 10:35–45; Matt 20:20–28; Luke 22:24–27).[56] Further, Elliott speaks of "striking parallels between Jn 21:15–23 and 1 Pet 5:1–5," listing nine such parallels.[57]

These parallels, according to Elliott, "do not indicate any literary dependency of the Synoptics upon 1 Pt or vice versa. They do, however, suggest two other possibilities: Petrine reminiscences or Petrine tradition."[58] Here Elliott evidences familiarity with the Gundry-Best debate. And while he notes that genuine Petrine remembrances must be left open to possibility, Elliott sides with Best, arguing that all that is *necessary* to explain the text (and Gundry's parallels) is that there was a "Petrine tradition."[59] Such a tradition, Elliott argues, would likely have developed and would have been accessible to a Petrine disciple who may have penned 1P.[60]

Elliott furthered developed this perspective in his influential article, "The Rehabilitation of an Exegetical Step-Child: 1 Peter in Recent Research," which highlights the trajectories of scholarship on 1P. In that article, he noted the then-current state of discussion concerning 1P's use of Jesus' words. He did so, however, by summarizing the scholarship in two opposite camps as well as by suggesting his own path forward between these camps:

---

52. While the survey so far has been chronological, this work has been displaced in order for the Best-Gundry debate to be presented together.

53. Elliott, "Ministry and Church Order," 367–91.

54. Elliott, "Ministry and Church Order," 372–73.

55. See the appendix for a full list. Elliott, "Ministry and Church Order," 386.

56. In regard to that dispute, he notes that 1P has affinities to each of the Gospel traditions, even in places where the traditions uniquely differ (Elliott, "Ministry and Church Order," 375).

57. Elliott, "Ministry and Church Order," 383–84.

58. Elliott, "Ministry and Church Order," 387.

59. Elliott's reluctance to see the significant parallels as indicating genuine Petrine remembrances stems from "the structure and style of 1 Pt and the difficulties they pose for Petrine authorship" along with "the type of tradition and manner of its usage in 1 Peter" (Elliott, "Ministry and Church Order," 387n81).

60. Elliott, "Ministry and Church Order," 387–88.

My own position assumes a middle ground between that of Spicq and Gundry, on the one hand, and Best and Brown, on the other. The textual affinities demonstrate only commonality of tradition but not authenticity of either sources or Petrine redaction. However, the prominence of Simon Peter in this tradition and the coalescence of the tradition, especially on discipleship and ministry, in 1 Peter clearly suggest the existence and development of a specific Petrine body of material.[61]

Future scholarship, Elliott suggests, should not focus on authorship, for "literary affinities and the use of tradition cannot provide the main proof for either apostolic, Silvanine, or pseudonymous authorship."[62] Instead, authorship is a secondary issue to the what is clear; namely, there is a Petrine body of material from which the author of 1P drew his source. He concludes, "Ultimately, then, the issue of authorship is subordinate to, and should be seen in the context of, the content and the historical-ecclesiastical context of 1 Peter itself."[63]

GERHARD MAIER

In a volume of essays on the use of JT outside the Gospels, Gerhard Maier contributed an extensive essay on the JT in 1P.[64] In the introduction, Maier highlighted two issues that he believed had so far hindered a proper understanding of the JT in 1P. First, most scholars focused attention on the use of individual sayings, but that left the three substantial short catechisms (1:18–21; 2:21–25; 3:18–22) without explicit discussion. Second, Maier believes the hypothesis that Q is the basis of the JT in 1P has had an inhibiting effect on scholarship.[65] Without explicit argumentation, Maier, citing the work of Gundry, assumes genuine Petrine authorship.

Maier's article is organized in two major parts. The first considers the individual saying parallels between 1P and the Gospel tradition, while the second considers the relation between the short catechisms and the Gospel tradition. Because the exchange between Gundry and Best was the most extensive expression of the individual sayings, Maier uses this as his starting point in the first section. After summarizing four major points of difference

---

61. Elliott, "Rehabilitation," 248.
62. Elliott, "Rehabilitation," 248.
63. Elliott, "Rehabilitation," 248.
64. Maier, "Jesustradition," 85–128.
65. Maier, "Jesustradition," 85.

between Best and Gundry,⁶⁶ Maier considers thirteen passages that were debated between the scholars. Afterward, he considers twelve passages that were not in dispute between Gundry and Best, but that nevertheless may be derive from *dominical logia*.⁶⁷ After his analysis of the twenty-five passages, Maier offers a series of nine conclusions.

1. The frequency of parallels is more than Best allowed.
2. References to *dominical logia* in 1P excludes parables, sign acts, and events.
3. Three blocks of material are discernible: (1) the Sermon on the Mount; (2) eschatological and farewell speeches; (3) passion and resurrection reports.
4. The parallels include surprising amounts of contact with Johannine material.⁶⁸
5. The Christian tradition was established before 1P, and this epistle shows that all four Gospels trace back to approximately equal ancient tradition.
6. In light of the above, there are three options concerning the author: (1) he was an eyewitness, drawing from personal experience; (2) he was dependent on oral tradition or written records, making him equivalent to the Gospel-writers; (3) he was dependent on the canonical Gospels, requiring the epistle to be very late or the Gospels to be very early.
7. In striking difference to the Gospels, Peter never directly quotes Jesus. This follows the pattern of other NT epistolary writers.
8. If one asks why an apostle would use tradition, the answer is that he was a part (and a chief originator) of much of the oral tradition. As part of this group, Peter knew this tradition and had no reason to state it differently, even if he was an eyewitness.⁶⁹
9. First Peter is "saturated" with the words of Jesus, making clear that the *dominical logia* were a "unique authority" for the author.⁷⁰

---

66. The four are as follows: (1) Gundry argues for Petrine authorship, while Best argues against it; (2) Gundry believes 1P refers to both events and sayings, while Best allows only sayings; (3) Gundry allows for twenty parallels, while Best limits it to a third of that amount; (4) Gundry believes there is a connection between 1P and John's Gospel, while Gundry rejects this association (Maier, "Jesustradition," 86).
67. For a list of the parallels suggested by Maier, see the appendix.
68. Maier, "Jesustradition," 103.
69. Maier, "Jesustradition," 104.
70. Maier, "Jesustradition," 105.

The second major section of Maier's article concerns the three short catechisms in 1P (1:18–21; 2:21–25; 3:18–22). He highlights five elements present in these catechisms: Jesus' pre-existence, passion, resurrection, exaltation, and mediation. Each element is best explained, Maier argues, by going back to Jesus' teaching and actions, which provide the source of the shared tradition of the church.

In conclusion to the second section, Maier makes nine additional observations in light of the short catechisms. While each is interesting, the following are important for our purposes.

1. The catechisms are so brief, the narrative had to be previously known.
2. These catechisms are influenced by Jesus' statements.
3. The only explanation for the similarity between 1P and John's Gospel is that Peter knew John's tradition in oral or pre-Gospel form.[71]

RAINER METZNER

Metzner presents a unique argument in the history of this topic. He believes that the letter of 1P was literarily influenced by the Gospel of Matthew. Reliance is revealed in the way the author adapted and interpreted the Matthean Gospel tradition for his audience in a new social and historical situation.[72] Metzner's thesis comes in three major sections. First, he argues that there is evidence of direct historical influence in five passages of 1P. Four are from the Sermon on the Mount (2:12 [Matt 5:16]; 3:9 [Matt 5:38–48]; 3:14 [Matt 5:10]; 4:13 [Matt 5:11–12]), while the fifth passage concerns the Temptation of Christ (5:6–9 [Matt 4:1–11]).

The second section of Metzner's work concerns the theological influence of Matthew's Gospel on 1P. The prior section is designed to give further support to this section, for if Peter shows direct reliance on Matthew's Gospel, it should not be surprising to find theological influence as well. Alternatively, if this section is persuasive, it gives further reason to believe the textual arguments from the first section are accurate. Four trajectories of theological influence are explored by Metzner: the image of Peter, ecclesiology, Christology, and eschatology.[73]

The final section of the work argues that early Christian writings of the first two centuries of the church show that Matthew was well known and

---

71. Maier, "Jesustradition," 117.
72. Metzner, *Rezeption des Matthäusevangeliums*, 283.
73. Metzner, *Rezeption des Matthäusevangeliums*, 283.

popular in Rome and Asia Minor.[74] This is significant because, as Metzner argues, it is likely that 1P was produced in Rome and sent to Asia Minor. The significance of this third line of reasoning is only seen when it is considered together with the first two sections. That is, Metzner has attempted to make a three-fold argument for the use of Matthew's Gospel in 1P. Each argument serves to strengthen the others, though if any of the arguments are found to fall short, the entirety of the argument is weakened.

Metzner draws a few conclusions from his research. First, he suggests that the type of reliance demonstrated goes beyond oral tradition and makes direct reliance the likely option.[75] Second, due to such reliance, First Peter is one of the earliest witnesses to the Gospel of Matthew among early Christian witnesses.[76]

THERON K. WONG

In 2008, Theron Wong wrote a dissertation on "The Use of Jesus' Sayings in 1 Peter."[77] As the title suggests, Wong's study is closely aligned with the present study; nevertheless, his focus and conclusions are substantially different from those reached in this study.

Wong rightly recognizes that advancements in intertextuality in recent years have opened the door to the study of JT in 1P once more. His study is an attempt to verify the allusions to the words of Jesus in 1P using more refined categories than those used by those who came before—particularly, Gundry, Best, and Maier. In order to establish a comparative basis for how the author of 1P uses traditional material, Wong engages in two lengthy studies before engaging the question of the use of Jesus' words. First, Wong investigates the way Peter alludes to the OT. Second, he considers how James and 1 Clement allude to Jesus' words. In regard to the first, Wong believes that there may be some overlap between how the author uses the OT and how he uses the JT. In regard to the second, Wong suggests that studying two (somewhat) contemporary letters of 1P will aid modern interpreters in recognizing when Peter alludes to the JT.[78]

---

74. Metzner, *Rezeption des Matthäusevangeliums*, 293.

75. Significantly, he is unsure whether 1P is directly reliant on a written text or whether he has recalled Matthew's Gospel by memory (Metzner, *Rezeption des Matthäusevangeliums*, 274).

76. Metzner, *Rezeption des Matthäusevangeliums*, 283.

77. Wong, "Use of Jesus' Sayings."

78. Wong's chapters contribute little to the fundamental question he investigates. This is due to two factors. First, as Wong himself admits, the difference in text base (use

Having established a basis for how one might expect allusions to work in 1P, Wong investigates seventeen proposed allusions to the JT in 1P. The selection of the parallels is not arbitrary; rather, he investigates only those allusions recognized by at least two of the following three scholars: Gundry, Maier, and Best.[79] The standard of measure to determine the presence of an allusion is that there must be at least one (though preferably two) "*clear corresponding lexical element.*" Further, the allusion should have "smooth integration into the text and a use that is *reasonably* consistent with that in the Gospel settings."[80]

After applying his standard of measure, Wong concludes that there are only seven allusions "strong enough to be defensible."[81] Consequently, Wong allows less allusions to the JT than Best, who even Wong calls "quite pessimistic."[82] Further, while Best suggests the author knew blocks of tradition similar to that found in Luke's Gospel, Wong concludes that the author more likely knew a tradition similar to Matthew's Sermon on the Mount.[83]

---

of a standardized text for OT compared to the oral tradition basis for the JT) is substantially different and leads one to question how the observations in one field can rightly apply to the other. The same can be said in reference to the author's contemporaries; i.e., it is not clear that Peter uses Jesus' words in the same way James and 1 Clement did. Second, the conclusions from these chapters are not significantly used in the chapter on the use of JT in 1P. Indeed, the dissertation focuses on the use of Jesus' words in 1P, but only thirty-seven pages actually considers the potential allusions (less than 20 percent of the dissertation). In sum, in light of the challenges presented above, it seems better to examine the potential parallels at length, which is the approach taken in this study (Wong, "Use of Jesus' Sayings," 16, 135).

79. This results in an investigation of the following seventeen proposed parallels: 1:3, 23; 2:2 (John 3:3, 7); 1:4 (Luke 12:33; Matt 6:20); 1:8 (John 20:29); 1:10–12 (Luke 24:25–27; Matt 13:17); 1:13 (Luke 12:35); 1:22 (John 13:34; 15:12); 2:4 (Mark 12:10; Matt 21:42); 2:12 (Matt 5:16); 2:13–17 (Matt 17:25–27); 2:19–20 (Luke 6:32–35); 3:9 (Luke 6:27–28; Matt 5:39); 3:14 (Matt 5:10); 4:7–8 (Luke 21.31–36); 4:10 (Luke 12:42); 4:13–14 (Luke 6:22; Matt 5:10–11); 5:3–5 (Mark 10:42–45; Luke 22:25–30; Matt 20:20–27); 5:8–9 (Luke 22:31–32).

80. Wong, "Use of Jesus' Sayings," 191. Emphasis added.

81. The following are those seven: 1:8 (John 20:29); 1:13 (Luke 12:35); 2:4 (Mark 12:10; Matt 21:42); 2:12 (Matt 5:16); 2:19–20 (Luke 6:32–35); 3:14 (Matt 5:10); 4:13–14 (Luke 6:22; Matt 5:10–11). Wong, "Use of Jesus' Sayings," 225.

82. Wong, "Use of Jesus' Sayings," 225.

83. "Though a block of tradition might be identified, it is not in Luke but in Matthew's Gospel" (Wong, "Use of Jesus' Sayings," iv, 225).

SUMMARY OF THE STATE OF THE RESEARCH

Much scholarship on the use of JT in 1P has focused on the question of authorship. Some (Scharfe, Chase, Schattenmann, Spicq, Gundry, Tenney, and Maier) have found the JT indicative of genuine apostolic authorship, while others (Jülicher, Soden, Harnack, Best, and Brox) have concluded the opposite.[84] The arguments for apostolic authorship focus on the similarity between the JT in 1P and the analogies 1P uses (Chase), the theological themes of 1P (Spicq), the "ear-witness" nature of references in 1P (Selwyn, Schattenmann), and the historic events and sayings of 1P and their relation to the historic apostle (Gundry). The arguments against apostolic authorship highlight that an apostle would not have cited tradition that occurred in tradition blocks, would not have cited developed tradition, would not know the tradition in Greek, and would have used JT in places where 1P does not.[85]

A third path is offered by John Elliott, who suggests that the question of authorship should not be primary. The evidence of the JT in 1P cannot bear the weight of the authorship question;[86] nevertheless, it does clearly indicate that there is a Petrine tradition. In this light, future research should focus less on who the author was and what the Petrine tradition communicates via the JT.[87] And while Wilkes is personally convinced of apostolic authorship, he likewise suggests that scholars should be able to agree concerning the Petrine tradition of the text and seek to advance scholarly knowledge from that mutually accepted vantage point.

This work will follow this perspective. In addition to the benefits noted by Elliott, such a position also allows us to recognize the point made by Frankemölle—regardless of whether Simon Peter was the author, the biographical details of Peter's life inform the letter.[88] In other words, this work will assume that the writer wrote from the perspective of Peter, and the

---

84. Jülicher, *Introduction to the New Testament*, 210; Soden, *Hand-commentar zum Neuen Testament*, 114; Harnack, *Geschichte der Altchristlichen Litteratur bis Eusebius*, 451.

85. All of these arguments are developed by Best.

86. Achtemeier agrees, noting that "such evidence is most convincing to those who on other grounds assume Simon Peter to be the author." The opposite could be said as well; such evidence is least convincing to those who on other grounds reject Simon Peter as the author (Achtemeier, *1 Peter*, 12n109).

87. Craddock indicates that the issue of authorship has lost importance, for it is clear that "this letter represents the teaching and preaching of Simon Peter and extends that ministry into Asia Minor, whether or not Simon penned it, dictated it, or was the source of the content used by a follower of his" (Craddock, *First and Second Peter*, 13).

88. Frankemölle, *1 Petrusbrief*, 9.

readers were understood to read the text as though from Peter. In embracing this position, we follow Feldmeier who says that since the text indicates Petrine authorship, such a vantage point "must always be taken into account as one reads this work."[89]

A second concern of scholarly attention to JT in 1P has been the question of source; from where does 1P derive its JT? Of course, this question is significantly influenced by the question of authorship, for it is possible that the author's use of JT derives from his historic experiences and does not reflect any other traces of tradition. Nevertheless, even scholars who hold to apostolic authorship suggest traces of other tradition.[90] This is explained in various ways. For Scharfe, the answer seems to be the preeminent place of Peter in the early church as one of the founders of the tradition that would subsequently be recorded in various Gospels.[91] Gundry, likewise, argues that Peter may have been a fountainhead of much of the tradition, and he adds that Peter may have accommodated his own retelling to the popular ways the JT had spread in the early church.[92]

Many early scholars, including Spicq, Selwyn, and Brown, argue that 1P was reflective of the Q tradition.[93] Some recent scholars have not been as committed, for various reasons. Maier questions whether such a document ever existed. And even if it did exist, the vagueness of its content, he argues, has produced an inhibiting effect on discerning the use of JT in 1P.[94] Wilkes, while acknowledging Q as an option, believes the evidence in its favor could also support oral tradition, which he finds more likely.[95] Watson, without explicit argumentation, rejects 1P's use of a written Q source.[96]

The Gospel of Mark has not been seriously considered as a source for 1P's JT, despite the connection between Mark's Gospel and 1P in early church history.[97] Selwyn believes Mark's Gospel was centered on the narra-

---

89. Feldmeier, *The First Letter of Peter*, 51.

90. Schattenmann may be an exception, for he seeks to establish the original content of the tradition recorded in Mark 13 on the basis of Peter's witness. Nevertheless, his essay does not directly address the question at hand.

91. Scharfe, *Die petrinische Strömung*, 183–84.

92. Gundry, "Further Verba," 212.

93. This is not to say that modern interpreters do not hold to Q, for Michaels does. Michaels, *1 Peter*, xli.

94. Maier, "Jesustradition," 119.

95. Wilkes, "The Synoptic Tradition," 92–93.

96. Watson, "Early Jesus Tradition," 151; Watson and Callan, *First and Second Peter*, 13.

97. Varhenhorst notes that only the tradition established by Papias leads interpreters to find connections, since "the texts themselves give no evidence" (Vahrenhorst, *Der Erste Brief Des Petrus*, 41n159).

tive (*haggada*), unlike Matthew and Mark, which focused on Jesus' teaching (*halakhah*). Thus, connections between 1P and Mark, if they exist, would likely be observed through similarity of the development of the Gospel narrative,[98] precisely what some scholars have noted.[99]

Neither Luke's Gospel nor John's Gospel has gained traction as the source of 1P's JT. As for Luke, Best argues that 1P does show awareness of its developed tradition, but only in very limited selections.[100] And while Tenney suggests numerous parallels between John's Gospel and 1P, he argues that these are best explained by common tradition in the church, tradition that the apostles Peter and John likely discussed with one another.

Recently, Rainer Metzner has made a bold proposal that Matthew's Gospel is the source of the JT in 1P. Nevertheless, scholarly reception has not been favorable.[101] Three problems have been emphasized. First, Metzner has not provided sufficient evidence for literary reliance.[102] In Elliott's words, Metzner "has attempted to construct a dependency mountain from a similarity molehill."[103] Second, both Elliott and Davids agree that even the minimal evidence given is unpersuasive.[104] Finally, Metzner shortcuts his argument, not sufficiently establishing the points necessary to defend his position.[105]

---

98. Note should be made of an article by Dodewaard, which was a distillation of from his dissertation in which he attempted to determine the influence of Peter and Paul on Mark's Gospel from linguistic analysis. He concludes that Paul's writing displays few similarities to Mark's Gospel, while Peter's shows much similarity (Dodewaard, "Die Sprachliche Übereinstimmung," 229).

99. Scharfe and Wilkes argued for this thesis as noted above (see also Elliott, "The Roman Provenance," 181–94). Boring, however, argues that 1P "shows no connections to the Gospel of Mark" (Boring, *1 Peter*, 35–36).

100. Charles Bigg, likewise, suggested that Luke's Gospel was the closest relation to 1P of all the Gospels. Nevertheless, he agrees with Soden that 1P evidences allusions that are pre-canonical (Bigg, *Epistles of St. Peter*, 23).

101. Travis Williams described John H. Elliott's review as a "devastating critique" of Metzner's thesis (Williams, *Persecution in 1 Peter*, 24n53; see also Vahrenhorst, *Der Erste Brief Des Petrus*, 42–44).

102. Peter Davids notes, "Unfortunately, Metzner tries to establish his thesis on the basis of five passages in 1 Peter comprising ten verses" (Davids, "Review," 388).

103. Elliott, "Review," 382.

104. Davids notes that most of the material is from the Sermon on the Mount, which scholars have suggested is Q material. As such, a pre-Matthean source is possible, but was not sufficiently ruled out (Davids, "Review," 388; Elliott, "Review," 380–81).

105. For instance, Metzner assumes that 1P is later than the Gospel of Matthew, but he does not argue that it is (Elliott, "Review," 388).

Most modern scholars do not propose that 1P is following any particular written tradition.[106] Since most scholars date 1P around the time that the Gospel traditions were being codified into canonical form,[107] many see 1P as an independent witness of early, primarily oral church tradition—particularly through a Petrine lens.[108] For some, that lens is the lens of an authentic, apostolic witness, while others believe that lens is the lens of an authentic Petrine tradition which had formed in the early church. In either case, 1P offers independent witness of the Gospel tradition in the early church, even if at certain points elements of the other Gospel traditions are evident in 1P. Consequently, 1P should not only be viewed in light of the tradition retained in the Gospels, but the Gospels should be viewed in light of the tradition retained in 1P.[109]

By viewing 1P as an independent witness to early JT, multiple avenues of exploration are opened. First, some have attempted to trace the lineage of this tradition, focusing on its epicenter in Rome (Metzner, Watson, Best).[110] Second, Horrell has attempted to contribute to the study of the Historical Jesus by means of the JT in 1P, an avenue relatively unexplored in Jesus studies. By asking, what picture of Jesus is present in the tradition preserved in 1P, Horrell is suggesting that the material in the four Gospels can be supplemented with the tradition preserved in the Epistles. Third, some scholars are studying the intersection of traditions, seeing how the early JT was merged with OT tradition (Horrell) or Jewish tradition (Watson).

In light of the above summary, there are two lacunas in scholarship on the JT in 1P. First, a surprising gap in the history of research on the JT in 1P is the rarity of formal criteria for discerning the use of JT.[111] Early on, Selwyn

106. See the analysis by Vahrenhorst, who concludes that 1P is not dependent on any NT text (Vahrenhorst, *Der Erste Brief Des Petrus*, 50).

107. First Peter is generally dated between AD 60–80, while the Gospels are generally dated between AD 50–90 (Gundry, *Survey of the New Testament*).

108. As Elliott notes, similarities between 1P and other texts, including the Gospels are "the result not of literary dependency but of a common, varied use of a wide stream of oral and written tradition" (Elliott, *1 Peter*, 28). Leonhard Goppelt agrees, noting that "the ecclesiastical tradition in which I Peter arose traveled the same road of development as did the Synoptic Jesus tradition" (Goppelt, *A Commentary on I Peter*, 34).

109. Some scholars observe that the reliability of Gospel tradition can be strengthened in light of 1P. For example, Gundry suggests 1P gives credibility to the traditions found in the Gospels (Gundry, "'Verba Christi' in I Peter," 350). Similarly, Maier believes the parallels with John's Gospel are particularly striking in this regard (Maier, "Jesustradition," 154).

110. See also Elliott, *1 Peter*, 24; Michaels, *1 Peter*, xliv.

111. This problem has not gone unnoticed. Brox criticized Spicq for his lack of explicit criteria, and Goppelt criticized Best for not delineating and recognizing the importance of the criteria (Brox, "Erste Petrusbrief," 188; Goppelt, *A Commentary on*

noted that the JT in 1P was "below the surface" and many have recognized that 1P never formally cites *dominical logia*. Best rightly notes that if the words of Jesus are cited in a way similar to the way 1P cites the OT, then such citations would be without clear markers.[112] Despite these recognized challenges, clear criteria have rarely been established or used in relation to the JT in 1P. Years ago, Bauckham highlighted this as a primary problem in the study of Gospel traditions outside the canonical Gospels, indicating the need for "methodological work... listing the kinds of criteria which should count in establishing allusions and arguing for their relative importance." He highlighted that "a more self-conscious and disciplined use of clearly defined criteria could reduce the subjective element considerably."[113] The need for criteria is evident in the history of scholarship on this issue, for there are substantial differences among scholars concerning which passages reflect the use of *dominical logia* in 1P (e.g., Gundry and Best).[114]

I Peter, 34n96).

112. Best, "I Peter and the Gospel Tradition," 196.

113. Bauckham, "Study of Gospel Traditions, 384.

114. The need is not only to identify criteria, but also to indicate how those criteria are to be judged. This is the main difference between the present study and that of Theron Wong. As noted above, the conclusions reached in the present work vary significantly from those proposed by Wong. It will be helpful here to consider why. Wong himself recognizes that "in the search, identification, and evaluation of alluded material, one must be aware that optimism and skepticism can significantly influence one's conclusions" (Wong, "Use of Jesus' Sayings," 13). In regard to the history of research, Gundry and Maier are firmly in the camp of "optimism" while Best is firmly in the "skepticism" camp. For Gundry and Best, the difference in attitude was based, in part, on historical and theological factors. For Wong, the pessimistic approach comes primarily from carefulness (though, it is also possible that Wong's view that "the high authority of [Jesus'] sayings was not recognized immediately by the early churches" plays a part in his pessimism. Wong, "Use of Jesus' Sayings," 234). He quotes Paulien in reference to his stance towards identifying allusions: "it seems wise to err on the side of caution, to apply bias towards minimalism" (Paulien, "Criteria and the Assessment of Allusions," 128, quoted in Wong, "Use of Jesus' Sayings," 62).

Such a stance is somewhat odd in light of the strong case Wong makes for a community of tradition which was taught to recognize and hear allusions (Wong, "Use of Jesus' Sayings," 42–47.) The present study differs from Wong not so much in the standard of measure to determine the presence of allusion, but rather in the overall attitude towards the presence of allusion. In light of various factors that will be discussed below, there is good reason to believe early Christian communities would have been tuned towards hearing allusions and seeing their significance. Ironically, Wong himself recognizes this: "There is a real possibility that ancient readers had a heightened sensitivity to allusions especially with more limited and anchored literary canons, a sensitivity that modern readers may lack" (Wong, "Use of Jesus' Sayings," 43–44). In light of this, a more optimistic approach is warranted.

A second lacuna is found in the lack of extended consideration of how 1P uses the words of Jesus rhetorically within the development of the epistle. Other traditions in 1P, particularly the use of the OT, have been studied at length,[115] while the *dominical logia* remain relatively unexamined. If, as many scholars have argued, 1P is saturated with reflections on the teaching of Jesus, then a study dedicated to unearthing the author's use of such tradition is overdue.

---

115. Glenny, "Hermeneutics"; McCartney, "Use of the Old Testament"; Green, "Use of the Old Testament," 276–89; Greaux, "To the Elect Exiles"; Woan, "Use of the Old Testament."

3

Assumptions, Criteria, and Method

"To some, study of allusions and echoes of Jesus may appear the height of folly."[1] So says Michael Thompson in his notable study on the use of JT in Romans 12–15. What he found problematic also concerns the present study: "Not only is it impossible to *prove* that [a NT author] is depending upon a tradition in the absence of quotation formulae or explicit statements to that effect, but questions about the availability and authenticity of the tradition seems to rule out the endeavor entirely."[2] Two distinct problems are highlighted by Thompson, and both will need to be addressed in this chapter. First, we will address the issue of the availability and authenticity of the JT. Second, we will address the matter of identifying the presence of Jesus' words in 1P. In a concluding section to the chapter, we will summarize the methodology used to evaluate the role of JT in 1P.

AVAILABILITY AND AUTHENTICITY OF THE JESUS TRADITION

A crucial question in intertextual study is whether the source text was available to the author. The challenge for the present study relates to the lack of knowledge modern scholars have concerning the JT, especially in relation to 1P, an epistle of unknown date. A related problem concerns the *authenticity* of the JT recorded in the Gospel material. Some scholars suggest that the early church was largely responsible for the creation of JT. If so, 1P's

1. Thompson, *Clothed with Christ*, 22.
2. Thompson, *Clothed with Christ*, 22.

references to the JT may actually be references to early church teaching and not to Jesus at all. We will discuss these problems in order.

Availability of the Jesus Tradition

The availability of the JT depends on multiple factors. First, the JT had to be spread among early Christians.[3] Second, for 1P to allude to the JT, the epistle must be dated after the spread of the JT. Chronologically speaking, the second issue is not much of a challenge, for nearly all scholars suggest a date for 1P later than AD 60.[4] This makes it possible that not only oral tradition, but even Mark's Gospel may have been known by Peter's readers.[5]

But even if they did not know Mark's Gospel, there is substantial reason to believe the JT spread in such a way that they knew the traditions of Jesus' sayings. First, it is nearly inconceivable to imagine the congregations addressed in 1P believed in and submitted to a risen Jesus without also knowing something of his teaching. Martin Hengel ably argues this point:

> The assertion that Paul and earliest Greek-speaking Christianity were completely uninterested in the historical Jesus and knew hardly anything of him can be refuted by the simple consideration that in antiquity it was quite impossible to proclaim as *Kyrios*, Son of God and Redeemer a man who had been crucified a few years before—i.e. an alleged criminal—without saying something about who this man was, what he taught and did and how and why he died.[6]

---

3. While the term "Christian" is likely an anachronism in regard to the early Jesus-followers addressed in this letter, it is used here for convenience.

4. Those who maintain genuine Petrine authorship propose dates in the early 60s in light of the early church record that Peter was martyred around that time (Himes, *Lexham Bible Guide*). Those who embrace psuedepigraphal authorship generally suggest a date before Domitian's reign in AD 93 (Elliott, *1 Peter*, 138).

5. The date of Mark's Gospel is debated. Some recent works have argued for a date prior to AD 60 (Won, "The Date of Mark's Gospel"; Crossley, *The Date of Mark's Gospel*). If this is accurate, then Bauckham's argument that the Gospels were written for the purpose of wide dissemination becomes important. When added to Thompson's argument that the early church communities were in conversation with one another, the possibility that Mark's Gospel had spread to the area designated by 1P is quite possible (Bauckham, "For Whom Were the Gospels Written?," 9–48; Thompson, "The Holy Internet," 49–70).

6. Hengel, *Between Jesus and Paul*, 178n73. See also James D. G. Dunn, who says, "It must surely be considered highly likely that the first Christian communities were interested in, not to say highly fascinated by the figure of Jesus" (Dunn, "Jesus Tradition in Paul," 156).

Dunn argues along the same lines from a sociological perspective, indicating that it is most probable that the early church was dependent on the core teachings of Jesus in order to distinguish their new group from other religious groups. Thus, as Dunn notes, "it would be surprising if early congregations who placed themselves under the name of Christ were not concerned to learn and cherish what was known about this Christ, to rehearse it in their communal gatherings for worship, to draw on it in instruction of new converts, and to use it in discussion with those outside the group."[7]

Stated succinctly, the establishment of a new community based on the resurrection of a recently crucified man would require not only a narrative of what he did, but also an accounting of what he said. It is inconceivable that such a new community could exist without the JT, which surely supplied the necessary cohesion for the early church.

First Peter also gives reason to believe that the JT was known by the readers. For instance, Maier, after considering the way the short catechisms are used in 1P, argues that their brevity requires that the readers already knew the full narrative.[8] Further, Horrell, considering 1P 2:21–25, suggests that 1P may give evidence of "early traditions, perhaps independent of, even prior to, the Synoptic Passion Narratives, or at least in a form not directly derived from them."[9] If the author of 1P could assume the audience's knowledge of the acts of Jesus, it is likely that he could assume the audience's knowledge of the words of Jesus as well.

The lack of direct reference to Jesus' words may be taken to imply that the author was unaware of Jesus' teaching. But 1P follows the broad pattern of early epistolary literature, which prefers allusion to the JT over direct reference. For example, Paul's literature alludes to the words of Jesus often, but directly references it only six times.[10] Likewise, scholars have noted that the book of James often alludes to Jesus' words, but the author nowhere directly references them.[11] Thus, lack of explicit reference cannot be taken as evidence that 1P was unaware of the JT.

---

7. Dunn, "Jesus Tradition in Paul," 157.

8. Maier, "Jesustradition," 114.

9. Horrell, "Jesus Remembered," 147.

10. There is significant debate concerning the use of the JT in Paul's literature, especially in relation to how often he alludes to the words of Jesus. Unfortunately, we cannot survey the well-trodden landscape here (Kim, "Sayings of Jesus," 474–92; Allison, "Pauline Epistles," 1–32; Capes, "Jesus Tradition in Paul"; Dunn, "Jesus Tradition in Paul"; Hiestermann, "Paul's Use of the Synoptic Jesus Tradition"; Stuhlmacher, "Jesus Tradition Im Römerbrief," 240–50; Walter, "Paul and the Early Christian Jesus-Tradition," 51–80; Wedderburn, "The Problem of Continuity," 189–203; Wedderburn, "Similarity and Continuity," 161–82).

11. Debate likewise surrounds the identification of allusions to Jesus in the letter

The question concerning why early church authors preferred indirect over direct reference deserves more consideration than can be given here.[12] One recent explanation comes from John Kloppenborg, who has suggested that early Christian authors engaged in the rhetorical practice of *aemulatio*, in which the author takes the words of a prior tradition and puts them in his own words. They did this because, "verbatim repetition of predecessor texts was not always desireable" and it was not expected. Instead of direct citation, the author would use a known tradition as a "resource for rhetorical performance."[13] Peter Davids agrees, noting that in *aemulatio* the author "expects that his ideal reader will recognize the source and view the restructuring of the source as an honoring of the source and at the same time a skilled use of the source."[14] As we will see, the present study suggests that *aemulatio* is a rhetorical strategy employed by the author of 1P throughout the letter.

In conclusion, whether for rhetorical or sociological reasons, it is clear that other epistolary material prefers to reference the words of Jesus indirectly. Thus, if we find reference to Jesus' words in 1P, we should actually expect to see them indirectly referenced (i.e., through allusion or echo).

---

of James. For the most detailed analysis, see Deppe, "Sayings of Jesus." See also Batten, "Jesus Tradition," 381–90; Bauckham, *James*; Davids, "James and Jesus," 63–84; Hartin, "James and the Jesus Tradition," 55–70; Kloppenborg, "Reception of the Jesus Tradition," 71–100; Wachob and Johnson, "Sayings of Jesus," 431–50; Wachob, *The Voice of Jesus*.

12. Dunn argues that the sociological situation of the early church explains the use of allusion, for "in communities bonded by such common experience and language there is a whole level of discourse which consists of allusion and echo. It is the very fact that allusions are sufficient for much effective communication which provides and strengthens the bond; recognition of the allusion/echo is what attests effective membership of the group." In this light, Dunn argues that what we find "is just what we would expect. It would be surprising were it otherwise" (Dunn, "Jesus Tradition in Paul," 177). Dale Allison suggests that the JT was handled differently when it was first given and then when it was later referenced. In reference to Paul, Allison notes that "tradition was something given during the period when the apostle himself was present with the community.... The epistles, however, presuppose another *sitz im Leben*. Their context is not initiation into tradition but subsequent affairs" (Allison, "The Pauline Epistles," 21–22). Goppelt and Stuhlmaker argue that the different circumstances of Jesus' context and the early church context demanded a transposition of the sayings "into not only a historically but also salvation-historically different situation" (Goppelt, *Theology of the New Testament*, 2:45; Stuhlmacher, "Jesus Tradition Im Römerbrief," 242). Such transpositions may have led the authors to indirect reference, with the audience recognizing the JT applied to present life situations.

13. Kloppenborg, "Emulation of the Jesus Tradition," 133.

14. Davids, "What Glasses Are You Wearing?," 763.

Authenticity of the Jesus Tradition

In light of the above, there is substantial reason to believe both the author and audience of 1P knew the JT. This leads us to consider Thompson's second concern—authenticity. In one sense, this question could simply be put to the side, for there is evidence that by the time 1P was written, accounts like those recorded in the Synoptic Gospels were widely considered to be the words of Jesus.[15] Nevertheless, due to the importance of the topic, it may be helpful to consider it more directly.

Despite the ongoing presence of the form-critical assumptions of a long, drawn out process of development of the JT, which was formed chiefly by the needs of the early church communities, such assumptions have come under substantial criticism in recent years—even to the point that Bauckham has announced their death.[16] A survey of such criticisms is beyond the purview of this work;[17] nevertheless, the alternative models that have been suggested each offer substantial credibility to the idea that the words recorded in the Gospels trace back to Jesus. These alternatives have been offered in reference to rabbinic education methods,[18] on the basis of oral tradition,[19] and in relation to the role of eyewitnesses.

---

15. Similarly, Thompson says, "What is clear is that by the time the Synoptics were written, the communities in which the Gospels arose had sufficient confidence to accept the teachings (in their Greek translation) as words of Jesus" (Thompson, *Clothed with Christ*, 24).

16. "I discovered the death of form criticism and reported it. I did not attempt to kill it; I had only to report its death" (Bauckham, *Jesus and the Eyewitnesses*, 590).

17. For a concise and helpful summary of the criticisms, along with the major authors and works, see Bird, *The Gospel of the Lord*, 113–24; Bauckham, *Jesus and the Eyewitnesses*, 246–49.

18. Gerhardsson popularized the view of his teacher, Harald Riesenfeld, that the tradition contained in the Gospels is best understood as a product of a process similar to that used in rabbinic schools, where pupils memorized their master's works (Gerhardsson, *Memory and Manuscript*; Gerhardsson, *The Reliability of the Gospel Tradition*). This view has been widely criticized for its reliance on late material for its description of earlier practices, a problem found in most analogies with rabbinic methods (Davids, "The Gospels and Jewish Tradition," 75–99). Further, even granting the idea that authoritative tradents could interpret and slightly modify the tradition, the model does not appear to answer the questions posed by the differences in the Synoptic accounts. Nevertheless, this account is to be noted as more historically grounded than the form-critical assumptions that preceded it.

19. That the traditions about Jesus were passed orally has always been considered in the history of this question. Nevertheless, the work of Kenneth Bailey brought the nature of oral tradition into sharper focus, both in regard to its communal role and for its capacity for preserving the traditions of a community (Bailey, "Informal Controlled Oral Tradition," 34–54; Bailey, "Middle Eastern Oral Tradition," 363–67). Bailey's work has been picked up by notable scholars such as N. T. Wright and James Dunn, who

Richard Bauckham's work on the role of eyewitnesses has potential to aid in the present study. He argues,

> the actual variation in the versions of the Jesus traditions that we have in our extant sources can be adequately explained on the hypothesis of a formal controlled tradition in which the eyewitnesses played an important part, and do not require the form-critical hypothesis of a long period of uncontrolled, creative development by anonymous community processes.[20]

Such a hypothesis attempts to do what Dunn suggests is possible; namely, to merge the developed insights scholars have gained concerning community-oriented oral tradition and the significance of eyewitnesses who provide the tradition and, in some ways, also regulate the tradition.[21]

According to Bauckham, the Gospels contain testimonies of Jesus as remembered by eyewitnesses.[22] Consequently, he concludes that "the texts of the Gospels are close to the way the eyewitnesses told their stories and transmitted the sayings of Jesus."[23] The relation to the present study is

---

find the idea of a fixed core, yet flexible incidentals in storytelling a helpful system for understanding the present form of the Synoptic Gospels. Nevertheless, criticism has come from various directions. The most significant criticisms concern whether there is a universal "oral culture" that can be analyzed, or whether each oral culture is unique (e.g., see the critique of "orality" and "oral culture" in Derico, *Oral Tradition and Synoptic Verbal Agreement*). If each is unique—as many scholars are now suggesting—Bailey's anecdotal evidence may indicate little about the world of the NT. This is one significant reason studies on oral tradition will not have a significant role in the present study.

20. Bauckham, *Jesus and the Eyewitnesses*, 594. Bauckham uses "formally controlled" from Bailey's work. The latter defines such tradition in the following way: "It is formal in the sense that there is a clearly identified teacher, a clearly identified student, and a clearly identified block of traditional material that is being passed on from one to the other. It is controlled in the sense that the material is memorized (and/or written), identified as 'tradition' and thus preserved intact" (Bailey, "Informal Controlled Oral Tradition," 5).

21. Dunn, *Oral Gospel Tradition*, 209.

22. Bauckham recognizes John's Gospel as unique, while maintaining its similarity with the other Gospels as eyewitness testimony. He speaks of the fourth Gospel as "idiosyncratic testimony of a disciple whose relationship to the events, to Jesus, was distinctive and different. It is a view from outside the circles from which other Gospel traditions largely derive, and it is the perspective of a man who was deeply but distinctively formed by his own experience of the events. In its origins and in its reflective maturation this testimony is idiosyncratic, and its truth is not distinguishable from its idiosyncrasy" (Bauckham, *Jesus and the Eyewitnesses*, 411).

23. Bauckham, *Jesus and the Eyewitnesses*, 603. Bauckham has been criticized for attempting to get back to the "Jesus of History," as though the testimony of eyewitnesses can establish verifiable historical fact. Bauckham has responded to such a misunderstanding of his work by noting that such testimony from eyewitnesses "give us Jesus

obvious; if the traditions of Jesus' words were not untethered and amorphous but were communicated *as* Jesus' words from eyewitnesses and were preserved in the Gospels, then we are justified in assuming that the references to the JT in 1P were understood by both the author and audience to be the words of Jesus.[24]

In conclusion, the authenticity of the sayings of Jesus cannot be established beyond scholarly doubt. Nevertheless, there is enough warrant to continue this study with the view that the author and audience of 1P had access to, knew, and valued the sayings attributed to Jesus that are also recorded in the Gospels.[25] As such, while the relation between these sayings

---

interpreted—interpreted from the perspectives of the eyewitnesses and the Gospel writers. They give us representations of Jesus but representations whose historical basis can be tested. My claim is that they transcend the dichotomy between the Jesus of history and the Christ of faith. They give us the Jesus of testimony" (Bauckham, *Jesus and the Eyewitnesses*, 615).

24. Donald Hagner comes to the same position from a different angle. In his study of the JT in the apostolic fathers, he found that the JT reflected there is consonant with oral tradition more than the Gospels. His conclusion to the article is worth sharing: "the implication of [the use of JT in the Apostolic Fathers] for the historical reliability of the words of Jesus as recorded in the Synoptic Gospels is not insignificant. It may plausibly be argued that, if the tenacity and relative stability of oral tradition in the first half of the second Century was as impressive as we have seen it to be, the trustworthiness of that oral tradition in the middle decades of the first Century was, if anything, even more substantial. The very fact that the oral tradition reflected in the Apostolic Fathers and Justin Martyr was so similar to the sayings of Jesus as contained in the written Gospels thus, at the same time, confirms the reliability of the latter which were of course themselves originally dependent on oral tradition. The basic agreement between the written accounts of Jesus' words and the oral tradition later than the Gospels is evidence both that the words of Jesus were treasured from the beginning and that they were handed down with the utmost care. We may have a high degree of confidence, then, that the sayings of Jesus in our Synoptic Gospels are true representations of what our Lord himself spoke" (Hagner, "The Sayings of Jesus," 259; cf. Young, *Jesus Tradition in the Apostolic Fathers*).

25. Special comment should me made concerning the Gospel of John. Scholars have argued that both its availability and authenticity are to be questioned. As for its availability, the traditions recorded in John's Gospel are often unique, not being referenced in the other Gospels. This leads to the view that its traditions were not as well known in the early church. Further, the unique voice of Jesus in John's Gospel lead many to consider John's Gospel as an interpretive retelling of the Gospel narrative. Despite these challenges, if Bauckham is right to consider the author an eyewitness, we need only suggest that similarities between 1P and John's Gospel derive from shared tradition of Jesus' words, a shared tradition we must assume is broader than what is recorded in all of the Gospels (John 21:25). Thus, while we will not suggest JT in places where there is no Gospel parallel, we will justifiably suggest JT where there is resonance between 1P and the Gospels. For a fuller defense of using Johannine material in 1P see the helpful appendix in Wong's dissertation pertaining to this topic (Wong, "Use of Jesus' Sayings," 241–54).

and the figure of the historical Jesus must remain a point of scholarly debate, this thesis need only suggest that the author and audience of 1P recognized the sayings as the words of Jesus.

INTERTEXTUALITY: LOCATION, DEFINITION, AND CRITERIA

While we have noted the scholarly uptick in interest in intertextuality, this should not be taken to say that scholars of previous generations were not interested in the question of sources, for they certainly were. A difference, however, is that modern interpreters have attempted to place more careful limits on the method of identifying sources, seeking to avoid the charge of parallelomania.[26] For a premier example, one may consider the work of Alfred Resch who proposed an astronomical number of parallels (upward of a thousand) between the words of Jesus and Paul's literature.[27] Porter calls Resch the classic "whipping boy" in consideration of incorporated material,[28] for many have critiqued the lack of control that led to such an astonishing number.[29] Speaking more generally of the eagerness of prior scholarship to find source materials, Beetham says, "the good examples of source investigation were nearly outweighed by the poor and embarrassing ones."[30]

In relation to the JT in 1P, it is clear that there are vast differences in how scholars have determined the presence of Jesus' words. Notably, in the significant debate between Gundry and Best concerning the words of Jesus in 1P, neither author offered criteria or definitions. The results of their study revealed that their approach to the pertinent questions differed dramatically. Likewise, the appendix to this thesis shows that while the question of the *dominical logia* in 1P has been of interest to many scholars over the years,

---

26. While Samuel Sandmel did not create the term, he popularized it in his presentation at the Society of Biblical Literature critiquing the lack of scholarly methodological control on identifying parallels (Sandmel, "Parallelomania," 1–13).

27. Resch, *Paulinismus und Die Logia Jesus.*

28. Porter, "Use of the Old Testament," 88.

29. Thompson notes that the study of JT has been impeded by Resch, for the latter provided "a lasting caricature of the potential excesses" in source study (Thompson, *Clothed with Christ*, 19). Of course, lack of controls characterized other intertextual fields. For example, Jon Paulien, in his study of intertextual resonances within the seven trumpets of revelation, found that ten commentaries suggested two hundred and eighty-eight OT allusions. Shockingly, all ten commentaries agreed on only one allusion (Paulien, "Elusive Allusions," 37).

30. Beetham, *Echoes of Scripture*, 11.

few have attempted to establish the criteria by which to judge whether such *logia* are in fact present, nor have many attempted to distinguish between the various levels of reliance (quotation, allusion, echo, etc.). This thesis, and particularly this chapter, seeks to fill such a gap.

Despite the increased attention to definitions and methods in modern scholarship, it is clear that there is no consensus on definitions or criteria, as the following chapter will reveal. Thus, Porter rightly notes that

> In order to undertake any such investigation it is imperative that one define the categories under discussion, and then apply them rigorously. Ideally, a common language would be found that all could willingly use, but this is an unreasonable expectation. Therefore, short of a common language, interpreters should be clear in their own terminology and the application thereof.[31]

The following chapter will seek to capitalize on the scholarly advances made in defining terms and delineating criteria.[32]

This section will progress in three parts. First, we will consider the fundamental question concerning the role of the author, text, and audience in relation to intertextuality. Second, we will define key terms such as quotation, allusion, echo, and trace. Finally, we will delineate the criteria by which we will determine the role of proposed JT in 1P.

Intertextuality: Location

One of the key questions in consideration of intertextuality concerns the locus of identification for such intertextual references. Put differently, what determines that an intertextual reference has been made? Three major options will be considered:[33] authorial intention, textual presence, or reader identification.

In his seminal study, Hays asked the same question and essentially came to the same three possibilities as we note above.[34] Hays avoids a decision, opting instead to "hold them all together in creative tension."[35] But, as

---

31. Porter, "Use of the Old Testament," 94–95.

32. Use will be made of resources that speak to intertextuality in relation to non-biblical literature, in relation to the OT and the NT, in relation to OT within the OT, and in relation to the JT in various other books (e.g., JT in Paul and JT in James).

33. Hays, *Echoes: Paul*, 27–28.

34. He actually listed five possibilities, but his first three correlate with "reader" according to our categories above: the original readers, the present reader, a community of interpreters, the author, or the text (Hays, *Echoes: Paul*, 27–28).

35. Hays, *Echoes: Paul*, 27–28.

Porter says, "it is not at all apparent how one can hold all five of these positions together in tension, unless the rules of contradiction and exclusion are suspended."[36] It will be argued that Hays's attempt to hold all in tension is the result of recognizing strengths in each category; nevertheless, it will also be argued that the category of authorial intention can be understood to incorporate many of these strengths.

Perhaps the most serious concern with authorial intention is the specter of the intentional fallacy.[37] This fallacy suggests that one cannot *know* the intention of an author. While admitting that modern readers cannot access the intricacies of the thought process which led to the production of a text, we must also admit that the production of a text *is* the result of an intentional process.[38] Therefore, the text itself is the public record of the intention of the author.[39] Further, in the case of 1P, it can be assumed that the author is seeking to effectively communicate with the readers, giving further reason to believe the text encodes the intention of the author.[40]

Because of the importance of Hays's work on intertextuality, his critique of authorial intention should be considered. He warns that it is mistaken "to limit our interpretation of Paul's scriptural echoes to what he intended by them," for doing so "is to impose a severe and arbitrary hermeneutical restriction."[41] How so? Hays argued that "echoes are acts of figuration. Consequently, later readers will rightly grasp meanings of the figures that may have been veiled from Paul himself."[42] Put differently, Hays is arguing that "texts can generate readings that transcend . . . the conscious intention

---

36. Porter, "Allusions and Echoes," 37.

37. Wimsatt and Beardsley, "The Intentional Fallacy," 468–88.

38. Hirsch, *Validity in Interpretation*, 1–23.

39. See also Beetham, who says, "we are not trying to get into the 'mind' of the author (as if that were possible). All we have is the written expressions of the author, which in this study are taken as an author's attempt to render meaning in written form" (Beetham, *Echoes of Scripture*, 14). Kyne likewise argues that such considerations are "built not from assumptions about the author's psychology based on criteria external to the text, but from the text itself, [and thus] avoids running aground on the intentional fallacy" (Kynes, *My Psalm Has Turned into Weeping*, 33).

40. While authors can intend to deceive, and thereby encode in a text something that is opposite their true intention, this is a special case of communication, which we need not develop here. For a helpful critique of the concerns often mentioned in regard to the intentional fallacy, see Juhl, *Interpretation*, 45–65.

41. Hays gives two reasons. The first is that the identification of the author's intention is "a matter of historical speculation." Since this argument has been addressed by the comments above, we will only consider his second argument here (Hays, *Echoes: Paul*, 33).

42. Hays, *Echoes: Paul*, 33.

of the author."⁴³ These occur, he says, when "texts speak through us in ways that could not have been predicted, ways that can be comprehended only by others who hear the voice of the text through us—or, if by ourselves, only retrospectively."⁴⁴

Hays appears to be arguing that an author can unintentionally make verbal, syntactical, or ideological parallels with a text, which while unintentional nevertheless produce some intertextual resonance. In such a case, the connection between the texts is merely accidental and yet meaningful.⁴⁵

A few things should be considered in this regard: first, the following pages will show that the author of 1P deeply imbibed from the *dominical logia*. As such, it is hard to imagine that modern readers could find legitimate resonances between 1P and JT for which the author was ignorant.⁴⁶ Second, some critics of authorial intention (including Hays and Sommer) speak of identifying intertextual references by the presence of their rhetorical effect in the text. It is not clear, however, how an author could strategically use a text unintentionally.⁴⁷ Stated differently, many commentators seek to remove authorial intention as a necessary element of intertextual reference, but when they speak of identifying such references they do so from the primary perspective of how the author could have been using the reference for a strategic end, tacitly accepting authorial intention.⁴⁸

Finally, even if accidental resonance were to exist, it is not clear how modern readers could distinguish between *unintentional* intertextual links that cause resonance and *intentional* intertextual links that cause resonance. If Vanhoozer is right that "a text must be read in light of its intentional context, that is, against the background that best allows us to answer the question of what the author is doing," then the discovery of such resonances leads to the conclusion that the author intended them.⁴⁹ Therefore, it will

---

43. Hays, *Echoes: Paul*, 33.

44. Hays, *Echoes: Paul*, 33.

45. It is conceivable, however, that someone could make the argument that the divine nature of Scripture allows for *sensus plenoir* in regard to allusions, just as some theologians argue for *sensus plenior* in regard to the meaning of the OT. If so, the argument would be that while the human author did not intend such intertextual references, the divine author did (cf. Brown, *The Sensus Plenior of Sacred Scripture*).

46. In this light, it is ironic that Hays notes that modern interpreters, who are not as familiar with the OT as the original readers, are often deaf to many of the resonances created by interaction of a text with the OT. For if Paul would have been able to discern the tradition easier than modern readers, then it is unlikely modern readers could discern what Paul could not (Hays, *Echoes: Paul*, 31).

47. Kynes, *My Psalm Has Turned into Weeping*, 30n80.

48. For a similar point see, Porter, "Use of the Old Testament," 93.

49. We cannot fully develop the philosophical debate surrounding the question of

be the position of this thesis that if intertextual references cause resonance which adds to the meaning of the text, there is sufficient reason to believe such resonances were intentional.

In conclusion, this thesis will pursue intertextual references from the perspective that they are discoverable because they are authorially intended. Such intention is encoded in a text, and is, in principle, able to be recognized and understood by the audience. Therefore, while the origin of intertextual references is grounded in the intention of the author, such intention leaves marks on the text[50]—marks which, when combined with a robust consideration of the source material, reveal to responsible readers resonances between the two texts.

Intertextuality: Definitions

In the interest of simplicity, this thesis will limit the use of categories to the following: quotation, allusion, echo, and trace. "Parallel" will continue to be used to refer to pre-categorized proposed intertextual references. As noted above, interpreters have defined these categories in contrasting ways, and so it will be necessary to state clearly what each means within this thesis. Nevertheless, it should be mentioned that neat, impenetrable borders cannot always be maintained. The categories are best understood on a spectrum in which there is a level of fluidity between their borders.[51]

Most scholars have organized intertextual references according to their level of clarity. For instance, Hays suggests that "Quotation, allusion, and echo may be seen as points along a spectrum of intertextual reference, moving from the explicit to the subliminal."[52] Likewise, Stead provides a chart expressing the ascending "identifiability" of intertextual references.[53] On the other hand, Hollander and Beetham organize their categories on what they call a "rhetorical hierarchy."[54]

This distinction between clarity and rhetoric is significant and reveals two distinct ways of thinking about the categories of intertextual reference.

---

authorial intention, but the central role of authorial intention is ably defended in Vanhoozer, *Is There a Meaning?*, 201–80, here 265.

50. As Vanhoozer says, "Intention is enacted and embodied in the text" (Vanhoozer, *Is There a Meaning?*, 262).

51. Stead, *Intertextuality of Zechariah 1–8*, 22; Sommer, *Prophet Reads Scripture*, 17.

52. Hays, *Echoes: Paul*, 23.

53. His categories include: trace, echo, allusion, quotation, and citation (Stead, *Intertextuality of Zechariah*, 21).

54. Hollander, *Figure of Echo*, 64; Beetham, *Echoes of Scripture*, 16–20.

Organizing according to clarity appears to be a more objective enterprise, for some of its proponents lean towards quantitative measures of determination. Porter is of this camp, and he proposes distinctions among the groups primarily based on quantitative verbal similarity.[55] Thus, the distinction between a quote and an allusion is the number of words paralleled. No distinction exists between allusion and echo, except concerning what is being referenced.[56] Porter seems to want to separate *identification* from *interpretation*, reserving the latter until the former has been completed.[57]

Rhetorical significance, on the other hand, delineates the categories chiefly through qualitative means, on the basis of the degree to which the intertextual reference impacts the text. While quotation and allusion may still be distinguished by quantitative measures, the distinction between allusion and echo is based on how the new text interacts with the source text. If the significance is minimal, it is an echo, but if the significance is palpable, then it is an allusion. Accordingly, Hays and Beetham bring together *identification* with *interpretation*; i.e., interpretation is a necessary part of identifying intertextual parallels.

Earlier we noted that Hays aligns his categories from more explicit to less explicit. This appears to align him with the clarity organizational scheme. Nevertheless, Hays criteria of identification of allusions and echoes turns significantly on interpretation. Porter criticizes him at exactly this point, suggesting that Hays has confused interpretation with identification.[58] But Hays, like Beetham who follows him, suggests that identification comes, in part, through the interpretive process. This is in keeping with the authorial intention position advocated above. If an author intends to make an intertextual reference, such a reference is generally made because of the author's desire to cause some form of resonance between the alluded text

---

55. Porter, "Further Comments, 107–9.

56. Porter distinguishes them in the following way: "Whereas allusion invokes a specific person, place, or literary work, the notion of echo may be used for the invocation by means of thematically related language of some more general notion or concept" (Porter, "Allusions and Echoes," 39).

57. In his criticism of Hays's criteria, Porter suggests that four of Hays's seven criteria "are less criteria for determining echoes than they are attempts to establish the interpretation of these echoes." In regard to Hays's comment that the most important criteria concerns satisfaction, Porter notes, "It is perplexing that the most important criterion is not in fact a criterion for discovering echoes, but only for interpreting them, leaving the question of definition and determination unresolved" (Porter, "The Use of the Old Testament," 83).

58. See comments in prior footnote.

and the allusive text.⁵⁹ Thus, one characteristic feature of an intertextual reference is that it causes ripples of resonance between the two texts.

This thesis proceeds on the assumption that both quantitative (e.g., verbal or conceptual similarity) and qualitative (interpretive significance) measures are necessary to understand the full range of intertextual references.⁶⁰ On the far-left end of the spectrum, quantitative measures are most helpful, while the farther one moves to the right, qualitative measures become more significant. With these distinctions in mind, we will define the significant terms. After defining the terms, we will discuss the primary and secondary criteria by which we will determine where a proposed parallel fits within the spectrum of intertextual references. Finally, we will conclude by giving examples of each of the categories.

Figure 3.1: Measures for Intertextual References

Importance of Quantitative Measures		Importance of Qualitative Measures
Quotation	Allusion	Echo

Quotation

While 1P has no quotations of Jesus, it is nevertheless helpful to define this category. First, defining the category will aid in contrasting quotation from allusion, echo, and trace.⁶¹ Second, 1P does quote the OT, and thus this is a rhetorical category which the author of 1P utilized, though not in regard to the JT. Consideration will later be given to the rhetorical consequence of 1P's choice in this regard.

---

59. Clearly, an author may make an intertextual reference without regard to intertextual resonance. But if he does, it is not clear that a present reader can distinguish such a reference from accidental similarity. See the example of a trace below.

60. Verbal and conceptual similarity as well as interpretive significance will be more fully analyzed below. For now, it is enough to say that *verbal similarity* exists where a word is used in a source text and reproduced in the new text. *Conceptual similarity* exists when a distinctive, recognizable idea is repeated between the alluding and allusive text. *Rhetorical significance* exists where the source text is designed to influence the way the reader understands the new text. This rhetorical significance can be major or minor; it can entirely change the meaning of the text for one who recognizes the intertextual reference, or it can simply add greater significance to the new text without modifying the meaning. Examples will be supplied below.

61. Porter argues that the definition of allusion is best given in relation to how it differs from quotation (Porter, "Use of the Old Testament," 95).

Hollander defined a quotation as "The literal presence of a body of text" by which he meant that a quote reproduces the wording of an earlier text.[62] There are two categories of quotation, differing on whether they are explicitly identified by an introductory formula. First, there are *formulaic quotations*, which are accompanied by introductory formulas. First Peter contains only a few formulaic quotations of the OT:[63] διότι ("for"; 1:24, citing Isa 40:6–8); διότι γέγραπται ("for it is written"; 1:16, citing Lev 19:2); διότι περιέχει ἐν γραφῇ ("for it stands in Scripture"; 2:6, citing Isa 28:16; Ps 118:22; Isa 8:14); γὰρ ("for"; 3:10, citing Ps 34:13–17).

The second form of quotations lack such formulas, though in other ways they are identical to formulaic quotations. Porter persuasively argues that these must also be called quotations, for "labels have a heuristic value, and end up shaping the interpretation of the evidence at hand."[64] In this light, this study has refrained from using the terminology of citation,[65] choosing instead to refer to quotations that lack a formula as *non-formulaic quotations*.[66] These quotations differ from allusion in their directness of reference, observed primarily in their verbatim (or near verbatim) reference to a prior text.[67] Scholars differ concerning the necessary length of non-formulaic quotations.[68] For this study, a non-formulaic quotation consists

62. Hollander, *Figure of Echo*, 64.

63. Peter appears to quote from a textual tradition similar to the LXX tradition.

64. Porter, "Use of the Old Testament," 92.

65. "Citation" is not clearer than quotation, and it has been used in past studies to refer to both formulaic quotations and non-formulaic quotations. (Hoffman, "Technique of Quotation and Citation," 72.

66. Porter suggests the title "direct quotation," but following his own suggestion that titles have heuristic value, we have avoided such a designation. "Direct quotation" falsely suggests the alternate is indirect. Non-formulaic, while not aesthetically pleasing, is nevertheless clear. Beetham's titles, "formal" and "informal," are also possible, but they have the potential to communicate a difference in the author's attitude towards the quotation (Beetham, *Echoes of Scripture*, 16).

67. Such a definition is similar to Stanley's definition: "any series of several words that reproduces with a reasonable degree of faithfulness the general word order and at least some of the actual language of an identifiable passage from an outside text" (Stanley, *Paul and the Language of Scripture*, 36). Changes in minor elements of grammar (e.g., case, gender, mood, preposition) are what is meant by "near verbatim."

68. Porter suggests three, while Beetham suggests six (Porter, "Further Comments," 107; Beetham, *Echoes of Scripture*, 16–17). Both recognize that the number selected is arbitrary. The problem with making the number too large is that lower numbers may be excluded when it is otherwise clear that the author is intending to directly reference a source text (e.g., when four unique words are used from a source text). The problem with the number being too small is that the smaller the number, the greater the chance of unintended similarity. This study has chosen a smaller number because it is easier to rule out an unintended similarity (by revealing a lack of intertextual resonance) than to

of a verbatim (or near verbatim) reference to a source text of four or more words.[69]

In sum, a quotation is a direct reference to a source text with verbatim (or near verbatim) imitation of four or more words. The *formulaic quotation* is made even more explicit by accompanying terminology which either mentions the source text or signals that a source text is being referenced. The *non-formulaic quotation* lacks the formula but evidences direct lexical similarity.

Allusion

In his widely influential *A Handbook to Literature*, William Harmon defines an allusion as

> A figure of speech that makes brief reference to a historical or literary figure, event, or object. . . . Strictly speaking, allusion is always indirect. It seeks, by tapping the knowledge and memory of the reader, to secure a resonant emotional effect from the associations already existing in the reader's mind. . . . The effectiveness of allusion depends on a body of knowledge shared by writer and reader.[70]

Harmon's definition highlights three necessary elements of an allusion. First, allusions are "always indirect." This element distinguishes allusions from quotations, for in a quotation the verbatim reference calls direct attention to the referenced text, while in allusion such references are, in the words of Earl Miner, *tacit references*.[71] Ben-Porat highlights the centrality of indirect reference by saying it is the "common base of all allusions."[72] As Hollander notes, indirectness can be accomplished in primarily two ways.[73] First, the author can paraphrase the source text, using different words to suggest the same meaning. Second, the author can fragment the source text,

---

justify excluding extended verbatim agreement.

69. In rare circumstances, one may argue for a quotation of less than four words, but it must be exceedingly clear that the author is intending the audience to recognize the prior text. For example, in John 8:58 Jesus uses only two words (ἐγώ εἰμί [I am]) to refer back to Exodus 3:14, but the context is clear both from the content of the speech as well as the audience's response that Jesus intended to make an intertextual reference.

70. Harmon, "Allusion," 14.

71. Miner, "Allusion," 11.

72. Ben-Porat, "Poetics of Literary Allusion," 109.

73. Hollander suggests allusion, in distinction from quotation, can be "fragmentary or periphrastic" (Hollander, *Figure of Echo*, 64).

using the same words but not in the same order. In either case, the reader's attention is drawn to the source text, but in an indirect manner.[74]

A second necessary element of an allusion is the presence of meaningful resonance between the alluded text and the allusive text. Ben-Porat likewise defined allusion in this regard, noting that allusion is, at bottom, "a device for the simultaneous activation of two texts."[75] Sommer adds that an allusion is not merely similarity between a source text and a newly formed text, but rather consists "in the utilization of the marked material for some rhetorical or strategic end."[76] It is at this point that authorial intention surfaces in regard to allusions, for it is the author who intends the relation of the texts and their resonant effects.[77]

Further, allusions, according to the definition used in this thesis, *require* the resonance with the source text in order for the text to be properly understood. As Hays says, "the meaning of a text in which an allusion occurs would be opaque or severely diminished if the reader failed to recognize the implied reference to the earlier text."[78] Beetham helpfully adds that "Even if the audience does miss the allusion . . . contextual clues may be present to help the reader piece together a partial understanding of what the author has signified."[79] Thus, it is not necessary to an allusion that the meaning of the text is incomprehensible without recognizing the source text; rather, the presence of allusion will mask the full meaning of the text unless the alluded text is comprehended.

The third essential element of an allusion is that the intended audience can, in principle, recognize the allusion.[80] This implies two things. First, if an author knows the source text is not known to an audience, then the author cannot intend to use the intertextual reference for a strategic end,

---

74. The imprecise barrier between quotation and allusion can be seen in the space that exists between non-formulaic quotations of four words and allusions of only three words. For if the three words are unusual words, one could make a case that *direct* reference is being made.

75. Ben-Porat, "Poetics of Literary Allusion," 107.

76. By marked material, Sommer means the element in the new text that draws the reader to consider the relation between it and the source text (Sommer, *A Prophet Reads Scripture*, 15).

77. For this reason, Irwin indicates authorial intention is necessary for allusion (Irwin, "What Is an Allusion?," 294). Likewise, Beetham notes that an allusion is an "Intentional, conscious attempt by an author to point a reader back to a prior text" (Beetham, *Echoes of Scripture*, 18).

78. Hays, *Echoes: Gospels*, 10.

79. Beetham, *Echoes of Scripture*, 19.

80. In the words of Harmon, it is necessary that "the associations already [exist] in the reader's mind" (Harmon, "Allusion," 14).

and therefore it cannot function as an allusion. Second, authors intend for the audience to understand the reference, and consequently, they encode the text with this purpose in mind.[81]

This final essential element highlights the possibility that an allusion may fail. That is, despite the intention of the author to allude, the process may not reach its intended end. Thus, it is helpful to consider what is necessary for a *successful* allusion. Michael Thompson, following Camille Perri, gives the following criteria: "In order for the allusion to be successful, the audience must *recognize* the sign, *realize* that the echo is deliberate, *remember* aspects of the original text to which the author is alluding, and *connect* one or more of these aspects with the alluding text in order to get the author's point."[82] Similarly, Ben-Porat indicates the audience must accomplish the following for an allusion to succeed:

(1) Recognition of a marker (something evoking the source text)[83]

(2) Identification of the evoked text

(3) Interpretation of the text in light of this marker[84]

Each of these authors highlight the central importance of the reader, particularly his or her knowledge of the source text, ability to recognize the markers, and intention to correlate the source text with the text he is reading.[85] Without these, an allusion may exist, but it cannot be successful.

---

81. Again, in the words of Hollander, "Intention to allude *recognizably* is essential to the concept" (Hollander, *Figure of Echo*, 64).

82. Thompson, *Clothed with Christ*, 29; Perri, "On Alluding," 301.

83. A marker is "an element or pattern belonging to another independent text" (Ben-Porat, "Poetics of Literary Allusion," 108). In other words, it is something introduced in the new text which serves to direct the intended audience to consider a particular source text. A marker could be a distinctive combination of words, a distinctive thematic connection, or a unique contextual correspondence. In sum, it is that which draws the intended audience to see the connection between the source text and the new text.

84. Ben-Porat identifies a fourth element as "the activation of the context of the alluded text and its intertextual patterns expressed within the alluding text." He suggests that only some allusions will include this final element (Ben-Porat, "Poetics of Literary Allusion," 110–11).

85. Thus, Perri notes that the difficulty of allusion is that to be successfully completed, it requires "the reader's knowledge of [the alluding text's] source text's intension sufficient to enable him—actively and comprehensively—to complete the allusion's unstated significance" (Perri, "On Alluding," 299).

Before concluding the definition of allusion, it should be noted that an author may allude to more than a text.[86] In reference to the JT, 1P may allude to the *words* of Jesus or the *acts* of Jesus.

In summary, an allusion is a recognizable indirect reference to a source text, event, tradition, person, or thing which is intended by the author to produce an intertextual resonance essential to fully understanding the meaning of the text.

Echo

The current state of scholarship on the distinction between echoes and allusions is deeply divided. While most agree the border between the two is fluid,[87] there is little agreement as to the exact distinction between the two forms of intertextual reference. Some interpreters do not define the terms, though they use both.[88] Others use the terms synonymously.[89] While still others use strictly quantitative means to differentiate them.[90] Porter offers a unique distinction based on the element being referenced.[91] Most who maintain the category recognize it as either being less clear than an allusion or being less rhetorically significant than an allusion.[92]

---

86. Beetham, *Echoes of Scripture*, 18.

87. Sommer, *Prophet Reads Scripture*, 17; Stead, *The Intertextuality of Zechariah*, 22.

88. Porter criticized Dunn on this account, noting that sometimes Dunn makes them synonymous and at other times he seems to make echoes a subordinate term (Porter, "Use of the Old Testament," 82; Dunn, "Jesus Tradition in Paul").

89. Hollander can use the term "allusive echo" suggesting no firm distinction between the two words (Hollander, *The Figure of Echo*, 63. See also Miner, "Allusion"; Wagner, *Heralds of the Good News*, 9n36; Beale, *Handbook*, 29–36).

90. For example, Stead notes the following distinctions: "a 'quotation' typically involves four or more shared vocabulary features, an 'allusion' involves two or three features, and an echo, one or two" (Stead, *The Intertextuality of Zechariah*, 22n22. See also Schultz, *The Search for Quotation*, 205; Thompson, *Clothed with Christ*, 32).

91. "Whereas allusion invokes a specific person, place, or literary work, the notion of echo may be used for the invocation by means of thematically related language of some more general notion or concept" (Porter, "Allusions and Echoes," 39).

92. Hays notes that distinguishing allusions and echoes is a hard procedure in light of the distance between modern readers and the ancient audience. This is because we cannot determine with sufficient clarity what they would have known. Thus, Hays concludes that "the difficulty of deciding how to classify [echoes and allusions] illustrates my reasons for using the terminology flexibly: I make no systematic distinction between the terms. In general . . . allusion is used of obvious intertextual references, echo of subtler ones" (Hays, *Echoes: Paul*, 29). Beale suggests that the distinction may not be helpful, but if there is one, "an echo is an allusion that is possibly dependent on an OT text in distinction to a reference that is clearly or probably dependent" (Beale, *Handbook*, 32).

This thesis will follow those scholars who define an echo as less interpretively significant than an allusion. Whereas in allusion recognition of the source text is essential to proper interpretation, echoes can be missed without significantly altering the reader's understanding of the text.[93] This is not to suggest that the author intends the reader to miss the echo; rather, the author encodes the text sufficiently to point the reader to the source text, yet the resonances discovered in this textual fusion do not *fundamentally* shape the way the passage is understood. Stated differently, recognizing echoes may add substantial richness to a text, but understanding them is not necessary to grasping the author's meaning.[94]

In sum, an echo is a recognizable indirect reference to a source text, event, tradition, person, or thing which is intended by the author to produce an intertextual resonance *non-essential* to fully understanding the meaning of the text.

Trace

Whereas the allusion is central to the interpretation of a passage and echo adds additional nuance and color to the interpretation of a passage, the trace shows only lexical or stylistic similarity to another text. Indeed, the trace is best recognized as a lexical or stylistic similarity that is unaccompanied by rhetorical significance. These occur because of an author's familiarity with source material,[95] yet their appearance within a new text does not intentionally draw the reader back to the origin text; rather, the use of the language or style is merely imitative and not functional.[96]

---

93. While Hays can be read to distinguish echoes and allusions in various ways, he does sometimes suggest a distinction similar to the one we make here: "the meaning of a text in which an allusion occurs would be opaque or severely diminished if the reader failed to recognize the implied reference to the earlier text. . . . Ordinarily, however, the surface meaning of the text would be intelligible to readers who fail to hear the echoed language" (Hays, *Echoes: Gospels*, 10). Nevertheless, he seems to suggest that echoes go beyond the "literal sense" of the text, a claim not made in this study.

94. Similarly, Sommer identifies echoes as intertextual references "where elements of an earlier text reappear in a later one, but the meaning of the marked sign in the source has little effect on a reading of the sign with the marker of the alluding text" (Sommer, *A Prophet Reads Scripture*, 16). Cf. Beetham who indicates that while echoes are not essential to interpretation, recognizing them "deeply enhances and colors the understanding of the new context" (Beetham, *Echoes of Scripture*, 22).

95. In other words, these may occur because an author has deeply imbibed of the source text to the degree that the source text has shaped his lexical choices.

96. This is the opposite of how Wolfgang Iser defines allusions: "functional, not merely imitative" (Iser, *The Act of Reading*, 79).

In sum, a trace is an indirect reference to a source text which is not intended to draw the reader back to the source text and thus is imitative rather than functional. As with quotations, no traces are suggested in this study.

Intertextuality: Criteria

As noted above, both qualitative and quantitative criteria are used to evaluate intertextual presence. As much as the distinctions on the left side of the spectrum are chiefly differentiated by quantitative means (presence of a formula, number of words shared), they are easier to identify. But since distinctions on the right side are chiefly defined by qualitative measures (the interpretive significance of the reference), it is there where scholarly subjectivity cannot be avoided.

References to Jesus' words in 1P never rise to the level of quotation, and thus are, at most, allusions. Stated differently, this study will predominantly rest on the differences between the right side of the spectrum (between allusions and echoes), and consequently will necessarily include some level of subjectivity. This admission should not be surprising, for nearly all interpreters recognize that there is both art and science in recognizing allusions and echoes.[97]

Despite the lack of objective, clinical methodology that can neatly classify alleged intertextual references, the modern interpreter is not left in despair.[98] Garner powerfully makes this point on the first page of his work on allusion:

> Poetic allusions—this is part of their power to charm and to frustrate—cannot be proved or disproved. At first this elusiveness seems disastrous to the critic. Upon reflection, however, the problems seem less threatening: little that readers value in poetry responds reliably to the arid analysis of axiom and corollary, or even to the more pragmatic pins and tools of dissection that serve so well to examine the earth-worm or affix the butterfly to the board once it can no longer fly.[99]

---

97. Beetham, *Echoes of Scripture*, 35; Sommer, "Exegesis," 486; Thompson, *Clothed with Christ*, 30; Garner, *From Homer to Tragedy*, 1; Hays, *Conversion of the Imagination*, 29.

98. Sommer encourages his readers to avoid despair by pointing them to Garner's work (Sommer, "Exegesis," 486).

99. Garner, *From Homer to Tragedy*, 1.

In other words, the literary nature of allusion and echo require artistic interpretation.[100] It is for this reason that Hays suggested the most important criteria for identifying echoes and allusions was his most subjective criteria, what he called satisfaction.[101]

Porter criticized Hays in this regard: "It is perplexing that the most important criterion is not in fact a criterion for discovering echoes, but only for interpreting them, leaving the question of definition and determination unresolved."[102] But as we noted above, Hays believes determination comes through interpretation. That is, it is only as an alleged allusion's or echo's resonance is heard by an informed interpreter that it can truly be identified. In the words of Hays,

> We do not make much progress in reading such figures if we confine our inquiry to asking questions like, "Is Eliot's line an allusion to Augustine, yes or no?" and "Can we prove that the *Confessions* was a source for *The Waste Land*?" (I'm afraid that many readers trained in the usual methods of biblical studies might insist that Eliot intended no reference to the "cauldron of unholy loves," because he did not actually quote that part of the line!) We attain an illuminating reading of Eliot's text only when we follow the play of allusion and see where it leads.[103]

In light of the above, the following criteria are not to be understood as scientifically rigorous principles which deliver certainty to their practitioners. Some of the criteria are more objective (e.g., the availability of a source text to an author), and the failure to meet these criteria eliminate the possibility of authorial intention. Other criteria (e.g., significance) are more subjective and require the reader to hear the proposed resonances between 1P and the *dominical logia*. These latter cannot be avoided, and as Hays rightly notes, are of great importance.

---

100. Further, it is the very nature of allusion and echo as literary modes to make tacit reference. Their nature is indirect, and while the author is not seeking to hide the allusion or echo, bringing the source text into the open would have eliminated the intended purpose of the literary mode. This leaves the modern interpreter with only degrees of certainty.
101. Hays, *Echoes: Paul*, 31.
102. Porter, "Use of the Old Testament," 83.
103. Hays, *Conversion of the Imagination*, 33.

Primary Criteria[104]

This thesis will divide the criteria for detecting allusions and echoes into two types. Primary criteria are those essential for identifying allusions and echoes. The confirming criteria are supplemental in that while they may be present when an intertextual reference is made, they are not *necessary* for intertextual reference. No criteria are given for the identification of quotation, for they are absent in 1P's use of the JT.[105]

If an allusion is a *recognizable* indirect reference to a source text which is intended by the author to produce intertextual resonance *essential* to fully understand the meaning of the text, then the criteria for identification should be based on this definition. Three primary criteria are offered here. The first two—availability and agreement—are necessary in that allusions make *recognizable* reference to source texts. Significance, the third primary criteria, derives from the fact that the resonance is *essential* in understanding the alluding text.

Availability

Because allusion is an authorially intended reference to a source text, it is necessary that the author had access to the source text. This criterion is objective in that if it can be proved that an author did not know the source text (e.g., the alleged source text is chronologically later than the purported allusion), allusion can be ruled out. Further, since allusion is encoded by the author for the audience to recognize it, the author must also have reason to believe the audience had access to the source text.[106]

The case for both 1P's author and audience having access to the JT has been made above, and consequently will be assumed at this point. It is enough here to say that our procedure will be to assume that traditions recorded in the Gospels were recognized by both the audience and author of 1P to be the words of Jesus.

---

104. In making two levels of criteria, we follow, Beetham, *Echoes of Scripture*.

105. Clearly the challenge of the flexibility of the wording of the JT in the early church plays a significant role here. It is possible that Peter does attempt to provide a nonformulaic quotation, yet the present records we have never show that he does. Stated differently, none of the passages in 1P contain a verbatim (or near verbatim) reference to a Gospel text of four or more words.

106. Porter rightly criticizes criteria that require the audience know the allusion (Porter, "Further Comments," 103). In the present case, the requirement is simply that the author *believe* the audience had access, for how could he intend to meaningfully allude unless he believed his audience knew the allusion?

Agreement

Because an allusion is a *recognizable* reference to a source text, there must be some textual evidence that an allusion is intended.[107] We will suggest three ways an author can express agreement in a text so that a reader can identify the alluded text: verbal agreement, structural agreement, and conceptual agreement.[108]

Verbal agreement is, in the words of Michael Thompson, the "clearest sign of possible allusion."[109] As noted above, the difference between intertextual reference categories is fluid. Thus, while extended verbal agreement makes a quotation, allusion consists of verbal agreement that falls short of quotation. In this thesis, quotation has been defined as a series of four or more verbatim or near verbatim words in order. Thus, allusion is likely present where three identical or very similar words are used in order, or where substantially similar words are used in combination that distinctively reflects the source text.

The variability of the JT as evidenced by the Synoptic writer's use of the JT causes some difficulty here. Such varied use suggests that a saying of Jesus may be stated in different ways and yet be understood as the words of Jesus.[110] This variability does not eliminate the possibility of identifying the words of Jesus, as though the tradition was infinitely flexible. Nevertheless, it does highlight the need for contextual understandings of the sayings. Thus, we will find that verbal agreement is less helpful in discovering

---

107. Hays defines this criteria as "volume" by which he means to ask "how insistently the echo presses itself upon the reader" (Hays, *Conversion of the Imagination*, 35). Porter criticized Hays for using a metaphor (volume) to define a metaphor (echo; Porter, "Use of the Old Testament," 83). Hays's clarification indicates that "volume" includes many of the same items we consider in the category of "agreement" (Hays, *Conversion of the Imagination*, 35–37).

108. For instance, Paulien calls the three categories structural, thematic, and verbal parallels, while Thompson calls them verbal agreement, conceptual agreement, and formal agreement (Paulien, "Elusive Allusions," 43; Thompson, *Clothed with Christ*, 31–33). Beale also recognizes these three categories, though he organizes them differently: "The telltale key to discerning an allusion is that of recognizing an incomparable or unique parallel in wording, syntax, concept, or cluster of motifs in the same order or structure" (Beale, *Handbook*, 31).

109. Thompson, *Clothed with Christ*, 31.

110. Such variability may be the product of the flexibility of oral tradition, the multiple ways Jesus said something, the varied uses of the Gospel writers, and translation variants (if Jesus did not teach in Greek) (Porter, "Did Jesus Ever Teach in Greek?," 199–235; Gleaves and Cloud, *Did Jesus Speak Greek?*).

allusions to JT than it is in discovering allusions in the OT, which has a more solid base of comparison.[111]

Structural agreement occurs when a text imitates the language or themes of a prior text by reflecting the same ordering of material.[112] For example, Beale suggests that the book of Daniel provides the broad structure for the book of Revelation, with the latter intentionally patterning the order and structure of the former.[113] On a much smaller scale, Paulien argues that Revelation 9:1–11 is structured according to the pattern of Joel 2:1–11.[114] In both cases, Beale and Paulien strive to show that there are enough markers in the new text to distinctively reflect the source text for those aware of the source text. In regard to JT, structural agreement is difficult to prove for the same reason verbal agreement is difficult to prove—both rely on a stable base of comparison. In the Synoptic Gospels, narratives are rearranged for rhetorical purposes and thus identification of structural agreement is hindered.

What we have called conceptual agreement, Beetham calls "rare concept similarity."[115] By this name he highlights that an author can signify to the reader that an intertextual reference is present by using a concept that is unique to a previous text or is so rare that reference to it draws the reader back to the source text. For example, 1P speaks about the blessing (μακάριος) of persecution (4:14), an idea uniquely emphasized by Jesus, particularly in the Sermon on the Mount (Matt 5:11). Early church listeners would have been drawn back to Jesus' sermon, and this invites consideration of the resonances that may exist between the context of Jesus' statement and the context of 1P's text. While verbal and structural agreement are the chief means of determining indirect reference in OT in the NT studies, the nature of JT makes conceptual agreement a vital element in discovering JT.

One of these three—verbal, structural, or conceptual agreement—is necessary for the identification of an allusion. Nevertheless, the presence of *agreement* with an *available* source text does not guarantee the presence of an allusion. One more thing must be true of higher-level intertextual relations; they must have *significance*.

---

111. Of course, in the case of the OT, things are not simple either. The author may be referring to the Hebrew or the Greek, and the textual traditions in both of those categories are quite diverse.
112. Paulien, "Elusive Allusions," 43.
113. Beale, *John's Use of the Old Testament*, 75.
114. Paulien, *Deep Things of God*, 146–47.
115. Beetham, *Echoes of Scripture*, 29.

SIGNIFICANCE[116]

Allusions must have interpretive significance for the text in which they are found. That is, allusive texts can only be *fully* understood in relation to the alluded text. Consequently, identification of allusions is inescapably tied to interpretation. If detection of allusions is both a science and an art, the prior two criteria—availability and agreement—are the science, while significance is the art. This is another way of saying that this criterion is more subjective than the others, for it requires a "hearing ear" which can discern the degree to which a proposed intertextual reference creates resonances which inform the referencing text.[117]

There are various levels of significance, and it is here that the distinctions among intertextual references are found. Allusion, echo, and trace all require the first two criteria, confirming that the intertextual reference was available to the author and that there is some form of agreement. The allusion is the most rhetorically significant, for if an allusion is missed the text's meaning remains veiled.[118] An echo, on the other hand, may be missed without hindering the interpreter from grasping the meaning of the text. Nevertheless, the echo has significance, adding vibrancy and color to the text by evoking another textual world, allowing for deeper appreciation for the meaning of the text. Finally, the trace shows no interpretive significance, and thus only meets the first two criteria.

A few examples will help clarify the preceding distinctions. Since 1P offers no traces, we will examine an example from Pauline literature. In Philippians 1:19, Paul reproduces, with five consecutive words, the exact Septuagint rendering of Job 13:16: "τοῦτό μοι ἀποβήσεται εἰς σωτηρίαν" ("this will turn out for my deliverance"). Nevertheless, Beale and Carson

---

116. Significance, as we are defining it here, is similar to Hays's criteria of satisfaction. For Hays, the criterion of satisfaction answers the following questions positively: "does the proposed reading make sense? Does it illuminate the surrounding discourse? Does it produce for the reader a satisfying account of the effect of the intertextual relation?" (Hays, *Echoes: Paul*, 31). Indeed, one can say that a proposed intertextual reference is "satisfying" when "the resultant reading ... is clarified and enhanced by an awareness of the proposed intertexts" (Hays, *Conversion of the Imagination*, 44).

117. So Wong: "When one tests an allusion as to how well it 'coheres with the text itself,' the interpreter is also determining if there is an overall sense that the proposed contribution fits and is not contrived or forced. This overall sense is subjective, but is appropriate if assessing allusions is an art and not just application of criteria" (Wong, "Use of Jesus' Sayings," 59).

118. Beetham notes that proposed references are allusions when they answer positively to the following question: "Does the alleged source have a component that, when brought forward to the alluding text, unlocks the riddle of the alluding text?" (Beetham, *Echoes of Scripture*, 30).

note that "most commentators, even if they notice the striking verbal correspondence, appear to see *little significance* in it."[119] In other words, the turn of phrase does not appear to point the reader back to Job; rather, it may be the byproduct of Paul's saturation with Scripture.[120] Thus, despite being quantitatively rich, this reference is ultimately categorized as a trace, because it lacks qualitative richness.[121]

An example of an echo can be seen in 1P 1:18–19a, where the text says, "You know that you were ransomed from the futile ways inherited from your ancestors, not with perishable things like silver or gold, but with the precious blood of Christ." The suggested source text, Isaiah 52:3, says, "For thus says the Lord: You were sold for nothing, and you shall be redeemed without money." The conceptual similarity is obvious, but there are verbal similarities with the Septuagint as well. For instance, both texts speak of being ransomed (λυτρόω) by silver/money (ἀργύριον). And while these two words are not uncommon in biblical literature, the combination of lexical and ideological similarity leads to the conclusion that the author is directing the reader to consider the source text. It is beyond the purpose of this paper to detail how extensively the resonances reverberate through this text; nevertheless, 1P's attribution of terminology originally given to Israel suggests that the text may see a parallel between the redemption offered to Israel and the redemption provided for its readers.[122] That this is an echo is confirmed in that the central meaning of the passage can be understood without reference to the echoed text. In other words, readers who miss the echo will not miss the meaning of the text, though they may miss some of the richness of the text.

Finally, many commentators find an allusion in the first verse of 1P, where the author indicates the audience is composed of ἐκλεκτός

---

119. Beale and Carson, *Commentary on the New Testament*, 836.

120. Incidentally, Porter is probably correct when he notes that Hays "has trouble seeing Job 13:16 as anything more than a faint echo—even though there are five words cited—apparently because he cannot figure out why Paul is citing these words." Porter, "Further Comments," 105. This example highlights the difference between Hays's approach and Porter's approach.

121. Such an extreme example shows the necessary limitations of the quantitative and qualitative measures we are using. While they are generally in agreement, this example shows that they are not always so. Indeed, we might call this text a "trace quote" for it qualifies as a quote by quantitative measures, but it operates as a trace in its lack of intertextual resonance. These examples are exceedingly rare in the biblical corpus, chiefly because the natural purpose of imitating the words of a source text (evidenced by quantitative measures) is to make some resonance between the source text and the current text (evidenced by qualitative measures).

122. See Karen Jobes's commentary for more consideration of this echo: Jobes, *1 Peter*, 116–20.

παρεπίδημος (elect exiles) in the διασπορά (dispersion). In what sense are they elect exiles, and in what sense are they in the dispersion? The sense is clarified in 2:11, where 1P combines παρεπίδημος with πάροικος in noting that the audience is composed of those who are both "aliens and exiles." These two terms are used together in the OT in reference to Abraham, who at that time was seeking a burial place for Sarah (Gen 23:4).[123] By drawing the reader back to Abraham prior to the possession of the land, 1P is encouraging the readers to see themselves as those, like Abraham, elected by God who are on a journey awaiting their final homeland. While some have argued that the use of these words (παρεπίδημος, πάροικος, and διασπορά) is compatible with a non-metaphorical interpretation of people who are literally in exile,[124] the similar use of ideas and terminology in Hebrews 11:13 give further credence to the metaphorical view.[125]

It is beyond the ability of this study to develop the way the author of 1P develops this heavenly-exilic theme in reference to the identity of the readers. But granted its presense, the audience cannot fully comprehend the meaning of this language in 1P, particularly in 2:11, unless they have grasped the allusion. Thus, to the extent one interprets the text without reference to the allusion, one has missed the *full* meaning of the text.[126]

---

123. They are also used together in LXX Psalm 38:13, but it is not clear 1P is referring to this Psalm.

124. The chief proponent of this view has been John Elliott (Elliott, *A Home for the Homeless*). Since Elliott's groundbreaking work, there is no scholarly consensus. Himes helpfully summarizes the scholarship, which has split into three camps: the historically dominant position that the terms are metaphorical; those following Elliott in seeing a non-metaphorical use of the terms; and those following Jobes in seeing both a metaphorical and non-metaphorical sense (Himes, *Lexham Bible Guide*; Chin, "Heavenly Home for the Homeless, 96-112; Elliott, *1 Peter*, 312-15; Jobes, *1 Peter*, 23-41).

125. John Pryor likewise finds the Hebrews passage relevant: "Considering the way the Epistle to the Hebrews makes use of the Abraham story (11.8-9, 13) as a paradigm of the pilgrim outlook that has always characterised God's covenant people, we can with confidence suggest that Peter also has in mind the confession of Abraham" (Pryor, "First Peter and the New Covenant (2)," 46.

126. Elliott helpfully interprets 2:11 in reference to Genesis 23:4, though he argues that others are mistaken when they "introduce and impose an alien cosmological contrast not in the original Greek text and not consistent with the social rather than cosmological orientation of this letter" (Elliott, *1 Peter*, 461). But the reference to Abraham suggests the cosmological orientation, as Davids has eloquently argued: "The knowledge that they do not belong does not lead to withdrawal, but to their taking their standards of behavior, not from the culture in which they live, but from their 'home' culture of heaven, so that their life always fits the place they are headed to, rather than their temporary lodging in this world" (Davids, *First Epistle of Peter*, 95).

Confirming Criteria

These criteria are less significant than the former in that while the former address issues necessary for allusions and echoes, these criteria are merely suggestive. Where these are, an intertextual reference may not exist, though their presence increases the likelihood that an intertextual presence might be found.

History of Modern Interpretation

In light of the research done in the NT, it would be foolish to engage in a study of intertextuality without at least considering the recent history of scholarship on the topic. Thus, these sources will be mined concerning their understanding of how 1P used the JT.

Hays suggests that this criterion is best used to find, not exclude: "this criterion should rarely be used as a negative test to exclude proposed echoes that commend themselves on other grounds."[127] Or, as he says elsewhere, "this criterion may serve more to expand than to veto."[128] Hays is concerned that prior scholarship will be used to limit further exploration, for he argues that past scholars have not always been attuned to the potential source texts to the degree needed to hear the echoes.

Ironically, Beetham suggests this same criterion for the opposite reason. For Beetham, the criterion acts as a check on rogue interpretation, for this criterion should cause a scholar to act with "caution if no one has observed the proposed allusion heretofore."[129]

Hays and Beetham highlight two helpful elements of this criterion. First, it operates as a guide to consider those places where prior scholars have found JT in 1P.[130] Second, it acts as a check against rampant subjectivity. Thus, while we will examine some areas where few scholars have suggested JT, such passages will come under greater scrutiny.

Multiple Attestation

In reference to Pauline literature, Dale Allison highlighted that the reference to Jesus' words often occurred in recognizable patterns: "Pauline parallels

127. Hays, *Echoes: Paul*, 31.
128. Hays, *Conversion of the Imagination*, 43.
129. Beetham, *Echoes of Scripture*, 32.
130. Accordingly, the appendix charts where prior scholars have suggested the presence of JT in 1P.

are not randomly scattered throughout our Gospels. Most come from a handful of relatively brief, well-defined sections which are widely held to reproduce early blocks of tradition."[131] Further, he recognized that most of the parallels are clustered together in Paul's writings.[132] These observations—that Paul clustered his citations and that Paul preferred to cite from certain sections of the tradition—form the basis for the criterion of multiple attestation. Though Allison wrote in reference to Paul, the principles apply more broadly, as we will see.

Allison's article ably demonstrates the significance of the criterion of multiple attestation, which is established on the idea that where a particular JT logion is referenced once, it is more likely to be referenced again.[133] We will categorize multiple attestation into three levels, which are organized according to descending importance: references within the same work; references by the same author; and references within the early church more broadly.

If an author clearly references a saying of Jesus in one passage, the likelihood is increased that he references another saying of Jesus in the near context. Further, if it has already been shown than an author alludes to a certain element of the JT, say the Sermon on the Mount/Plain, then the case for another allusion from that same tradition block is enhanced. This is partly because the readers know the author had access to that particular tradition but is more reflective of the psychological fact that authors are more likely to cite a tradition that was just referenced, for such a reference is still on the author's mind.

Because an author is likely to emphasize certain teachings and sayings more than others, it is often helpful to compare the works of the same author, looking for observable patterns in the author's use of a particular tradition. Of course, the debate over the authorship of both epistles attributed to Peter causes some difficulty. Further, though Acts records the sermons of Peter, many scholars believe the speeches are severely redacted (or simply created) beyond the ability to recover the Petrine voice. Nevertheless, there is reason to suggest the usefulness of both 2 Peter and the Acts speeches of Peter. In the former case, even if the letter is considered psuedepigraphal, the author intended the audience to consider his words the words of Peter, and it appears he may have known the first letter (2 Pet 3:1). Thus, it may

---

131. Allison, "Pauline Epistles," 11.

132. Allison, "Pauline Epistles," 10.

133. Sommer notes the importance of this criteria when he asserts that "the argument that an author alludes, then, is a cumulative one: assertions that allusions occur in certain passages become stronger as patterns emerge from those allusions" (Sommer, *Prophet Reads Scripture*, 485).

give evidence to what an early author (Petrine circle?) believed Peter would have said. As for Acts, whatever degree of redactional activity is present, many have observed the similarities between the epistle and the speeches.[134] Thus again, we have reason to believe this early tradition reflects the Petrine voice. In light of the above, JT reflected in 2 Peter and the Petrine speeches in Acts will be used as aids in looking for the use of JT in 1P.

While multiple attestation is most helpful in consideration of how a particular author uses a source text, the criterion can also be helpful more broadly. Just as a particular author tends to value and appropriate prior source texts in an uneven fashion, so does the early church. This is another way of recognizing that some passages, like the Sermon on the Mount/Plain or the Olivet Discourse, were more referenced than other passages. Consequently, as Travis Williams has recently noted, "If a source was widely known and commonly quoted by other authors during a given time period, this can increase the chances that it was cited by the author in question."[135]

In conclusion, it is important to emphasize that multiple attestation is only a confirming criterion. There need be no other epistolary reference in all of early church literature for a particular *dominical logion* to be identified in 1P. Nevertheless, the popularity of a logion, whether to the author or the early church more broadly, makes the use of that same logion in 1P more probable.

Textual Disturbance

The final confirming criterion recognizes that the presence of a source text in a newly written text sometimes leaves traces of disturbance. These range from obvious to nearly imperceptible. On the obvious side, Thompson draws attention to those times the text uses words referring to tradition in the surrounding context of the proposed intertextual reference (e.g., ὁμολογεῖν, πιστεύειν, πίστις, ἀρτυρεῖν, μάρτυς, παραλαμβάνειν, παραδιδόναι), or where the name of Jesus (or Lord) is used in the surrounding context.[136] On the less obvious side, grammatical or stylistic changes[137] might be observed in places where the author attempts to bridge between his conceptions and that of a prior source.[138]

---

134. Gourbillon and Buit, *Première Épitre de Saint Pierre*, 10.
135. Williams, "Intertextuality," 179.
136. Thompson, *Clothed with Christ*, 35.
137. In the case of 1P, the minimal amount of text modern scholars have from the author limits the ability to recognize disturbances in grammar and style.
138. See also Gisela Kittel, who suggests that particular terseness of expression

Intertextuality: Frustration and Opportunity

As we conclude the section on the identification of intertextual references, we must reemphasize that the study of a text's indirect reference to another text is the source of both frustration and opportunity. This is because the efficacy of allusions and echoes "depends partly upon their initial obscurity."[139] The above criteria will help guide us in clearing the fog of obscurity, but they cannot produce dogmatic answers. This is because "there is an element of intuition and judgment in the detection and verification of echo. Such is the nature of this type of investigation, that it is both art as well as science."[140] As has been shown above, most scholars in the field recognize that there is an inevitable element of subjectivity in the detection of allusions and echoes.[141] Nevertheless, there are degrees of subjectivity and the application of the above criteria will help to avoid what Hays has called "rampant subjectivity and misinterpretation."[142]

Having noted that allusions and echoes cause some frustration for the scholar, we should also recognize that they are also one of the more exciting and ripe fields of research. This is because the identification of intertextual resonances opens the door to interpretive exploration.[143] Allusion and echo draw the reader into the intersection of two textual worlds, and sometimes what is found opens new vistas of consideration. In regard to the present study, the intertextual resonances between 1P and the JT have not been thoroughly explored, and this provides exciting opportunities of research.

This thesis is not an exercise in creative reading, though that is a danger that must always be avoided;[144] rather, it is seeking to uncover the

---

might indicate the presence of source material (Kittel, "Geschichtliche Ort des Jakobusbriefes," 91–92n39).

139. Hays, *Conversion of the Imagination*, 33.

140. Beetham, *Echoes of Scripture*, 35.

141. Porter, however, continues to seek for more objective measures. In his critique of Thompson's work on the JT in Romans, Porter claims that Thompson's work is both subjective and unworkable (Porter, "Use of the Old Testament," 187). The core difference between Porter and the scholars mentioned above, has already been noted. Namely, Porter seems to believe the identification of intertextual references must precede interpretation, while these other scholars believe intertextual references can be discovered through interpretation.

142. Hays, *Conversion of the Imagination*, 29.

143. Hays, *Echoes: Paul*, 17. Cf. Perri, "On Alluding," 293.

144. Hollander, in his classic study on allusion suggests that "we must always wonder what our own contribution was—how much we are always being writers as well as readers of what we are seeing" (Hollander, *The Figure of Echo*, 99). The criteria-based approach used here seeks to limit the reader's contribution.

meaningful intersections of the vast intertextual world in which the reader and author shared. In conclusion, we agree with Beetham that while great care must be exercised in the discernment of intertextual references, "we need not shy away from presenting what we hear, that is, what we think *an author* has done, in the text."[145]

Intertextuality: Expectations

Before turning to an investigation of the text of 1P, it will be helpful to address one more issue—the present writer's expectations. The history of research on the presence of Jesus' words in 1P reveals that the investigator's perspective matters significantly in the discovery of allusions and echoes. Because echoes and allusions exist on the less obvious side of intertextual references, this is not surprising. Stated differently, if one thinks it highly likely that 1P would allude to the JT, the threshold of evidence needed to identify an allusion is proportionally established. On the other hand, if one believes it unlikely that Jesus words would be alluded to in 1P, the threshold is also proportionally established.[146]

This study will take a decidedly optimistic view of the presence of Jesus' words in 1P. Such a stance comes from a confluence of factors.[147] First, we have noted above the central and important role that the JT would have had in the early church. As Wenham has noted, "the idea that the early church . . . [was] uninterested in, or uniformed about, the teaching and history of Jesus is a priori improbable."[148] On the contrary, as Dunn has argued, such teaching would have been central for it set the church apart as a community.[149] Consequently, the early Jesus communities would have had frequent

---

145. Beetham, *Echoes of Scripture*, 35. Emphasis added.

146. The history of research clearly reveals this. Gundry found many allusions while Best found few. For Gundry, the author was Peter the apostle and therefore the likelihood of allusion increased dramatically. For Best, Peter was likely not the author, and whoever the author was, he likely had little knowledge of Jesus' words.

147. Authorship does appear to be a factor that leans in favor of a positive attitude towards references to the JT. Of course, if the apostle Peter is the author, it is likely he would allude to the significant and impactful words of Jesus (as Gundry argues). On the other hand, Schreiner proves that even if someone thinks Peter is the author, this does not necessarily lead to the conclusion that Peter alludes to Jesus' words often (Schreiner, *1, 2 Peter*, 31). But even if Peter was not the author, a pseudepigraphal author would likely refer to Jesus' words in order to sound authentic. Seen in this light, the primary question is not whether Peter was the author; rather, it is whether the author knew the JT and expected the audience to know it.

148. Wenham, "Paul's Use of the Jesus Tradition," 29.

149. Dunn, "Jesus Tradition in Paul," 177.

and significant exposure to the teachings of Jesus, increasing the possibility that Peter would reference such traditions and that the readers would expect to hear them.

Considering how the JT would have been handled in the early church provides further reason to maintain an optimistic attitude towards the presence of allusions and echoes to Jesus' words. If the early church modeled their gatherings after the synagogues, then a central portion of the gathering concerned the recitation of authoritative material. Of course, in the synagogue the material would have been the OT scriptures, but in the early Jesus communities this would have certainly been combined with the reading of Gospel material or the recitation of oral traditions concerning Jesus.[150] This would have resulted in "oral literacy," even if conventional literacy was lacking.[151]

It is likely that such oral literacy was taught to the early church communities. Allison notes that "inner-biblical allusion was a cultural convention in Judaism" to the degree that "a Jewish audience must have been accustomed to catching allusions."[152] It appears that Paul taught this even to his gentile audiences, for he often makes suggestive allusions to the OT, expecting that they will recognize the allusion and make the proper interpretation.[153] Of course, some of these readers may have been acquainted with the OT prior to conversion, but certainly not all of them were. Instead, Paul introduced his readers to the OT and prepared them by acquaintance with the writings to recognize his allusive use of them. If Paul did so with the OT, it is likely that he and others did the same with the JT.

Community reading would reinforce such allusive references.[154] Wong rightly notes that "Oral reading in the context of community renders a

---

150. It is not necessary to argue that the congregations written to in 1P had access to the four Gospels in the NT canon. The transition from oral tradition to written Gospels certainly did not occur in a moment, but rather it is likely that there were other written testimonies which were later incorporated into the canonical Gospels (Luke 1:1).

151. There is significant debate concerning the literacy rates in the first century. In this discussion, however, the issue is relatively unimportant, for one significant way the JT was spread and remembered was through oral proclamation. Such an observation silences the critique who might claim that early Jesus followers would not have had the literary sophistication to recognize echoes and allusions.

152. Allison, *Intertextual Jesus*, 17.

153. Harry Gamble notes that "the frequency, variety, and subtlety of Paul's recourse to Scripture presumes not only that the communities he addressed acknowledged the authority of Jewish Scripture, but also that they were sufficiently familiar with it to understand and appreciate his appeals to it, subtle and diverse as they were" (Gamble, *Books and Readers in the Early Church*, 212–13).

154. "It is plausible that on subsequent readings of revelation in the churches that the audience would be able to discern more of the allusions than on merely hearing the

completely different dynamic than in private, individual, silent reading."[155] Where an individual member may miss an allusion or echo, the community may aid in revealing it. Further, the original letter reader would also likely help the readers understand allusive connections.

Combining these prior points, it is likely that the early churches were grounded in the JT and they were taught, by means of their frequent exposure to the JT, to naturally recognize allusion and echoes.[156] Such a situation provides rich opportunity for allusive use of the JT. It is for this reason that Allison indicates that modern readers might not be the best judges of the presence of allusion, for "Time deletes. Things that were obvious can, as a text's audience changes, evaporate."[157] He provides numerous examples, including the place of the King James Version (KJV) in English. It was once the case that the KJV was recognizable to all who heard its distinctive sound. Thus, C. S. Lewis observes that

> For three centuries the Bible was so well known that hardly any word or phrase, except those which it shared with all English books whatever, could be borrowed without recognition. If you echoed the Bible everyone knew that you were echoing the Bible. And certain associations were called up in every reader's mind—sacred associations. All your readers had heard it read, as a ritual or almost ritual act, at home, at school, and in church.[158]

Lewis indicates that such an age was quickly passing, and Allison illustrates that echoes and allusions to the KJV are now regularly missed unless explicitly stated in footnotes.[159] The point is that familiarity—perhaps especially religiously motivated—leads to a world of resonance in which those who do not share such familiarity will likely miss the cues.

Allison helps us consider the significance of an ancient reader's familiarity:

---

first reading (this is based on the known fact in the second century and the probability in the first century that letters were read repeatedly in the early church)" (Beale, *John's Use of the Old Testament*, 70).

155. Wong, "Use of Jesus' Sayings," 46.

156. Kelli O'Brien suggests that the early church, by means of constant exposure to the passion narrative in combination with the OT, was "taught to see the allusions" (O'Brien, *Use of Scripture*, 64). Such teaching wold prime the listeners for further allusions.

157. Allison, *Intertextual Jesus*, 5.

158. Lewis, "Literary Impact of the Authorised Version," 141.

159. Allison, *Intertextual Jesus*, 4–5.

> Ancients who attended religious services and who heard the same sacred texts read or chanted throughout their lifetimes probably had little difficulty catching some allusions that modern readers, who are acquainted with many more books and not intimately familiar with the texts in their original languages, have often missed.¹⁶⁰

In other words, since these early Jesus-followers were deeply familiar with a limited amount of material, resonances with that material were more likely to bring to mind allusions and echoes. Allison continues: "Ancient audiences, with their much smaller textual world, may very well have been *more accustomed to paying keener attention to linguistic details than most of us*, who live in an age of verbal inflation and speed reading, an age in which people take in texts with their eyes, not their ears."¹⁶¹

In sum, deep familiarity with the JT through constant oral repetition leads to a rich world of opportunity for allusion and echo. Dunn argued that such allusive use of Jesus' words was intentional, for it was a part of bonding the community together.¹⁶² By alluding to and echoing those words, the author was able to bring the rich words of Jesus to bear on the contemporary situation of the readers. Modern audiences—particularly scholarly critics—who are distantly removed from such a setting may have a "bias against the implicit and subtle,"¹⁶³ requiring too much evidence for an allusion. But if we were exposed to the words of Jesus as those in the first century likely were—i.e., if they were the central words of significance for our lives—it is probable that such words were heard even when "implicit and subtle."

Theron Wong, in his dissertation on the use of Jesus' words in 1P, took an exceptionally conservative approach, seeking to avoid *adding* significance to 1P by seeing allusions where none exist.¹⁶⁴ But the possibility exists that such a "conservative approach" *negates* significance that the original readers would have heard. While seeking to avoid finding what was not intended to be there, this study approaches the potential use of Jesus' words in 1P from the perspective that the JT was an authoritative body of material well-known by early Christians and ripe for allusive reference.¹⁶⁵ Such a stance does not

---

160. Allison, *Intertextual Jesus*, 14.
161. Allison, *Intertextual Jesus*, 14.
162. Dunn, "Jesus Tradition in Paul," 177.
163. Allison, *Intertextual Jesus*, 14.
164. Wong, "Use of Jesus' Sayings."
165. Graham Stanton, in his article on the use of Jesus' words in the early church, rightly notes that "a decision on the extent of allusions to traditions of the life and teaching of Jesus is inevitably based partly on presuppositions. Scholars who insist that most early Christian writers took it for granted that their readers had an extensive knowledge

lead to the automatic acceptance of every potential reference; rather, it gives serious consideration where evidence suggests a relationship.

METHOD FOR INTERPRETING JESUS' WORDS IN 1 PETER

The purpose of this thesis is to investigate how 1P uses the words of Jesus. This chapter has set the stage for such an exploration by giving credibility to the fact that the JT was known and valued as the words of Jesus by both the author and audience of 1P. Further, it has established the definitions of intertextual reference that will be used in the study and has provided criteria for how intertextual references will be identified. This final section of the chapter addresses how the rest of the thesis will seek to answer to the core question noted above.

The following chapters are divided according to the major textual sections of 1P.[166] Unfortunately, space restraints prevent an exhaustive exegetical treatment of the text. Nevertheless, broad exegetical overviews based on scholarly consensus of Peter's message will be provided for each section. After this initial exegetical overview, detailed investigation will be given to parallels that have been proposed in the history of research.[167]

The three elements necessary to intertextual references are availability, agreement, and significance. Accordingly, our study will proceed by examining each. Because we have covered the topic of availability in this chapter, it will not always be necessary to discuss it in regard to each passage. Nevertheless, occasional comments will be made when necessary.

As for agreement, we will provide detailed investigations designed to compare the text in 1P to the parallels proposed by scholars from the Synoptic Gospels and/or the Gospel of John. These parallels are not primarily examined to discover textual reliance (as though Peter knew any of the canonical Gospels as they are presently codified), though we must remain

---

of traditions about the teaching and actions of Jesus are naturally more willing to accept a considerable number of allusions. A very different view is taken by those who claim either that before about AD 150 interest in the earthly life of Jesus was less prominent in Christian preaching and teaching than we might suppose, or Jesus traditions did not circulate in all early Christian communities" (Stanton, "Jesus Traditions," 565). This study falls firmly within the first camp.

166. It is beyond the scope of this study to detail the organizational structure of 1P. Instead, we will follow the work of Lauri Thurén: chapter four covers 1:1–2; chapter five, 1:3–12; chapter six, 1:13—2:10; chapter seven, 2:11—3:12; chapter eight, 3:13—4:11; and chapter nine, 4:12—5:14 (Thurén, *Argument and Theology*, 88–185).

167. The appendix charts the proposed parallels and the origin of those parallels.

open to that possibility. Instead, the parallels are assessed with the assumption that even if there was flexibility in the expression of a particular logion, there often remains an identifiable core which can be discerned by a careful reader/listener.

In order to assess the significance of the proposed parallel, it will sometimes be necessary to develop the meaning of the *dominical logion* in its context(s).[168] This will require an exegetical consideration of one or more Gospels, allowing us to see the meaning the Gospels give to the logion, and provide a basis for comparison with 1P's usage. Further, since some allusions invoke the context of a source, this exegetical treatment will allow us to discover this deeper layer of significance.

Once the dominical saying has been understood in its context(s), attention will be given to the way the JT is used in 1P, establishing whether the proposed parallel is an allusion (essential for proper interpretation), echo (non-essential, though has significance), or trace (merely imitative, non-functional). Often this will require an examination of the intersection of the two contexts with the purpose of discerning whether there are resonances the author intended the audience to perceive.

Finally, after considering all of the proposed JT references, each chapter will conclude with a summary of 1P's use of the JT in that section. A final chapter will conclude the thesis by summarizing how 1P uses the words of Jesus to instruct, encourage, warn, and strengthen the readers.

---

168. A clear challenge faced in this regard concerns the flexibility of the ordering of JT as evidenced by the Gospel literature. Nevertheless, it is clear that some of the tradition was communicated in block format (e.g., the sayings in the Sermon on the Mount), and some of the other sayings may have also been communicated with a structure. Each passage will have to be considered on its own merits.

4

First Peter 1:1–2

SPICQ CALLED 1P AN "epistle of tradition,"[1] and subsequent studies have confirmed that assessment.[2] It is not the purpose of this thesis to investigate all of the traditions used by the author, but Travis Williams has recently pointed out something that aids our study: "The chances of literary borrowing increase when a given author has demonstrated a tendency to use source materials in other written works, and/or in the text in question."[3] When Peter's penchant for referencing external source material is combined with our earlier sociological arguments concerning the necessity and value of the JT for the early churches, there is substantial reason to think 1P would reference this body of material.

It is the burden of this chapter to explore the first two verses of the letter, discerning where Peter reflects the words of Jesus and expressing the rhetorical significance of those references.

---

1. Translated from "Peut être caractérisée comme une 'Épître de la Tradition.'" (Spicq, *Épîtres de Saint Pierre*, 15).

2. Horrell, in a chapter dedicated to examining the traces of tradition in 1P confirmed that "using modern terminology, we might say that [1P] is richly intertextual, that is to say, that the fabric of its own text is constructed with the threads of many other (pre-)texts and traditions woven into it" (Horrell, *1 Peter*, 41).

3. Williams, "Intertextuality," 179.

EXEGETICAL CONSIDERATIONS

The terse nature of 1P 1:1-2 has led to numerous exegetical possibilities and therefore numerous interpretive differences. This section of the paper will provide an exegetical examination of these verses to give credence to the view that 1P echoes the traditions found in the Gospels.

The Audience

One of the most foundational issues for the interpretation of 1P concerns the nature of the audience. We have already considered whether the author intended παρεπίδημος (exile) to be understood literally or metaphorically. Consequently, here we will assume the metaphorical interpretation; Peter presents his readers as spiritual exiles, no longer at "home" in the world (1:1; 2:11). On the basis of election, they no longer are at home in this world, for they follow Christ (2:21), yet this following includes ethical transformation (1:2) leading to tension with their previous relations in the world (4:4).

The debate over whether the readers are literal or figurative exiles comes to bear in these introductory verses. In fact, the way one takes this potential metaphor significantly influences the way the prepositional phrases in 1:2 are understood. As commentators have noted, 1P does not clearly reveal the referent of the three prepositions. It is possible that they refer back to πέτρος (Peter), but few scholars have even considered this as an exegetical option. Most scholars argue that the phrases refer back to ἐκλεκτός (elect), but many years ago Hort rightly noted that "It is . . . by no means natural that so much weight should belong to a single word unmarked for special emphasis by order or particle, divided from *v.* 2 by eight words, and itself preceded by four words."[4]

It is better to understand the phrases to refer back to the entire experience of the readers as both elect *and* exile.[5] On this reading, the text is indicating that the readers are elect-exiles in the dispersion

- according to the foreknowledge of God
- through the sanctification of the Spirit

---

4. Hort, *First Epistle of St. Peter*, 18. Hort's solution was to make the phrases refer back to the elect as well as apostle. Himes notes the problem with Hort's proposal: "Yet for three prepositions to point to both a singular *and* a plural noun would surely be asking too much" (Himes, *Foreknowledge and Social Identity*, 137).

5. "The three prepositional phrases of v. 2 modify Peter's identification of his audience as 'chosen' and 'strangers'" (Green, *1 Peter*, 18-19; cf. Grudem, *First Epistle of Peter*, 54).

- for the obedience-and-sprinkling of the blood of Christ.

The Third Preposition

Each of these prepositions are rich in significance, but the third is the most important for our purposes. After expressing that the reader's elect-exile situation is according to God's eternal plan and is enacted by the Spirit at conversion, Peter turns to consider the work of Jesus.[6] There are three interpretive problems with the third preposition: (1) the meaning of εἰς, (2) the relationship between obedience (ὑπακοήν) and sprinkling (ῥαντισμόν), and (3) the relationship of Ἰησοῦ Χριστοῦ (of Jesus Christ) to both obedience and sprinkling.[7]

Two major positions have been taken on the force of εἰς. Most interpreters argue that it has a telic sense (*for* obedience). However, Elliott, following Agnew,[8] has championed the view that the preposition should be taken as having causative force, resulting in the reading, "elect exiles in the dispersion *because* of the obedience of Christ and the sprinkling of his blood."[9] The persuasiveness of this position rests heavily on the balance it provides to the three phrases. On this reading, the Father's foreknowledge is the origin of the election, the Spirit's setting apart is the application of election, and the Son's obedience is the basis for election.

The weakness of this view is that εἰς is not used this way elsewhere in 1P, and it is only debatably used this way in the NT. In regard to 1P, Agnew himself recognizes that though the preposition occurs forty-two times in 1P, it is never causal elsewhere.[10] Further, his position is not helped by the fact that in the next few verses (3–5) Peter uses the same preposition three times, all with the telic sense.[11] More broadly, Sydney Page, points out that "The possibility that εἰς can have a causal force is not even mentioned in LSJ, Thayer, or Louw and Nida. It is mentioned in BDAG but is not endorsed there."[12]

---

6. The work of the Spirit referenced here is the initial act of the Spirit at conversion which transfers the elect into a position of holiness. Such an act ultimately results in ethical change, making one holy as God is holy (1:16) (Jobes, *1 Peter*, 69).

7. Jobes, *1 Peter*, 71.

8. Agnew, "An Alternative Translation," 68–73.

9. Elliott, *1 Peter*, 319.

10. Agnew, "An Alternative Translation," 70.

11. Achtemeier, *1 Peter*, 87.

12. Page, "Obedience and Blood-Sprinkling," 295.

One of the reasons Agnew proposes a causal interpretation is based on the second problem we noted above. Namely, if we take a telic view of the preposition, then it would appear that the genitive Ἰησοῦ Χριστοῦ (of Jesus Christ) is used in two ways at one time: obedience to Jesus Christ (objective genitive) and the sprinkling of the blood of Christ (subjective genitive). Achtemeier notes that such a double use is "something of a grammatical monstrosity."[13]

There is a reading that solves both the genitive problem and the balance problem. This is the view that 1P is using both terms to refer to a single idea (hendiadys).[14] On this reading, the third prepositional phrase is read as follows: *elect exiles of the dispersion . . . for the obedience-and-sprinkling of the blood of Christ.* Justification for this hendiadys comes from the OT account of the establishment of the Mosaic covenant in Exodus 24:3–8. Jobes explains,

> the newly formed people of Israel first pledge their obedience (24:3, 7) and then are sprinkled with the blood of the sacrifice (24:8). In this ceremony both sides of the essential nature of the covenant are represented: the people pledge obedience to God, and the blood of the covenant is applied to them. Thus the phrase "obedience and sprinkling of blood" can serve as a hendiadys to refer to God's covenant relationship with his people.[15]

While there are three places in the OT where blood is sprinkled on people,[16] Jobes is correct that the covenant episode in Exodus 24 is in view here.[17] This connection makes the words of Jesus in Mark 14:24 much more significant: "This is my blood of the covenant, which is poured out for many." James Edwards rightly notes that "the 'blood of the covenant' cannot be understood apart from the first covenant that Moses instituted by throwing blood on the people (Exod 24:3–8)."[18] Luke 22:20 makes the connection between the blood and the New Covenant (NC) even more explicit: "This cup that is poured out for you is the *new* covenant in my blood" (cf. Matt 26:28).

---

13. Achtemeier, *1 Peter*, 87..
14. Beare, *First Epistle of Peter*, 76–77; Jobes, *1 Peter*, 72.
15. Jobes, *1 Peter*, 72.
16. Exod 24:5–8; 29:21; Lev 14:6–7 (Grudem, *First Epistle of Peter*, 56).
17. So pervasive is the opinion that Exod 24 is in view, that John Pryor can say, "This link with Ex. 24 is well recognized by all commentators" (Pryor, "First Peter and the New Covenant (1)," 3). This view is confirmed by the emphasis on obedience as well as from the hints in the surrounding context that 1P is referring to the NC.
18. Edwards, *Gospel according to Mark*, 426.

Thus, the JT affirmed that Jesus' blood was connected to the NC. The observance of the Lord's Supper, as evidenced by 1 Corinthians 11:25, suggests that the early church often called to remembrance these words of Jesus. It is no surprise, then, that Michaels argues 1P's connection to the NC:

> Without speaking explicitly of a "new covenant" or the "blood of the covenant" (which may in his circles have been reserved for the Eucharist, cf. Mark 14:24; 1 Cor 11:25), Peter relies on language that had perhaps become already fixed among Christians as a way of alluding to the same typology. To "obey" was to accept the gospel and become part of a new community under a new covenant; to be sprinkled with Jesus' blood was to be cleansed from one's former way of living and released from spiritual slavery by the power of his death.[19]

By combining *obedience* with *the sprinkled blood of Christ*, 1P is calling to mind the relation between the establishment of the Mosaic Covenant and the establishment of the NC through Christ's blood.[20] Consequently, the three prepositional phrases can be understood in the following way: Peter's readers are elected exiles of the dispersion *according to* (κατά) God's foreknowledge, *through* (ἐν) the sanctification of the Spirit, *for the purpose of* (εἰς) being cleansed and obedient members of the NC.

THE WORDS OF JESUS AND 1 PETER 1:1-2

In light of the exegetical examination above, we will argue that 1P 1:1-2 shows some reliance on the JT. Indeed, the presence of the JT in 1P's introduction is not limited to a recognition of the acts of Jesus (e.g., his sacrificial death), but appears to depend on the words of Jesus. We will argue for two connections between the words of the Lord and 1P 1:2.

1 Peter 1:2 and Mark 14:23; Matthew 26:28; Luke 22:20b

As we have noted above, 1P is concerned with highlighting the identity of the readers as elect-exiles. They are undergoing some form of persecution, which appears to be primarily social in nature (2:12; 3:16; 4:4). Thus, they are experiencing rejection from the broader world. First Peter is concerned with explaining their identity and offering hope in light of that identity.

---

19. Michaels, *1 Peter*, 12-13.
20. Cf. Spicq, *Épîtres de Saint Pierre*, 43; Schelkle, *Die Petrusbriefe*, 21.

How does such an identity depend on the words of Jesus? The following table compares the texts.[21]

Table 4.1: 1 Peter 1:2 and Mark 14:23; Matthew 26:28; Luke 22:20b

1 Peter 1:2	Mark 14:23	Matthew 26:28	Luke 22:20b
κατὰ πρόγνωσιν θεοῦ πατρὸς ἐν ἁγιασμῷ πνεύματος εἰς ὑπακοὴν καὶ ῥαντισμὸν *αἵματος* Ἰησοῦ Χριστοῦ, χάρις ὑμῖν καὶ εἰρήνη πληθυνθείη.	καὶ εἶπεν αὐτοῖς· τοῦτό ἐστιν τὸ *αἷμά* μου τῆς διαθήκης τὸ ἐκχυννόμενον ὑπὲρ πολλῶν	τοῦτο γάρ ἐστιν τὸ *αἷμά* μου τῆς διαθήκης τὸ περὶ πολλῶν ἐκχυννόμενον εἰς ἄφεσιν ἁμαρτιῶν.	τοῦτο τὸ ποτήριον ἡ καινὴ διαθήκη ἐν τῷ *αἵματί* μου τὸ ὑπὲρ ὑμῶν ἐκχυννόμενον

In regard to the accessibility of this teaching, it occurs at the Last Supper, a tradition that would likely have been well-rehearsed among early believers. The significance of this episode for the early church is confirmed in that each of the Gospels detail the Lord's Supper, and this particular teaching is expressed, albeit slightly differently, in each of the Synoptic Gospels (Mark 14:23; Matt 26:28; Luke 22:20). Further, as we will note in the pages to follow, it appears that Peter reflects traditions within this larger tradition-block elsewhere in his epistle (3:22; 5:2-4, 8-9), making a reference to it here more likely.

The only significant lexical agreement is the reference to blood (αἷμα). Unfortunately, this is a frequent word in the NT and thus cannot give certainty that Peter is reflecting these words of Jesus. Nevertheless, the lexical similarity is strengthened by the ideological parallels between the passages. First, it is specifically the blood of Jesus. In the Gospels, Jesus says "my blood" (αἷμά μου), which comports with 1P as it speaks of "the blood of Jesus" (αἵματος Ἰησοῦ Χριστοῦ). Second, this blood is clearly connected to the covenant, as we argued above.

One potential challenge concerns whether Peter simply reflects Exodus 24 and not the JT. A few responses can be given. First, as we will note in the pages to follow, Peter often considers OT passages through the lens of Jesus' sayings. In other words, Peter will reflect passages that Jesus has reflected. Second, is it more likely to think Peter's audience would consider the Exodus text alone or that they would do so through reflecting on the words of Jesus? In light of the fact that these words are given at the Last Supper which was frequently reflected on in the early church (perhaps daily;

---

21. The Greek text used here and throughout this work is the Nestle-Aland 28th edition. See Aland et al., *Nestle-Aland*.

1 Cor 11:25), it seems likely that Peter's readers would link his language to Exodus *through* the teaching of Jesus. In this way, Jesus' words act as a bridge between the contexts.

A connection between these passages may be further defended by considering the significance of the connection. As Blomberg notes concerning the Gospel sayings, "The covenant language implies the creation of a community, now to be constituted of those who in their eating and drinking identify with the benefits of Jesus' sacrificial death."[22] By invoking these words of Jesus, repeated at their fellowship meals where the sociological bond was frequently strengthened, Peter reinforces their identity.

Further, each of the Gospel remembrances of the words at the Last Supper stress two elements (Mark 14:24; Matt 26:28; Luke 22:20). First, they stress the now-past sacrificial work of Christ which secures the forgiveness of sins: "this is my blood of the covenant which is poured out for many" (Mark 14:24). Accordingly, 1P can say, "You know that you were ransomed from the futile ways inherited from your ancestors, not with perishable things like silver or gold, but with the precious blood of Christ, like that of a lamb without defect or blemish" (1:18–19). In other words, their transfer from an old way of life (inherited from the forefathers) to the new way of life (elect-exile status from the Father) occurred because of the shed blood of Christ. Thus, who they are (identity) is based on the covenant-making blood-work of Jesus Christ,

Second, each of the Synoptic Gospels stresses a future element of the Lord's words, for Jesus notes that he will not drink of wine again until he does so in the kingdom. By the addition of "with you," Matthew's Gospel clarifies that the purpose of waiting is so that the members of the NC will share with Christ at the Messianic table (26:28). By echoing the words of Jesus at the Last Supper, 1P invites readers to consider their future as elect sojourners. While it is true that they must endure suffering, this is only for a little while (1:6; 5:10). Their hope should be "on the grace that Jesus Christ will bring ... when he is revealed" (1:13). This new identity has made them strangers to this land, yet expectant sojourners of another land. Each time they celebrate the Lord's Supper, they are reminded that it is because of Jesus' blood that they are both elect and exiled. Yet such an exilic status is no reason for despair, for rejection of the world evidences acceptance by God (4:13–15).

In Matthew and Mark Jesus notes that his blood was shed "for many" (ὑπὲρ πολλῶν). By referencing them as "*elect* exiles," Peter encourages them to view themselves as those for whom Christ died and for whom Christ

---

22. Blomberg, *Matthew*, 391.

established the NC. This self-reflection will be critical to their survival in a foreign land, inhabited by those who disobey the word (2:8) and inhabited by an enemy who seeks to consume them (5:8).

This intertextual reference is best classified as an echo. While recognizing the reference strongly reinforces the theme of identity, those who recognize the Exodus 24 reference would also see such an implication, albeit with less color.

1 Peter 1:2 and Matthew 28:18-20

Some commentators have also found an echo of Matthew 28 here. For example, Selwyn highlights that "the baptismal formula of Matt. 28 . . . has had some influence upon 1 Pet. 1:2."[23] Such dependence, he argues, is not directly literary, for "Were it dependent directly upon the Matthaean charge, it would presumably have been verbally closer to it."[24] Goppelt, likewise, says 1 P 1:2 is "probably related to Mt 28:19."[25]

Table 4.2: 1 Peter 1:2 and Matthew 28:19-20

1 Peter 1:2	Matthew 28:19-20
κατὰ πρόγνωσιν θεοῦ *πατρὸς* *ἐν ἁγιασμῷ πνεύματος* εἰς ὑπακοὴν καὶ ῥαντισμὸν αἵματος Ἰησοῦ Χριστοῦ, χάρις ὑμῖν καὶ εἰρήνη πληθυνθείη.	19 πορευθέντες οὖν μαθητεύσατε πάντα τὰ ἔθνη, βαπτίζοντες αὐτοὺς εἰς τὸ ὄνομα τοῦ *πατρὸς* καὶ τοῦ υἱοῦ καὶ τοῦ *ἁγίου πνεύματος*, 20 διδάσκοντες αὐτοὺς τηρεῖν πάντα ὅσα ἐνετειλάμην ὑμῖν· καὶ ἰδοὺ ἐγὼ μεθ' ὑμῶν εἰμι πάσας τὰς ἡμέρας ἕως τῆς συντελείας τοῦ αἰῶνος.

While some might consider this episode a rhetorical flourish of Matthew's pen, the similarities with Luke 24 (particularly v. 47) suggest that "the universal mission is no Matthean innovation.[26] As we noted earlier in this study, we will proceed with the assumption that the Gospels record traditions that the early church received as the words of Jesus. But in favor of the historical accuracy of an account similar to what Matthew records, we could note that the substantial outreach of the early church to Gentiles probably requires something like what is recorded here.[27]

---

23. Selwyn, *First Epistle of St. Peter*, 248.
24. Selwyn, *First Epistle of St. Peter*, 247.
25. Goppelt, *Commentary on I Peter*, 70. Cf. Beare, *First Epistle of Peter*, 76.
26. Nolland, *Gospel of Matthew*, 1266.
27. Morris, *Gospel according to Matthew*, 744.

What is the basis for arguing for an intertextual link here? First, both passages contain a "Trinitarian formula,"[28] though the formulation is not precisely the same in both texts. The order is different in 1P (Father, Spirit, Son) than in Matthew's Gospel (Father, Son, Spirit).[29] Further, 1P makes reference to *Jesus* not to *Son*, though the latter identity is implied by the term Father. Finally, the activities implied in the two texts are different. The focus of the Matthew text is on disciple-making, while the focus of the 1P text concerns the identity of the readers as elect-exiles. Nevertheless, the words of Jesus were given in the *past* in regard to those who would *one day become obedient*, and Peter speaks of the *present* blessing of those who have, by the power of the Spirit, *become obedient*. These themes meet in the experience of Peter's readers.

A second connection is not as obvious, though we have argued for it above. Both Matthew 28:16–20 and 1P 1:2 call baptism to the minds of the readers. Matthew's Gospel references baptism explicitly, but as we have argued above, the prepositional phrases of 1P 1:2 would have invoked the idea of baptism as well. The significance of baptism language again highlights the identity of the readers. It was through baptism that the readers identified with Christ and the church (cf. Acts 2:41). As Bromiley says, the significance of baptism is in its "marking a step from darkness and death to light and life. Recipients are thus confirmed in the decision they have taken, *brought into the living company of the regenerate, which is the true church.*"[30] The significance of Matthew 28 becomes even more pronounced in that the readers are encouraged to see themselves as the fulfillment of the Lord's words, a point we will now turn to.

A third connection concerns obedience. Both contexts identify disciples taken from the nations who will express obedience to Jesus Christ. Matthew's passage speaks of the original disciples taking the teachings of Jesus

---

28. While it may appaear anachronistic to call this a Trinitarian formula, texts like these are the reason the Trinitarian doctrine was established. Brox suggests that such terminology can be used, even if later Trinitarian dogmas are not to be read back into the text (Brox, *Erste Petrusbrief*, 58).

29. Schelkle suggests that the order in 1P may be due to a lack of early consensus on the ordering, or it could be based on the economy of salvation in 1P, from the origin in the Father through the mediation of the Spirit for the purpose of communion in the Son (Schelkle, *Die Petrusbriefe*, 24). Importantly, some have recognized a trinitarian cast to 1:3–12, and that is ordered Father, Son, Spirit, suggesting that the order here is based on the needs of the context (Boismard, "Liturgie Baptismale (1)," 183; Elliott, *1 Peter*, 326). Unnik argues that the order is reflective of the OT reference, since the order follows "the way in which the Lord made Israel His own people at Mount Sinai" (Unnik, "Christianity according to 1 Peter," 114–15).

30. Bromiley, "Baptism," 109; emphasis added. Cf. Clerck, "Baptism," 154.

to the nations for the purpose of leading them to obedience to Jesus, while 1P speaks of a section of people from the nations who have been called out for obedience to Jesus in the NC. One interesting resonance that occurs due to this connection concerns the readers as the fulfillment of the charge given by Jesus in Matthew 28. That is, if 1P is echoing the tradition preserved in Matthew 28, the text encourages the readers to see their identity in light of what has come to be called Jesus' Great Commission. They are who they are because, as 1P 1:25 says, they have believed the word of "the good news that was announced to [them]." In this light, they are only a small part of what God is doing throughout the world. This makes sense of the fact that 1P encourages the readers by reminding them that the sufferings they are enduring are being endured by the brotherhood throughout the world (5:9). If they need a portrait of their identity, it is found in the final words of Jesus to his disciples—i.e., they are the product of Jesus' resurrection victory, who have become obedient through the Spirit as evidenced by their baptismal entry into the new community of God's people.

There are certainly challenges to seeing an intertextual reference to Matthew 28. First, only Matthew's Gospel contains the Great Commission in this form, and thus one might ask whether such a tradition was available to the readers of 1P. Of course, as Elliott notes, "The combination of sanctifying action with Spirit, together with the triadic form of 1:2a–c, suggests the influence here of primitive Christian baptismal tradition."[31] If one asks what the source of such a tradition is, the answer is likely a tradition similar to Matthew 28. Second, the agreement between the texts is not verbal, but ideological. The challenge is that such ideological similarities are shared in other early Christian teaching (e.g., 2 Thess 2:13), making a non-debatable connection between the texts difficult to substantiate. Finally, while the connections between these texts are highly suggestive and rich in potential resonance, it is clearly not necessary to understand 1P 1:2 in reference to Matthew 28:18–20. Thus, it is possible that 1P is echoing the tradition found in Matthew 28, but it is not possible to prove such an echo.

CONCLUSION TO 1 PETER 1:1–2

The influence of the words of Jesus on 1P 1:1–2 may be easy for the modern reader to miss, but we have sought to show that the echoes of Jesus' words in these verses reverberate with significance for those who listen for them. The readers are called to view themselves in light of the unfolding plan of God in history. While they once were not a people, they have now been called

---

31. Elliott, *1 Peter*, 318–19.

through Christ's shed blood to be members of a NC. Further, 1P may be encouraging the readers to see themselves as the fruit of the Great Commission given to the disciples of Jesus. While they are exiles, they are *elect* exiles, chosen from the nations to be obedient to Jesus Christ.

5

First Peter 1:3–12

THE FIRST TWO VERSES of 1P served to identify the readers as members of the New Covenant through the Father's choice, the Spirit's sanctifying action, and the Son's covenant-making work. 1:3–12 turns away neither from the identity of the readers nor the Trinitarian formulation. In reference to the identity of the readers, these introductory verses highlight that the paradoxical situation they presently live in (suffering because rejected by the world, blessed because chosen by God) is the result of their new birth, and is part of the God's plan. While they must suffer for a little while (1:6), such suffering is a badge of identity with God, for as 1P will reveal, the suffering of God's people is expected in light of the suffering of Christ (2:21). Further, such suffering will result in praise, glory and honor when Jesus returns. Indeed, their place within the history of redemption is enviable, both to the prophets as well as to the angelic witnesses (1:10–12).

The organizational structure of these introductory verses is complex. In Greek, the entire section is composed of one extended sentence.[1] Commentators have divided the passage in different ways, but it appears that 1P is continuing to develop the identity of the readers in a triadic fashion. Just as 1:1–2 was structured according to a Trinitarian pattern, so these verses are as well (Father [vv 3–5], Jesus [vv 6–9], and Holy Spirit [vv 10–12]).[2] Our consideration of the passage below will follow this triadic pattern.

---

1. Brox rightly calls this complex sentence "skillful" and "impressive" (Brox, *Erste Petrusbrief*, 60).

2. Elliott, *1 Peter*, 329. Cf. Boismard, "Liturgie Baptismale (1)," 183.

This opening section situates the identity of the readers both theologically and hermeneutically.[3] Theologically, they are born again by the rich mercy of God through the resurrection of Christ for a secure, eternal inheritance (1:3–5). Hermeneutically, they are the generation who experiences the fulfillment of the prophecies promised beforehand, and they, like Christ, are destined for suffering before future glory (1:10–12). These two realities contextualize the present experience of suffering, for such suffering is only for a little while and is experienced alongside great hope and joy (1:6–9). The future-redemptive element is highly stressed in this section, for each of the sub-sections concludes with a consideration of salvation.[4]

The importance of this section to the letter has been recognized in various studies. Kendall, for instance, argues that 1:3–12 "provides the foundation for *all* of the author's subsequent remarks."[5] Fika van Rensburg, following Kendall, suggests that 1P is organized around these introductory verses, with the rest of the epistle being four extended inferences flowing out from these initial considerations.[6]

In light of this structure, if Peter is concerned to ground the message of the letter in JT, it is likely that we will find reference to Jesus' words here. The rest of this chapter will consider three subsections (1:3–5, 6–9, 10–12), paying particular attention to the influence of *dominical logion*.

1 PETER 1:3–5

Verse 3 begins with a doxology concerning the Father who has mercifully given new birth to the readers. Three prepositional phrases, introduced by εἰς provide expansive explanation of this new birth, which is *for* a living hope, *for* an inheritance, and *for* salvation. The living hope is clarified by the addition that such hope is grounded in the resurrection of Jesus from the dead. The second prepositional phrase is expanded in extensive consideration of the type of inheritance gained through the new birth. This inheritance is described by three adjectives (imperishable, undefiled, and unfading) and expanded upon by a participial clause that indicates the inheritance is kept in heaven for the readers. Consideration of the readers in light of the inheritance leads the author to encourage the readers that they are guarded by God's power through faith. The final prepositional phrase indicates that the salvation gained through new birth is not a fully realized

---

3. Jobes, *1 Peter*, 79.
4. Green, *1 Peter*, 22.
5. Kendall, "Literary and Theological Function," 106.
6. Rensburg, "Outline of 1 Peter," 41.

salvation; rather, it will be revealed in the last time. We will consider two proposed parallels within this section of 1P: 1:3 and John 3:3-7; 1:4; Luke 12:33; Matthew 6:20.

1 Peter 1:3 and John 3:3-7

First Peter's use of ἀναγεννάω (to cause to be born again) has sometimes been understood to reflect the tradition also found in John 3, concerning the necessity of being born again.[7] However, as the following table reveals, the dependence is not based on precise textual similarities.

Table 5.1: 1 Peter 1:3 and John 3:3

1 Peter 1:3	John 3:3
Εὐλογητὸς ὁ θεὸς καὶ πατὴρ τοῦ κυρίου ἡμῶν Ἰησοῦ Χριστοῦ ὁ κατὰ τὸ πολὺ αὐτοῦ ἔλεος *ἀναγεννήσας ἡμᾶς* εἰς ἐλπίδα ζῶσαν δι' ἀναστάσεως Ἰησοῦ Χριστοῦ ἐκ νεκρῶν	ἀπεκρίθη Ἰησοῦς καὶ εἶπεν αὐτῷ· ἀμὴν ἀμὴν λέγω σοι, ἐὰν μή τις *γεννηθῇ ἄνωθεν*, οὐ δύναται ἰδεῖν τὴν βασιλείαν τοῦ θεοῦ.

As noted earlier, every alleged reference to the Gospel of John in 1P is open to scholarly doubt concerning the availability of the JT.[8] Nevertheless, 1P may provide evidence of early church awareness of the JT as preserved in John's Gospel.[9] Further, Bauckham is correct to note that more significance needs to be given to the claim that the Gospel of John was penned by an eyewitness.[10] This, along with the observation that the early church was interconnected,[11] suggests that this narrative, in at least oral form, is likely to have been known in the early church.[12]

---

7. Gundry, "'Verba Christi' in I Peter," 339; Maier, "Jesustradition," 89; Jobes, *1 Peter*, 83; Michaels, *1 Peter*, 17-18; Bigg, *Epistles of St. Peter*, 100; Boismard, "Liturgie Baptismale (1)," 203.

8. See the earlier discussion for more general comments on the issue.

9. For example, Feuillet finds the evidence in 1P of the use of material in John's Gospel as evidence that the traditions contained in the fourth Gospel are legitimate. For Feuillet, the use of Fourth Gospel material in 1P "suggests that although this tradition was recorded in a gospel much later, it is not a creation and a theological speculation of the end of the first century" (translated from, "Cela suggère que si cette tradition n'a été consignée dans un évangile que beaucoup plus tard, elle n'est pas pour autant une création et une spéculation théologique de la fin du premier siècle [Feuillet, "Quelques Reflexions," 242, 247]).

10. Bauckham, *Jesus and the Eyewitnesses*, 358-83.

11. Thompson, "The Holy Internet."

12. Gundry finds Titus 3:5 to be another text reflective of the Nicodemus narrative

What form of agreement exists between 1P 1:3 and John 3:3? Initially, the lexical evidence looks sparse, for 1P has ἀναγεννήσας, while John 3 has γεννηθῇ ἄνωθεν. Nevertheless, Justin Martyr when commenting on John 3 used a form of ἀναγεννάω, suggesting the lexical equivalence of γεννηθῇ ἄνωθεν to ἀναγεννάω.[13] Further, the use of the term in John 3 is part of a word-play in which the reading can be either *born again* or *born from above*. Thus, the use of γεννηθῇ ἄνωθεν was necessary for such a rhetorical device.[14] 1P lacking such a device, can use the compound ἀναγεννήσας to communicate the idea of being born again.[15] Indeed, if 1P 1:3 and John 3:3–7 are based on a similar tradition, it is not necessary that they use precisely the same verbage. In the words of Gerhard Maier, "light differences in formulation must be expected."[16] What must exist for our purposes, however, is that the language is sufficiently similar to identify the connection, a sufficiency we find here.[17]

Before examining the relationship between 1P and the tradition recorded in John 3, it is necessary to recognize that prior scholars have suggested other fountains of tradition for the "begotten anew" conception. Perdelwitz, for instance, argued that the source of the tradition was the mystery religions.[18] Scholars widely reject this conclusion today, not only because it lacks sufficient evidence,[19] but also because there are closer, more

---

(Gundry, "Further Verba," 219).

13. "For the Christ also said, Unless you are born again [ἂν μὴ ἀναγεννηθῆτε], you will never enter the kingdom of heaven" (Martyr, *Apology*, 1.61).

14. Likewise, Michaels says, "γεννᾶν ἄνωθεν is perhaps a Johannine adaptation making possible either the meaning 'born again' or as the use of ἄνωθεν in John 3:31 suggests—'born from above'" (Michaels, *1 Peter*, 17).

15. Silva argues that "the compound ἀναγεννάω in 1 Pet 1:3 (act.) and 23 (pass.) clearly means, 'to beget again, give new birth,' and the sense is very similar to that of γεννάω in John 3:3–8" (Silva, *New International Dictionary*, s.v. "γεννάω," 1:559–64). Likewise, Ernest Best in his debate with Gundry over this text recognizes that though the words used are different, "the conception is the same" (Best, "I Peter and the Gospel Tradition," 98).

16. Translated from, "Geringe Unterschiede der Formulierung muß man geradezu erwarten" (Maier, "Jesustradition," 89).

17. Gundry adds that the differences in the way new birth is spoken of are "easily explicable as a variant in translation from Aramaic or Hebrew or as a difference in preference as to Greek style" (Gundry, "Further Verba," 218).

18. Perdelwitz, *Mysterienreligion und Das Problem*, 42–45; cf. Shimada, "Formulary Material in First Peter," 175–76; Goppelt, *Commentary on I Peter*, 81–82.

19. Silva, for instance, notes that despite the popularity of the view within the German school, there is no evidence prior to the fourth century of the verb ἀναγεννάω in such mystery religions (Silva, *New International Dictionary*, s.v. "γεννάω," 1:559–64).

likely candidates for the tradition.²⁰ As Michaels says, "Certainly the Gospel tradition, is a nearer and more plausible source for Peter's terminology than, e.g., the pagan mystery religions."²¹

Some scholars have traced the begotten-anew concept back to Jewish sources. Selwyn, for instance, notes similar conceptions in rabbinic literature.²² Nevertheless, as is the case with much of the rabbinic material, it is not clear that this teaching was in circulation in the first century,²³ and the sparse data seems to indicate that even if it was, it was not a significant conception in the Jewish world.²⁴ Goppelt connects the begotten-anew conception to the Essenes, though he cannot reproduce a text that uses similar terminology. Instead, he merely suggests a connection between new creation, which was attested in Essene literature, and new birth, which is not attested in the literature.²⁵

In light of the above, Brox is right to conclude that the attempt to derive the begotten-anew concept from Jewish backgrounds or a Hellenist Mystery religion context fails.²⁶ The Petrine use of the idea that one is begotten again and therefore born again, is distinctive to the teaching of Jesus, even if there are analogous concepts in the surrounding culture (whether Hellenistic or Jewish). And despite the analogous concepts, Jobes is right to say that "the most immediate source for the new-birth concept is found in the first-century Christian tradition that originated in the teachings of Jesus himself."²⁷

Gundry and Best debated the relationship between 1P 1:3 and John 3:3ff. Best offered four reasons to believe the traditions behind John 3:3–7 and 1P 1:3 were different. First, he argued that the language was insufficiently similar, a point we have addressed above. Second, he argued that "though the idea of rebirth is similar the *modus operandi* is different, and

20. Schelkle notes that the use of the word ἀναγεννάω "is so far away from the Mysteries that [the author of 1P] did not directly and deliberately borrow the word from there" (translated from "Den Mysterien steht er so ferne, daß er das Wort nicht unmittelbar und absichtlich von dort entlehnt hat" (Schelkle, *Die Petrusbriefe*, 31; cf. Gustave, *Enseignement de Saint Pierre*, 74).

21. Michaels, *1 Peter*, 17–18; cf. Maier, "Jesustradition," 89.

22. Selwyn, *First Epistle of St. Peter*, 306.

23. Shimada, "Formulary Material," 175; Neusner, "Use of the Later Rabbinic Evidence," 215–28.

24. Elliott also suggests that "whereas the rabbis speak of divine 'begetting' but never of divine 'regeneration,' our author repeatedly employs only the latter concept (1:3, 23; 2:2a)" (Elliott, *1 Peter*, 333).

25. Goppelt, *Commentary on I Peter*, 82–83.

26. Brox, *Erste Petrusbrief*, 61.

27. Jobes, *1 Peter*, 83.

it is an important difference."[28] Stated differently, Best argues that rebirth comes through the resurrection (1:3) and word (1:23) in 1P, while it comes through the Spirit and baptism in John 3. Gundry responded in three ways: (1) the connection between the resurrection and new birth is not made explicit until after the resurrection; (2) the ideas of resurrection and baptism are closely related in the early church; (3) and if the author of 1P could suggest new birth comes through *both* the word (1:23) and the resurrection (1:3), "why should a difference in *modus operandi* be thought crucial?"[29]

Best's third criticism of the relationship between the traditions is that "rebirth is found in the NT apart from the direct influence of the teaching of Jesus ... Titus 3:5 cannot be directly linked to John 3:3ff."[30] In response, Gundry offers a number of reflections that show the connection between John 3:3–7 and Titus 3:5–7,[31] but it is not necessary to defend such a connection. For even if the only similarity between Titus 3:5–7 and John 3:3–7 was the similar idea of new birth, one must ask where the idea derived, and the tradition recorded in John 3 would still be most likely.[32]

This leads to the consideration of Best's final critique, a form of an argument we have addressed above. He indicates that there no reason to think the idea of regeneration was unique to Jesus, for "it was, in fact, part of the religious atmosphere of Asia Minor."[33] Yet surely, *even if* there were similar ideas in the surrounding culture that are clearly analogous (a debatable point), one should first look to the JT before speculating about other sources. This is another way of saying, with Maier, that "similarities must first be examined in the inner-Christian or inner-New Testament space."[34]

In sum, it is quite likely that the idea of regeneration derives from the words of Jesus and that both 1P 1:3 and John 3:3 derive from the same tradition. In regard to significance, both passages connect the new birth to the NC. First Peter does so by means of the consideration of the blood of Christ and the work of the Spirit as expressed in 1:2. John 3:5 does so in regard to

---

28. Best, "I Peter and the Gospel Tradition," 98.

29. Gundry, "Further Verba," 218–19.

30. Best, "I Peter and the Gospel Tradition," 98.

31. Gundry, "Further Verba," 219.

32. Boismard has made a substantial case for a relationship between Titus 3:5 and 1P 1:3 (Boismard, "Liturgie Baptismale (1)," 186; cf. Shimada, "Formulary Material," 176–82). If he is correct, such a connection may strengthen the idea of a shared tradition that is likewise reflected in John's Gospel.

33. Notably, Best provides no argument for this claim (Best, *1 Peter*, 98).

34. Translated from, "Zusammenhänge zuerst im innerchristlichen bzw. innerneutestamentlichen Raum untersucht werden müssen" (Maier, "Jesustradition," 89; cf. Wong, "Use of Jesus' Sayings," 194).

mentioning the necessity of being born "of water and Spirit" (ἐξ ὕδατος καὶ πνεύματος). Undeniably, John 3:5 has a long history of interpretive debate. Nevertheless, most interpreters recognize the influence of Ezekiel 36:25-27, one of the chief passages detailing the benefits of the NC.[35] In both 1P and John 3, then, there is a direct connection between the blessings of the NC and the new birth. This serves to highlight that when 1P turns from 1:2 to 1:3, the author is not abandoning the NC conception or the explicit description of the identity of the readers. Instead, the new birth analogy is merely another way of speaking of the reader's entrance into the NC, a place where the readers have been set apart by the renewing of the Spirit.

As Linda Belleville has noted, "Spiritual 'birth' of the individual with God as 'Father' is unique to the NT."[36] Thus, while the NC work of the Spirit was anticipated, the way Jesus develops that tradition is distinctive. Such unique expression is of critical importance in 1P, for as we noted above, the idea of rebirth is central to the development of the book.[37]

In sum, 1P is calling the readers to identify themselves as members of the NC on the basis of the choice of the Father, the blood of Christ, and the work of the Spirit. This work of the Spirit has set them apart, giving them a new birth into a new family with God as the Father.[38] The rest of the epistle develops the implications of this identity. Important for our purposes is that two of the major motifs used to explain the identity of the people—members of the NC and newborns—are based on the words of Jesus.[39] In both cases, these complex ideas are presented without explanation, suggesting that the stock of shared tradition already explained these motifs. The author of 1P could simply mention the blood, expecting the readers to recognize the reference to the words at the Last Supper connecting the blood to the New Covenant. Likewise, the author simply mentions new birth, expecting his readers *not* to experience the same confusion as Nicodemus, but

---

35. McCabe, "Meaning of 'Born of Water,'" 92-93; Beasley-Murray, "John 3:3, 5," 168-69; Carson, *Gospel according to John*, 192-96.

36. Belleville, "'Born of Water and Spirit,'" 137. As we noted above, some Jewish conceptions come close, particularly in regard to seeing initiates like newborn children. Nevertheless, the idea that God is the Father and that there is a new begetting is not found in any Jewish tradition.

37. Rensburg, "Outline of 1 Peter," 41.

38. After analyzing new birth language in 1P, the Gospel of John, 1 John, and James, Shimada concludes, "it appears probable that, at least in some quarters of the early Church the idea of rebirth (-new birth) was common enough to find different formulations or usage to designate the new status of Christians" (Shimada, "Formulary Material," 191).

39. A third motif is that the readers are exiles and foreigners, an idea sourced in the OT (see above).

instead recognizing that the work of the Spirit grants new life and identity. Since the author assumes the audience's knowledge of this metaphor, it is likely he is intentionally alluding to it. Indeed, without previous knowledge of Jesus' development of the new birth motif, this passage would be difficult to comprehend.[40]

1 Peter 1:4 and Luke 12:33; Matthew 6:20

First Peter 1:4 speaks of the invaluable inheritance reserved for those who have been born again. Michaels suggests that the connection from 1:3 is natural, for "it is likely that Peter's thought is still being shaped by the traditional saying of Jesus about rebirth that seems to underlie v 3: 'Unless you are born again, you will not *inherit* the kingdom of heaven.'"[41] But Selwyn suggests that the theologically rich word "inheritance" (κληρονομία) drew the readers to consider the OT.[42] Achtemeier recognizes (with Michaels) that the passage may reflect the JT, but ultimately suggests (with Selwyn) that it is more reflective of the OT.[43] Many others have suggested the influence of Jesus' words on this passage, particularly the teaching of Luke 12:33.[44] So which is the source—the teaching of Jesus or the OT tradition?

It is not clear one has to choose between them. If we remember that 1P is presenting the readers as members of the NC, then we can affirm that 1P compares the promises of the prior covenant to the NC promises in light

---

40. It is not necessary to argue that Peter's readers knew the entirety of the Nicodemus narrative. What is necessary is that the audience had been exposed to teaching on the new birth, a teaching harmonious with the way the concept is developed in the Nicodemus narrative.

41. Emphasis added. Michaels says, "Peter's use of the term, however, is most closely related to NT passages that speak of "inheriting" (κληρονομεῖν) either "the kingdom" . . . or "eternal life" . . . or an equivalent" (Michaels, *1 Peter*, 20)."

42. "The use of the term κληρονομία [inheritance] would have awakened deep chords of religious patriotism in all who cherished the memories of Israel's past." Selwyn, *First Epistle of St. Peter*, 71.

43. Achtemeier, *1 Peter*, 96.

44. Gundry, "'Verba Christi' in I Peter," 337; Gundry, "Further Verba," 223; Best, "I Peter and the Gospel Tradition," 103-4; Wilkes, "Synoptic Tradition," 77; Michaels, *1 Peter*, 20-21; Selwyn, *First Epistle of St. Peter*, 124-25; Gourbillon and Buit, *Première Épître de Saint Pierre*, 47; Fronmüller, *Epistles General of Peter*, 15; Boismard, "Liturgie Baptismale (1)," 118.

of the words of Jesus (Matt 25:34),[45] the one whose redemptive work made the NC possible.[46]

The following table reveals the similarity of thought and language between 1P 1:4 and Luke 12:33, along with Matthew 6:20, a close parallel to the Luke passage.

Table 5.2: 1 Peter 1:4 and Luke 12:33b; Matthew 6:20

1 Peter 1:4	Luke 12:33b	Matthew 6:20
εἰς *κληρονομίαν* ἄφθαρτον καὶ ἀμίαντον καὶ ἀμάραντον τετηρημένην *ἐν οὐρανοῖς* εἰς ὑμᾶς	ποιήσατε ἑαυτοῖς βαλλάντια μὴ παλαιούμενα, *θησαυρὸν* ἀνέκλειπτον *ἐν τοῖς οὐρανοῖς*, ὅπου κλέπτης οὐκ ἐγγίζει οὐδὲ σὴς διαφθείρει	*θησαυρίζετε* δὲ ὑμῖν *θησαυροὺς ἐν οὐρανῷ* ὅπου οὔτε σὴς οὔτε βρῶσις ἀφανίζει καὶ ὅπου κλέπται οὐ διορύσσουσιν οὐδὲ κλέπτουσιν

That both Luke and Matthew record this tradition suggests its wide purchase in the early church, strengthening the case for its availability to the author and audience of 1P (cf. Col 1:5, 12). Further, this teaching resides in a text block frequently referenced by Peter (1:6, 13; 2:11–12; 3:9; 4:10; 5:7), making a reference to it here more likely. The agreement of the Gospel passages to the text of 1P has been a point of debate, however. Boismard, for instance, finds the relationship between the texts so compelling that he says, 1P 1:4 "is without doubt a reminiscence of the words of Christ in Luke 12:33."[47] Maier, on the other hand, argues that, in light of the lack of verbal similarity between Luke 12:33 and 1P 1:4, we must leave the question open.[48]

There are numerous reasons to suggest a shared tradition behind these verses. First, both passages contrast the imperishable, future, heavenly (ἐν οὐρανοῖς) rewards of those who follow Christ with present, perishable, earthly possessions. Second, as Gundry has noted, "1P's ἄφθαρτον ('imperishable') gives in a single word the thought of Luke's short clause οὐδὲ

---

45. A few commentators suggest a connection between Matt 25:34 and this passage: "Then the king will say to those at his right hand, 'Come, you that are blessed by my Father, inherit the kingdom prepared for you from the foundation of the world.'" Such a passage shows that the inheritance is the kingdom (Chase, "Peter, First Epistle," 788; Spence, *1 Peter*, 1:20; Achtemeier, *1 Peter*, 10).

46. Grudem, *First Epistle of Peter*, 62.

47. Translated from, "Au v. 4, l'idée de l'héritage incorruptible, gardé dans les cieux, est sans doute une réminiscence de cette parole du Christ rapportée en Lc., xii, 33" (Boismard, "Liturgie Baptismale (1)," 188).

48. Maier, "Jesustradition," 87.

σὴς διαφθείρει ('neither moth causes to perish')."[49] Third, both share the concept that the inheritance is secure.[50] Fourth, while κληρονομια (inheritance) and θησαυρὸν (treasure) are not translation equivalents as Gundry initially argued,[51] Best rightly recognizes that there is reason to believe 1P would modify *treasure* to *inheritance*: "1 Peter stresses the continuity of the church with the OT People of God and therefore the change to 'inheritance' is a likely modification."[52] Finally, as Selwyn has highlighted, both passages lead to "the practical exhortation to vigilance and hope (Luke 12:35; 1P 1:13)."[53]

Gundry overstates the case when he says that "almost every word and phrase in 1P 1:4 has its counterpart in Luke 12:33."[54] Two of the three descriptive adjectives from 1P 1:4 are not paralleled in Luke 12:33. Nevertheless, this passage is one of the few that Best poses as possibly related to the Gospel tradition. In his assessment, 1P reflects a Lukan or pre-Lukan reading.[55] In response, Gundry denies 1P's direct reliance on Luke. By highlighting the similarity between 1P 1:4 and Matthew 6:20, Gundry argues that the similarities amongst the three passages (1P 1:4; Matt 6:20; Luke 12:33) is best explained by the known tradition of the words of Jesus.[56] Similarly, Selwyn argues that 1P 1:4 "recalls the striking passage in Luke 12:22-40, which probably underlies it, though not directly but mediately through the tradition."[57]

---

49. Gundry, "'Verba Christi' in I Peter," 337.

50. 1P's kept (τηρέω) in heaven may compare to Luke's analogy of the absence of the thief.

51. Gundry initially said they were translation variants (Gundry, "'Verba Christi' in I Peter," 337). Best corrected him, and Gundry acknowledged his error (Best, "I Peter and the Gospel Tradition," 104; Gundry, "Further Verba," 223).

52. Best, "I Peter and the Gospel Tradition," 104. Further, Gundry has shown that "the two words are closely associated, as shown in the story of the rich young ruler, who asked what he might do to 'inherit' eternal life and received answer that he should sell all and give to the poor to have "treasure in heaven" (Mark 10:17-21; par. Luke 18:18-22; Mt 19:21)" (Gundry, "Further Verba," 224. Cf. Wilkes, "Synoptic Tradition," 77).

53. Selwyn, *First Epistle of St. Peter*, 124-25.

54. Further, Gundry's association of 1P's "for you" (εἰς ὑμᾶς) with Luke's "for yourselves" (ἑαυτοῖς) is not persuasive (Gundry, "'Verba Christi' in I Peter," 337).

55. Best, "I Peter and the Gospel Tradition," 105.

56. Gundry is not against suggesting that 1P's language reflects the known tradition, for he asks, "are we so sure a firsthand hearer would not have used a modified form [of a Jesus saying]?" (Gundry, "Further Verba," 223-24).

57. Selwyn, *First Epistle of St. Peter*, 124.

Earlier we noted that Maier cast doubt on the relation between these passages. He could only say that "the thought of the two passages is related."[58] What makes him hesitant to see a connection is that the rich images of the moth and thief are missing from 1P. Clearly, this would be a significant change, for 1P is quite fond of pictorial images.[59] But there is good reason to believe 1P purposefully bypassed the images attached to both Matthew 6:20 and Luke 12:33. While 1P is fond of rich images, the author is also fond of wordplay, with both alliteration and assonance in this passage.[60] The three adjectives are alpha-privatives (ἄφθαρτον, ἀμίαντον, ἀμάραντον), forming what Michaels calls "a classic negative way of characterizing persons or things that strain one's descriptive powers."[61] In other words, 1P describes the inheritance this way for rhetorical effect, for in doing so the author implies that "he can only set forth what it is by declaring what it is not."[62]

Despite the rich similarity between these passages, the lack of matching imagery (moth, rust, thief) leads to the conclusion that the author may not have been pressing for his readers to overtly recognize the reference. Further, it is clearly not necessary to the interpretation of the passage to recognize the words of Jesus. Therefore, this intertextual reference is best classified as an echo. But, as we noted earlier, even echoes have significance. One primary reason an author uses the words or ideas of a previous text are due to the resonances that exist between the prior context and the present context. Thus, we may ask, what resonances exist between these texts? Since the tradition is appropriated in different ways by Luke and Matthew, and because it is not clear that 1P is following either text directly, we are on safest ground by limiting our comments to those elements shared by both Gospel passages.

A theme highlighted in both Gospel passages is the transient nature of earthly goods and the eternal, enduring significance of the heavenly inheritance. In terms of 1P, the readers appear to have lost their social standing in light of their association with Christ. This would undoubtedly have been connected to the loss of earthly privilege and riches. Is such a life worth the cost? By recalling the words of Jesus, 1P notes that the inheritance gained as newly born members of God's family far surpasses what they have lost (cf.

---

58. Translated from, "Außerdem ist die Gedankenführung beider Stellen miteinander verwandt" (Maier, "Jesustradition," 87).

59. See the extensive list as detailed by Elliott, *1 Peter*, 66.

60. Beare notes that the "paronomasia of the three verbals is most effective" (Beare, *First Epistle of Peter*, 83). Elliott notes that the author has a "rhetorical sensitivity for assonance" (Elliott, *1 Peter*, 345).

61. Michaels, *1 Peter*, 20; cf Spicq, *Épîtres de Saint Pierre*, 46.

62. Trench, *Synonyms of the New Testament*, 239.

Mark 10:30). If Jesus' original listeners were encouraged to *begin* investing in eternity, 1P's readers needed to be encouraged in light of their *already* costly investment. In both cases, the reward far outweighs the investment.

Further 1P is seeking to encourage the audience to view themselves in light of their new identity as members of the NC, who have been born again into a new family, with God as Father. This identity puts them on a new path, one with an alternative destination. As Jesus indicated in Matthew 25:34, the inheritance of those who trust in him is the kingdom. In this light, Hort is correct to note that κληρονομία (inheritance) directly complements their identity as "exiles,"[63] for their new identity is the reason they are both exiled and possessors of a heavenly inheritance.[64]

1 PETER 1:6–9

The second section of the opening to 1P (1:6–9) continues considering the significance of the new birth. The two occurrences of "rejoice" (ἀγαλλιᾶσθε; 1:6, 8) provide structure to these four verses. The author encourages the readers to rejoice in light of the new birth leading to inheritance just mentioned,[65] yet he cannot simply tell them to rejoice without also considering their present suffering. Thus, Michaels identifies the entire discussion between the verbs (6b–8b) as a digression from the author's main point, which is that the readers should rejoice in the inheritance for they will receive final salvation.[66]

Nevertheless, to call the verses on suffering and testing a digression appears to diminish their importance. Instead, as Achtemeier has noted, these verses put the epistle's opening comments concerning Christians as dispersed exiles in fuller perspective: "It is precisely because they are a new people that they no longer fit in well with the society in which they were once at home."[67] Thus, the digression is not accidental, but rather serves as a necessary explanation of the current experience of the audience. They are

---

63. Hort, *First Epistle of St. Peter*, 35; cf. Feldmeier, *First Letter of Peter*, 71–72.

64. Though a few commentators suggested a parallel between 1:4 and the tradition preserved in Mark 12:7; Matt 21:38; and Luke 20:14, the only significant similarity is the use of the word κληρονομία (inheritance), which Foster rightly recognizes as too common a word to connect these passages (Foster, *Literary Relations*, 499).

65. There is substantial debate concerning the nature of the relative pronoun here (ἐν ᾧ). It is best to see the antecedent referring to the entirety of the preceding thought.

66. Michaels, *1 Peter*, 26. See also McKnight, *1 Peter*, 71.

67. Achtemeier, *1 Peter*, 99.

elect and therefore should rejoice in the promised inheritance, but they are also *exiles* and therefore experience present suffering.[68]

1 Peter 1:6 and Matthew 5:10-12; Luke 6:22-23

Rejoicing in suffering is a theme prevalent in NT epistolary literature (Rom 5:3 5; Heb 10:32-34; Jas 1:2).[69] There is substantial debate concerning the origin of this thought in regard to the text of 1P, and we must enter that discussion here. Before doing so, it will be helpful to provide a table comparing the wording of the proposed Gospel parallel passages to the text of 1P.

Table 5.3: 1 Peter 1:6 and Matthew 5:10-12; Luke 6:22-23

1 Peter 1:6	Matthew 5:10-12	Luke 6:22-23
ἐν ᾧ <u>ἀγαλλιᾶ-σθε</u> ὀλίγον ἄρτι, εἰ δέον ἐστίν, λυπηθέντας ἐν ποικίλοις πειρασμοῖς	μακάριοι οἱ δεδιωγμένοι ἕνεκεν δικαιοσύνης, ὅτι αὐτῶν ἐστιν ἡ βασιλεία τῶν οὐρανῶν. 11 μακάριοί ἐστε ὅταν ὀνειδίσωσιν ὑμᾶς καὶ διώξωσιν καὶ εἴπωσιν πᾶν πονηρὸν καθ' ὑμῶν [ψευδόμενοι] ἕνεκεν ἐμοῦ. 12 χαίρετε καὶ <u>ἀγαλλιᾶ-σθε</u>, ὅτι ὁ μισθὸς ὑμῶν πολὺς ἐν τοῖς οὐρανοῖς· οὕτως γὰρ ἐδίωξαν τοὺς προφήτας τοὺς πρὸ ὑμῶν.	μακάριοί ἐστε ὅταν μισήσωσιν ὑμᾶς οἱ ἄνθρωποι καὶ ὅταν ἀφορίσωσιν ὑμᾶς καὶ ὀνειδίσωσιν καὶ ἐκβάλωσιν τὸ ὄνομα ὑμῶν ὡς πονηρὸν ἕνεκα τοῦ υἱοῦ τοῦ ἀνθρώπου· 23 χάρητε ἐν ἐκείνῃ τῇ ἡμέρᾳ καὶ σκιρτήσατε, ἰδοὺ γὰρ ὁ μισθὸς ὑμῶν πολὺς ἐν τῷ οὐρανῷ· κατὰ τὰ αὐτὰ γὰρ ἐποίουν τοῖς προφήταις οἱ πατέρες αὐτῶν.

Before addressing the issue of agreement between 1P 1:6 and the Gospel parallels, it is necessary to address the origin of this joyful-suffering tradition. Brox, for instance, while agreeing that 1P stands in an "early Christian persecution tradition" also indicates that "this tradition is not a

---

68. Maier suggests parallels between 1P 1:7 and Luke 17:26ff and between 1:9 and Matt 16:25ff and Mark 8:35ff (par. Luke 21:19). Since these proposed parallels lacked sufficient agreement with 1P they were not considered here (Maier, "Jesustradition," 97).

69. Gerhard Barth notes that joy in suffering is a "relatively strong tradition that runs through almost the entire NT" (translated from, "eine relativ festgeprägte Tradition handelt, die sich fast durch das ganze Neue Testament zieht" [Barth, "1 Petrus 1, 3-9, 151]).

Christian novelty, but is present in early Jewish literature."[70] Boismard, likewise, suggests that "the tradition can be traced back to the Jewish milieu."[71]

Nauck's article, "Joy in Suffering: The Problem of a Primitive Christian Tradition,"[72] has been significant in the history of interpretation of 1P's joyful-suffering passages (1:6–8; 4:13). Nauck argues that the suffering tradition evident in 1P is dependent on Jewish conceptions, especially those developed during the Maccabean period.[73] Proponents of this position highlight a number of Jewish parallels with the joyful-suffering tradition found in 1P (Wis 3:4–6; 2 Bar 52.6–7; 2 Macc 6:28–30; 4 Macc 7:22; 9:29; 11:12; Jdt 8:25–27; Sib. Or. 5.269–70).

While the relative strength of the analogies between these texts and the NT theme can be debated, it is not necessary to deny the presence of a joyful-suffering theme in Jewish literature.[74] Indeed, Jesus' teaching was often consistent with the themes of other Jewish teachers.[75] The important question here centers on whether it is more reasonable to assume that 1P *directly* derives from the theme present in the broader Jewish literature, or whether the theme derives from the words of the Lord, directly or mediately?[76]

It is important to note that Nauck's article is concerned to show that the ultimate source of the tradition is Jewish, not to reject the intermediary influence of Jesus' words on 1P. In fact, Nauck highlights that the tradition is taken up in Christianity and given a new emphasis.[77] Importantly, the two themes he emphasizes (suffering *for* Christ and the *present* reward) are sourced out of Jesus' words (in Matt 5:10–12; Luke 6:22, 23; Mark 10:30), and they are present within 1P. Therefore, to the degree that 1P stresses these themes, it appears to be reflecting the tradition as developed by Jesus. For this reason, Davids notes, "It is true, of course, that such sayings, including those of Jesus, are rooted in a wider Jewish persecution tradition flowing

---

70. Translated from, "Und diese Tradition ist kein christliches Novum, sondern schon in frühjüdischer Literatur nachweislich" (Brox, *Der Erste Petrusbrief*, 64).

71. Translated from, "Cette tradition peut remonter aux milieux juifs d'où le christianisme est issu" (Boismard, "Liturgie Baptismale (2)," 165).

72. Nauck, "Freude Im Leiden," 68–80.

73. Nauck, "Freude Im Leiden," 77–79.

74. Though see Gundry's criticism of Nauck's article (Gundry, "'Verba Christi' in I Peter," 343n1).

75. Young, *Meet the Rabbis*.

76. The role of the words of Jesus throughout this letter adds support to the presence of Jesus' influence here. Further, the sociological arguments we have previously noted concerning the significance of Jesus' teaching to the early church communities also provides evidence for the source being the words of Jesus.

77. Nauck, "Freude Im Leiden," 76–77.

from the Maccabean persecution. But the specific joy-in-suffering form of this tradition that we encounter here is specifically Christian and thus most likely to stem from Jesus."[78]

The case for the presence of an echo is strengthened by the use of μακάριος (blessed) in 1P 3:14 and 4:14, for this word is strongly connected to the JT joy-in-suffering traditions (Matt 5:10–12; Luke 6:22–23) and is relatively rare in epistolary literature.[79] Consideration of the influence of the JT in those passages must wait until we can examine those passages in detail, but the fact that 1P clearly references this joy-in-suffering tradition two other times suggests that it is influencing the text at this point as well. Further, we have just argued that Peter referenced a tradition that was passed down, at least in its Matthean form, as part of the Sermon on the Mount. This tradition is likewise included in the same sermon.

What significance do the words of Jesus have in this context? Clearly, it is not necessary to recall the words of Jesus in order to understand the text. Nevertheless, that this is an echo of Jesus explains the development of this pericope. On the surface, the structure of this section appears to make an abrupt shift. That is, 1P's point concerns rejoicing in light of the blessings of new birth, and the comments on suffering appear to interrupt the rejoicing. But as one considers Jesus' words in both Matthew and Luke, 1P's train of thought makes sense. Both Gospel texts point to the reward reserved in heaven for those who are Jesus' disciples,[80] a reward both texts intimately connect with suffering. Thus, when Peter considers the inheritance in heaven, he is drawn to one significant way Jesus indicated disciples can become recipients of reward—through suffering.

Like Jesus, the author of 1P is indicating that the inheritance is intimately connected to suffering. This can be seen in that the first-class conditional (εἰ δέον ἐστίν; v.6) indicates that it is necessary for the readers, as born again inheritors of the kingdom, to suffer.[81] This same word, δεῖ (it is necessary), is used elsewhere in the NT to reference the suffering of Christ and those who followed him (Mark 8:31; Luke 17:25; 24:7, 26; John 3:14; 12:34; Acts 3:21; 14:22; 17:3).[82] Thus Michaels finds it "entirely appropriate

---

78. Davids, *First Epistle of Peter*, 55.

79. It is only present in the following epistolary verses: Rom 4:7, 8; 14:22; 1 Cor 7:40; 1 Tim 1:11; 6:15; Titus 2:13; Jas 1:12, 25; 1P 3:14; 4:14.

80. Κληρονομία (inheritance) and μισθός (reward) are not identical concepts, but the similarity of thought can be seen in the way they are paralleled in LXX Psalm 126:3 "ἰδοὺ ἡ κληρονομία κυρίου υἱοί, ὁ μισθὸς τοῦ καρποῦ τῆς γαστρός (behold sons are the inheritance of the Lord, the reward of the fruit of the womb)."

81. Brox, *Erste Petrusbrief*, 64.

82. Elliott, *1 Peter*, 339–40.

that Peter's first explicit reference to the sufferings of the Asian churches puts these sufferings in a similar framework."[83]

In sum, the words of Jesus connecting the future inheritance in heaven with suffering in the present explain why 1P naturally flows from a consideration of rejoicing in the new birth to a consideration of the suffering associated with the new birth. In all of this, the identity of the readers is still forefront. They are elect-exiles, elect in regard to the inheritance in heaven and exiles in relation to the suffering they experience as sojourners in this world.

1 Peter 1:8 and John 20:29

Scharfe notes that when hearing the words of 1P 1:8, "one is instinctively reminded of the words of the risen Lord in John 20:29."[84] Maier adds that, in light of the similarities between the texts, "there can be hardly any doubt about the connection to the Johannine literature."[85] The following table reveals the commonalities and differences between the texts.

Table 5.4: 1 Peter 1:8 and John 20:29

1 Peter 1:8	John 20:29
ὃν οὐκ ἰδόντες ἀγαπᾶτε, εἰς ὃν ἄρτι μὴ ὁρῶντες, πιστεύοντες δὲ ἀγαλλιᾶσθε χαρᾷ ἀνεκλαλήτῳ καὶ δεδοξασμένῃ	λέγει αὐτῷ ὁ Ἰησοῦς· ὅτι ἑώρακάς με πεπίστευκας; μακάριοι οἱ μὴ ἰδόντες καὶ πιστεύσαντες.

As we have argued above, 1P appears to have access to traditions that are also recorded in John's Gospel. Consequently, we may turn to considering what similarities exist between to the two passages that suggest a shared tradition. A discernible challenge in this regard is the fact that the tension between faith and sight is "often found in the NT"[86] and can be described as

---

83. Michaels, *1 Peter*, 29.

84. Translated from, "Ebenso wird man doch durch die Worte 1:8 unwillkürlich an jenes Wort des Auferstandenen Joh. 20, 29 erinnert" (Scharfe, *Die petrinische Strömung*, 139).

85. Translated from, "Jedenfalls kann an der Verbindung zur johanneischen Tradition kaum ein Zweifel bestehen" (Maier, "Jesustradition," 88). Other scholars have also recognized a connection between these verses (Streeter, *Primitive Church*, 132–33; Hort, *First Epistle of St. Peter*, 45; Gundry, "'Verba Christi' in I Peter," 338; Tenney, "Possible Parallels," 377; Foster, *Literary Relations*, 526; Feuillet, "Quelques Reflexions," 244).

86. Davids, *First Epistle of Peter*, 59. Cf. Michaels, *1 Peter*, 33.

"commonplace in early Christian teaching" (Mark 15:32; John 4:48; 6:30; 2 Cor 4:18; 5:7; Heb 11:1, 3, 27).[87]

That 1P 1:8 reflects the tradition also reflected in John 20:29 is supported by the following. First, both passages use the same two words to refer to sight (ὁράω and εἶδον). Second, both texts move in the same direction; one does not see, yet he believes (πιστεύω). And while commentators are right to note a NT theme concerning the tension between not seeing and believing, it is only in these verses that *not seeing Christ* is related to *belief in the risen Christ*.[88] Third, both passages uniquely connect not seeing with belief *and joy*.[89]

A few arguments in favor of a relationship between these verses rests on the similarity of Johannine language to 1P 1:8. For instance, the use of πιστεύω for *belief in*, though not exclusive to Johannine literature, is certainly distinctive of it.[90] Further, Maier argues that 1P's use of *love* and *joy* alongside *believing* is due to the strong connection amongst these words in John's Gospel.[91] This is not to argue that Peter knew the text of John's Gospel, but rather that the traditions embodied in that Gospel were known by Peter, who in reflecting on the distinctive tradition of that text reflects the terminology of that stream of tradition.

In light of these similarities, Foster went so far to say that "the sequence of thought and the similar phraseology make a strong argument for dependence."[92] While we are not arguing for direct literary reliance as Foster does, it is important to note that the reason Foster found literary reliance a possibility is due to the significant similarities between the texts.

---

87. Achtemeier, *1 Peter*, 102.

88. This was a point of controversy between Best and Gundry. For Best, the idea of belief in spite of not seeing "is one that would have arisen easily once the relationship to Jesus of those who had not known him on earth was considered" (Best, "I Peter and the Gospel Tradition," 98). Gundry responded noting that "in the face of inability to see Jesus, sorrow rather than joy would be the idea to arise more easily" (Gundry, "Further Verba," 2:218).

89. Gundry notes that "The contrast between faith and sight is common in the New Testament, but only these two verses relate the not-seeing-yet-believing specifically to Christ and add the thought of spiritual happiness" (Gundry, "'Verba Christi' in I Peter," 338).

90. Tenney says, "In this instance the use of πιστεύω εἰς is so close to that of the fourth gospel that a connection seems likely" (Tenney, "Possible Parallels," 373).

91. Maier notes that 1P uses the same formula twice, "replacing 'faith' with 'love' in a very Johannine way of speaking (John 3:18ff)" (translated from, "wird dieselbe Formel zweimal gebraucht, wobei in geradezu johanneischer Redeweise 'glauben' durch 'lieben' ersetzt wird [vgl. dazu Joh 3,18f]" [Maier, "Jesustradition," 87–88]).

92. He further believed that the parallels in 1P 1:9 and John 20:31b strengthened the connection here (Foster, *Literary Relations*, 526).

It is not necessary to recognize the reference to make sense of the text. Thus, this is best categorized as an echo. That 1:6 also echoed a beatitude of Jesus (blessed are those that are persecuted) strengthens the case for the echo of another beatitude here. Those who have been born again are truly blessed and should therefore rejoice. Two potential reasons for despair are provided—they have not seen Jesus and they are being persecuted. By echoing the words of Jesus, 1P is addressing both of these issues with the words of Christ. He has called those who are persecuted blessed, and he has called those who believe despite their lack of seeing blessed. Further, the recognition that 1P reflects two of Jesus' beatitudes in 1:6–9 supports the triadic theme many commentators have argued is present. That is, 1:6–9 centers on Jesus, and as it does so it is fitting that the author is naturally drawn to a consideration of the words of Jesus. In sum, Peter's use of this echo is rhetorically significant, for it reminds the readers that their Lord calls them blessed, despite the challenging circumstances.

1 PETER 1:10–12

The final section of the opening passage develops the significance of the σωτηρία (salvation) mentioned at the conclusion of both previous sections (vv. 5, 9). Having expressed praise to God for the blessings of the new birth (vv. 3–5) and showing why the readers are blessed in spite of present challenges (vv. 6–9), these verses now add a past-historical dimension to the passage.[93]

This section of the text situates the readers historically within the eternal plan of redemption. The readers are not accidentally in their present situation; rather, they are elect sojourners because of God's predetermined work in the world. Such consideration brings comparison with both the OT prophets and even the angels.

In terms of the prophets, their prophecies concerned the grace that was to be obtained by 1P's readers. Further, these prophets knew that their prophecies served a future generation, a generation that has now come to fulfillment in these readers. Thus, the readers stand in a historically privileged position, despite the present challenges. Further, their privilege is likewise revealed in that the Gospel they have embraced is of great cosmic interest to the celestial beings. Brox helpfully highlights the connection between this passage and the identity of the readers:

---

93. Achtemeier, *1 Peter*, 105.

The Christian mission is the accomplishment of the universal event of salvation. This series of thoughts makes the people addressed "important" in their own eyes within the history of salvation. They recognize themselves as the representatives of the blessed, holy end to which the story planned by God has come. So, they are not what they seem: an abandoned, frightened, resigned minority. The self-assessment described on the basis of apocalyptic dimensions shows them clearly the true order of magnitude, which gives nothing but cause for hope.[94]

Numerous connections between Jesus' sayings and these verses have been proposed. Quite a few are possible, though since the evidence for the agreement of some of them is slim, we cannot consider them here.[95] Instead, we will focus on the following two echoes: (1) 1P 1:10 and Matthew 13:16-17; Luke 24:25-27; (2) 1P 1:11 and Luke 24:25-27.

1 Peter 1:10 and Matthew 13:16-17; Luke 10:23-24

Few commentators highlight a connection between these passages, and those who do generally mention the similarity of idea without extended discussion.[96] Nevertheless, Foster notes that this is "a suggestive parallel,"[97] and Hort calls the derivation of this passage from Jesus' saying "highly probable."[98] We will offer reasons to believe 1P is reflecting the words of Jesus here.

---

94. Translated from, "Die christliche Mission ist Vollzug des universalen Heilsgeschehens. - Diese Gedankenreihe macht die Angesprochenen in ihren eigenen Augen heilsgeschichtlich wichtig. Sie erkennen sich als die Repräsentanten des glücklichen, heilvollen Endes, an das die von Gott geplante Geschichte gelangt ist. Sie sind also nicht, was sie scheinen: eine verlassene, verängstigte, resignierte Minderheit. Die beschriebene Selbsteinschätzung aufgrund apokalyptischer Dimensionen zeigt ihnen einleuchtend die wahre Größenordnung, die nichts als Anlaß zum Hoffen gibt" (Brox, *Erste Petrusbrief*, 72).

95. For example, 1P's turn from a consideration of suffering to the prophets may be due to the connection in the tradition recorded in Matthew 5:10-11, where with the consideration of suffering is a consideration of the prophets who likewise suffered. See also the potential connections between 1P 1:11 and John 12:41, and 1P 1:12 and Luke 15:10.

96. E.g., Achtemeier, *1 Peter*, 108; Brox, *Erste Petrusbrief*, 70.

97. Foster, who argues for this tradition in Q, notes that "the thought is not close enough to make [literary reliance] probable" (Foster, *Literary Relations*, 493).

98. Hort, *First Epistle of St. Peter*, 49.

Table 5.5: 1 Peter 1:10 and Matthew 13:16–17; Luke 10:23–24

1 Peter 1:10–12	Matthew 13:16–17	Luke 10:23–24
περὶ ἧς σωτηρίας ἐξεζήτησαν καὶ ἐξηραύνησαν <u>προφῆται</u> οἱ περὶ τῆς εἰς ὑμᾶς χάριτος προφητεύσαντες . . . εἰς ἃ <u>ἐπιθυμοῦσιν</u> ἄγγελοι παρακύψαι.	ὑμῶν δὲ μακάριοι οἱ ὀφθαλμοὶ ὅτι βλέπουσιν καὶ τὰ ὦτα ὑμῶν ὅτι ἀκούουσιν. 17 ἀμὴν γὰρ λέγω ὑμῖν ὅτι πολλοὶ <u>προ-φῆται</u> καὶ δίκαιοι <u>ἐπεθύ-μησαν</u> ἰδεῖν ἃ βλέπετε καὶ οὐκ εἶδαν, καὶ ἀκοῦσαι ἃ ἀκούετε καὶ οὐκ ἤκουσαν.	Καὶ στραφεὶς πρὸς τοὺς μαθητὰς κατ' ἰδίαν εἶπεν· μακάριοι οἱ ὀφθαλμοὶ οἱ βλέποντες ἃ βλέπετε. 24 λέγω γὰρ ὑμῖν ὅτι πολλοὶ <u>προφῆται</u> καὶ βασιλεῖς ἠθέλησαν ἰδεῖν ἃ ὑμεῖς βλέπετε καὶ οὐκ εἶδαν, καὶ ἀκοῦσαι ἃ ἀκούετε καὶ οὐκ ἤκουσαν.

The agreement among these passages concerns the ideological parallel of the OT prophets desiring to know what Jesus' disciples have come to know through Jesus' message. The idea that the OT prophets longed to see what NT saints now see is a distinctive idea,[99] shared uniquely in these passages. It is, of course, true that 1P does not use precise verbal parallels with the wording of either Matthew or Luke. Nevertheless, it should be noted that even Matthew and Luke differ in multiple ways, yet they are clearly reflecting the same tradition.[100] And since 1P is not seeking to detail the life of Jesus as the Gospels did, it is not surprising to find the same tradition expressed in words consistent with the context of 1P's overall message.

Along with sharing the distinctive prophet-longing idea, there are a few other reasons to believe 1P is echoing the words of Jesus. First, Matthew 13:16 and Luke 10:23 both begin with a beatitude. If we are correct in finding two of Jesus' beatitudes reflected above (Matt 5:10; John 20:29), the case for another beatitude here is strengthened. Second, while the contexts of this tradition differ in the two Gospels, both focus on the blessing the disciples of Jesus have in comparison to OT saints, the very point 1P is seeking to make.

---

99. Though some have advanced the proposal that 1P speaks of NT prophets here (Selwyn, *First Epistle of St. Peter*, 134, 258–68; Warden, "Prophets of 1 Peter," 1–12), most scholars rightly argue for a reference to the OT prophets (Achtemeier, *1 Peter*, 108; Elliott, *1 Peter*, 346; Davids, *First Epistle of Peter*, 60–61).

100. The following are representative: Matthew speaks of righteous people, whereas Luke has kings; Matthew speaks of both eyes and ears at the beginning and the end, while Luke speaks of eyes at the beginning and both eyes and ears at the end; Matthew is more particular in speaking of the disciples with Jesus, while Luke generalizes the statement to include others who will come afterward; Matthew amplifies the saying with ἀμὴν (truly), while Luke does not; Matthew uses a verb for desire (ἐπιθυμέω), while Luke uses a similar but different word (θέλω).

First Peter may reflect knowledge of the tradition similar to the way it is recorded in Luke's Gospel. The seventy disciples had just returned rejoicing over the power they had been granted over demons (10:17-19). Jesus encouraged them to *rejoice* over their names being *written in heaven* (v. 20). Before expressing to the disciples the beatitude, Luke records the prayer of Jesus to the Father in which Jesus rejoiced *in the Spirit* and praised the Father for the Father's *gracious revealing* of the truth to *"infants"* (νήπιος; v. 21). After this prayer, Jesus turned to the disciples privately and gave the beatitude. The italicized themes above are all significant in 1P 1:1-12. Peter has called his readers to *rejoice* because of their *new birth*, accomplished through the sanctification of the *Spirit*, granting them an inheritance *in heaven* by the *mercy of God*. That such a new birth implies an infant analogy is confirmed in 1P 2:2, where the readers are compared to newborn infants (ἀρτιγέννητα βρέφη).¹⁰¹

In light of the reasons provided above, 1P may reflect a tradition similar to that recorded by Luke. Nevertheless, that the saying is also located within Matthew's explanation of the Parable of the Sower gives further understanding of the original meaning of the beatitude.¹⁰² While Luke's Gospel implies the need for spiritual perception, Matthew's Gospel more clearly speaks of the necessity of spiritual perception.¹⁰³ It does this by contrasting the disciples with Jesus' opponents, who Jesus indicated were the fulfillment of Isaiah 6:9-10. For the opponents, Jesus spoke in parables so that "seeing they do not perceive, and hearing they do not listen, nor do they understand" (Matt 13:13; cf. Isa 6:9). On the other hand, his disciples are blessed, for they both see and hear, implying that they also understand.

The emphasis on spiritual perception fits the context of 1P well, for the readers have been born again by God's act. They, unlike others (2:8-9), have been blessed by God with spiritual insight, for they are able to hear the word (1:23). Nevertheless, even in Matthew, the beatitude also focuses on the historical advantage disciples of Jesus have, for they live during the flowering of God's unfolding purpose. Leon Morris succinctly describes Jesus' emphasis in the latter half of the beatitude:

> Jesus is saying that his mission in the world is the culmination
> of the purpose of God made clear in prophecies from of old.

---

101. Νήπιος is a translation equivalent of βρέφος. This can be seen in that Hebrews, using the same milk analogy says "for everyone who lives on milk, being still an infant (νήπιος), is unskilled in the word of righteousness" (5:13).

102. 1P also agrees with Matthew in the use of ἐπιθυμέω, a relatively rare word in the NT. Nevertheless, 1P has the angels longing to look, while Matthew has the prophets looking.

103. Marshall, *Gospel of Luke*, 438.

The servants of God in olden times may have looked for these days and desired to be involved in them. But that was not their privilege. Let the disciples accordingly appreciate what God is doing before their very eyes.[104]

One argument against the presence of a *dominical logion* here is that both Gospel passages stress seeing *and* hearing, while 1P only speaks of hearing. Nevertheless, that 1P only focuses on hearing makes good sense. First Peter 1:8 has just argued, on the basis of another beatitude, that the readers are blessed despite their current lack of seeing Jesus. To reference the sight of the readers at this point might invite confusion—do they or do they not see Jesus? Instead of muddying the water, 1P focuses on the hearing of the Good News.

Since the passage is understandable without explicit reference to the saying of Jesus, this is an echo. The reverberations are, nevertheless, significant. First, those who hear the echo recognize that the believer's advantage is not only historical but also redemptive. In other words, their blessing is *both* that they live in an advantaged time-period (the post-Messiah age), but also that they have been granted ears to hear and accept the Good News (cf. Matt 16:17). This is implied in that 1:10–12 is still developing the blessing from verse 3 but is made more explicit by hearing the echo of Jesus' words. Such considerations confirm that Peter is still developing their identity as *elect* exiles in this exordium.

Second, while not evident on the surface, Peter has combined three statements from Jesus that declare certain people blessed (μακάριος). As many have noted, μακάριος is a challenging word to translate into English, for it pertains to "being fortunate or happy because of circumstances" and also to "being especially favored, blessed, fortunate, happy, privileged."[105] These ideas are not incompatible with one another, but rather the cause for rejoicing is due to the privilege granted.[106] In regard to the present passage, it is true that Peter does not use the word (though see 1P 3:14; 4:14), but the context is ripe with its overtones. Particularly important is the connection between eschatology and present experience in regard to μακάριος. These statements are almost exclusively used in regard to eschatological blessing

---

104. Morris, *Gospel according to Matthew*, 344.

105. Bauer et al., BDAG, s.v. "μακάριος," 610–11.

106. Silva notes that μακάριος is used in the NT in a way similar to its use in Hebrew thought, pertaining to "religious happiness consisting in Yahweh's favor and earthly happiness through the Creator's gifts" (Silva, *New International Dictionary*, s.v. "μακάριος," 3:206–9).

(as here),[107] yet as Silva notes, in these passages, "the promised future always involves a radical alteration of the present."[108] By the multiplication of the echoes of Jesus' beatitudes, Peter amplifies their cause for rejoicing. They are exceedingly favored, and therefore have much cause for rejoicing.

1 Peter 1:11 and Luke 24:25-27

Feuillet lists the relationship between 1P 1:11 and Luke 24:25-27 as one of Peter's "most remarkable references to the Synoptic tradition."[109] Goppelt suggests that the idea present in this verse, "appropriates a basic line of the NT coming from Jesus himself," and he notes that the idea is "especially prominent" in Luke 24.[110] Gundry adds that the similarities between the texts are "impressive."[111] The following table reveals the similarities and differences.

Table 5.6: 1 Peter 1:11 and Luke 24:25-27

1 Peter 1:11	Luke 24:25-27
ἐραυνῶντες εἰς τίνα ἢ ποῖον καιρὸν ἐδήλου τὸ ἐν αὐτοῖς πνεῦμα Χριστοῦ προμαρτυρόμενον τὰ εἰς Χριστὸν <u>παθήματα</u> καὶ τὰς μετὰ ταῦτα <u>δόξας</u>.	Καὶ αὐτὸς εἶπεν πρὸς αὐτούς· ὦ ἀνόητοι καὶ βραδεῖς τῇ καρδίᾳ τοῦ πιστεύειν ἐπὶ πᾶσιν οἷς ἐλάλησαν οἱ προφῆται· 26 οὐχὶ ταῦτα ἔδει <u>παθεῖν</u> τὸν χριστὸν καὶ εἰσελθεῖν εἰς τὴν <u>δόξαν</u> αὐτοῦ; 27 καὶ ἀρξάμενος ἀπὸ Μωϋσέως καὶ ἀπὸ πάντων τῶν προφητῶν διερμήνευσεν αὐτοῖς ἐν πάσαις ταῖς γραφαῖς τὰ περὶ ἑαυτοῦ.

There is little direct verbal similarity between the texts, making literary borrowing unpersuasive. Nevertheless, the parallels are significant and appear to be consistent with shared tradition.[112] The following five similarities are notable:[113]

1. Reference to prophet's predictions

---

107. "Because of their eschatological motivation the NT makarisms appear consistently as prophetic-apocalyptic address or instruction" (Strecker, "μακάριος").

108. Silva, *New International Dictionary*, s.v. "μακάριος," 3:206-9.

109. Translated from, "références les plus remarquables à la tradition synoptique" (Feuillet, "Quelques Reflexions," 242).

110. Goppelt, *Commentary on I Peter*, 96, 97n72.

111. Gundry, "Further Verba," 228. See also Unnik, "The Teaching of Good Works in I Peter," 98; Selwyn, *First Epistle of St. Peter*, 29; Bigg, *Epistles of St. Peter*, 110.

112. Stanton, while recognizing the lexical limitations, nevertheless notes that there are "a number of similarities" between the verses (Stanton, "Jesus Traditions," 569).

113. Gundry, "'Verba Christi' in I Peter," 338; Maier, "Jesustradition," 88.

2. The statement of both suffering (πάθημα) and glory (δόξα)
3. The decisive movement from suffering to glory
4. "The formal use of Χριστός alone"[114]
5. The shared demonstrative pronoun, ταῦτα, in reference to the suffering

Despite exposure to these similarities, Best offered three reasons to believe the two texts are genetically unrelated. First, Best argued that the Lukan passage displays features that suggest it is a creation of the Gospel author and not a genuine saying of the Lord. Second, if 1P knew the Lukan tradition, it is strange that 1P changed the singular δόξαν to the plural δόξας. Third, "The two statements could arise quite independently since from the very beginning the Christians explained the death and resurrection/glory of Jesus in OT terms, and as fulfilment of OT prophecy."[115]

In response to Best's first argument, it is necessary to distinguish a Gospel writer's retelling of a narrative to the fabrication of a narrative.[116] This is not to deny "Lukanisms" in the text, but is rather to suggest that inclusion of Luke's favorite words or themes does not indicate an a-historical tradition. In the end, the striking similarities with 1P suggest either that this is not a Lukan creation or that Peter knew portions of Luke's Gospel. Best ascribes to the latter,[117] and we will argue for the likelihood of the former (see the concluding chapter).

Gundry turned Best's second argument around by suggesting that the tradition included the difficult plural, which 1P kept, while Luke smoothed it out.[118] Nevertheless, there is some reason to believe Peter would have made the singular plural. Since the sufferings are multiple, it makes sense that the glories would be multiple likewise.[119] And since Peter is contextually stressing the significance of the inheritance for those who are elect-exiles, the plural of glory serves to highlight the significance of the reward. Stated

---

114. Gundry, "Further Verba," 228.

115. Best, *1 Peter*, 108.

116. Best offers no argument for the presence of Lukanisms, though he does reference the following works: Conzelmann, *Theology of St. Luke*; Flender, *St. Luke*.

117. Best, "I Peter and the Gospel Tradition," 111.

118. "The difficult plural δόξας instead of Luke's singular supports the allusion [to Jesus in 1P], for the more difficult reading is more likely original" (Gundry, "Further Verba," 228).

119. Bigg suggests that the plural "may refer to the successive manifestations of Christ's glory—Resurrection, Ascension, Pentecost, Miracles, Judgment" (Bigg, *Epistles of St. Peter*, 110). Similarly, Kelly says that the glories refers to "His resurrection, ascension, enthronement on high and, not least, His final 'revelation' as judge of living and dead" (Kelly, *Commentary on the Epistles of Peter*, 61.)

succinctly, Jesus endured sufferings and received glories, and therefore the reader's sufferings should also anticipate glories (cf. 2:21).

Best's argument that the traditions could have arisen independently appears to ignore the significant connections detailed above. While it cannot be denied that the themes present in this text were part of the broad themes in the early church, the specific commonality of these texts suggests that there resides behind both the same tradition. In the words of Maier, "The more obvious explanation is that both agree on the same logion (that is to the risen Jesus)."[120]

Having addressed the agreement between the texts, it is necessary to consider the significance of the reference. That this is an echo can be seen in that it is unnecessary to recognize the reference to make full sense of the passage. Further, Peter does not seem to be evoking the broader context of Luke 24. Nevertheless, there may be an implied contrast with the way Luke 24 uses the tradition and its use in 1P. In Luke 24, the men on the road to Emmaus were criticized for their slowness of heart in believing all that was proclaimed by the prophets. But in 1P, the readers have accepted, by means of the Spirit, the message of the prophets. Indeed, they are like the prophets in that the Spirit (of Christ) revealed to both parties the suffering-glory path of the Messiah.[121] Such similarity between the present readers and the prophets has been hinted at through previous echoes of Jesus' words, for the readers, like the prophets, were persecuted (Matt 5:12). Thus for the OT prophets, the Spirit of Christ testified *beforehand* to the suffering-glory path, while for the present readers Jesus testified *afterhand* by means of the tradition being referenced (through "those who brought you the good news") and such testimony was confirmed by the Spirit. Nevertheless, the readers are in a privileged position, for the OT prophets could not know the fullness of what has now been revealed to Peter's readers.

CONCLUSION TO 1 PETER 1:3–12

Six intertextual resonances were identified in this opening section (1:3–12), consisting of five echoes and one allusion (see table below). Following the introductory verses (1:1–2), Peter desires his readers to recognize the

---

120. Translated from, "Die näherliegendere Erklärung ist doch die, daß beide auf dasselbe Logion (des. auf erstandenen Jesus) zurückgehen" (Maier, "Jesustradition," 88).

121. "The Spirit of Christ" is a rare designation which occurs infrequently in the NT (here; Rom 8:9; cf. Acts 16:7; Gal 4:6; Phil 1:19). It expresses a close connection between Jesus and the Spirit.

importance of their identity as elect-exiles. In regard to their election, they are those who have been granted new birth (John 3:3–7) by the Father. Such an identity grants them privileges as God's children, particularly an inheritance reserved for them (Luke 12:33; Matt 6:20). Nevertheless, this identity also makes them exiles, estranged from their forefathers.

Table 5.7: Intertextual Resonances to *Dominical Logia* in 1 Peter 1:3–12

1P Reference	Gospel Reference	Type of Reference
1:3	John 3:3–7	Allusion
1:4	Luke 12:33; Matt 6:20	Echo
1:6	Matt 5:10–12; Luke 6:22–23	Echo
1:8	John 20:29	Echo
1:10	Matt 13:16–17; Luke 20:23–24	Echo
1:11	Luke 24:25–27	Echo

Despite the blessing of their identity, the readers face two challenges. First, their sociological position leads to persecution, which is a distinctive badge of their identity with Christ (Matt 5:10–12; Luke 6:22–23). Second, they are called to believe in Jesus despite their lack of seeing Jesus (John 20:29). At first, the connection between these challenges is obscure. But the connection is made clearer when the words of Jesus are taken into account. In both cases, Jesus calls his disciples *blessed* (μακάριος). In this text, Peter is encouraging his readers to rejoice despite these challenging circumstances. They are to rejoice because their experience of these challenges are, according to Jesus, evidence of divine blessing. When they are persecuted and when they show forth faith and love to Jesus without seeing him, they are evidencing their identity as those whom the Father has privileged, and thus they should rejoice.

Having considered the privilege the readers have in the future (1:3–6) and in the present (1:7–9), Peter considers the privilege they have in respect to the past (1:10–12), particularly in regard to the prophets. These prophets, who were likewise the recipients of the world's persecution (Matt 5:12), desired to see and hear what was now revealed to Peter's readers. This occasions Peter's third reference to a beatitude of Jesus, for Jesus also noted that his disciples should rejoice for being the recipients of divine favor in living in a unique period of revelation, in which God was opening eyes and ears to truth (Matt 13:16–17; Luke 20:23–24). Indeed, while the Spirit revealed to the prophets of old the suffering-to-glory path of the Messiah (Luke 24:25–27), the same Spirit has now revealed to the readers the same suffering-to-glory path, yet in a fullness OT prophets could only distantly gaze after.

In sum, each of the major themes of this opening section are supported by the words of Jesus. In only one case is an explicit allusion identified here, and it is likely that Peter depended on his reader's knowledge of a tradition like John 3 to make sense of his text. In the five other occasions, the similarity of concepts strongly suggest that Peter was deriving his thought from the words of Jesus. And, as we have argued above, the resonances that exist between the echoes and the echoed text appears to support their presence.

6

First Peter 1:13—2:10

FIRST PETER DIVIDES INTO three sections in the main body. 1:13—2:10, the section we are considering in this chapter, is the body opening, followed by the body middle (2:11—4:11) and the body closing (4:12—5:11).[1] By beginning 1:13 with διό (therefore), Peter connects the material in the body opening to the introductory verses (1:3-12), drawing moral implications from the extended introduction.[2]

The change from indicative to imperative verbs is significant and follows other early Christian letters.[3] Stated theologically, Peter is grounding the imperatives of this section in the indicatives of the last.[4] The five imperative verbs in these verses stress that, in light of the new birth and its consequent blessings, the readers must:[5]

---

1. For more detail see, Schutter, *Hermeneutic and Composition*, 24-27; Martin, *Metaphor and Composition*.

2. Elliott, *1 Peter*, 355; Vahrenhorst, *Erste Brief Des Petrus*, 84.

3. "As a paraenesis, 1 Peter structures the composition of its body-middle by the interplay of the ontological status of its readers with the appropriate exhortations" (Martin, *Metaphor and Composition*, 270).

4. Achtemeier, *1 Peter*, 115. See also Schreiner, *1, 2 Peter*, 77.

5. It is lexically possible that 2:5 contains an imperative (οἰκοδομεῖσθε; "let yourselves be built"), but the form could also be indicative (you are built), and, in light of the context speaking of the work that God does for the believer, most believe the verb is an indicative (e.g., Achtemeier, *1 Peter*, 155; Davids, *First Epistle of Peter*, 87; Elliott, *1 Peter*, 413; Michaels, *1 Peter*, 100). Few scholars argue that it is imperative (e.g., Bigg, *Epistles of St. Peter*, 128; Goppelt, *Commentary on I Peter*, 140; Perkins, *First and Second Peter*, 43).

- Set their hope on the grace coming at the revelation of Jesus (1:13)
- Be holy as God is holy (1:15)
- Conduct themselves with fear during their exile (1:17)
- Love one another earnestly (1:22)
- Crave spiritual milk (2:1-3)

Peter's return to the indicative in 2:5, wherein he further describes the identity of the audience, sandwiches the imperatives between statements of identity.

The duality of elect-exile has not been forgotten in these verses. For, as Green highlights, "The section as a whole has as its boundaries a dual emphasis on 'call' or 'election' (1:15; 2:9–10; cf. 1:20; 2:4, 6) and holiness (1:15–16; 2:9; cf. 2:5)."[6] They are called to holiness as a consequence of their election, and it is this call to holiness that distinguishes the readers from the rest of the world.[7] In light of their new identity, it is unsurprising that Peter uses familial and relational language throughout this section,[8] seeking to give the readers solidarity in their sociological situation, even while he encourages them to cultivate those traits that make them exiles in the world.

Peter calls the readers to be consistent with who they have become in Christ;[9] that is, to live out the identity that has been provided to them through the new birth. And as newborn children, they are to reflect their Father (1:15), the one who has given them new birth (1:3). As Peter encourages his readers to live out their identity, he does so by appealing to numerous traditions.[10] McKnight highlights that "from his biblical heritage *and the teachings of Jesus*" Peter has learned to "ground his exhortations in the

---

6. Green, *1 Peter*, 33.

7. These verses stress the "central theme of the letter. . . . Christians must behave in accordance with their new reality in Christ, which means living in a way at odds with their former lifestyle"(Achtemeier, *1 Peter*, 118).

8. In this section, Peter makes effective use of "familial language and terms of endearment: 'children' (1:14), 'brotherly love' (1:22), 'born anew' (1:23), 'parentage' (or 'seed,' 1:23), 'newborn babies' (2:2), 'to mature as children' (2:2), and 'house/household' (2:5)." Further, Peter calls God Father (1:17) and speaks positively of his audience as a "'holy/royal priesthood' (2:5, 9), 'holy nation' (2:9), and 'God's (own) people' (2:9, 10)" (Green, *1 Peter*, 34).

9. Jobes, *1 Peter*, 107; cf. Vahrenhorst, *Erste Brief Des Petrus*, 86.

10. Jobes highlights the preponderance of OT terminology in this section of the letter, and suggests Peter is applying the hermeneutical principles he expressed in the opening verses. More specifically, "Allusions to the exodus event, quotations from the Holiness Code of Leviticus and from Isaiah, and echoes of Ps. 34 are woven together to create a new-covenant context" (Jobes, *1 Peter*, 107).

character and actions of God."[11] The following chapter will consider how Peter takes up the words of Jesus in the opening to the body of the letter.

1 PETER 1:13-16

Following the exordium, these verses provide the first responses the readers should have to the blessings delineated in 1:1–12. The imperative (ἐλπίσατε) indicates that the readers must set their hope on the grace coming at the revelation of Jesus. The two participles indicate the way the readers will accomplish this command; by preparing their minds for action (ἀναζωσάμενοι τὰς ὀσφύας τῆς διανοίας ὑμῶν) and by being sober-minded (νήφοντες).[12]

The second imperative of this section (ἅγιοι ... γενήθητε), calls the readers to live up to their new birth. Since they have God as Father, they must be holy as God is holy. Building on the analogy of new birth, Peter indicates that the readers are to be obedient children (τέκνα ὑπακοῆς), not conforming to the ignorant passions of their prior life.[13]

While numerous parallels to Jesus' words from this passage have been suggested in the history of scholarship,[14] only one has enough merit to be considered here: 1P 1:13 and Luke 12:35–45.

Table 6.1: 1 Peter 1:13 and Luke 12:35, 45

1 Peter 1:13	Luke 12:35, 45
Διὸ <u>ἀναζωσάμενοι</u> τὰς <u>ὀσφύας</u> τῆς διανοίας ὑμῶν νήφοντες τελείως ἐλπίσατε ἐπὶ τὴν φερομένην ὑμῖν χάριν ἐν ἀποκαλύψει Ἰησοῦ Χριστοῦ.	Ἔστωσαν ὑμῶν αἱ <u>ὀσφύες περιεζωσμέναι</u> καὶ οἱ λύχνοι καιόμενοι· ... 45 ἐὰν δὲ εἴπῃ ὁ δοῦλος ἐκεῖνος ἐν τῇ καρδίᾳ αὐτοῦ· χρονίζει ὁ κύριός μου ἔρχεσθαι, καὶ ἄρξηται τύπτειν τοὺς παῖδας καὶ τὰς παιδίσκας, ἐσθίειν τε καὶ πίνειν καὶ μεθύσκεσθαι.

---

11. McKnight, *1 Peter*, 84. Cf. Gourbillon and Buit, *Première Épitre de Saint Pierre*, 56.

12. Schreiner, *1, 2 Peter*, 77–78.

13. This description of the audience suggests that they are mainly Gentile (Brox, *Der Erste Petrusbrief*, 76).

14. See the appendix for a full listing of the proposed parallels and the scholars who argued for them. There appears to be a connection between 1P 1:15 and Matt 5:48 (Stibbs, *First Epistle General of Peter*, 87; Kistemaker, *Exposition of the Epistles of Peter*, 61; Davids, *First Epistle of Peter*, 69; Vahrenhorst, *Erste Brief Des Petrus*, 88–89), but the language could easily derive from the OT and the linguistic evidence does not clearly indicate that Peter was referencing the words of Jesus.

Peter begins the body of his text with a figure of speech concerning "girding the loins of the mind."[15] Michaels notes that "the most likely immediate source of the metaphor is the saying of Jesus preserved in Luke 12:35."[16] Gourbillon adds that here "Saint Peter undoubtedly alludes to the words of Jesus Himself."[17] Others have suggested a connection between these passages as well.[18]

Though sharing the relatively rare ὀσφῦς (eight occurrences), the other lexical similarity between the texts is not exact. First Peter has a form of ἀναζωσάμενοι, while Luke has περιεζωσμέναι. The difference in prefix causes no definite conceptual difference,[19] but since 1P chooses a rarer form,[20] it may suggest 1P is not evidencing textual reliance on Luke's Gospel. The ideological parallels are quite significant, however. First, both passages use the same metaphor of girding up the loins. As some have noted, such a metaphor was common and therefore need not of itself imply a connection between the passages.[21] But, importantly, only these two passages in Scripture associate the girding of the loins with the eschatological waiting for the revelation of Jesus, the Messiah.[22] Thus, while the metaphor itself may have been used widely, its eschatological application is unique to these two passages.

Another connection between the passages is Peter's call for the readers to be sober-minded (νήφοντες). This word, in its literal sense, refers to not being intoxicated, though it is used widely in its figurative sense of

---

15. A modern form of the metaphor would be "rolling your sleeves up for work" (Cranfield, *First Epistle of Peter*, 32).

16. Michaels, *1 Peter*, 54.

17. Translated from, "Saint Pierre vient sans doute de faire allusion à cette parole de Jésus lui-même" (Gourbillon and Buit, *Première Épitre de Saint Pierre*, 57).

18. Vahrenhorst, *Erste Brief Des Petrus*, 85; Feuillet, "Quelques Reflexions," 242; Watson and Callan, *First and Second Peter*, 32; Witherington, *Letters and Homilies for Hellenized Christians*, 94; Senior and Harrington, *1 Peter, Jude, and 2 Peter*, 40; Boring, *1 Peter*, 73; Boismard, "Liturgie Baptismale (2)," 197–98; Beare, *First Epistle of Peter*, 96; Bigg, *Epistles of St. Peter*, 112; Maier, "Jesustradition," 89–90; Goppelt, *Commentary on I Peter*, 108n23; Delling, "Bezug Der Christlichen Existenz," 98.

19. It appears that Gundry understood Best to argue for a conceptual difference on the basis of the prefix. Nevertheless, Best seemed to be arguing for a broader contextual difference (Gundry, "Further Verba," 224; Best, "I Peter and the Gospel Tradition," 104).

20. Ἀναζώννυμι is a *hapax-legomena*, and it occurs only twice in the LXX. Luke's περιζώννυμι occurs six times in the NT and thirteen times in the LXX.

21. In his commentary on the passage, Best said, "in view of its obvious nature and its frequent use there is no need to see dependence of the metaphor on Lk 12:35" (Best, *1 Peter*, 84; see also Foster, *Literary Relations*, 501).

22. Maier, "Jesustradition," 89; Gundry, "Further Verba," 224.

being self-controlled.²³ In this light, one can see that νήφοντες may find its equivalent in Jesus' parable in Luke 12:42-46.²⁴ In this latter text, Jesus warns about servants who, not faithfully waiting for the return of the master of the house, begin to "beat the other slaves, men and women, and to eat and *drink* and get *drunk*" (12:45).²⁵

The bridge between the command to be watchful and the parable of the Unfaithful Slave is also significant (Luke 12:41). The occasion for the telling of the parable was *Peter's* question, when he asked whether the dominical teaching was for the disciples or for everyone. Again, whether the author was Peter or one speaking in his name, the connection between this text and Peter in the tradition of Jesus' sayings is significant.²⁶ Thus, the association of Luke 12 and Peter in the JT increases the likelihood of an association of Luke 12 and 1P 4:10, 14.

A few other arguments can also be made in favor of seeing a reference to Jesus' words here. Boismard draws attention to the structure of 1P 1:13, suggesting that it not only contains the same elements as Luke 12:35-46 (girding loins and being sober in expectation of the Master, who is the Messiah), but that it provides the elements in the same order.²⁷ Further, 1P likely references this same block of tradition elsewhere (see 1P 1:4, 17; 4:10, 14), strengthening the case for the possibility of reference to it here.²⁸ Finally, this passage contains three statements of blessing (μακάριος) from Jesus (12:37, 38, 43) to the servants who wait patiently for the Master. In light of Peter's three echoes to Jesus' other beatitudes above, the beatitude here provides further support for a connection.

---

23. Silva, *New International Dictionary*, s.v. "νήφω," 3:389-91.

24. Bigg, *Epistles of St. Peter*, 112.

25. Schelkle finds that "The admonition to sobriety is reminiscent of the synopsis, which does not use that word in eschatological parable, but factually makes the same demand (Luke 12:45)" (Translated from, "Auch die Mahnung zur Nüchternheit erinnert an die Synopse, die in eschatologischer Gleichnisrede zwar jenes Wort nicht gebraucht, aber sachlich die gleiche Forderung stellt (Lk 12,45)" [Schelkle, *Die Petrusbriefe*, 44]).

26. The argument would be as follows. Since the author is seeking to speak like Peter (1:1), he would naturally include elements of the tradition in which Peter was present. Therefore, since the JT indicates Peter's concern in this passage, it is likely the author of 1P would refer back to it.

27. Boismard, "Liturgie Baptismale (1)," 197-98.

28. "The author of 1 Peter may then have known Luke 12:32-45 in a condition similar to that which it possesses now in the Gospel" (Best, "I Peter and the Gospel Tradition," 105). Best changed his mind by the time of the writing of his commentary where he says, "In view of its obvious nature and its frequent use there is no need to see dependence of the metaphor on Luke 12:35 or in any special way on the Exodus event" (Best, *1 Peter*, 84).

A potential reason to argue against a reference to the words of Jesus here is that Peter's source for the loin-girding metaphor seems to be the OT. In Exodus 12:11, the Israelites were told to eat the Passover meal with their loins girded (περιεζωσμέναι), prepared for departure. In light of 1P's pilgrim theme, the association of Israel with believers in Jesus, and the quotation from the holiness code in 1:15, some have found this OT passage to be the source of Peter's allusion.[29] Despite these rich connections, the difference in verb from the LXX leads away from a direct reference, for as Achtemeier notes, the lack of agreement is "surprising if our author wants deliberately to recall the Exodus verse since he is quite capable of reproducing exactly the language of the LXX when he wishes."[30] If, instead, Peter is reflecting the oral tradition of Jesus' saying, the change in prefix is more likely.

Further, the eschatological element strongly connects this passage with Jesus' words, an element lacking in the Exodus passage.[31] Indeed, Wong notes that the eschatological emphasis "is the decisive factor" in favor of a *domincal logion*.[32] However, that Peter derives the eschatological emphasis from Jesus does not indicate that there are no echoes of the Exodus passage here. Indeed, Jesus' statement is itself an echo of the Exodus,[33] and thus Peter may be pointing back to the Exodus through Jesus. Consequently, with Michaels, we may argue that "Peter is indebted to the Gospel tradition not for the precise vocabulary and not even for the metaphor in itself, but for the application of the metaphor to the Christian eschatological hope."[34]

It is unnecessary to recognize the *dominical logion* in order to understand the passage. Thus, this is best categorized as an echo of the words of Jesus. The reverberations of the echo help to reveal the significance of Peter's language. Both the result of their obedience and disobedience is emphasized by reference to the source text. As for obedience, Luke 12:37–38 stresses that the faithful slaves will be blessed. Μακάριοι occurs at both the beginning (v. 37) and end (v. 38) of these verses and surrounds the ultimate expression of this blessing—the Master will serve the slaves. Obviously, this

---

29. See, e.g., Davids, *The First Epistle of Peter*, 66; Michaels, *1 Peter*, 52–53.

30. Achtemeier, *1 Peter*, 118.

31. Others have noted this as well. Beare, for instance, notes that rather than in reference to Exodus, "It is more directly reminiscent of Luke 12:35, where the figure is related, as here, to the eschatological expectation" (Beare, *First Epistle of Peter*, 96). Goppelt adds that "the closest parallel in content to I Pet. 1:13 is Lk. 12:35" (Goppelt, *A Commentary on I Peter*, 108n23).

32. Wong, "Use of Jesus' Sayings," 202.

33. Green, *Gospel of Luke*, 500. Cf. Strobel, *Untersuchungen zum eschatologischen Verzögerungsproblem*, 209n4.

34. Michaels, *1 Peter*, 54.

turns the entire social paradigm upside down, for the slaves were to serve the master. In regard to 1P, this may be hinted at in that Jesus will *bring grace* to the readers. Those who recognize Jesus' words here rightly see the truth of Jesus' words: "Blessed is that slave whom his master will find at work when he arrives" (12:43).

The significance of the intertextual reference also highlights the penalty for disobedience. While Peter will encourage the readers to live in reverent fear in light of the coming impartial judgment (1:17), it is by hearing the rich overtones of Luke 12 that the significance of this warning is recognized. The slave who fails to obey and instead engages in unbelieving actions—beating other slaves, getting drunk, and other things Peter associates with "the desires you formerly had in ignorance" (1:14)—will be "cut in pieces" and will be counted among the "unfaithful" (Luke 12:46). Others, who do not engage in such actions, but fail to properly prepare and do good will be beaten. Significantly, Jesus suggests that these different slaves are judged on the basis of their actions, which aligns with 1P's "according to their deeds" (1:17).

The conclusion to the Lukan parable indicates that those who have been given much will be required much (12:48). In relation to 1P, Peter has just delineated the richness of the blessings they have received from God in Christ. While the readers can call God Father, they must not ignore that such a relationship requires much from them (1:17). If they will be blessed, they must be faithful children.[35]

1 PETER 1:17–21

Verses 17–21 consists of one long, complex sentence in Greek. The imperative, "live in reverent fear" (ἐν φόβῳ . . . ἀναστράφητε),[36] reveals the theme of the section. The opening first-class conditional (εἰ πατέρα ἐπικαλεῖσθε; "if you invoke as Father"),[37] does not introduce doubt that the readers call on God as Father; rather, it draws the reader into the consideration of what should happen in light of their calling on God as Father. Stated differently, this conditional indicates that because they call on God, the impartial judge,

---

35. Peter has now used four beatitudes of Jesus. The first three promised blessing for things the readers had no direct control over (persecution, not seeing Jesus, seeing what the prophets could not see), but this beatitude concerns a blessing they must seek after.

36. While φόβος can refer to reverence or dread, its use in 1P suggests reverent fear in regard to God (Hillyer, *1 and 2 Peter, Jude*, 51).

37. The first-class conditional indicates that something is assumed true for the sake of argument (Wallace, *Greek Grammar*, 690–94).

as Father, they should live in reverent fear. In the rest of the sentence, Peter provides two further reasons to live in reverent fear. First, the knowledge that the readers have been ransomed away from their former lifestyle by a perfect, priceless sacrifice should lead to an obedient lifestyle. Second, they should live in reverent fear, because their "faith and hope are the result of God's eternal plan to raise and glorify Christ."[38]

The participle in verse 18 (εἰδότες ὅτι; "you know that") is used elsewhere in the NT to refer to basic Christian teaching.[39] Used here, it precedes a number of subordinate clauses, indicating that Peter believes the readers already know the information he is presenting.[40] Consequently, it is not surprising to find fundamental Christian tradition in these verses. Because of the presence of this tradition, some have suggested this section is a hymn or a pre-written body of material Peter utilized for his own purposes. But since Peter shows creativity elsewhere in the merging of sources, there is little reason to suggest he is not the author of this unique adaptation as well.[41]

The merging of diverse traditions, a characteristic of 1P, is amplified in this passage. Michaels agrees and highlights the associated difficulty: "In few other places is the character of 1 Peter as an epistle composed out of earlier traditions better demonstrated than in vv. 13–21, *but the recovery of the individual units out of which the section is composed is now virtually impossible.*"[42] Though commentators are sure prior sources are central to the formulation of this section of text, the general nature of the admonitions make any specific correlations difficult to sustain.[43]

Due to the way Peter has merged his sources into the epistle, many of the proposed parallels fall short of the evidence needed to identify intertextual reference.[44] Nevertheless, we will argue that a few passages suggest

38. Jobes, *1 Peter*, 115.

39. Elliott notes that this NT phrase "introduces material, frequently elementary Christian teaching, providing the reason or reasons for a preceding imperative (Elliott, *1 Peter*, 369).

40. "This phrase seemingly suggests, at least to our Petrine writer, and possibly to his intended readers, that what follows ὅτι is already a well-known statement" (Shimada, "Formulary Material," 233–34).

41. Achtemeier agrees, noting that it is "not beyond the linguistic capacity of the author of this letter to construct such felicitous phrases without necessary dependence on early formulations" (Achtemeier, *1 Peter*, 131).

42. Michaels, *1 Peter*, 53. Emphasis added.

43. Achtemeier, *1 Peter*, 123.

44. The appendix reveals many proposed parallels. A potential parallel exists between John's use of "lamb" (ἀμνός; John 1:29, 36) and 1P's use of the same word (1:19); nevertheless, the use of ἀμνός in LXX Isaiah 53:7 makes the connection with John less substantial.

common reliance on shared dominical traditions. Particularly, we will argue that 1:17 evidences knowledge of the tradition found in Matthew 6:9 and Luke 11:2, while 1:18 evidences knowledge of a tradition similar to Mark 10:45 and Matthew 20:28.[45]

1 Peter 1:17 and Matthew 6:9; Luke 11:2

Peter indicates that he believes his readers "call on the Father" (εἰ πατέρα ἐπικαλεῖσθε). Ἐπικαλέω, generally meaning "to call upon deity for any purpose,"[46] suggests that such calling is accomplished in prayer.[47] Commentators express various levels of certainty concerning whether Peter's statement derives from Jesus' pattern of prayer (Matt 6:8–9; 11:25–26). Michaels and Schreiner call it "likely,"[48] Hort says it is "very likely,"[49] while Spicq and Achtemeier say it is "almost certain."[50]

Table 6.2: 1 Peter 1:17 and Matthew 6:9; Luke 11:2

1 Peter 1:17	Matthew 6:9	Luke 11:2
καὶ εἰ <u>πατέρα</u> ἐπικαλεῖσθε τὸν ἀπροσωπολήμπτως κρίνοντα κατὰ τὸ ἑκάστου ἔργον, ἐν φόβῳ τὸν τῆς παροικίας ὑμῶν χρόνον ἀναστράφητε	Οὕτως οὖν προσεύχεσθε ὑμεῖς· <u>Πάτερ</u> ἡμῶν ὁ ἐν τοῖς οὐρανοῖς· ἁγιασθήτω τὸ ὄνομά σου	εἶπεν δὲ αὐτοῖς· ὅταν προσεύχησθε λέγετε· <u>Πάτερ</u>, ἁγιασθήτω τὸ ὄνομά σου· ἐλθέτω ἡ βασιλεία σου

Achtemeier distinguishes between finding the source of Peter's statement in the overall pattern of Jesus' prayer and finding it in the specific instruction to pray (Matt 6:9; Luke 11:2). In reference to the latter, he notes that associating Peter's words directly with the Lord's Prayer "is questionable" because the language had become common in the early church.[51] Schreiner makes the same distinction, noting that the former is "likely" while

---

45. First Peter 1:17–21 is one of the passages identified by Maier as a "short catechism." He seeks to show the reliance of the entire section on the JT, but since our purposes are more limited, we will only examine individual passages that appear dependent (Maier, "Jesustradition," 105–8).

46. Bauer et al., BDAG, s.v. "ἐπικαλέω," 373.

47. Elliott, *1 Peter*, 365.

48. Schreiner, *1, 2 Peter*, 82; Michaels, *1 Peter*, 60.

49. Hort, *First Epistle of St. Peter*, 73.

50. Spicq, *Épîtres de Saint Pierre*, 65; Achtemeier, *1 Peter*, 124.

51. Achtemeier, *1 Peter*, 124.

the latter is "harder to discern."⁵² Nevertheless, in light of the importance Jesus' instructions for prayer were to the early church, it is likely that the tradition recorded in both Matthew and Luke was known to the audience (cf. Rom 8:15; Gal 4:6). Thus, when Peter speaks of calling on God as Father, it is likely his audience would have recognized *both* the pattern of Jesus' prayer and Jesus' instructions for his disciples.⁵³

The agreement between 1P and the Gospel passages is primarily ideological. In this case, a characteristic trait of Jesus (and uncharacteristic of others at that time) points the reference back to Jesus. In his study on Jesus' use of *'Abbā* in prayer,⁵⁴ Jeremias argues that the use of *'Abbā* in prayer to God is characteristic of Jesus and entirely absent in Judaism.⁵⁵ While believing Jeremias has overstated his case, Dunn nevertheless agrees that Jesus' use of *'Abbā* distinguishes him from all contemporaries.⁵⁶ Dunn explains the significance: "It is *excessively difficult* to avoid the conclusion that it was a characteristic of Jesus' approach to God in prayer that he addressed God as *'abba'* and that the earliest Christians retained an awareness of this fact in their own use of *'abba.'"*⁵⁷

Accordingly, the ear attuned to the words of Jesus would likely be reminded of Jesus' teaching here. What significance does such an echo have? By calling on God as Father, the readers are following in the steps of Jesus, the Son of God. Jeremias shows the importance of Jesus' use of this language: "The complete novelty and uniqueness of *'Abbā* as an address to God in the prayers of Jesus shows that it expresses the heart of Jesus' relationship to God. He spoke to God as a child to its father; confidently and securely, and yet at the same time *reverently and obediently*."⁵⁸ Stated differently, as the readers consider the life of Christ, who called God Father, they, likewise calling God Father, must live as Jesus lived (2:21). And while Jesus embraced the closeness of relationship afforded by sonship, he also lived as an obedient child.

---

52. Schreiner, *1, 2 Peter*, 82.

53. That the prayer is included in Matthew's Sermon on the Mount, a tradition block familiar to the Petrine author (1:4, 6; 2:11–12; 3:14; 4:13–14; 5:7), reinforces the strength of this proposed parallel.

54. Αββα is Aramaic. In Greek the translation would be πατερ.

55. Jeremias notes that the cry from the cross (Matt 27:45–46) seems to be the only exception, but there the reference to the OT passage explains the lack (Jeremias, *New Testament Theology*, 66; see also Edwards, *Gospel according to Luke*, 322).

56. Dunn, *Christology in the Making*, 27.

57. Dunn, *Christology in the Making*, 26. Emphasis added.

58. Jeremias, *New Testament Theology*, 67. Emphasis added.

1 Peter 1:18 and Mark 10:45; Matthew 20:28

In verse 18 Peter indicates a second reason the readers should live in reverential fear during their exile; namely, they have been ransomed (λυτρόω) by the blood of Christ. The concept of ransom has a rich history, both in the OT and in Roman society.[59] Significantly, it is also a concept Jesus used in reference to his own death as recorded in both Matthew and Mark.

Table 6.3: 1 Peter 1:18 and Mark 10:45; Matthew 20:28

1 Peter 1:18	Mark 10:45	Matthew 20:28
εἰδότες ὅτι οὐ φθαρτοῖς, ἀργυρίῳ ἢ χρυσίῳ, <u>ἐλυτρώθητε</u> ἐκ τῆς ματαίας ὑμῶν ἀναστροφῆς πατροπαραδότου	καὶ γὰρ ὁ υἱὸς τοῦ ἀνθρώπου οὐκ ἦλθεν διακονηθῆναι ἀλλὰ διακονῆσαι καὶ δοῦναι τὴν ψυχὴν αὐτοῦ <u>λύτρον</u> ἀντὶ πολλῶν	ὥσπερ ὁ υἱὸς τοῦ ἀνθρώπου οὐκ ἦλθεν διακονηθῆναι ἀλλὰ διακονῆσαι καὶ δοῦναι τὴν ψυχὴν αὐτοῦ <u>λύτρον</u> ἀντὶ πολλῶν

While some have doubted the authenticity of this *dominical logion*, there have been numerous and substantial defenses made in favor of it.[60] Shimada, after surveying the evidence, indicates that "the burden of proof is to be borne by those who hold views contrary to its authenticity."[61] And Rainer Riesner, following the lead of scholars before him, concludes that the *logion* was well-known and well-utilized in the early church.[62]

What evidence suggests that Peter is echoing Jesus' words here? Peter appears to reference this same tradition in 5:2–4, strengthening the case for its presence here. The chief agreement, however, rests with the cognates λυτρόω and λύτρον. But some have denied the association, noting that the idea presented here could simply derive from Isaiah 52:3.[63] And while there is certainly a reference to Isaiah, Michaels is correct to note that "the dominant echoes here are not of Isa 53."[64] This is confirmed in that Peter highlights the λύτρον terminology, which comes from Mark 10:45 but is absent from Isaiah 53."[65] Further, Achtemeier highlights that derivation from the

---

59. Unfortunately, it is beyond the scope of this work to develop the details from either side. For a good summary as well as substantial bibliography, see Silva, *New International Dictionary*, s.v. "λυτρόω," 3:179–87.

60. Riesner, "Back to the Historical Jesus, 171–99; Jeremias, "Lösegeld Für Viele," 216–29; Stuhlmacher, *Biblische Theologie*, 120–30; Gundry, *Mark*, 586–93.

61. Shimada, "Formulary Material," 257.

62. Riesner, "Back to the Historical Jesus."

63. Brox, *Erste Petrusbrief*, 81.

64. Michaels, *1 Peter*, 63–64.

65. Michaels does recognize the presence of λυτρόω in the LXX, but he says "To his

OT is "second hand . . . since the author's language (εἰδότες) makes clear he intends to appeal to an already existing Christian tradition."[66]

That Peter is echoing Jesus' self-reflection does not mean the text does not reflect other traditions. Indeed, this passage displays Peter's skill in weaving together multiple streams of thought. Feldmeier notes three potential motifs introduced by the ransom language: "redemption of slaves, freeing from exile, and atonement through Jesus' death."[67] The first is based on the broad use of ransom language in Greek culture,[68] the second is based on Isaiah 52:3 and the thought of freedom from foreign exile,[69] and the third is based on Jesus' statement in Mark 10:45 (Matt 20:28). After highlighting the possibility of each, Feldmeier suggests an intentional combination of the three in which each motif serves to strengthen the others.[70]

While Feldmeier is right to see the convergence of three streams of thought, there is reason to believe the reference to Jesus' words is primary. That is, the motive for Peter to speak of ransom in the first place is likely because Jesus has referred to his own sacrifice in that regard. Davids has recently argued that Peter often references OT passages that Jesus interpreted (e.g., 1:24-25; 2:6-9; 3:10-12; 4:18; 5:5).[71] In this case, Peter develops the OT motif of ransom, because Jesus himself suggested it.

Further, as Peter echoes Jesus' words, he is encouraging the reader to consider Jesus' interpretation of the OT text. Here, many commentators convincingly argue that Jesus is alluding to Isaiah 53 and interpreting his upcoming death in light of that text.[72] That Peter is referring to Isaiah

---

Gentile readers, ἐλυτρώθητε may have suggested not so much the language of the LXX as that of the Roman custom of sacral manumission, a legal fiction by which a slave (or his benefactor) paid money into a temple treasury so that the god honored at that temple would 'purchase' or 'ransom' him from his master" (Michaels, *1 Peter*, 63-64).

66. Achtemeier, *1 Peter*, 127.

67. Feldmeier, *First Letter of Peter*, 117.

68. Jobes also notes this connection, explaining that "in Greco-Roman culture [ransom language was used] to refer to the manumission of a slave. The slave would receive his or her freedom after depositing money in the temple of a god or goddess. . . . The sum of money paid for the redemption was referred to as the τιμή (*timē*, price), and the slave was considered to have been redeemed by the deity" (Jobes, *1 Peter*, 116-17). Significantly, Peter calls Jesus' sacrifice τίμιος (precious), a play on τιμή, and he refers to his readers as "free people" who are also "servants of God" (2:16).

69. Jobes also recognizes this aspect, developing the point that "in the LXX the Greek verb λυτρόω (lytroō, redeem) most frequently translates the Hebrew verbs אָגַל (gā'al, redeem) and פָּדָה (pādâ, ransom), which are both used to refer to the liberation of God's people from foreign exile" (Jobes, *1 Peter*, 117).

70. Feldmeier, *First Letter of Peter*, 117.

71. Davids, "Exalted Lord and Suffering Servant," 262.

72. There is debate concerning whether Mark 10:45 is an allusion to Isaiah 53. There

53 through Jesus is confirmed in that he alludes to Isaiah 52:3 and that he speaks of a sacrificial lamb (ἀμνός), likely in reference to Isaiah 53:7.[73] Peter appears to assume his readers will recognize the teaching (εἰδότες ὅτι; for you know) and this seems to be confirmed when he summarizes, from Isaiah 53, the substitutionary death of Christ (2:23–25) in such a succinct manner that one must assume the audience was already familiar with the teaching.[74] If the audience knew the teaching, from where did they learn it? This question leads us back to the traditions concerning Jesus' self-reflection (Mark 10:45). As Maier notes, "a leap in the historical tradition over the *dominical logion* is unlikely."[75]

While it may appear that Peter does not capitalize on the practical application Jesus gives for the ransom saying in the Gospel accounts (i.e., the disciples ought to serve others in light of Jesus' service), such application is given in verse 22. The intervening verses address the significance of Jesus' sacrifice, but after developing that significance, Peter turns to how the readers ought to live in light of their redemption. His chief command is to "love one another," which provides in imperative form what Jesus provided through example. That is, since Jesus gave himself for others in love (the chief example of love; John 15:13), so the readers must give themselves to others in love. Love through service is a point Peter will again stress later in the letter (4:8–11).

Further significance of this echo is found in the way the reflection on Jesus' words leads the reader back to Isaiah 53. And this provides rich avenues of exploration. In light of Isaiah 53, the ransom is the release from the penalty of sin, and this release logically includes the release from the power of sin.[76] In terms of 1P, this is thought of chiefly in connection to the escape from the patterns of their old life ("the futile ways inherited from your ancestors"; v. 19).

Finally, Jesus' statement that he came as a ransom "for many" (ἀντὶ πολλῶν) suggests the important place the current readers have in God's plan of redemption. They have already been told that the prophecies of old were given in regard to them (1:12), now they are told that the sacrifice planned

---

have been substantial critiques of the existence of this allusion (Hooker, *Jesus and the Servant*; Barrett, "The Background of Mark 10:45," 1–18). Nevertheless, the allusion has been ably defended by others (France, "Servant of the Lord," 26–52; cf. France, *Gospel of Mark*, 419–21; Watts, "Jesus' Death," 125–51).

73. Kelly, *Peter and Jude*, 75. Further, 1P uses the relatively rare word for lamb here (ἀμνός), which is also used in Isaiah 53:7.

74. Maier, "Jesustradition," 114.

75. Maier, "Jesustradition," 107.

76. Maier, "Jesustradition," 107.

from before the foundation of the world was for their sake (1:20). They are among the "many."

1 PETER 1:22-25

These verses provide a summarizing element to Peter's argument, echoing many of the themes developed to this point.[77] The lone imperative on which the structure of this section is built commands the readers to love (ἀγαπάω) the brotherhood (φιλαδελφία). The familial reference continues the emphasis on the new birth and broadens the believer's moral duties; they not only must live in right relationship with their Father, but they must also live in a loving relationship with their spiritual siblings.

The imperative is accompanied by two participles, both giving reasons the readers must show love.[78] First, they must love because they have purified their souls by obeying the truth.[79] Second, they must love because their new birth is the product of an imperishable seed, meaning that they have a new birth from God Himself.[80] Implied in this latter point is what has already been referenced; namely, the readers should be holy because God is holy. Accordingly, the readers must love because God, their Father, loves.

Verse 24 begins an extended reference to Isaiah 40:6b-8. After the citation, Peter notes that the word which brought them new birth is the Gospel concerning Jesus. Importantly, he notes that this Gospel is "for you" (εἰς ὑμᾶς). Michaels draws out the implications:

> The placement of εἰς ὑμᾶς at the end of the section gives emphasis to what has been a major theme in the epistle's first chapter at least since the εἰς ὑμᾶς of v 4: everything that God planned from the beginning, everything that he accomplished through the death and resurrection of Jesus Christ, everything still waiting to be revealed, is for the sake of the Christians in Asia Minor

---

77. For detail on how Peter echoes the earlier themes see, Achtemeier, *1 Peter*, 135.

78. Jobes, *1 Peter*, 123.

79. That such obedience is grounded in God's election is assumed on the basis of 1:2 and on the parallel reference to the act of God in giving them birth in this text. Davids says that the reader's obedience and God's action are "kept in creative tension" here (Davids, *The First Epistle of Peter*, 78).

80. The connection between the concept of new birth and the imperative to love is not clear. One potential meaning is provided in the text above. Spicq, however, believes the metaphor is used to stress that the impossible command can be accomplished because of the new life granted through the enduring word (Spicq, *Épîtres de Saint Pierre*, 75).

who read Peter's words. . . . The repeated pronouns help build the readers' identity, and begin to call them to responsibility.[81]

The last sentence of Michael's quote highlights a theme within these verses, which is a part of Peter's broader argument; who the readers are (born-again, obedient children) implies what they should do (love the brotherhood).[82]

The distinctive Isaiah 40 quotation here serves to reinforce Peter's point concerning the enduring nature of the word. Further, the comparison serves a rhetorical function by contrasting the fleeting nature of the reader's past with the enduring nature of their new birth in Christ. The wording of the quotation suggests Peter was referencing a text like the LXX.[83] One significant difference appears intentional, however. Instead of the reading, "word of God" (θεοῦ), as indicated in both the Masoretic Text and the LXX, Peter has the word of the Lord (κυρίου). This serves to connect the word to Jesus directly, for Peter prefers to use Lord (κύριος) in reference to Jesus (1:3; 2:3, 13; 3:15).[84]

In light of the lack of evidence that any known text available to Peter read "word of the Lord" (ῥῆμα κυρίου), it is appropriate to ask why Peter may have made the change. Michaels suggests an intentional parallel with a statement of Jesus: "Heaven and earth will pass away, *but my words will not pass away*" (Mark 13:31; cf. Matt 24:35; Luke 21:33).[85] Nevertheless, while the availability of the saying is strong (occurring in each of the Synoptic Gospels), there are no verbal clues (only ideological similarity) and little significance exists between the use in 1P and the three Synoptic contexts. Therefore, while this is a possible echo, it would be helpful to explore other possibilities.

Whatever explanation is given must account for Peter's use of "word of God" (λόγου . . . θεοῦ) in verse 23. In light of the use of both "word of God" and "word of the Lord," it is possible Peter is seeking to equate the words of the Father with the words of the Son—both are enduring.[86] Thus, Peter

---

81. Michaels, *1 Peter*, 79–80.

82. Achtemeier, *1 Peter*, 135.

83. Vahrenhorst suggests that while the quote in 1P "is largely identical to the LXX," it "may reflect a revision that brings it closer to the Masoretic text" (Translated from, "Dieser Schriftrekurs ist weitgehend mit dem Text der LXX identisch, spiegelt aber möglicherweise eine Rezension, die sich dem masoretischen Text angenähert hatte" [Vahrenhorst, *Erste Brief Des Petrus*, 96]).

84. Michaels, *1 Peter*, 79.

85. Michaels, *1 Peter*, 79; cf. Balz and Schrage, "*Katholischen*," 81.

86. Peter Davids, in comments on an earlier draft of this study, noted that it is possible that Peter was simply following Greek rhetoric in varying his referent. The result is ambiguous, for both Jesus and the Father can be called Lord.

would be implying that Jesus' words are of great significance. And, as we noted above, one of the confirming criteria for determining the presence of JT is contextual clues that the author may be referencing the words of Jesus. Here, reference to "the word of the Lord" makes it more likely to find those words cited. Further, since Peter refers again to new birth (1:23), which we earlier argued derives from *dominical logion* (see 1:3 above), Peter appears to be appealing to JT in these verses. With these points in mind, we will consider the following potential parallels: (1) 1P 1:22 and John 13:34–35; John 15:12; and (2) 1P 1:23–25 and the Parable of the Sower (Mark 4:3–20; Matt 13:1–23; Luke 8:4–15).

1 Peter 1:22 and John 13:34–35; 15:12

In verse 22, Peter calls the readers to love one another. While this command is not unique to the teaching of Jesus, it is certainly distinctive of his teaching. As Wong notes, such a phrase "easily evokes the teaching of Jesus as found in John's Gospel."[87] Unsurprisingly, some have sought to trace the lineage of this dependence back to its source in the teaching of Jesus, particularly in regard to the teachings recorded in John's Gospel.[88]

Table 6.4: 1 Peter 1:22 and John 13:34–35; 15:12

1 Peter 1:22	John 13:34–35	John 15:12
Τὰς ψυχὰς ὑμῶν ἡγνικότες ἐν τῇ ὑπακοῇ τῆς ἀληθείας εἰς φιλαδελφίαν ἀνυπόκριτον ἐκ καθαρᾶς καρδίας ἀλλήλους ἀγαπήσατε ἐκτενῶς.	Ἐντολὴν καινὴν δίδωμι ὑμῖν, ἵνα ἀγαπᾶτε ἀλλήλους, καθὼς ἠγάπησα ὑμᾶς ἵνα καὶ ὑμεῖς ἀγαπᾶτε ἀλλήλους. 35 ἐν τούτῳ γνώσονται πάντες ὅτι ἐμοὶ μαθηταί ἐστε, ἐὰν ἀγάπην ἔχητε ἐν ἀλλήλοις.	Αὕτη ἐστὶν ἡ ἐντολὴ ἡ ἐμή, ἵνα ἀγαπᾶτε ἀλλήλους καθὼς ἠγάπησα ὑμᾶς.

The availability of this teaching is difficult to challenge. As Kistemaker notes, this command is reflected by three apostles: Paul (I Thess 3:12; 4:9; 2 Thess 1:3), Peter (1 Peter 1:22; 2:17; 3:8; 4:8), and John (1 John 3:23).[89] Nevertheless, the wideness of this tradition creates another problem; how can

---

87. Wong, "Use of Jesus' Sayings," 203.

88. E.g., Lohse, "Paränese und Kerygma," 85n93; Hort, *First Epistle of St. Peter*, 90; Kistemaker, *Exposition of the Epistles of Peter*, 71; Gundry, "'Verba Christi' in I Peter," 340; Maier, "Jesustradition," 90; Spicq, *Épîtres de Saint Pierre*, 150; Feuillet, "Quelques Reflexions," 244; Foster, *Literary Relations*, 527; Tenney, "Possible Parallels," 374.

89. Kistemaker, *Exposition of the Epistles of Peter*, 71.

we be sure the reference goes back to Jesus and is not dependent on early church teaching? Foster provides two reasons to believe it does. First, since this context frequently points to the words of Jesus (cf. 1:19, 21, 22a, and 23), the likelihood that Peter is referring to Jesus' words here increases.[90] Second, the context of John speaks explicitly of Peter (13:31–32, 36).[91] Foster doubts genuine Petrine authorship, but his argument assumes that someone writing in Peter's place would likely reflect traditions associated with Peter.

Best argues that John's Gospel records a redacted form of Jesus' original command, "love your neighbor." The only evidence Best gives is the following *reductio ad absurdum*: "If we argue that the author of 1 Peter knew the teaching of Jesus as originally given in the form of John we should also have to argue that Paul did so and was presumably, therefore, a disciple."[92] But why should Paul's knowing the tradition require that he be an original disciple? Is it not possible that Paul heard the tradition as passed on by eyewitnesses? Largely on the strength of his *reductio*,[93] Best supplies what he believes is a superior alternative: "It is much easier to conclude that a variant of the logion 'love your neighbour' existed in the early church in the form 'love one another' and was known to Paul, 1 Peter, John, 1 John."[94] But why is that easier to conclude? Indeed, Maier has come to the exact opposite conclusion: "Logically, it is easier to imagine that the *dominical logion* [love one another] was handed down from the early church, thus reaching both Paul and 1 Peter."[95]

Significantly, Best and Gundry do agree that the passage in 1P refers back to the traditions of the teaching of Jesus, whether genuine (Gundry)

---

90. Foster, *Literary Relations*, 527; cf. Michaels, who makes the same point, while defending the reliance of 1P 1:22 on Matt 11:29. Evidence for the connection with Matthew fell short of the criteria for this study (Michaels, *1 Peter*, 74).

91. "The context of John suggests 1 Peter (cf. 13:31–32), even mentioning Peter by name, v. 36" (Foster, *Literary Relations*, 527).

92. Best, "I Peter and the Gospel Tradition," 97.

93. Best also indicates that the presence of ἀνυπόκριτος in many of the texts (Rom 12:9; 2 Cor 6:6; 1P 1:22) supports his point. Nevertheless, Gundry disarms the argument with a legitimate question: "why should the association of ανυπόκριτος imply the unoriginality of 'love one another?'" (Gundry, "Further Verba," 216). Thompson argues that the presence of ἀνυπόκριτος in Rom 12:9 is based on the words of the Lord (Matt 7:5; Luke 6:42), and the same argument could be made here. Thus, the presence of the ἀνυπόκριτος may strengthen the case for Peter's dependence on the words of the Lord more generally here (Thompson, *Clothed with Christ*, 92–94).

94. Best, "I Peter and the Gospel Tradition," 97.

95. Translated from, "Logisch kann man es sich leichter vorstellen, daß ein Wort Jesu von der Urgemeinde tradiert wurde und auf diese Weise sowohl zu Paulus als auch in den 1. Petr gelangte" (Maier, "Jesustradition," 90).

or redacted (Best).⁹⁶ The primary lexical similarity is the repetition of the phrase "love one another" (ἀγαπᾶτε ἀλλήλους).⁹⁷ Of course, these words are not rare or unique; nevertheless, the centrality of the love command in Jesus' teaching suggests that both Peter and the readers would have traced such a command back to Jesus.⁹⁸

Since this is an echo, it is not necessary to reflect on the origin of the words in order to understand the meaning of the passage. Nevertheless, reflection provides rich sources of significance. Earlier we noted that Best has not proved that the command, "love one another," is a redacted form of "love your neighbor."⁹⁹ Nevertheless, it would be artificial to disconnect the two commands. The love of the brotherhood is a specific application of loving one's neighbor,¹⁰⁰ and in terms of 1P, there are reasons to suggest Peter would emphasize love for the brothers.¹⁰¹ Accordingly, the reader's love as a consequence of their obedience to the truth results in the fulfillment of a "great" commandment (Mark 12:30). First Peter 4:8 seems to suggest this when Peter says, "*Above all* (πρὸ πάντων), maintain constant love for one another." In light of such language, Furnish suggests that readers "might expect in this context a reference to Jesus's Great commandment or at least to the love command of Lev. 19:18, but there is no use, direct or indirect, of either of these anywhere in I Peter."¹⁰² Nevertheless, Peter's pattern is not to directly cite Jesus; instead, Peter assumes the core teachings of Jesus and

---

96. Gundry recognizes this and suggests that Best's position is not incompatible with his own: "Accepting the dictum for the sake of argument, however, we may recall that even an apostle might occasionally use a developed and accepted form of a dominical saying" (Gundry, "Further Verba," 216).

97. Best notes that "No objection can be offered because of the use in 1 Peter of the aorist imperative of ἀγαπαω since the writer has a definite predilection for this tense in the imperative mood" (Best, "I Peter and the Gospel Tradition," 97).

98. "Undoubtedly this command of Jesus was remembered by all of his apostles, since it was a cardinal aspect of his teaching" (Tenney, "Possible Parallels," 374).

99. Bultmann likewise believed these verses were Johannine redaction (Bultmann, *Gospel of John*, 525n1, 542n1). Wong rightly notes, however, that such a position "ignores the unusual aspect of Jesus' teaching in John 13:33-35 where the command is 'new' and that newness lies with the manner of loving one another—as he has loved them, a point noted by more than one commentator" (Wong, "Use of Jesus' Sayings," 203n35).

100. Furnish, speaking specifically about John's Gospel and its concern for loving those within the community notes that such a command "is neither a softening nor a repudiation of the command to love the neighbor, but a special and indeed urgent form of it" (Furnish, *Love Command in the New Testament*, 148).

101. The most important is the sociological fact that the audience is under great persecution, and they need the fellowship and love offered in the Christian community.

102. Furnish, *Love Command in the New Testament*, 161.

builds on them. Thus, the very expectation Furnish admits may be seen as evidence that Peter expected the early readers to also think of this teaching of Jesus.

There are other connections between the present text and John 13:31–35 that prove instructive. First, that Jesus calls the command "new" may be explained by recognizing that the speech is occurring at the Last Supper.[103] While John does not record the words, it is here that the Synoptics indicate that Jesus spoke of the blood of the new covenant (Matt 26:28; Luke 22:20). In this light, Carson notes that the "new" command in John's Gospel may be an "indirect allusion to the new covenant that was inaugurated at the last supper (1 Cor. 11:25; cf. Lk. 22:20)".[104] Others have noted that the reference to obedience in verse 22 reflects 1:2, which we argued speaks of the readers as members of the NC. This connection may also explain the existence of the textual variant addition "obedience to the truth *through the Spirit.*"[105] Such a reading further explains how the apparent tension between the reader's obedience and the new birth can be resolved. On a cursory reading it appears that the readers are responsible for the purification of their souls, yet it is difficult to resolve this in reference to the new birth. But if the text is read in light of the NC context, such a purification occurs through the work of the Spirit, a work dependent on God's grace. In this light, Peter is saying, "Now that you have purified yourself by becoming holy, obedient, spirit-indwelt members of the NC, fulfill the great command of Jesus to love another."

Carson reveals another NC aspect when he notes that in John's Gospel, the new command is

> not only the obligation of the new covenant community to respond to the God who has loved them and redeemed them by the oblation of his Son, and their response to his gracious election which constituted them his people, it is a privilege which, rightly lived out, proclaims the true God before a watching world. That is why Jesus ends his injunction with the words, *All men will know that you are my disciples, if you love one another.*[106]

Such a theme fits nicely within Peter's evangelistic thrust (2:12; 3:13–17) and is consonant with the prophecies concerning the NC (Ezek 36:23).

---

103. That the command is not out of accord with prior revelation is recognized also in 1 John 2:7–8.

104. Carson, *Gospel according to John*, 484–85.

105. While a few witnesses contain the phrase (e.g., P 5. 307. 442. 642 vgms), the most significant do not ($\mathfrak{P}$72 ℵ A B C Ψ), and it is likely not original.

106. Carson, *Gospel according to John*, 485.

For those who hear the echo of Jesus' teaching here, the standard of love is powerfully expressed. Peter calls the readers to a fervent (ἐκτενῶς) love, which is explained by the tradition recorded in John's Gospel; fervent love is the love Jesus showed towards his disciples: "Just as I have loved you, you also should love one another" (13:34).

1 Peter 1:23–25 and the Parable of the Sower (Mark 4:3–20; Matt 13:1–23; Luke 8:4–15)

Peter speaks of the word of God as a seed which brings new life. Such language is similar to the parable of the sower recorded in each of the Synoptic Gospels. While many others have noted the potential allusion, none appear to have developed the significance of it.[107] Because of the length of the parable, a table will not be provided in comparison of the texts. Nevertheless, we will walk through the three elements of an allusion—availability, agreement, and significance—arguing that Peter is alluding to the parable.

The case for availability is bolstered by the fact that the tradition is present in all three Synoptic Gospels. Added to this, the content of the tradition—the accounting of the various responses to the Christian message—would certainly have been of interest to a nascent group of evangelistic believers. Further, there is reason to believe other NT texts refer to the parable (e.g., Jas 1:18, 21; 1 Cor 9:11),[108] suggesting its wide purchase in the early church. Finally, this is a tradition which focuses on the teaching of Jesus directly to the disciples (Mark 4:10; Matt 13:10; Luke 8:9), something likely to be passed on.

Agreement exists at the linguistic and ideological levels. Linguistically, both texts speak of the seed (σπορά/σπόρος), which is identified as the word of God (λόγος τοῦ θεοῦ; Luke 8:11; 1P 1:23).[109] Further, Mark's Gospel speaks of the planted seed growing up (αὐξάνω; 4:8), and 1P 2:2 speaks of the new life produced by the seed growing (αὐξάνω) into salvation.[110] Ideo-

---

107. Maier, "Jesustradition," 98; Hunter and Homrighausen, *First Epistle of Peter*, 104; Kokot, "Znaczenie 'Nasienia Niezniszczalnego,'" 41; Michaels, *1 Peter*, 76; Blgg, *Epistles of St. Peter*, 123; Riesenfeld, *Gospel* Tradition, 193; Elliott, *1 Peter*, 389, 392; Frankemölle, *1 Petrusbrief*, 40; Spicq, *Épîtres de Saint Pierre*, 75.

108. Riesenfeld develops the influence of the parable on NT texts, particularly in reference to Paul's epistles (Riesenfeld, *Gospel Tradition*, 190–93. See also Mayor, "Reminiscences of the Parable of the Sower," 407–14).

109. Though σπορά normally refers to the process of sowing, it can by metonymy also refer to the seed itself (Bauer et al., BDAG, s.v. "σπορά," 939). Accordingly, there is no functional difference between the terms used.

110. Goppelt notes the connection between these passages, but suggests the Petrine

logically, the identification of the seed with the word of God is substantial. This is not to say that there were no precedents for such language in the OT, but it is to say that the most likely origin of the identification is in Jesus' parable.[111]

One of the clues that an intertextual reference is being made is that the context of the passage has some ambiguity. In this case, it is not clear whether Peter is speaking of human seed or agricultural seed. As Michaels notes, "Both σπορά and σπέρμα can be used either of raising plants or of human procreation, and there is no way to be absolutely certain which metaphor Peter has in mind here."[112] The analogy of new birth in verse 23 and in 2:1–3 suggests human seed, while the citation of Isaiah 40 suggests agricultural seed. A way to resolve this is by reference to the teaching of Jesus, for while Jesus uses the agricultural analogy, he also refers to the new life produced by the word in people, a reality he elsewhere refers to as new birth. Reference to the teaching of Jesus may offer one way to explain why Peter so easily vacillates between the metaphors.

Finally, we argued above that 1P 1:10 echoed the beatitude of Jesus as expressed in Matthew 13:16. Significantly, that beatitude is expressed directly between the telling of the parable of the soils (vv. 3–9) and its explanation (vv. 18–23), strengthening the case for both that echo and this allusion.

As noted above, this has been labeled an allusion to the teaching of Jesus. Unlike an echo, an allusion is required to fully understand the meaning of the passage at hand. In this case, reflection on the parable of the sower helps us to understand Peter's meaning. Why does Peter call the seed imperishable and stress the living and enduring nature of the word? These questions are answered by considering a broader issue in 1P. Martin has argued that while 1P does not explicitly warn against apostasy, this is one of the main themes of the letter. In the words of Martin, Peter stresses the necessity of endurance by "utilizing a rhetorical strategy of suppression," meaning Peter "stresses notions antithetical to defection as he attempts to move the mind of his readers away from scandal and defection to hope, sobriety, and steadfastness."[113]

In relation to the present passage, Peter may be invoking the parable of the sower in an attempt to encourage his readers to continue in the faith.

---

passage refers to endurance, while the Markan passage refers to growth. Nevertheless, the idea that growth is necessary to endurance is taught elsewhere in the NT (2 Pet 1:8) and may stand behind this passage (Goppelt, *Commentary on I Peter*, 132n49).

111. Maier, "Jesustradition," 98.

112. Michaels, *1 Peter*, 76.

113. Martin, *Metaphor and Composition*, 275. See also Thurén, *Argument and Theology in 1 Peter*, 224.

Jeremias rightly recognizes that the parable of the sower, as expressed in the Synoptic Gospels, provides a "warning to the converted against a failure to stand fast in time of persecution and against worldliness."[114] As Peter alludes to this passage, he expects his readers to grasp the central meaning of the parable. They have heard the word of God and have received the seed. Indeed, they have ingested the word, and the seed has been planted, producing what appears to be new life. But, as the parable reveals, some who receive the seed do not continue on to produce fruit that evidences salvation (Luke 8:11). Peter's emphasis on the imperishable seed and the enduring word gives every reason for the readers to believe they will continue on in the faith, reaching maturity and ultimate salvation (2:2).[115] Nevertheless, Peter indicates that they must embrace good behavior (love and pursue spiritual milk; 1:22; 2:2) and avoid negative behavior (malice, guile, etc.; 2:1) to be the type of seed that grows up (αὐξάνω) into salvation.

1 PETER 2:1–3

First Peter 2:1 starts with "therefore" (οὖν) showing the continuity of thought between this section and the last. It is the new birth and the obedience to the truth of the gospel that makes sense of the removal (ἀποτίθημι) of certain vices and the longing for (ἐπιποθέω) the spiritual milk. Significantly, the vices the readers are to remove destroy community and are antithetical to the love for the family to which Peter has called the readers (1:22).[116]

The sole command in these verses concerns the necessity to long for (ἐπιποθέω) the pure spiritual milk. The identity of the milk has long been a point of debate.[117] For the purposes of this study, it is not necessary to resolve the issue. It is enough to see that Peter is using the language metaphorically because of its relation to the new birth motif he has developed since the beginning of the letter. Further, the reference to LXX Psalm 33 was chosen partly because its reference to taste fits the metaphor under

---

114. Jeremias, *The Parables of Jesus*, 150.

115. Michaels notes that the use of σωτηρία in this context is not well-suited to the metaphor. His explanation is that Peter wants to connect 2:2 with the salvation being referenced in chapter 1. This is accurate, but it may be that Peter uses the word because of its use in Jesus' description of the parable of soils (Luke 8:11) (Michaels, *1 Peter*, 89).

116. Helm notes that these vices "have one thing in common. They all undo other people. They destroy relationships" (Helm, *1 and 2 Peter and Jude*, 69; cf. Green, *1 Peter*, 48; Schreiner, *1, 2 Peter*, 93).

117. Most commentators believe it refers to the word of God and some specific studies have defended this position (McCartney, "Λογικός," 128–32; Tite, "Nurslings," 371–400).

consideration.[118] Thus, the metaphor concerning new birth, begun in 1:3, continues to have an important role even here. While many potential parallels have been offered in the history of research, only one will be considered here: 1P 2:3 and Luke 6:35.[119]

First Peter 2:3 is a citation of LXX Psalm 33:9. Peter edited the citation to remove "and see" (καὶ ἴδετε) which did not fit the analogy to milk he was presenting and conflicted with the fact that his audience had not seen Christ (1:8). That Peter is referencing the OT leads many to conclude that he is not echoing Jesus' words. Nevertheless, Maier and Michaels have made such a connection and we will seek to strengthen the case for the connection here.[120]

Table 6.5: 1 Peter 2:3 and Luke 6:35

1 Peter 2:3	Luke 6:35
εἰ ἐγεύσασθε ὅτι <u>χρηστὸς</u> ὁ κύριος.	πλὴν ἀγαπᾶτε τοὺς ἐχθροὺς ὑμῶν καὶ ἀγαθοποιεῖτε καὶ δανίζετε μηδὲν ἀπελπίζοντες· καὶ ἔσται ὁ μισθὸς ὑμῶν πολύς, καὶ ἔσεσθε υἱοὶ ὑψίστου, ὅτι αὐτὸς <u>χρηστός</u> ἐστιν ἐπὶ τοὺς ἀχαρίστους καὶ πονηρούς

The connection between these passages is chiefly tied to the rare word χρηστός.[121] Of course, Peter's choice of this word is influenced by the LXX Psalm 33:9;[122] nevertheless, this does not eliminate the possibility that Peter is also echoing the words of Jesus. The clear OT citation, however, does demand greater support for a dominical echo.

That Peter is echoing Luke 6:35 can be defended in the following ways. First, it would not be surprising to find an echo from the traditions found in Luke 6, for as we suggest in this study, Peter elsewhere refers to this same tradition block five other times (1:6; 2:18–21; 3:9, 14, 16; 4:13–14).[123]

---

118. Susan Woan develops the importance of LXX Psalm 33 for 1P in an article and dissertation (Woan, "The Psalms in 1 Peter," 213–30; Woan, "Old Testament in 1P," 141–59; See also Jobes, "'O Taste and See,'" 241–51.

119. Other proposed parallels can be seen in the appendix.

120. Maier, "Jesustradition," 98–99; Michaels, *1 Peter*, 90–91.

121. The word occurs only seven times in the NT (Matt 11:30; Luke 5:39; 6:35; Rom 2:4; 1 Cor 15:33; Eph 4:32; 1P 2:3).

122. Directly after the section Peter quotes, the Psalm goes on to say, "blessed (μακάριος) is the man who hopes (ἐλπίζω) in him." As noted above, Peter appears to have an affinity for verses stressing God's blessing (μακάριος), and the expression of hope merges quite well with the theme as it is developed in 1P.

123. Cf. Michaels, *1 Peter*, 91.

Second, χρηστός would likely have been pronounced identically to χριστός (Messiah) in Koine Greek,[124] drawing the reader's attention to Jesus.[125]

Third, the similarity of theme between 1P 2:3 and Luke 6:35 can be seen in two areas. First, while it is true that Peter is speaking of love for the brethren and Luke 6 is speaking of love for enemies, the latter reinforces the former. Stated differently, if Jesus loved his enemies—a trait the readers are also called to emulate (3:9)—love for the brethren is tacitly implied.[126] Thus, both passages are calling the reader to love. Second, Luke indicates that those who love their enemies are "sons of the most High," which accords well with Peter's connection between the reader's love and new birth (1:23), and which accords with the command to be obedient children by modeling the heavenly Father (1:14).

While these connections cannot prove Peter is echoing Jesus' words in Luke 6, the case appears strong.[127] What significance could Peter have intended by this echo? To answer that question, it is necessary to recognize that the first-class conditional (*if* you have tasted) is not designed to introduce doubt, but is used as a "causal clause with the positive force of 'since,' 'because,' 'seeing that.'"[128] Accordingly, the clause can be understood in the following way: "since you have tasted that the Lord is kind [crave the milk]." Peter is assuming that the readers have in fact tasted the kindness of the Lord. When did they do so? They did so when they were enemies of God in bondage to the ways of their forefathers (1:14). That is, the readers experienced the grace of God through the new birth planned in election from the foundation of the world (1P 1:12, 20); nevertheless, prior to their calling, they were among those whom God turned his face against (3:12).

Thus, this echo brings the discussion back to the imperative that began the paragraph: love one another (v. 22). They are being called to love one another on the basis of the love that was shown them in Christ, a love that embraces even those who are enemies. From this perspecive, the command to love *one another* (1:22) is shown to be comparatively light. Further, it is by means of such love that Jesus says they will "be the children of the Most

---

124. Achtemeier, *1 Peter*, 148n72.

125. This is based on the principle that where the name of the Lord is mentioned, the likelihood of consideration of his words increases.

126. In the Gospel context, Jesus is calling the readers beyond love for those close to oneself to a greater love that embraces enemies (Luke 6:27–34). Thus, the love for enemies assumes the love for those close.

127. Maier is right to note that "we do not go beyond a certain possibility" (translated from, "kommen wir über eine gewisse Möglichkeit nicht hinaus" [Maier, "Jesustradition," 99]).

128. Elliott, *1 Peter*, 402.

High," a compatible conception with the new birth motif Peter has been developing. The point is not that they will earn such a title, but rather that by modeling such love, they will show themselves to be the children of God. Finally, such love results in that which Peter has already held out in hope for his readers—a blessed inheritance (1:4).

1 PETER 2:4-10

While not focusing exclusively on the new birth, 1:3—2:3 has primarily developed that motif. In 2:4-10, the conclusion to the opening of the letter, Peter offers another set of metaphors that focus on the communal element resulting from the new birth: they are living stones fashioned together to create a spiritual house in which they function as a holy priesthood,[129] offering spiritual sacrifices to God through Jesus Christ (2:4-5).

That the audience's identity is based on the identity of Christ is first formally introduced here (2:4). Nevertheless, it has been anticipated since the first verse of the letter. Just as Jesus is chosen by God (ἐκλεκτός), so Peter has already described his audience as those chosen by God (ἐκλεκτός; 1:1) and will describe them as a chosen race (ἐκλεκτός; 2:9). That Jesus was rejected by men also finds its counterpart in the experience of Peter's readers, which has been hinted at up to this point (1:6-9) but will become a focus in his upcoming exhortations (2:21-23; 3:17-18; 4:12-19).

First Peter 2:4-5 sets the stage for 2:6-10, one of the lengthiest compilations of OT texts in the NT.[130] The metaphor of the stone, used in verse 4, is developed more fully in verses 6-8, while the readers' identity as a spiritual priesthood, introduced in verse 5, forms the basis for verses 9-10.[131] Further, the development of the stone motif (vv. 6-8), which emphasizes the distinction between God's elect and the disobedient, forms the basis for Peter's descriptive language in 9-10. Stated theologically, who they are as chosen in Christ (vv. 4-8) is the foundation for the privileges expressed in verses 9-10.

The use of τίθημι (v. 6) to describe those God has chosen for salvation bookends with ἐτέθησαν (v. 8) concerning those who do not believe. Such

---

129. Davids highlights three stages of the stone imagery: "(1) Christ as stone and human beings as builders to (2) Christians as stones and part of the building to (3) Christians as priests serving in the building" (Davids, *First Epistle of Peter*, 86).

130. Jobes notes that Peter is "quoting or alluding to six LXX passages: Ps. 117:22 (118:22 Eng.); Exod. 19:5-6; Isa. 8:14; 28:16; 43:20-21; and Hos. 2:25 (2:23 Eng.)" (Jobes, *1 Peter*, 142).

131. Achtemeier, *1 Peter*, 150.

an inclusion serves to focus the whole of verses 6–8 on the concept of divine election, some to honor and others to dishonor. Peter masterfully weaves the three "stone" texts together to highlight this distinction.[132] Isaiah 28:16 is his chief text to refer to the positive side of election, first applied to Christ and through him to the stones which come to life in Him. Psalm 117:22 and Isaiah 8:14, on the other hand, are combined to note the negative side of election. Nevertheless, even while emphasizing God's role in placing the stone, Peter never loses sight of the personal failure of those who will experience eschatological shame to believe in Christ (v. 7b) and to obey the word (v. 8c). These two failures are not disconnected, for it is the failure to obey the word that ultimately leads to the failure to believe in Christ, the stone. Consequently, those who fail to obey will ultimately trip over the stone.[133]

While Peter clearly grounds these assertions in the OT, it appears he is also reflecting the words of Christ. Here we will consider the relationship between 1P 2:4–8 and Mark 12:10, 11; Matthew 21:42, 43; Luke 20:17, 18.[134]

The "Stone Passages" of the OT—two in Isaiah (8:14; 28:16), one in Psalms (118:22), and one in Daniel (2:34–35)—provide substantial interpretive fodder for New Testament exposition. Jesus references two of the passages (Mark 12:10–11; Matt 21:42; Luke 20:17–18), Luke ascribes to Peter's sermon one reference (Acts 4:11), Pauline literature directly references two in Romans and makes an allusion to one in Ephesians (Rom 9:30–33; 10:10; Eph 2:20–22), and in this text, Peter references three of them at once (1P 2:6–8).

The relationship between 1P's use of the stone passages and other NT uses of those passages is complex. Four notable similarities exist between Paul's use and Peter's use of the stone passages: (1) Both use καταισχύνω (to shame); (2) both provide the inclusion ἐπ' αὐτῷ (in him); (3) both omit the negative participles; and (4) both substitute σκάνδαλον for πτώματι.[135]

---

132. Unfortunately, space prevents an extended exegetical treatment of the three stone passages. It can simply be stated here that each of the stone passages focuses on the consequences of trusting in or alternatively disobeying the stone.

133. Thus, while the focus is on election, Peter maintains a tension between divine sovereignty and human responsibility, a tension present elsewhere in the New Testament (Acts 2:22–23; 4:27–28; Rom 9–10; Phil 2:12).

134. See the appendix for a list of other possible JT influences here, of which 1P 2:9 and Matt 5:13–16; John 8:12; 12:35, 46 is probable, though not clear enough to be considered here. Further, while Peter may be reflecting a Johannine theme as he speaks of the rejected λόγος, the author of the Fourth Gospel does not suggest that Jesus called himself the λόγος, and thus while there may be thematic coherence here, Peter does not seem to be deriving this theme from the words of Jesus.

135. Oss notes the unique similarities between Peter and Paul on these texts (Oss, "Interpretation," 187).

In light of these striking similarities, some have argued for literary dependence, usually with Peter relying on Paul.[136] Nevertheless, the difficulties of such a position are hard to overcome.[137] The more probable explanations center on either a written *testimonia*,[138] which both men had access to, or common oral tradition. The latter would more easily explain some of the divergences and would be consistent with the way the JT was transmitted.[139] Regardless of the similarities between Peter's use of the passages and Paul's, the application of the stone passages here evidences authorial ingenuity, suggesting Peter is not merely mimicking prior considerations but has artfully combined the passages to express his distinctive purposes.[140]

That the Isaiah stone passages (8:14; 28:16) were read together is not unique to the NT. Wagner suggests that the Hebrew text of Isaiah led interpreters to read them together.[141] This may be verified by observing the ancient interpretive translation of the LXX, which borrows language from 8:14 (ἐπ' αὐτῷ) and reads it into 28:16.[142] Further, the LXX gives evidence that there existed a messianic interpretation of these texts prior to the NT.[143] Elliott has shown that other Jewish sources (Targums, Qumran) handled these texts similarly, leading him to conclude that the messianically-charged stone image "had already been prepared; the church simply had to make the application."[144]

The primary question that interests us concerns the role Jesus' words may have had on Peter's text, and how that influence may affect our reading of the text. The table on the next page compares Peter's text to the three Synoptic proposed parallels.

---

136. Beare, *First Epistle of Peter*, 120–21.

137. One significant difficulty is that Paul combines the Isaiah passages in a seamless and artistic way, and it is hard to imagine Peter separating these if he had access to Paul's text (Jewett, *Romans*, 612–13; Michaels, *1 Peter*, 94; Snodgrass, "I Peter II. 1–10," 99–101).

138. For a detailed development of the theory of a written *testimonia*, see Albl, *And Scripture Cannot Be Broken*.

139. Elliott notes that the "flexibility of this complex and the freedom with which its contents were adapted and interpreted argue against the existence of a written source and suggest rather *oral transmission*" (Elliott, *The Elect and the Holy*, 32).

140. Wilkes, "Synoptic Tradition," 154. Contra Best, "I Peter II 4–10," 284.

141. Wagner, *Heralds of the Good News*, 150.

142. Moyise indicates that the addition "already suggests a link with Isa. 28:16 in the eyes of the LXX translators" (Moyise, "Isaiah in 1 Peter," 179).

143. Compare Isaiah 28:16d in its LXX rendering with its Hebrew rendering: "and the one who believes *in him* will not be put to shame" (NETS); "one who trusts will not panic" (NRSV).

144. Elliott, *Elect and the Holy*, 26–28.

Table 6.6: 1 Peter 2:7-8 and Mark 12:10, 11; Matthew 21:42, 43; Luke 20:17, 18

1 Peter 2:7-8	Mark 12:10, 11	Matthew 21:42-44[145]	Luke 20:17, 18
⁷ ὑμῖν οὖν ἡ τιμὴ τοῖς πιστεύουσιν, ἀπιστοῦσιν δὲ *λίθος ὃν ἀπεδοκίμασαν οἱ οἰκοδομοῦντες, οὗτος ἐγενήθη εἰς κεφαλὴν γωνίας* ⁸ καὶ λίθος προσκόμματος καὶ πέτρα σκανδάλου·	Οὐδὲ τὴν γραφὴν ταύτην ἀνέγνωτε· *λίθον ὃν ἀπεδοκίμασαν οἱ οἰκοδομοῦντες, οὗτος ἐγενήθη εἰς κεφαλὴν γωνίας·* ¹¹ παρὰ κυρίου ἐγένετο αὕτη καὶ ἔστιν θαυμαστὴ ἐν ὀφθαλμοῖς ἡμῶν;	Λέγει αὐτοῖς ὁ Ἰησοῦς· οὐδέποτε ἀνέγνωτε ἐν ταῖς γραφαῖς· *λίθον ὃν ἀπεδοκίμασαν οἱ οἰκοδομοῦντες, οὗτος ἐγενήθη εἰς κεφαλὴν γωνίας·* παρὰ κυρίου ἐγένετο αὕτη καὶ ἔστιν θαυμαστὴ ἐν ὀφθαλμοῖς ἡμῶν; ⁴³ διὰ τοῦτο λέγω ὑμῖν ὅτι ἀρθήσεται ἀφ᾽ ὑμῶν ἡ βασιλεία τοῦ θεοῦ καὶ δοθήσεται ἔθνει ποιοῦντι τοὺς καρποὺς αὐτῆς. ⁴⁴ καὶ ὁ πεσὼν ἐπὶ τὸν λίθον τοῦτον συνθλασθήσεται· ἐφ᾽ ὃν δ᾽ ἂν πέσῃ λικμήσει αὐτόν.	ὁ δὲ ἐμβλέψας αὐτοῖς εἶπεν· τί οὖν ἐστιν τὸ γεγραμμένον τοῦτο· *λίθον ὃν ἀπεδοκίμασαν οἱ οἰκοδομοῦντες, οὗτος ἐγενήθη εἰς κεφαλὴν γωνίας*; ¹⁸ πᾶς ὁ πεσὼν ἐπ᾽ ἐκεῖνον τὸν λίθον συνθλασθήσεται· ἐφ᾽ ὃν δ᾽ ἂν πέσῃ, λικμήσει αὐτόν.

The case for the availability of the tradition is quite strong. First, this is a part of the triple tradition. Second, the tradition would have been important in the early church, for all three Synoptic Gospels connect the saying to the parable of the wicked tenants, which offered a prediction of the death of Jesus and offered an explanation of the Jewish rejection of Jesus.

On the basis of the usefulness the saying would have had in the early church, some argue that the teaching is a product of the church and is not genuinely dominical.[146] While the case for authenticity has been ably de-

---

145. Matt 21:44 is a textual variant, which while absent in a few important manuscripts (D, 33, itmss, syrs) is nevertheless present in nearly all the most significant (ℵ, B, C, K, L, X). But since it agrees so closely with Luke 20:18 many scholars believe it is an interpolation from there (Nolland, *Gospel of Matthew*, 865). Nevertheless, its placement in Matthew's text is awkward and not where one would expect if it were interpolated from Luke. For this reason, France argues it is original (France, *Gospel of Matthew*, 807n3). Further, Morris offers a plausible reason for the reading's absence in some manuscripts: "a copyist's eye might well have slipped from αὐτῆς at the end of verse 43 to αὐτόν at the end of the disputed verse, omitting everything in between" (Morris, *Gospel according to Matthew*, 544n70).

146. For arguments against its authenticity, see Best, "I Peter and the Gospel Tradition," 101; Goppelt, *Commentary on I Peter*, 138; cf. Dodd, *Parables of the Kingdom*

fended, it is not necessary to offer such a defense here. Since the three Synoptic Gospels record the parable along with a quotation of LXX Psalm 117, we can reasonably conclude that Peter had access to a tradition of like kind.

Before turning to the agreement that exists between 1P and the Gospel passages, it is helpful to note that some believe the reference to Peter as the "rock" increases the probability that the author would reference these Gospel passages. This is true whether one holds to Petrine authorship or not. If Peter is the author, then he has a vested interest in the motif.[147] If a pseudonymous author was writing in the name of Peter, it is likely he would seek to make historical connections with the traditions concerning Peter as well.[148]

Because the lexical agreement is sourced in the shared, identical citation of LXX Psalm 117:22, the agreement we will focus on here is ideological. A primary question is, where did Peter get the idea that *Jesus* is the stone upon which people will trust or upon which people will stumble and fall? In Harris's oft-cited opinion, "It is Jesus . . . who sets the Stone rolling."[149] While we have argued above that the stone passages were understood in a messianic sense prior to the NT, Longenecker notes that "Much of this 'stone' imagery of the OT seems to have been rather enigmatic to most Jews during the time of Jesus and Paul."[150] It was necessary for someone to highlight the connection between Jesus and the stone passages, and historically that connection was understood to be made by Jesus Himself.[151]

While it is possible Peter derived such thoughts directly from the OT or from other early church usage, Lea is correct to note that "The towering figure of Jesus should be allowed to loom over the literary or oral activity

---

128; Jülicher, *Gleichnisreden Jesu*, 385–406. Maier, however, suggests that "there are no striking arguments against this evangelist claim" (translated from, "Es gibt keine durchschlagenden Argumente gegen diese Behauptung der Evangelisten" [Maier, "Jesustradition," 91]).

147. Gundry, "'Verba Christi' in I Peter," 346. Cf. Spicq, "Ia Petri," 56; Stibbs, *First Epistle General of Peter*, 99.

148. Moule, an agnostic concerning Peter's authorship (Moule, *Nature and Purpose of 1 Peter*, 11), notes the connection between these sayings and Peter: "May not the name [of Peter], then, have been allowed to collect to itself all the 'stone' ideas? And if so, it is perhaps not for nothing that the first Epistle bearing Peter's name is at pains to present the alternatives of receiving or rejecting Christ in terms of the stone imagery, I Pet. ii. 4–8" (Moule, "Some Reflections," 57).

149. Harris, *Testimonies*, 96.

150. Longenecker, *Epistle to the Romans*, 843.

151. "Jesus Himself was the first to apply the metaphor of the stone to Himself" (Jeremias, *Theological Dictionary of the NT*, s.v. "λίθος," 274; cf. Stendahl, *School of St. Matthew*, 69, 212; Oss, "Interpretation," 183).

of other early Christian sources in producing the Old Testament insights which are found on the pages of Peter's writings."[152] One criticism of the view offered here concerns the difference in the stone passages referenced in each text. The Gospel texts refer to three OT stone passages (LXX Ps 117:22; Isa 8:14–15; Dan 2:34)[153] and Peter refers to three as well (LXX Ps 117:22; Isa 8:14–15; 28:16), but Peter fails to reference Daniel 2:34 and Peter adds consideration of Isaiah 28:16. Nevertheless, France is right to suggest that early Christian expositors likely searched the OT for stone passages that could be interpreted christologically. Importantly, France highlights the origin of this inclination: "it is likely that it was Jesus' use of Ps 118:22 which started the search."[154] Thus, just as Jesus merged separated stone passages, so Peter follows his example.

One agreement between 1P and the Gospel passages that is not present between Romans and the Gospel passages concerns the rejection of the stone. Paul chooses to emphasize the catastrophic result of the rejection of the stone, but he does not focus on the rejection itself.[155] On the other hand, the Gospel passages and 1P focus heavily on the Jewish leader's rejection of the stone. Lindars recognizing this use of the Psalm in 1P, said, "The inevitable conclusion is that the writer is familiar with Ps. 118:22 as a proof of the rejection of the Jews, just as it is found in the parable of the wicked husbandmen."[156]

Another way of expressing the last point is to highlight that 1P and the Gospel passages reference LXX Psalm 117, while Romans does not. This portion of the Psalm, which focuses on the rejection of the stone, does not appear to have ever been connected to the Isaiah stone passages prior to Jesus connecting them.[157] The importance of this point for our purposes is hard to overemphasize. Since Jesus is the first to associate LXX Psalm 117 within the other OT stone passages, when Peter also does so, it is likely he is following Jesus.

A final point of agreement between 1P and the Gospel parallels concerns the emphasis on building. This emphasis, however, does not come from any of the cited OT texts.[158] Instead, Michaels sees 1P reflecting tradi-

---

152. Lea, "How Peter Learned the Old Testament," 102.
153. Mark's Gospel only speaks in reference to LXX Ps 117:22, while Matt and Luke appear to refer to all three passages.
154. France, *Gospel of Matthew*, 817–18.
155. Gundry, "'Verba Christi' in I Peter," 346n1.
156. Lindars, *New Testament Apologetic*, 180.
157. Snodgrass, "I Peter II. 1–10," 106.
158. Michaels, *1 Peter*, 97.

tions likewise reflected in other Pauline texts (Eph 2:19-21; 1 Cor 3:9-17), which trace back to Jesus:

> Not only the decisive promise to Peter himself that 'On this rock I will build my church' (Matt 16:18), but the persistence of charges against Jesus that he intended to build a new temple (Mark 14:58 // Matt 26:61; cf. John 2:19) suggest that the building metaphor may have played a significant role in his self-consciousness and his vision of the future. *The use of Ps 117[118]:22 in Mark 12:10-11 // Matt 21:42-44 // Luke 20:17-18 confirms this impression with its tacit assumption that a process of building is under way in which the religious leaders of Israel will play no part.* . . . It appears likely that 1 Peter is drawing here on tradition common to Paul and the Gospel tradition, rooted in Judaism (e.g., Qumran) but especially important to the earliest Christians *because of its presence in their traditions of the words of Jesus.*[159]

Significantly, none of the stone passages from the OT suggest believers will become stones. This theme is expressed, however, in Jesus' words to Peter in Matthew 16:18. Best finds two problems with this association, however. First, Matthew 16:18 presents Peter as having a special position as "rock," while 1P has Jesus alone in a unique position.[160] Second, "the 'building' image of 1 Peter 2:4-10 was very common in the early church and can be traced back to Judaism."[161]

In response to Best's first argument, the author elsewhere appears to minimize Peter's importance, noting he is simply a fellow-elder (5:1). Accordingly, it is not surprising he does not stress the foundational role he and the other apostles played in the building of the church. Further, the purpose of this section is to highlight the role of Christ as the cornerstone. Inserting himself (and the other apostles) would have needlessly complicated the matter. As for Best's second argument, there certainly were building metaphors in Judaism, but that individual believers are *stones forming a temple* is not present in Judaism but is sourced out of the unique teachings of Jesus.

Having addressed the availability of the JT and the agreement between the Gospel passages and 1P 2:4-8, it is now helpful to consider how the echo of the Gospel tradition may influence a knowledgeable reader's understanding.[162] First, when 1P 2:4-8 is read in light of Jesus' teaching, the proposal

---

159. Michaels, *1 Peter*, 97. Emphasis added.
160. Best, "I Peter and the Gospel Tradition," 101.
161. Best, "I Peter and the Gospel Tradition," 101.
162. Though Lea argues that "Peter's views here cannot be understood unless they

that Peter is implicitly addressing Jewish unbelief becomes more probable. Such a position has been proposed in past scholarship,[163] but other scholars have argued that Peter's lack of direct mention of Jewish unbelief makes a general, non-ethnic application more likely.[164]

The case that Peter is hinting at Jewish unbelief is supported in multiple ways. First, no verses of Scripture more consistently or eloquently describe Christian readers in terms originally used in reference to God's chosen nation, ethnic Israel than 1P 2:9–10. And while Davids suggests that Peter uses the titles of honor with "no awareness or recognition of an 'old' Israel," Achtemeier is right to note that the deliberate multiplication of titles makes this unlikely.[165] Whatever Peter's view of the relationship between Israel and this new people of God,[166] it is clear that Peter intends to communicate that some blessings promised to Israel are now the possession of his readers because of their response to Jesus, the rock. If Peter's readers knew the OT (and Peter's extensive use of it suggests they did), they could not help but consider the fate of the Jewish people, and such considerations would lead them to recognize that the Jewish people were largely, though not exclusively, part of those who rejected the stone.

Another reason to suggest Jewish unbelief is implied in the text concerns the use of the stone sayings, both in the Gospels and outside the Gospels. Starting with the latter, we see that reference to LXX Psalm 117:22 in Acts 4:11 focuses directly on Israel's rejection of Jesus, even identifying the elders and the rulers of the people as the "builders": "This Jesus is 'the stone that was rejected *by you, the builders*; it has become the cornerstone.'"[167] Likewise, Romans 9:33, which masterfully combines Isaiah 8:14 and 28:16, appears within Paul's personal anguish over and explanation for Jewish unbelief.

---

are referred to the initial teaching which he received from Jesus in grasping the Old Testament background for these thoughts," we will argue that Peter's view could be properly understood, though some nuance of thought is lost without reference to Jesus' teaching (Lea, "How Peter Learned the Old Testament," 96).

163. Selwyn, *First Epistle of St. Peter*, 165; Calvin, *Commentaries on the Catholic Epistles*, 72–73; Beare, *First Epistle of Peter*, 126; Hort, *First Epistle of St. Peter*, 122–23; Reicke, *Epistles of James, Peter, and Jude*, 92–93.

164. Jobes, *1 Peter*, 156.

165. Achtemeier, *1 Peter*, 167n235.

166. Achtemeier suggests the following four possibilities, along with bibliographic detail each: continuation, fulfillment, reenactment, or replacement (Achtemeier, *1 Peter*, 167).

167. Jesus' description of the leaders of Israel as builders is not unique to him, for, as France has noted, "In rabbinic literature scribes and scholars are sometimes referred to as 'builders'" (France, *Gospel of Mark*, 463; cf. Nolland, *Gospel of Matthew*, 878).

That these non-Gospel passages, focusing on the rejection of Jesus by ethnic Israel, both reference the stone passages is likely due to the influence of the *dominical logion* recorded in the passages we have been discussing. Consequently, when 1P references the stone passages, particularly LXX Psalm 117:22, readers would also likely be drawn to a consideration of Jesus' use of the passage in regard to the memorable parable of the tenants,[168] which detailed the Jewish leader's unbelief.

A question remains: Why didn't Peter explicitly address Jewish unbelief? Perhaps the stone passages provide the reason. Elsewhere in the NT, the stone passages are used to defend the unity of Jew and Gentile in Christ. For instance, in Romans 10:11, Paul references Isaiah 28:16 a second time, but this time he uses it to note that there is no Jewish priority, for all who believe—whether Jew or Gentile—will not be put to shame. Likewise, the extended consideration of the unity between Jews and Gentiles in Ephesians 2:11–22 concludes with the description of the holy temple being built of Jewish and Gentile converts, in which Jesus is the cornerstone. These passages indicate that the stone passages were applied to the Jewish-Gentile problem in the early church. There could be unity, because both Jews and Gentiles were part of the same spiritual building project. Thus, when used by Peter, they implicitly draw attention to the Jewish "builders" failure to accept God's chosen cornerstone; nevertheless, they also express the unity of the *new* people of God. Seen in this light, Peter's lack of explicit mention of Jewish unbelief is likely intentional, for he desires to stress the unity that exists among the new people of God.

A second point of significance that might be implied by the echo of Jesus' words concerns jubilant praise for God's elective purposes. Two of the Gospel passages (Mark 12:11; Matt 21:42) include verse 23 from LXX Psalm 117: "This was the Lord's doing, and it is marvelous (θαυμαστός) in our eyes." Such an inclusion stresses God's elective purposes in both the "builders" rejection of the cornerstone and in God's placing it as the cornerstone. In regard to 1P, Peter seems to intentionally draw on this passage when he mentions in 2:9 that God has called Peter's readers into a marvelous (θαυμαστός) light.[169] By echoing this passage Peter places his readers on the positive end of God's election. They are not those who reject the stone; rather, they are those who see God's plan and find it marvelous.

---

168. Barnard rightly notes that Jesus' use of LXX Ps 117 "at the conclusion of a pointed parable which spoke of his impending passion and death ensured for it a special place in the mind of the early church" (Barnard, "The Testimonium," 306).

169. Michaels observes that θαυμαστός was "possibly suggested to Peter's mind by the θαυμαστή of Ps 117[118]:23 in the immediate context of one of his preceding quotations (cf. Matt 21:42 // Mark 12:11)" (Michaels, *1 Peter*, 111).

CONCLUSION TO 1 PETER 1:13—2:10

As with the letter opening and introduction, we have found that the words of Jesus are a substantial source for the concepts developed in the body opening. Indeed, each of the major sections of the body opening reflect the teaching of the Lord. We have argued for six echoes and one allusion.

Table 6.7: Intertextual Resonances to *Dominical Logia* in 1 Peter 1:13—2:10

1P Reference	Gospel Reference	Type of Reference
1:13	Luke 12:35, 45	Echo
1:17	Matt 6:9; Luke 11:2	Echo
1:18	Mark 10:45; Matt 20:28	Echo
1:22	John 13:34-35; 15:12	Echo
1:23-25	Parable of the Sower (Matt 13:1-23; Luke 8:4-15; Mark 4:3-20)	Allusion
2:3	Luke 6:35	Echo
2:4-8	Mark 12:10, 11; Matt 21:42, 43; Luke 20:17, 18	Echo

In these verses, Peter turns from an explicit consideration of the reader's identity in Christ to a call for the readers to act in conformity to that identity. In doing so, Peter uses the words of Jesus to great effect. By echoing Jesus' metaphor of girding the loins (Luke 12:35, 45), Peter places the teaching in an eschatological setting. Further, since the teaching also contains a beatitude of blessing for those who wait expectantly, Peter once more reinforces the importance of God's blessing. A second echo of the teaching of Jesus indicates the seriousness of their position. They have been granted a place in the family of God and can now call on God as Father (Matt 6:9; Luke 11:2); yet this familial relationship requires much of the readers, for they must model their Father in holiness, providing an example to all people of who God is.

By indicating that the readers have been ransomed by the blood of Jesus, Peter reminds them that their adoption was costly. Further, he reminds the readers that just as Jesus lived sacrificially for them (Mark 10:45; Matt 20:28), so they must live sacrificially for others. Indeed, echoing another teaching of Jesus, Peter indicates that the readers must love one another (John 13:34-35; 15:12). This is a fruit of their new birth and is evidence that they are a part of the new covenant community Jesus has established with his blood. And while Peter illustrates their new birth through the seed by means of an OT reference (Isa 40:6-8), he alludes to the parable of the sower, which indicates that the Word of God is a seed which brings new life. By means of this allusion, Peter encourages the readers to perseverance, for they must show themselves to be the seed which brings forth fruit and thus grow up into salvation.

Peter seamlessly transitions from the seed producing life to a young child in need of milk, a transition made possible by the parable of the sower. That Peter's readers are considered children is reflective of Jesus' teaching that only children will obtain the kingdom (Mark 10:14–15; Matt 19:14–15; Luke 18:16–17). And, unlike the authors of other milk analogies in Scripture, Peter does not anticipate a time when the readers will outgrow their need for the milk, for they must remain in the child-like phase to inherit the kingdom. As Peter continues the milk-metaphor he reflects LXX Psalm 33:9, which indicates that the reader has come to taste that the Lord is kind. But it is likely that Peter is also reflecting the teaching of the Lord here as well, for Jesus indicated that God is kind to the wicked. Of course, Peter's readers know this for God has looked kindly on them through Jesus even when there was a hostile relationship. Likewise, then, as they reflect their Father, they must also show love to others.

Finally, Peter echoes the memorable teaching of Jesus concerning the foundation stone of God's new building project. While it is clear Peter is reflecting an OT theme, it is also clear that he does so through the lens of Jesus' words. This echo would remind the readers that just as Jesus was rejected by men and yet chosen by God, so they are likewise. That they are a part of the building project indicates their intimate connection to Jesus, yet there is a tacit warning too; many who were original recipients of these promises failed to believe and obey and they tripped over the stone. Peter's readers, however, have great hope that since they have come to Christ, they are among those chosen by God to build a new community, reflecting love for one another.

These echoes and allusions to the teaching of Jesus do not show any discernible pattern. That is, Peter's reflections are not limited to certain tradition-blocks or a certain literary tradition. Instead, it appears that Peter is developing his own themes, while borrowing the language of Jesus to support and enhance his message.

7

First Peter 2:11—3:7

First Peter 2:11—4:11 constitutes the body middle,[1] which can be divided into two main sections.[2] The first (2:11—3:7) details the role of believers in regard to three specific social situations (to government, to human masters, and to spouses), while the second (3:8—4:11) details further requirements for all believers.[3] This chapter focuses on the first half of the body middle.

McKnight calls 2:11-12 "the pivotal passage in 1 Peter," because here Peter reminds the readers of their identity and derives how they are to live in society on the basis of it.[4] Peter recalls the identity of his readers from 1:2; they are aliens and exiles (παροίκους καὶ παρεπιδήμους). Such a description provides a bold contrast to the recent description of them as a holy nation

---

1. The following suggest a new section is beginning here. First, Peter addresses the reader directly for the first time. Second, by using a nominative plural of direct address, Peter signals a shift in his argument (cf. 4:12). Third, there is a noticeable change in content as Peter begins to develop societal obligations. Fourth, the glory of God forms an inclusio beginning with 2:12 and ending with 4:11 (Green, 1 Peter, 64). Finally, by addressing the readers as aliens and exiles (παροίκους καὶ παρεπιδήμους) he recalls 1:2 and contrasts their present experience with their calling as a holy nation (2:9).

2. Achtemeier, 1 Peter, 169-70.

3. The division of the body middle into two parts is an unfortunate necessity, and it presents a challenge. In one sense, Achtemeier is right to note that 3:7 concludes the household code (Achtemeier, 1 Peter, 169). Yet he is also right to note that 3:8 passage begins with "now finally all of you" (τὸ δὲ τέλος πάντες) and is structured in the same way as the preceding instructions (Achtemeier, 1 Peter, 220-21). Consequently, commentators divide the passage differently. Here, we will divide the chapters between 3:7 and 3:8, recognizing that this is a somewhat artificial division.

4. McKnight, 1 Peter, 124.

(2:9). Thus, we see the tension between the elect-exile motif emphasized once more. Whereas 2:4–10 has focused primarily (though not exclusively) on the election of the readers (*elect*-exiles), this passage focuses on the estrangement of these chosen believers (elect-*exiles*). In light of their election and the familial, national, and social ramifications of this fact, how should they presently live? The rest of the first half of the body middle answers this question. Peter begins with a consideration of his readers and government (2:13–17), before a consideration of slaves and masters (2:18–25). Afterward, he considers the role of wives (3:1–6) and then of husbands (3:7).

Interspersed at deliberate points in the body middle is consideration of Christ. Consequently, Achtemeier speaks of Peter's "strategic references to the suffering (2:21–24; 3:18–20, 22; 4:1) and triumphant (3:22) Christ as the basis for the exhortations to appropriate conduct in the midst of [the reader's] hostile environment."[5] Significantly, Peter's most extended reflection on the work of Christ occurs within his instruction to slaves (2:21–24). In light of the centrality of the person of Christ in these verses, the presence of *dominical logia* are rightly anticipated.

1 PETER 2:11–12

These transitional verses set the stage for Peter's instructions to his readers regarding their various social obligations. Despite the variance of people included in this section (slaves, wives, husbands), Peter calls them all—regardless of social position—beloved (ἀγαπητός), establishing equal footing as God's children. Peter appears to have two chief concerns for these elect-exiles. First, he desires that his readers would persevere in the war for their soul by abstaining from the passions of the flesh. Second, and more positively, he wants his readers to live in a morally superior way, performing good/honorable (καλός) deeds. By avoiding evil and doing good, Peter does not believe his readers will avoid all verbal attack; nevertheless, he does envision that their lifestyle may lead some unbelievers to offer glory to God.

First Peter 2:12 appears to echo or allude to Matthew 5:14–16, where in the Sermon on the Mount Jesus speaks of the evangelistic nature of good works performed by his disciples. Best identifies this as "the clearest parallel in the whole of 1Peter," adding that it is accepted "as such by almost all commentators."[6]

---

5. Achtemeier, *1 Peter*, 170.

6. Best, *1 Peter*, 109. Cf. Hort, *First Epistle of St. Peter*, 136; Selwyn, *First Epistle of St. Peter*, 171; Schelkle, *Die Petrusbriefe*, 71; Achtemeier, *1 Peter*, 177; Best, *1 Peter*, 112; Cranfield, *First Epistle of Peter*, 55; Jobes, *1 Peter*, 171; Davids, *First Epistle of Peter*,

Table 7.1: 1 Peter 2:12 and Matthew 5:16

1 Peter 2:12	Matthew 5:16
τὴν ἀναστροφὴν ὑμῶν ἐν τοῖς ἔθνεσιν ἔχοντες καλήν, ἵνα ἐν ᾧ καταλαλοῦσιν ὑμῶν ὡς κακοποιῶν ἐκ τῶν <u>καλῶν ἔργων</u> ἐποπτεύοντες <u>δοξάσωσιν</u> τὸν θεὸν ἐν ἡμέρᾳ ἐπισκοπῆς.	16 οὕτως λαμψάτω τὸ φῶς ὑμῶν ἔμπροσθεν τῶν ἀνθρώπων, ὅπως ἴδωσιν ὑμῶν τὰ <u>καλὰ ἔργα</u> καὶ <u>δοξάσωσιν</u> τὸν πατέρα ὑμῶν τὸν ἐν τοῖς οὐρανοῖς.

While Matthew records this saying within the Sermon on the Mount, the parallel passage in Luke's Gospel (14:34–35) lacks this saying. Nevertheless, as Foster recognizes, "it is quite natural to suppose that Matthew preserves a genuine logion of our Lord, which was current in the church, but which was not used by the other Synoptic writers."[7] One reason to believe this to be the case is the substantial agreement between 1P 2:12 and the Matthean saying.

There is both ideological and lexical agreement. Ideologically, both passages emphasize persecuted, verbally maligned believers (cf. Matt 5:11) whose faithful character shines with evangelistic power.[8] Goppelt notes the exceptionality of this thought in the NT, when he highlights that this idea is "expressed programmatically only in Mt. 5:16 and here."[9]

The surrounding contexts are also significant. Both statements are used as introductions to lists of good deeds to pursue and vices to avoid.[10] Further, both speak specifically to the responsibility of believers in regard to broader society. The metaphors of salt and light in Matthew clearly speak to the role of Christians in society.[11] And Peter's use of the latter metaphor likewise develops the same theme by showing how believers ought to engage in a hostile society.

First Peter 2:12 evidences strong lexical similarity to Matthew 5:16.[12] Both passages speak of good works (καλός ἔργον) that lead unbelievers to glorify (δοξάσωσιν) God. Since Peter prefers αγαθός, the use of καλός

97–98; Michaels, *1 Peter*, 118; Kelly, *Peter and Jude*, 105; Green, *1 Peter*, 69.

7. Foster, *Literary Relations*, 499–500. See also Nolland, *Gospel of Matthew*, 214.

8. Beare recognizes the "clear parallelism of thought" between the passages (Beare, *First Epistle of Peter*, 137. See also Luz, *Matthew 1–7*, 103).

9. Goppelt, *Commentary on I Peter*, 161–62.

10. Metzner, *Rezeption*, 285. For more on these lists see Wibbing, *Tugend- und Lasterkataloge*; Vögtle, *Tugend- und Lasterkataloge*.

11. Blomberg, *Matthew*, 103.

12. Beare notes that "the dependence in vocabulary is unmistakable" (Beare, *The First Epistle of Peter*, 137).

strongly evidences dependence on JT.[13] Further, Gundry notes that Peter's mention of light in 2:9 (φῶς) may have led him to consider Matthew 5:14–16, which likewise focuses on light (φῶς).[14] The verbal differences may be explained with regard to Matthean or Petrine development.[15]

The possibility that Peter is reflecting Matthew 5:16 is strengthened by the other echoes of Matthew 5 in 1P. While consideration of these will have to wait until later, it is quite probable that Peter reflects Matthew 5:10 in 1P 3:14 and Matthew 5:11–12 in 1P 4:13–14. This observation is consistent with Michaels, who notes that while it is unlikely Peter knew Matthew in its current form, "he was unquestionably familiar with parts of the Sermon as now preserved in Matthew and other parts as found in Luke."[16]

We will argue that this is an allusion to the words of Jesus, for recognizing the allusion unlocks the full meaning of the passage. It does this primarily by revealing the meaning of the enigmatic last line, ἐν ἡμέρᾳ ἐπισκοπῆς.[17] This phrase is translated in widely differing ways, from "in the day of visitation" (KJV) to "when he comes to judge" (NRSV). These translations reveal the interpretive challenge, for it is not clear whether Peter is referring to a future day of judgement or a present day of visitation. And this question is related to the broader question concerning *how* unbelievers will glorify God—through conversion or by forced confession of the righteousness of believers.

Three interpretive options are available: (1) unbelievers will remain unbelievers, and on the day of judgment they will be forced to offer words of glory to God in light of the good deeds of believers;[18] (2) unbelievers will become believers by means of the witness of believer's good deeds on a (non-eschatological) day when God visits them;[19] (3) unbelievers will be-

---

13. Best likewise indicates, "Peter's favourite words is αγαθός and his use of καλός here (only elsewhere at 4:10) strongly reinforces the suggestion of indebtedness to a common tradition" (Best, "I Peter and the Gospel Tradition," 110; cf. Metzner, *Rezeption*, 285).

14. Gundry, "'Verba Christi' in I Peter," 340.

15. For an incise consideration of the differences see, Michaels, *1 Peter*, 110. Best develops how such differences "are largely explicable in terms of normal Matthean and Petrine usage" (Best, *1 Peter*, 109–10; cf. Wong, "Use of Jesus' Sayings," 220–21).

16. Michaels, *1 Peter*, 119.

17. ἐπισκοπή is used only four times in the NT. Once here, twice in reference to an office in the church (Acts 1:20; 1 Tim 3:1), and once in Jesus' pronouncement of judgment on Jerusalem for its lack of proper response during the "time of visitation from God" (Luke 19:44).

18. Davids, *First Epistle of Peter*, 97–98.

19. Elliott, *1 Peter*, 471.

come believers by means of the witness of believer's good deeds and will offer glory to God on the day of judgment.

A full exegetical treatment of the issue is not possible here; instead, we will limit our discussion to a defense of the third option on the basis of the *dominical logion*. Stated differently, the allusion to the words of Jesus gives reason to believe the third option is correct. If Peter's readers were familiar with Jesus' teaching at this point, their interpretation of this passage would have been influenced towards the third view. As Luz rightly notes, the Lord's teaching in Matthew clearly indicates that the works of believers have an evangelistic power.[20] Jesus, as other early JT reveals, was known as the light of the world (John 8:12; 9:5), and Matthew has just recently spoke of Gentiles who sat in darkness receiving a great light (4:16). Now, as Jesus speaks of his disciples as lights in the world, they recognize that they have a "borrowed light;"[21] they are reflecting the light of God through their works, and this has the possible effect of introducing unbelievers to the God of light.

It is important to see that there are other confirming reasons to believe Peter is speaking of the conversion of unbelievers here. Schreiner, for example, marshals literary support for a salvific reading of the day of visitation (ἐν ἡμέρᾳ ἐπισκοπῆς).[22] Additionally, in 3:2 Peter speaks of unbelieving husbands seeing (ἐποπτεύω) the conduct of their wives and being brought to belief in Jesus. Importantly, this is the same word Peter uses here for unbelievers seeing (ἐποπτεύω) the good works of believers. Since the conduct of wives is one of the good works Peter is encouraging, it is hard not to conclude that he has the same end in mind; just as the unbelieving husband is possibly brought to belief in Jesus by means of the good works of his wife, so the unbeliever is possibly brought to belief in Jesus by seeing the believer's good works.[23]

In sum, the allusion to the words of Jesus confirms Peter's meaning. As Michaels notes, the hopeful, evangelistic reading of the passage makes sense when one recognizes that Peter "has made Matt 5:16 his starting point."[24]

Before leaving this passage, two other areas of significance should be mentioned. First, hearing the allusion to the words of Jesus would likely have resulted in a remembrance that every member of the new community was important. Jesus does not highlight certain individuals as prominent

20. Luz, *Matthew 1–7*, 208.

21. "*Your light* is, of course, a borrowed light. It is because they have received light from Jesus that the disciples can shine in the world" (Morris, *Gospel according to Matthew*, 106).

22. Schreiner, *1, 2 Peter*, 124.

23. Vahrenhorst, *Erste Brief Des Petrus*, 113.

24. Michaels, *1 Peter*, 119.

lights; rather, he speaks of the new community of believers as a unified city light, proclaiming far and wide the glory of the God they serve. This fits quite nicely with 1P, where even the disenfranchised in society (slaves, women) are empowered to "shine their lights." Second, Jesus' words stress the imperative nature of living out one's faith publicly. When Peter urges (παρακαλέω) them to avoid sin and do good, he is drawing on the command of the Lord. His readers would likely recall the futility of the light hidden under the basket and the Lord's command to let the light shine.

1 PETER 2:13-17

These verses detail what honorable conduct looks like in regard to the civil sphere. Whether to the emperor himself or his representative, the duty of Christians is to submit to the governing authority. Such a statement is necessary, for the believer's loyalty to Christ may be misconstrued as a license to disobey other, lesser authorities.[25] Peter explains that these civil leaders are established in order to punish wrongdoers and praise those who do right. And since Christians are to live praiseworthy lives, Peter stresses that God's will is that followers of Jesus do right. Notably, it is not only God's will that they do right, but further that *by doing right* the Christian will silence the ignorance of the foolish unbeliever.

Though Peter may compare the emperor to one who is "supreme" (ὡς ὑπερέχω), Peter also indicates the emperor is a mere mortal.[26] Read in light of Peter's prior comments, the point seems to be that believers, as members of a holy nation, have only one true ruler, the Lord Himself. It is for the sake of their Lord (διὰ τὸν κύριον) that they submit to other rulers, and while they honor other rulers, fear is reserved for God alone.[27] Consequently, in regard to civil society, believers are free; yet their freedom is constrained by their bond to Christ. Stated differently, their freedom leads to willing submission to civil authorities for the purpose of accomplishing God's will, which is that by being obedient, Christians will witness to the goodness of the Lord by their deeds.

---

25. Jobes, *1 Peter*, 174.

26. This is communicated both by the statement "human creature/institution" (ἀνθρωπίνῃ κτίσει; v. 13) and the parallel between honoring everyone and honoring the emperor (v. 17). Williams, *Good Works in 1 Peter*, 227.

27. Achtemeier notes that the "emphasis on the common humanity of the emperor probably reflects the growing prominence in Asia Minor of the cult of the emperor, and is designed to give Christians a reason for civil divorced from any notion of the emperor as a deity" (Achtemeier, *1 Peter*, 180).

Where does Peter derive his theology concerning the civil sphere? While there are some unique elements here, many have found the words of Jesus to be Peter's primary source.[28] Two Gospel passages have been identified as witnessing to the *dominical logia* that contribute to Peter's thought here: Matthew 17:25–27 and less clearly Matthew 22:21 (Mark 12:17; Luke 20:26).[29]

Table 7.2: 1 Peter 2:13–17 and Matthew 17:25–27 (cf. Matt 22:21)

1 Peter 2:13–17	Matthew 17:25–27	Matthew 22:21
Ὑποτάγητε πάσῃ ἀνθρωπίνῃ κτίσει διὰ τὸν κύριον, εἴτε βασιλεῖ ὡς ὑπερέχοντι 14 εἴτε ἡγεμόσιν ὡς δι' αὐτοῦ πεμπομένοις εἰς ἐκδίκησιν κακοποιῶν, ἔπαινον δὲ ἀγαθοποιῶν, 15 ὅτι οὕτως ἐστὶν τὸ θέλημα τοῦ θεοῦ ἀγαθοποιοῦντας φιμοῦν τὴν τῶν ἀφρόνων ἀνθρώπων ἀγνωσίαν, 16 ὡς <u>ἐλεύθεροι</u> καὶ μὴ ὡς ἐπικάλυμμα ἔχοντες τῆς κακίας τὴν <u>ἐλευθερίαν</u> ἀλλ' ὡς θεοῦ δοῦλοι. 17 πάντας τιμήσατε, τὴν ἀδελφότητα ἀγαπᾶτε, τὸν θεὸν φοβεῖσθε, τὸν βασιλέα τιμᾶτε.	λέγει· ναί. καὶ ἐλθόντα εἰς τὴν οἰκίαν προέφθασεν αὐτὸν ὁ Ἰησοῦς λέγων· τί σοι δοκεῖ, Σίμων; οἱ βασιλεῖς τῆς γῆς ἀπὸ τίνων λαμβάνουσιν τέλη ἢ κῆνσον; ἀπὸ τῶν υἱῶν αὐτῶν ἢ ἀπὸ τῶν ἀλλοτρίων; 26 εἰπόντος δέ· ἀπὸ τῶν ἀλλοτρίων, ἔφη αὐτῷ ὁ Ἰησοῦς· ἄρα γε <u>ἐλεύθεροί</u> εἰσιν οἱ υἱοί. 27 ἵνα δὲ μὴ σκανδαλίσωμεν αὐτούς, πορευθεὶς εἰς θάλασσαν βάλε ἄγκιστρον καὶ τὸν ἀναβάντα πρῶτον ἰχθὺν ἆρον, καὶ ἀνοίξας τὸ στόμα αὐτοῦ εὑρήσεις στατῆρα· ἐκεῖνον λαβὼν δὸς αὐτοῖς ἀντὶ ἐμοῦ καὶ σοῦ.	λέγουσιν αὐτῷ· Καίσαρος. τότε λέγει αὐτοῖς· ἀπόδοτε οὖν τὰ Καίσαρος Καίσαρι καὶ τὰ τοῦ θεοῦ τῷ θεῷ.

While the tradition of Matthew 17:25–27 is only recorded in that Gospel, the content would have been of great significance to the early church. The case for the availability of Matthew 22:21 is even stronger. It is a triple tradition saying (Mark 12:17; Luke 20:26) that is also evidenced in Romans 13:1–7.[30] Again, due to the nature of the teaching, it is quite likely to have spread among early Jesus followers.

---

28. Love, "First Epistle of Peter," 78; Russell, "Eschatology and Ethics in I Peter," 82; Leaney, *Letters of Peter and Jude*, 35; Gundry, "'Verba Christi' in I Peter," 340–41; Maier, "Jesustradition," 91–92; Spicq, "Ia Petri et Le Témoignage," 50–52; Selwyn, *First Epistle of St. Peter*, 174; Goppelt, *Commentary on I Peter*, 180.

29. Other proposed parallels may be seen in the appendix.

30. Bruce, "Paul and 'the Powers That Be,'" 111–20; Moo, *Epistle to the Romans*, 806n84.

The lexical agreement between Matthew 17:25–27 and this passage is based on the relatively rare ἐλεύθερος (free person). Significantly, only here and in Matthew 17 is the word used in reference to civil responsibility.[31] Spicq also notes the "unexpected" statement concerning the *freedom* of Peter's readers, and notes that it can "hardly be explained without reference to the logion of Capernaum, because *eleutheria* is never mentioned in the other NT traditional teachings on submission to established authorities."[32] That Peter was drawn to this text can be defended by the observation that Matthew 17:25 focuses on the identity of the *free people* as the children of God, a concept Peter has developed extensively. Indeed, it is based on the new identity of Peter's readers as the children of God who are a holy nation that necessitates consideration of their relationship to other civil structures.

Other ideological similarities suggest Peter is reflecting on these words of Jesus. Both passages are concerned with the way the children of God relate to the civil sphere,[33] particularly in regard to the way unbelievers view the actions of believers. In regard to Matthew 17 the focus is on avoiding offense, while in 1P the focus is on silencing foolish accusations. These are not incompatible, for the accusations against early Christians often focused on elements offensive to the broader culture.[34] In sum, we agree with Spicq who suggests that "Peter's insistence on the negative motive of this obedience: not to upset the pagans, not to lend themselves to criticism, to put an end to slander, seems to reproduce the surprising practical solution of Jesus."[35]

Finally, one might expect agreement between these passages due to the nature of the Gospel tradition. It was Peter who was asked by the collectors of the temple tax whether Jesus paid the tax, and he caught the fish. Those who believe the apostle is the author will recognize that such an event and the instructions from Jesus would not easily be forgotten. And those who believe Peter was not the author should recognize that a writer standing in his place would likely echo events associated with Peter. Thus, the

---

31. Gundry, "'Verba Christi' in I Peter," 341.

32. Translated from, "ce qui ne peut guère s'expliquer que par référence au logion de Capharnaum, car jamais cette eleuthéria n'est mentionnée dans les topoi traditionnels du N.T. sur la soumission aux autorités constituées" (Spicq, "Ia Petri et Le Témoignage," 51).

33. While Matthew 17 speaks about a religious tax, Jesus expands the context broader to taxation in general and thus invokes the civil sphere (v. 25; "From whom do kings of the earth take toll or tribute? From their children or from others?").

34. See, e.g., Felix, "The Octavius of Minucius Felix," 173–98.

35. Translated from, "L'insistance mise par Pierre sur le motif, surtout négatif, de cette obéissance: ne pas indisposer les païens, ne pas prêter flanc à la critique, faire cesser les calomnies, semble reproduire la solution pratique surprenante de Jésus" (Spicq, "Ia Petri et Le Témoignage," 51).

significance of Peter in the narrative in which this saying is located increases the probability that the text would echo the Gospel saying.

Despite the above agreements, some have argued against a reference to the *dominical logion*. Best, for instance, offers four counter-arguments to the claim that Jesus' words are referenced here. First, Matthew's text references a political situation involving those related to an earthly ruler, while 1P references a theological situation concerning spiritual foreigners. Second, Matthew's text is dealing with taxation, while 1P is much broader. Third, the passage in 1P is closely related to Romans 13 and is likely the product of a formal Haustafel (household code). Finally, even if Matthew 17:25–27 speaks about an original event, the development of the tradition prevents any clear statements about the original form of the tradition.[36]

It will be helpful to respond to each of these arguments. First, Best is correct to see the spiritual foreigner motif in 1P, yet it is precisely due to this motif that Peter must speak about current political realities. As Spicq noted, "It is likely that a certain number of Christians—on the grounds that they are children of God who have been regenerated or foreigners, simple residents passing through here below—were tempted to insubordination, if not contempt for pagan officials."[37] That Peter connects this freedom to the absence of sin illustrates the overall point in the paragraph; the relationship one has to Jesus should lead one to an exemplary life.[38] In regard to civil structures, the Christian has only one Lord, yet since God has called him to submit to the governing authorities, he may not claim his new spiritual status (as a member of the holy nation) as an excuse for insubordination and the exercise of evil in the present civil sphere.[39]

Maier argues that Best's second argument is one of his strongest, for Peter's application reaches "far beyond" that stated in Matthew.[40] Nevertheless, the argument is weakened by the recognition that taxation is one of the chief elements in the expression of a government. Thus, Gundry is right to

---

36. Best, "I Peter and the Gospel Tradition," 110–11.

37. Translated from "Il est vraisemblable qu'un certain nombre de chrétiens excipant de leur qualité d'enfants de Dieu régénérés ou d'étrangers, simples résidants de passage ici-bas, devaient être tentés d'incivisme, sinon de mépris pour les fonctionnaires païens" (Spicq, "Ia Petri et Le Témoignage," 51–52).

38. See also Selwyn, who notes that the idea of freedom derives from Matt 17:26, yet recognizes that Peter develops the idea of freedom in the dominant NT sense of freedom from sin (Selwyn, *First Epistle of St. Peter*, 174).

39. Of course, since believers follow civil leaders because of God's command, where civil leaders call for believers to contravene God's commands, the Christian must follow God.

40. Maier, "Jesustradition," 91.

suggest that "the extension is natural enough."⁴¹ Stated differently, if a state has the right to require financial dues (taxation), it likely also has the right to require obedience in other realms from that people.⁴²

Best's third argument—that Peter follows a Haustafel or is echoing Romans 13—is a significant challenge to the claim that Peter is dependent on the words of the Lord. Undoubtedly, the similarities between this passage and Romans 13:1-7 have led some to suggest Peter's dependence on Paul. But recent scholars are nearly unanimous in arguing that such commonalities merely evidence a common source.⁴³ Is it possible that the common source was a Haustafel known by both writers? The evidence seems to point in that direction. Gundry, for instance, allows for this text to come from a Haustafel, but he adds that it is necessary to "allow liberty for the kind of adaptation and interpolation typical of ancient writers."⁴⁴ Thus, the question concerns why Peter frames his writing the way he does, and the best answer concerns Jesus' words.

Finally, the argument that Matthew's tradition is "developed so much that we cannot be sure of its original form" is, as Maier notes, "still to be proved."⁴⁵ Best offers no arguments for this claim. In fact, Gundry argues the opposite way, suggesting that the connections with 1P suggest that the form may be more original than some have previously believed.⁴⁶ Further, even if the tradition in Matthew contains elements adapted by Matthew, Peter may have known this adaptation.

Despite making a case for the echo of Matthew 17:25-27 in this passage, Maier concludes that Matthew 17 is insufficient by itself.⁴⁷ Matthew

---

41. Gundry, "Further Verba," 230.

42. Spicq suggests that the broadening of the reference is inherent in the story itself, for "Jesus gives his disciple a short course in theology, whose formulation goes beyond the Galilean perspective" (translated from, "Cependant Jésus fait à son disciple un petit cours de théologie, dont la formulation déborde l'optique galiléenne" [Spicq, "Ia Petri et Le Témoignage," 50]).

43. Achtemeier says, "The differences in meaning are so pointed that any relationship between the two probably owes more to a common tradition . . . than to any kind of literary dependence" (Achtemeier, *1 Peter*, 180). Unnik adds that "a close comparison" between the passages shows that "Peter is not dependent on Paul, as is often thought, but that both are reproducing a generally accepted form of teaching in their own way." He then asks the logical question: "this raises the question whence it was derived" (Unnik, "A Parallel," 108; cf. Russell, "Eschatology and Ethics in I Peter," 81; Brox, *Erste Petrusbrief*, 121).

44. Gundry, "Further Verba," 230.

45. Maier, "Jesustradition," 91.

46. Gundry, "Further Verba," 230.

47. Maier, "Jesustradition," 92.

17 refers to the temple tax and is thus too narrow for Peter's purposes; nevertheless, Maier argues that there is a text that speaks about Jesus' attitude towards broader taxation. Thus, in order to supplement Matthew 17, Maier argues that Peter is also echoing Matthew 22:21 (cf. Mark 12:17; Luke 20:26). We discussed the availability of this logion above, so we can now turn to a discussion of the agreement between these passages: both concern the role of Jesus' disciples to civil authorities and both give room to civil authority and divine authority and give preference to the latter.[48] Even Best recognizes the similarity and suggests that from the traditions recorded in Mark 12:13-17 and parallels, "Peter might have deduced that obedience and honour were required towards the king."[49] Thus, the same ideological similarity noted above in reference to Matthew 17 is likewise noted here. This leads Meier to conclude that Peter was referencing Jesus' overall attitude to civil authority as expressed in both of these traditions.

Further, recognizing the influence of Matthew 22:21 and parallels clarifies the relationship between Peter's development of the topic and other NT expressions of the topic (Rom 13:1-7; 1 Tim 2:1-3; Titus 3:1-3). For example, the similarities between 1P 2:13-17 and Romans 13:1-7 are best explained by common reliance on a saying of Jesus similar to that recorded in Matthew 22:21 (and parallels).[50] Thus, like other NT authors, Peter reflects the tradition expressed in Matthew 22 (and parallels), yet the similarity in context between the sayings of Matthew 22 and Matthew 17 sufficiently explains why Peter also echoes that latter text.

What significance do the echoes to Jesus' teaching concerning civil authority have? Peter's echoing of these passages strongly reinforces the central point; Peter's readers should submit to the civil authorities *because Jesus—the King—did so and has called them to do so*. Matthew 17 stresses an additional point as well. Namely, Jesus has indicated the children of

---

48. Wand suggests that the lack of the authoritative phrase, "render unto Caesar the things that are Caesar's," indicates Peter may not have been referring back to the words of Jesus here. But Peter nowhere clearly quotes Jesus; consequently, this argument loses its force (Wand, *General Epistles of St. Peter and St. Jude*, 77).

49. Best ultimately argues against the logion as recorded in Mark, for he believes Peter would not have changed καῖσαρ to βασιλεύς. In response, it should be noted that καῖσαρ is used exclusively in the Gospels and Acts with one exception (Phil 4:22), while βασιλεύς is used widely both in the Gospels and Acts as well as in the rest of the NT (Best, "I Peter and the Gospel Tradition," 102).

50. So Goppelt: "The parenesis in I Pet. 2:13-17 overlaps with, among other passages in the NT, frequently with Rom. 13:1-7; I Tim. 2:1-3; and Tit. 3:1-3. There is apparently a common tradition behind these passages, which had its beginning in Jesus' saying on paying taxes to the emperor (Mk. 12:14-17 par.)" (Goppelt, *Commentary on I Peter*, 180).

God—an attribution Peter freely applies to his readers—are free in regard to civil structures; yet such freedom must be constrained by their desire not to cause offence. It is likely that Peter desires his readers to think in terms of their modeling the life of Christ (1:15–16; 2:21). Jesus, the premier son of God, submitted to the civil structures of his day in obedience to the Father in order to avoid causing offense. Thus, Peter's readers, who are also the children of God, must follow in the steps of Jesus by submitting for the sake of the Father.

1 PETER 2:18–25

In these verses, Peter continues developing the requirements of God's people in social relationships, specifically in regard to the relationship between masters and slaves. If the readers are free, what relationship should slaves have with their human masters? Peter calls them to obey with respect,[51] regardless of whether the master is kind or harsh (2:18). To encourage obedience, Peter argues that it is a credit to the slave who endures unjust suffering for the sake of the Lord, while it is no credit at all to endure suffering for sinning (vv. 19–20a). Indeed, those who endure unjust suffering evidence God's approval on their life, for followers of Jesus are called to suffer just as Jesus suffered (vv. 20b–21). While these verses are directly addressed to slaves, much of Peter's application is broader, applying to all Christians.[52] It is not only slaves who must suffer without retaliation, but it is the calling of all who follow Jesus.

Consideration of the steps of Christ leads Peter to develop one of the most extended Christological reflections in the epistle. Peter's reliance on Isaiah 53:7–9 for much of the language and thought of the passage implies that Peter saw Jesus as the suffering servant, an identity that explains why this Christological reflection is expressed in the instruction to slaves. After expressing the complete innocence of Jesus (v. 22), Peter records Jesus' response to unjust suffering; Jesus entrusted himself to the Father (v. 23). The application is clear: if Jesus, *the* innocent one, suffered without retaliating, Peter's readers should follow his steps.

---

51. Consideration of the use of φόβος (fear) throughout the epistle leads some to conclude that this fear is directed towards God (e.g., Elliott, *1 Peter*, 517; Balz and Schrage, "*Katholischen,*" 93). Nevertheless, it could refer to respect, and that would fit nicely here (Brox, *Erste Petrusbrief*, 131).

52. "This depiction of Christ is intended more generally as a model for all the letter's addressees, such that the slaves themselves become paradigmatic for the vocation and experience of the community as a whole" (Horrell, "Image of Jesus in 1 Peter," 307; cf. Brox, *Erste Petrusbrief*, 128).

Verses 24-25 explain the forgiveness of sins and a new opportunity for righteous living that resulted from Jesus' suffering. The significance seems to be that Peter's reader's suffering can likewise be redemptive. While their suffering is not spoken of as vicarious, such suffering may lead others to Jesus, where sins can be forgiven. In sum, Stibbs is right to see Peter calling his readers (whether slave or not) to follow the path of Jesus, for by suffering without retaliation, "divine commendation is obtained, and men previously hostile are moved to acknowledge God."[53]

In light of the significant Christological focus of this section, it is unsurprising that many have found the influence of dominical teachings here.[54] We will consider the following parallels: 1P 2:18-21 and Luke 6:32-35; and 1P 2:25 and John 10:11-18.

1 Peter 2:18-21 and Luke 6:32-35

Verse 18 begins Peter's admonition to slaves, which while addressing a particular problem some of his readers would face, also has broader application to all those who follow Jesus. The similarity of this section to Luke 6:32-35 has been observed by many and will be developed here.[55]

---

53. Stibbs, *First Epistle General of Peter*, 115.

54. See the appendix for a full list of suggested parallels. Due to its content, this passage offers a number of potential connections with Jesus' words. The following fell short of the evidence needed to be included in this study: 1P 2:18-21 and Matt 5:10; 1P 2:21 and Matt 10:38 (cf. Mark 8:34; Matt 16:24; Luke 9:23); 1P 2:22-25 and Luke 23:46.

55. Davids, *First Epistle of Peter*, 106-7; Spicq, *Épîtres de Saint Pierre*, 109; Kelly, *Peter and Jude*, 116; Brown, "Synoptic Parallels," 34; Frankemölle, *1 Petrusbrief*, 50; Best, "I Peter and the Gospel Tradition," 106; Selwyn, *First Epistle of St. Peter*, 89; Elliott, *1 Peter*, 518-20; Gundry, "'Verba Christi' in I Peter," 341.

Table 7.3: 1 Peter 2:18-21 and Luke 6:32-35

1 Peter 2:18-21	Luke 6:32-35
Οἱ οἰκέται ὑποτασσόμενοι ἐν παντὶ φόβῳ τοῖς δεσπόταις, οὐ μόνον τοῖς ἀγαθοῖς καὶ ἐπιεικέσιν ἀλλὰ καὶ τοῖς σκολιοῖς. 19 τοῦτο γὰρ χάρις, εἰ διὰ συνείδησιν θεοῦ ὑποφέρει τις λύπας πάσχων ἀδίκως. 20 ποῖον γὰρ κλέος, εἰ ἁμαρτάνοντες καὶ κολαφιζόμενοι ὑπομενεῖτε; ἀλλ' εἰ <u>*ἀγαθοποιοῦντες*</u> καὶ πάσχοντες ὑπομενεῖτε, τοῦτο <u>*χάρις*</u> παρὰ θεῷ. 21 εἰς τοῦτο γὰρ ἐκλήθητε, ὅτι καὶ Χριστὸς ἔπαθεν ὑπὲρ ὑμῶν ὑμῖν ὑπολιμπάνων ὑπογραμμόν, ἵνα ἐπακολουθήσητε τοῖς ἴχνεσιν αὐτοῦ	καὶ εἰ ἀγαπᾶτε τοὺς ἀγαπῶντας ὑμᾶς, ποία ὑμῖν <u>*χάρις*</u> ἐστίν; καὶ γὰρ οἱ ἁμαρτωλοὶ τοὺς ἀγαπῶντας αὐτοὺς ἀγαπῶσιν. 33 καὶ [γὰρ] ἐὰν <u>*ἀγαθοποιῆτε*</u> τοὺς <u>*ἀγαθοποιοῦντας*</u> ὑμᾶς, ποία ὑμῖν χάρις ἐστίν; καὶ οἱ ἁμαρτωλοὶ τὸ αὐτὸ ποιοῦσιν. 34 καὶ ἐὰν δανίσητε παρ' ὧν ἐλπίζετε λαβεῖν, ποία ὑμῖν χάρις [ἐστίν]; καὶ ἁμαρτωλοὶ ἁμαρτωλοῖς δανίζουσιν ἵνα ἀπολάβωσιν τὰ ἴσα. 35 πλὴν ἀγαπᾶτε τοὺς ἐχθροὺς ὑμῶν καὶ ἀγαθοποιεῖτε καὶ δανίζετε μηδὲν ἀπελπίζοντες· καὶ ἔσται ὁ μισθὸς ὑμῶν πολύς, καὶ ἔσεσθε υἱοὶ ὑψίστου, ὅτι αὐτὸς χρηστός ἐστιν ἐπὶ τοὺς ἀχαρίστους καὶ πονηρούς.

The availability of this tradition is strengthened by its presence in Luke's Sermon on the Plain (6:32-35) and the parallel in Matthew's Sermon on the Mount (5:38-39). Further, this tradition occurs within a group of sayings elsewhere reflected by Peter (3:16; 4:14). As has been noted above, even Best recognizes that the author knew the traditions contained in this tradition block.[56] Nevertheless, the differences between Matthew's recording of the tradition and Luke's recording of the tradition causes some challenge. As will be noted below, the two chief lexical similarities between 1P and Luke 6 are ἀγαθοποιέω (doing good) and χάρις (credit), but Matthew does not contain either word. Unnik concludes that while the author of 1P gets the idea of ἀγαθοποιέω from Jesus, he does not get the word from Him, for it is probably Luke's addition.[57] Likewise, Harnack argues that μισθόν (reward) is a more original reading than χάρις; consequently, Matthew's reading derives from Jesus and Luke's is redacted.[58]

Of course, it is possible that Luke has modified the tradition and Peter knows Luke's modification, or it is possible Luke is recording a tradition that has been modified by someone before him and that tradition is also known by Peter. But it is also not clear that Matthew's text is less redacted than Luke's. For instance, Gundry, based largely on the strength of the parallel with 1P, suggests that Matthew editorially excised ἀγαθοποιέω.[59] Also,

---

56. Best, "I Peter and the Gospel Tradition," 111.
57. Unnik, "Good Works in 1P," 110.
58. He further notes that χάρις occurs in Luke's Gospel twenty-five times, but it does not occur at all in Matthew and Mark (Harnack, *Sayings of Jesus*, 62).
59. Gundry, "'Verba Christi' in I Peter," 341n3.

Selwyn notes that μισθός occurs ten times in Matthew, but only four times in the other Synoptics (once in Mark, three times in Luke).[60] He further notes that Luke is not averse to using μισθός, for Luke uses it within the same passage (6:35).[61] The result of the preceding considerations is that one cannot be dogmatic concerning the original words used by Jesus. Nevertheless, that this passage is "the closest verbal parallel" with the Synoptic tradition is sufficient enough reason to believe Peter knew the tradition in a similar way as that recorded by Luke.[62]

As indicated above, there are two notable lexical similarities between 1P 2:18–21 and Luke 6:32–35. First, both passages reference ἀγαθοποιέω (good works), a rare word that occurs only in Luke's Gospel (6:9, 33, 35) and Peter's epistle (2:15, 20; 3:6, 17) with one exception (3 John 11). It is significant that all of the uses in Luke's Gospel are in chapter 6, within the Sermon on the Plain. Further, as Selwyn notes, there is a coordination of conception between 1P and the uses in the JT, for Jesus uses the word "in the same sense—that of active kindness and discharge of social duty—that the Epistle [of Peter] uses it."[63]

The second notable lexical similarity is the use of χάρις (grace, favor), which while far from a rare word, is used in both 1P 2:19 and Luke 6:32–35 in an uncommon way.[64] While some have attempted to understand Peter's use of the word in a theologically-Pauline way,[65] it is contextually best to read it in its Greek sense, referring to something *creditable* (NIV: commendable; NRSV: approved).[66] If it is asked why Peter uses the word in this way,

60. Selwyn, *First Epistle of St. Peter*, 176.

61. Selwyn, *First Epistle of St. Peter*, 176.

62. Wilkes, "Synoptic Tradition," 51.

63. Selwyn, *First Epistle of St. Peter*, 89. As to the origin of the concept, Unnik says, "In my opinion it goes back to and is a legitimate consequence from the teaching of Jesus. There are remarkable reminiscences of the Synoptic Gospels in this letter" (Unnik, "Good Works in 1P," 108). Best agrees, noting that it is likely "the author of 1 Peter remembered Luke 6:32–36. well because it contained his favourite word" (Best, "I Peter and the Gospel Tradition," 106).

64. Gundry refers to τοῦτο γάρ χάρις (for this is credit) as a "curious phrase" that finds its reason for use in the words of Jesus (ποία ὑμῖν χάρις ἐστίν [what credit is it to you]; Lk 6:32–35)" (Gundry, "'Verba Christi' in I Peter," 341).

65. Bigg warns of the danger of "pervert[ing] a remarkable saying in order to force the teaching of St. Peter into harmony with that of St Paul" (Bigg, *Epistles of St. Peter*, 143; see also Elliott, *1 Peter*, 518). Some have suggested that χάρις maintains its general NT sense here, usually because of the other uses of the term in 1P (e.g., Goppelt, *Commentary on I Peter*, 199–201; Schelkle, *Die Petrusbriefe*, 80; Jobes, *1 Peter*, 191).

66. Due, in part, to the clarity of the parallel with κλέος (fame), most commentators suggest Peter is using the word in its Greek sense (Elliott, *1 Peter*, 518; Achtemeier, *1 Peter*, 196; Davids, *First Epistle of Peter*, 107; Green, *1 Peter*, 80).

we are led back to the tradition of the words of Jesus. For, as Bigg notes, "only on two occasions is [χάρις] put in our saviour's mouth, and then only in its Greek sense."[67] Other early church writings also use χάρις in this way, and they likewise derive from the way Jesus used the word (*Did.* 1:3–5; Ign. *Pol.* 2:1; *2 Clem.* 13:4).[68]

The lexical similarities above are strengthened by one another.[69] That these two words (χάρις and ἀγαθοποιεῖν) are both used in their Greek sense in close proximity only in 1P and in the tradition associated with Jesus in Luke's Sermon on the Plain is striking and suggests some form of relationship.

Another clue to the relationship between this text and Luke 6:32–35 is the similar structure of the sayings. Elliott succinctly summarizes the similarities: "Each text states a principle for conduct (Luke 6:31 [declarative] / 1 Pet 2:19 [question]), followed by or including (1 Pet 2:19c) contrastive conditional clauses (Luke 6:32, 33, 34; 1 Pet 2:20bc, 20de) and a concluding statement (Luke 6:35–36/1 Pet 2:20f)."[70] Further, it is significant that this is the only rhetorical question in 1P. That the structure of the Lukan saying is built around Jesus' rhetorical questions offers a good explanation for Peter's unique use of the rhetorical question.[71]

Other contextual elements are present in the Lukan tradition that are consonant with the themes of 1P. For instance, Luke 6:35 says to those who love in the way Jesus calls his disciples to love, "Your reward will be great, and you will be children of the Most High." The first part of this verse picks up the theme of reward first introduced in 1:4 and hinted at throughout the text, while the second part picks up one of the macro-themes of the entire epistle. Additionally, we argued that Peter referenced this same tradition in 2:3, when he spoke of the kindness of the Lord.

One reason to doubt whether Peter is alluding to Jesus' teaching is the difference in overall theme. A comparison of the passages will show that they differ in the activity that is expected by the average person, in the activity that is recommended, and in the reward that results from the recommended action (Table 6.4). Maier argues that such differences imply that Peter cannot be referencing these words of Jesus.[72]

---

67. Bigg, *Epistles of St. Peter*, 144.

68. Elliott, *1 Peter*, 518.

69. As Selwyn has observed, in 1P "χάρις is used in close connection with ἀγαθοποιεῖν, exactly as in Lk. 6:32–5 and in exactly the same sense" (Selwyn, *First Epistle of St. Peter*, 89).

70. Elliott, *1 Peter*, 520.

71. Best, *1 Peter*, 106.

72. Maier will ultimately argue that 1P is dependent on JT, but on different passages

Table 7.4: Common Themes between 1 Peter 2:19-21 and Luke 6:32-35

	1 Peter 2:19-21	Luke 6:32-35
Normal Human Activity:	Endure when suffering for doing wrong.	Love those who love you, do good to those who do good to you, and only lend to those who can give back.
Above the Norm Command:	Endure unjust suffering for the sake of God.	Love enemies, do good to all, and give while not expecting payment in return.
Reward Promised:	Receive God's approval.	Receive a great reward and be the children of God, reflecting his character.

While the differences between the texts must not be minimized, their similarity of theme should also not be overlooked. Luke's Gospel provides three distinct examples of the normal response of humanity to life-situations. Peter, likewise, stresses the normal response of humanity to suffering when one does wrong. In each case, the response of the person is not commendable but is expected. On the other hand, the positive commands go beyond normal human activity. It is not expected that people would love their enemies, do good to all people, and give to those who cannot repay. In a similar way, Peter is arguing that submitting to a master who inflicts suffering unjustly is also beyond the norm of humanity.[73]

Finally, the result is similar as well. Jesus indicates that those who go beyond the normal human response will receive a reward and they will be recognized as children of God since they reflect his character. That Peter suggests both of these as well is not evident on the surface of the text, but the case can be substantially defended. First, Peter has been expounding on the significance of the sonship of his readers throughout the text. In 1:15, after calling them "obedient children" Peter said, "as he who called (καλέω) you is holy, be holy yourselves in all your conduct." Here in 2:21 he says, "to this you have been called (καλέω), because Christ also suffered for you, leaving you an example, so that you should follow in his steps." In both passages, Peter is exhorting his readers to follow the example set for them. As we noted above, Luke 6:36 is sometimes recognized as a source for 1P 1:15, for the Lukan text says, "Be merciful, just as your Father is merciful." Thus, both Luke 6:32-36 and 1P 2:18-21 call the audience to go beyond the natural human response and to follow the model provided. When the readers do so, they give evidence of their sonship. This is explicitly stated in Luke 6:35, but is strongly implied both by the parallel here and the overall context of 1P.

(Maier, "Jesustradition," 99-100).

73. Michaels, *1 Peter*, 135.

Second, while it may not initially appear that Peter has rewards in mind, there is good reason to believe he does. In order to see how, it is necessary to re-introduce the definition of χάρις. Earlier we noted the debate over how to translate χάρις in this text, whether it refers to God's commendation or whether it refers to God's grace. Schelkle argues that it must refer to grace, for "God never praises man before glory."[74] But perhaps Peter is using the phrase τοῦτο γὰρ χάρις in relation to the Gospel context. If so, the commendation (χάρις) in Luke 6:32–35 is the reward. In other words, Jesus is asking, what reward do you have if you love only those who love you? Such a reading harmonizes with Matthew 5:46-48: "If you love those who love you, what reward (μισθός) do you have?"[75] Schreiner, after making this same point, draws the appropriate conclusion: "When Peter said it is 'grace' for someone to endure suffering because of their relationship with God, his point was that those who suffer in such a way will receive a reward from God and that the reward in context is their eschatological inheritance—future salvation."[76]

In conclusion, while the content of Jesus' saying differs from Peter's saying, the core elements are the same. Both texts indicate that the listeners need to reflect the character of another (God/Jesus) by not responding in a normal human way, but by responding in the way that God/Jesus would, with the result that the readers obtain divine approval. Peter here simply applies Jesus' saying to a new context.

This is an echo, for recognizing the source text is not necessary, yet when recognized, the meaning is enhanced. The significance of the saying has been noted above but will be summarized here. When Peter asks what credit one will receive for being beaten when sinning, the Gospel context suggests that he is really asking what reward his readers should expect from it. Further, just as Jesus called his disciples to follow the example of their heavenly Father, so Peter calls the early Jesus followers to follow the steps of Jesus. In both cases, others will see that the activity goes beyond the normal human response and reflects the One the believer serves. In Peter's context, this suggests that such action provides further occasion for evangelistic opportunity.

---

74. Translated from, "vor Gott ist dem Menschen nie ein Rühmen verstattet" (Schelkle, *Die Petrusbriefe*, 81).

75. That Matthew's text clarifies the sense may suggest that Luke's reading is original. On the other hand, the improvement in Greek might suggest the opposite. Best argues the "Lukan verses go back very well into Aramaic and probably therefore represent better the Greek tradition from which Matthew derives" (Best, *1 Peter*, 106).

76. Schreiner, *1, 2 Peter*, 140.

1 Peter 2:25 and John 10:11–18

It is clear that Peter is alluding to Isaiah 53 in these verses (2:24–25).[77] Nevertheless, many have recognized that the order of events do not follow the Isaian text.[78] Indeed, "something other than engagement with Isaiah 53 drives the construction of this passage."[79] This "something" is clearly the order of the passion events.[80] Maier and Horrell offer extended reflection concerning the use of JT in these passages.[81] Since our focus is on specific echoes and allusions to the words of Jesus, the widespread and general nature of the ideas reflected in this passage becomes a challenge. Stated differently, many of the ideas in this passage find expression in numerous Gospel contexts and it is difficult to indicate which, if any in particular, Peter is echoing or alluding to.[82] Despite this challenge, we will argue that Peter is reflecting the JT in regard to the sheep/shepherd motif.[83]

Two potential echoes center on Peter's association of his readers with sheep and Jesus as shepherd.[84] Though 1P 2:25 reflects Isaiah 53:6 and a broad shepherding/sheep motif from the OT (Gen 48:15; Num 27:17; Ps

---

77. We cannot develop the debate concerning whether this passage is a pre-existing hymn or document. It seems most likely that this is Peter's reflection on Isa 53 through the lens of the JT (Osborne, "Guidelines for Christian Suffering," 381–408).

78. Further while verses 22 and 24 are clearly dependent on Isa 53, 2:23 appears to derive from some other tradition (Achtemeier, *1 Peter*, 200).

79. Horrell adds that "a good deal of the substantive content of the passage, while undoubtedly structured around selected phrases from Isaiah 53, is not at all derived from this source" (Horrell, "Jesus Remembered," 144).

80. Liebengood, *Eschatology of 1 Peter*, 91–92; Jobes, *1 Peter*, 194; Achtemeier, *1 Peter*, 193; Green, *1 Peter*, 85.

81. Maier, "Jesustradition," 105–11; Horrell, "Jesus Remembered."

82. For instance, Peter shares the Gospel idea that Jesus never sinned (Mark 14:55–56 [Matt 26:59–60]; Mark 15:14 [Matt 27:23]; Luke 23:4, 13–15, 41, 47; John 18:23; 19:4), but it is not clear that he derived the idea from any particular passage. Horrell further notes that there seems "little in 1 Pet. 2.21–25 that would demonstrate any direct literary dependence on one or other of the gospels and their Passion Narratives in particular" (Horrell, "Jesus Remembered", 135, 145; cf. Foster, *Literary Relations*, 528).

83. It is also possible that 1P 2:23 reflects Mark 8:31 (Matt 16:21; Luke 9:22). An earlier draft of this study argued for this echo, but it is on the faint end of the echo spectrum and so has been excised. The chief similarity is the word πάσχω (to suffer), which does not occur in Isa 53, but is present in these Gospel passages, which are also strongly associated with the person of Peter.

84. It is possible that shepherd refers to God the Father (Osborne, "Guidelines for Christian Suffering," 403–5; Brox, *Erste Petrusbrief*, 139). Nevertheless, the NT never refers to the Father as the shepherd, and the context of this passage suggests it is in reference to Jesus. Further, the reference to Jesus in 5:4 as the chief shepherd all but confirms that Jesus is the shepherd here (Achtemeier, *1 Peter*, 204).

23; Isa 13:14; 40:11; Jer 23:1–4; 31:10; Ezek 34; 37:24; Zech 11:4–17),[85] such a theme is consonant with the way the Gospels present Jesus as a shepherd and his people as the sheep (Mark 6:34; 14:27; Matt 9:36; 18:12; Luke 12:32; 15:4; John 10:2–30; 21:15–17). Indeed, it is likely that, as Davids suggests, "this tradition was mediated to the church through the teaching of Jesus."[86]

The breadth of this motif in the Gospels creates difficulty in identifying a particular passage Peter is echoing or alluding. Two passages are more likely than the others. First, while Jesus never directly identifies himself as a shepherd in the Synoptics,[87] in Mark 14:27 (Matt 26:31) he implies such an identity when he quotes a portion of Zechariah 13:7: "Strike the shepherd, that the sheep may be scattered." In both Mark and Matthew, Jesus' prediction of his disciples scattering is followed by the memorable account of Peter boldly proclaiming he would not desert and disown Jesus (Mark 14:29–31; Matt 26:33–35). Again, the association with Peter increases the likelihood that the author would reference these words of Jesus. Further, the content of the prediction fits precisely the passion context.[88] Nevertheless, the contextual differences make it difficult to substantiate Peter's echoing of this passage.[89]

A stronger case, however, can be made for an echo of John 10:11–18. While in the Synoptics Jesus does not directly call himself the shepherd, he does so explicitly in this tradition. The connections between these passages are suggestive, as even Best has recognized.[90] First, both refer to the death

---

85. It is unclear what OT texts were chiefly considered by Peter. Elliott makes a good case for the prominence of Ezek 34:4–11 (Elliott, *1 Peter*, 537). Others have made a case for the broader context of Is, particularly 6:10 (Achtemeier, *1 Peter*, 204).

86. Davids, *First Epistle of Peter*, 113–14; Wilkes, "Synoptic Tradition," 76.

87. Kelly, *Peter and Jude*, 125.

88. If Peter assumed his readers would recognize his reference to this saying of the Lord, it would help explain what Michaels calls an "abrupt shift" in 2:25: "Christ was last mentioned as wounded and carrying sins to the cross after much abuse, while the readers of the epistle were compared to a scattered flock of sheep. Now suddenly the sheep are back together, with Christ (very much alive) as the Shepherd who reunites them." This shift may be explained, Michaels suggests, by NT "passages where Christ fulfills the shepherd role precisely by virtue of his resurrection from the dead." Michaels mentions Mark 14:27–28 (Matt 26:31–32): "You will all become deserters; for it is written, 'I will strike the shepherd, and the sheep will be scattered.' *But after I am raised up, I will go before you to Galilee.*" In light of this connection, it is possible that Peter does not explicitly mention Jesus' resurrection because it is bound up in the words of Jesus he is echoing (Michaels, *1 Peter*, 151).

89. The Gospel context speaks of the disciples being scattered because of the death of Christ, while 1P describes the audience as straying sheep, who were astray not on the basis of Jesus' death, but because of their previous futile ways (1:18).

90. Best notes the "close association of words and ideas," though he ultimately

of Jesus as vicarious, resulting in life for his people. Jesus uses the metaphor of the shepherd laying down his life for the sheep so that the sheep might live (John 10:11), while Peter explains the reality pictured (2:24).[91] Second, the use of ἐπίσκοπος (guardian), especially in relation to ποιμήν (shepherd), images the care and protection described in detail in John 10:12–13.[92]

Table 7.5: 1 Peter 2:25 and John 10:11–18

1 Peter 2:25	John 10:11–18
ἦτε γὰρ ὡς πρόβατα πλανώμενοι, ἀλλ' ἐπεστράφητε νῦν ἐπὶ τὸν ποιμένα καὶ ἐπίσκοπον τῶν ψυχῶν ὑμῶν.	Ἐγώ εἰμι ὁ <u>ποιμὴν</u> ὁ καλός. ὁ ποιμὴν ὁ καλὸς τὴν ψυχὴν αὐτοῦ τίθησιν ὑπὲρ τῶν προβάτων· 12 ὁ μισθωτὸς καὶ οὐκ ὢν ποιμήν, οὗ οὐκ ἔστιν τὰ πρόβατα ἴδια, θεωρεῖ τὸν λύκον ἐρχόμενον καὶ ἀφίησιν τὰ πρόβατα καὶ φεύγει—καὶ ὁ λύκος ἁρπάζει αὐτὰ καὶ σκορπίζει— 13 ὅτι μισθωτός ἐστιν καὶ οὐ μέλει αὐτῷ περὶ τῶν προβάτων. 14 Ἐγώ εἰμι ὁ ποιμὴν ὁ καλὸς καὶ γινώσκω τὰ ἐμὰ καὶ γινώσκουσίν με τὰ ἐμά, 15 καθὼς γινώσκει με ὁ πατὴρ κἀγὼ γινώσκω τὸν πατέρα, καὶ τὴν ψυχήν μου τίθημι ὑπὲρ τῶν προβάτων. 16 καὶ ἄλλα πρόβατα ἔχω ἃ οὐκ ἔστιν ἐκ τῆς αὐλῆς ταύτης· κἀκεῖνα δεῖ με ἀγαγεῖν καὶ τῆς φωνῆς μου ἀκούσουσιν, καὶ γενήσονται μία ποίμνη, εἷς ποιμήν. 17 Διὰ τοῦτό με ὁ πατὴρ ἀγαπᾷ ὅτι ἐγὼ τίθημι τὴν ψυχήν μου, ἵνα πάλιν λάβω αὐτήν. 18 οὐδεὶς αἴρει αὐτὴν ἀπ' ἐμοῦ, ἀλλ' ἐγὼ τίθημι αὐτὴν ἀπ' ἐμαυτοῦ. ἐξουσίαν ἔχω θεῖναι αὐτήν, καὶ ἐξουσίαν ἔχω πάλιν λαβεῖν αὐτήν· ταύτην τὴν ἐντολὴν ἔλαβον παρὰ τοῦ πατρός μου.

Third, Michaels rightly notes that Peter seems to reflect Jesus teaching concerning the sheep "not of this fold" (John 10:16; 11:52).[93] Perhaps the reason Peter's perspective is similar to that expressed by Jesus is that Peter is intentionally reflecting those words of Jesus. In light of his extensive use of the OT, Peter likely knew the OT tradition concerning God as shepherd and Israel as sheep. The extension of a role given to God in the OT to Jesus in 1P is consonant with the NT generally and what we have seen in 1P specifically (1:25). The extension of a role first given to Israel to the ethnically diverse followers of Jesus follows the pattern Peter has established (2:4–10), but it may be based on the words of Jesus here. In other words, one of the reasons Peter may apply OT themes associated with ethnic Israel to Jesus-followers

---

appears to conclude that this is not an allusion (Best, *1 Peter*, 97).

91. Gundry, "Further Verba," 216.
92. Silva, *New International Dictionary*, s.v. "ἐπίσκοπος," 2:251.
93. Michaels, *1 Peter*, 150.

is because Jesus did so. Indeed, Peter seems to blur the distinction between ethnic Israelites and Jesus followers, and one basis for this may be Jesus' statement that there "will be one flock, one shepherd" (John 10:16).[94]

The shepherding motif may also explain why Peter does not explicitly cite the resurrection. In John 10:17–18 Jesus indicates that after laying down his life, he will take it up again—a clear reference to the resurrection. Thus, by simply calling to mind the shepherd motif, Peter can assume his readers will consider the spectrum of ideas associated with Jesus as shepherd, who will be struck, will die, and yet will rise from the dead and seek out his flock.

Those who recognized this echo would likely have been encouraged in the midst of their suffering. Their loving shepherd took the brunt of the suffering they deserved. He did not abandon them, but instead submitted to the unjust suffering for their sake. Further, John 10:18 reveals that the unjust suffering of the Son was the Father's plan. In like manner, the suffering the readers endure is not outside the will of God (3:17), but just as Jesus' suffering was used for the redemption of many, so their suffering may also be used for the conversion of others.[95] Finally, the echo draws the emotional weight of John 10:11–18 into the Petrine context. Stated differently, it is likely that the mention of the words guardian and shepherd would have drawn the entire dramatic shepherding metaphor into view. In answer to the question, "how can I endure unjust suffering?" Peter effectively answers, "remember that Jesus endured unjust suffering for you, and that he is presently leading and protecting you now. Follow your Shepherd for he cares for you and leads you in the right path."

In conclusion, 1P 2:22–25, due to its reflection on the passion, is heavily dependent on JT and may be sourced out of numerous sayings of Jesus.[96] Thus we agree with Davids that Peter is "solidly rooted in the teaching of Jesus when he refers to him as the 'Shepherd and Overseer'";[97] nevertheless, identifying precisely which *dominical logion* is being referenced is quite

---

94. Of course, this leaves open the question of the place for ethnic Israel in the eschatological unfolding of God's plan. Peter speaks here only of God's present work.

95. Peter has already indicated that God's will often involves the suffering of his people (1:6) and Peter will emphasize it more clearly in the passages ahead (3:9, 17). As noted above, such redemptive significance is not exactly parallel. In Jesus' case, he bore the sins of the people. In the case of the readers, they will reflect the love of God as they patiently endure unjust suffering. Such reflection, Peter argues, may result in the conversion of unbelievers (2:12).

96. Feuillet notes that this passage "recalls many biblical passages" (translated from, "Tout cela rappelle, nombre de passages bibliques,"), by which he means that it recalls many of the traditions associated with Jesus' teaching (Feuillet, "Quelques Reflexions," 244).

97. Davids, *First Epistle of Peter*, 114.

challenging. Thus, while we have made a suggestion of an echo to John above, it cannot rise above the level of probability.

1 PETER 3:1–7

Having described the social implications of being a Jesus-follower in regard to civil structures (2:13–17) and in regard to master-slave relations (2:18–25), Peter now turns to the social implications in relation to husbands and wives. In light of Jesus' relative silence on the duties of husbands and wives within the marriage relationship,[98] it is not surprising that there have only been a few proposed connections between Peter's text and Jesus' teaching. The most likely dominical reflection is from Matthew 5:5 and is contained within Peter's instruction to wives.

Table 7.6: 1 Peter 3:4 and Matthew 5:5

1 Peter 3:4	Matthew 5:5
ἀλλ' ὁ κρυπτὸς τῆς καρδίας ἄνθρωπος ἐν τῷ ἀφθάρτῳ τοῦ _πραέως_ καὶ ἡσυχίου πνεύματος ὅ ἐστιν ἐνώπιον τοῦ θεοῦ πολυτελές.	μακάριοι οἱ _πραεῖς_, ὅτι αὐτοὶ κληρονομήσουσιν τὴν γῆν.

Spicq argues that Peter's encouragement that right conduct may lead to the conversion of an unbelieving husband constitutes an "application of the blessedness of the meek who conquer the earth."[99] But it is not clear that the conversion of the husband is a coordinate concept with inheriting the earth.[100] Nevertheless, a connection between these verses has been suggested on the basis of the lexical similarity of πραΰς, which occurs only four times in the NT. Outside of its occurrence in this passage, it occurs twice on the lips of Jesus in Matthew's Gospel (5:5; 21:5) and once in a quotation of the OT, which is also recorded in Matthew (21:5).[101]

---

98. His teaching recorded in the Gospels focuses on divorce and remarriage (Mark 10:2–12; Matt 19:1–12; Luke 16:18).

99. Translated from the latter section of the following quote: "Lorsque les maris, réfractaires à la prédication de l'Evangile, sont gagnés au Christ par l'esprit de mansuétude et de calme de leur épouse, c'est encore un cas d'application de la béatitude des doux qui conquièrent la terre (Matt 5:4)" (Spicq, "Ia Petri et Le Témoignage," 43).

100. Silva, following David Hill, argues that the inheritance of the earth is another way of describing the inheritance of the new promised land (Silva, _New International Dictionary_, s.v. "πραΰς," 4:125; cf. Hill, _Gospel of Matthew_, 111–12).

101. An objection should be mentioned here. While the adjective for "meek" (πραΰς) is only present in Matthew and 1P, the noun form of "gentleness" (πραΰτης) is used eleven times. The distinction between the adjectival and noun form may not

The following may also be marshalled in favor of a reference here. First, Peter shows an affinity elsewhere for the Beatitudes (1:4, 6, 17). Second, the Matthean reference occurs within the Sermon on the Mount, a block of text likely referenced by Peter elsewhere (1:4, 6, 8, 10). Third, Maier suggests an ideological parallel: "the 'precious before God' in 1 Peter 3:4 corresponds to the eschatological reward in Mt 5:5."[102] Despite these points, there is not enough here to suggest Peter was echoing the words of Jesus. Stronger lexical and ideological parallels are necessary to establish this connection.

Because there are no other defensible dominical reflections in this text, we have spent time with the potential parallel of Matthew 5:5. In the end, we must admit that while this is a possible echo, it does not give enough evidence to be affirmed in this thesis. Consequently, 3:1–7 is one of the rare sections of 1P (see also 4:1–6) that nowhere clearly echoes or alludes to the words of Jesus.

CONCLUSION TO 1 PETER 2:11—3:7

Five intertextual resonances were identified in the first half of the body middle (2:11—3:7), consisting of three echoes and two allusions.

Table 7.7: Intertextual Resonances to *Dominical Logia* in 1 Peter 2:11—3:7

1P Reference	Gospel Reference	Type of Reference
2:12	Matt 5:14–16	Allusion
2:13–17	Matt 17:25–27	Echo
2:18–21	Luke 6:32–35	Echo
2:25	John 10:11–18	Echo

First Peter 2:11–12, a transitional passage in 1P, reminds the readers of their elect-exile status. Though Peter has described them as a holy nation (2:9), they are nevertheless still pilgrims on the earth. How then should they live? In answer to this question, Peter alludes to the memorable words of the Lord from Jesus' most famous sermon (Matt 5:14–16). While the readers

---

be enough to overcome the criticism that since meekness language had entered the language of the church, especially in virtue lists (Gal 5:23; Eph 4:2; Col 3:12; Titus 3:2), there is no need for direct dependence on Matthew 5:5 (Best, "1 Peter and the Gospel Tradition," 108). On the other hand, the source for the virtue of meekness is quite likely Jesus' own words, and the mention of it in the virtue lists may all point back to the distinctive teaching of Jesus.

102. Translated from, "dem 'kostbar vor Gott' in 1P 3:4 entspricht die eschatologische Belohnung in Mt 5:5" (Maier, "Jesustradition," 100).

avoid evil, they should act honorably in their social relations, allowing others to see their good works which may result in the unbeliever's conversion. This *dominical logion* establishes the foundation from which the rest of the body middle develops.

The relationship between Christians and the civil authorities is an area that Peter could likely not ignore. While there is much debate concerning the nature of the persecution experienced in 1P, it can hardly be doubted that the readers recognized the potential tensions with civil authorities. Further, since the readers were members of Jesus' kingdom, what right did any other civil ruler have over them? In answer to these unstated concerns, Peter appeals to Jesus' words and actions (Matt 17:25-27; 22:21). They should accept the authority of human rulers, since Jesus, their king, did so and commanded them to do so. He paid taxes in order to avoid offense, so by developed application, Peter's readers should submit to the civil authorities. Thus, again, Peter's appeal is supported by Jesus' words.

The next social reality Peter addressed was the master-slave relationship. In light of Jesus' identity as the suffering servant of Isaiah 53 and the reader's identity as followers of Jesus, Peter broadens the application from slaves to all believers. That is, just as Jesus was a suffering slave, so all his followers are called to be the same. It was noted above that the commonality of the ideas present in this section causes some difficulty. It is clear Peter is referencing the JT throughout, but it is not always clear where and if Peter has a particular saying of Jesus in mind. Nevertheless, a good case can be made for Peter alluding to Jesus' rhetorical questions in Luke 6:32-35 to argue for the necessity of his readers to imitate Jesus by operating in opposition to human expectations in order to draw attention to God. Further, the echo of John 10:11-18 reminds the readers that Jesus not only took the brunt of their suffering, but he is lovingly present with them in their suffering.

While some have argued for a dominical reference in 3:1-7, the evidence is not enough to justify the claim. Instead, we find here the first contextual unit in 1P that does not seek to develop the teaching of the Lord. Of course, it is possible that Peter is echoing or alluding to JT not recorded in the Synoptics, but if so we have no access to such teaching. The lack of consideration of Jesus' words here is explainable by a few factors. First, as noted above, the responsibilities of husband and wife was not one of the areas Jesus developed in his teaching. Second, it is necessary in a haustafel to address husbands and wives. Third, 2:11-12 placed each of the social relationships under the rubric of doing good deeds with the hope that such deeds will help lead to the conversion of others. In this case, Peter speaks explicitly of the wife doing good with the hope that her husband will see her good deeds and trust in Jesus. Consequently, while this particular paragraph may not echo or allude to the words of Jesus, the reason for its development is based on the words of Jesus.

8

First Peter 3:8—4:11

THE LAST CHAPTER EXAMINED the echoes and allusions to Jesus' words in the first half of the body middle (2:11—3:7). This chapter will consider their use in the rest of the body middle (3:8—4:11), which details the requirements for all believers regardless of their social position.[1]

While the first half of the body middle contained discernible units consisting of items usually discussed in a *haustafel* (household code), the structure of the second half is not as easily discerned. Many of the themes Peter has introduced in the prior chapters appears once more: the necessity of love, even to those who persecute believers (3:8, 9, 16; 4:8); the blessing of suffering according to God's will (3:9, 14); the evangelistic thrust of good works (3:16); and the imperative of following the example of Jesus (3:17-18; 4:1). In light of the multiple themes of this section, it has been variously identified: "The call to right conduct";[2] "Ethics in light of witness";[3] "Doing what is right in the face of hostility";[4] "The promise of vindication";[5] "Responding in a godly way to suffering";[6] and "Living as Christians generally."[7]

---

1. See the comments at the beginning of the last chapter concerning the necessity and difficulty of dividing the body middle.
2. Achtemeier, *1 Peter*, 169.
3. This is Himes's title for 3:8—4:6 (Himes, *Lexham Bible Guide*).
4. This is Elliott's title for 3:13-4 (Elliott, *1 Peter*, 618).
5. This is Michael's title of 3:13—4:6 (Michaels, *1 Peter*, xxxvii).
6. This is Schreiner's title for 3:13—4:11 (Schreiner, *1, 2 Peter*, 168).
7. This is Grudem's title for 3:8—4:19 (Grudem, *First Epistle of Peter*, 154).

Two elements are largely consistent through these verses. First, nearly every section concerns suffering. Second, each section gives instruction for a godly life. Thus, "godly living while suffering" appears to be a summative heading. This theme reveals that Peter is still expounding the identity of the readers as elect-exiles. Their election calls them to follow the steps of Jesus and imitate their heavenly Father with godly living, and their exilic status promises friction with the world at large.

It should be remembered that the body middle opened with 2:11–12, which emphasized both the avoidance of sin and the positive pursuit of honorable conduct. In reference to the latter, Peter was reflecting the words of Jesus, who indicated that his followers would be reflective of the Father's glory and thereby have opportunity to lead others to belief in Jesus. While the verses we are looking at may appear far distant from 2:11–12, they are nevertheless continuing to develop the same theme. Consequently, it would not be surprising to see Peter reinforce his points with allusions and echoes to Jesus' words, just as he has done with the first half of the body middle. The following chapter seeks to identify and then discern the significance of Peter's echoes and allusions to the words of Jesus.

1 PETER 3:8–12

First Peter 3:8–12 serve as a transition between the household codes and the various obligations required of all believers. Verse 8 addresses inter-community responsibilities, centering on love for one another,[8] while verse 9 speaks of the responsibility believers have to those who do not follow Jesus, focusing primarily on blessing the persecutors.[9] This section of 1P is clearly in line with other NT parenetic passages, yet its formulation is unique to Peter. This can be seen chiefly in that four of the five imperatival adjectives are unique to this epistle, but it can also be seen in that the themes present in these verses are consonant with distinct themes in 1P.[10]

As Peter does elsewhere, he concludes this section (vv. 10–12) with an OT citation. This citation, the longest of the letter, derives from Psalm 34, which Peter has referenced earlier (2:3). Since verses 10–12 reference a section of an OT passage that the Gospels do not reveal Jesus explicitly referencing, the focus of our study will be verses 8 and 9.

---

8. The centrality of love can be seen in that it occurs as the third of a series of five, placing it in the prominent position (Schreiner, *1, 2 Peter*, 162).
9. Jobes, *1 Peter*, 216; Green, *1 Peter*, 102.
10. Elliott, *1 Peter*, 600.

Many commentators have suggested a connection between 1P 3:9 and Luke 6:27-30 (Matt 5:38-44).[11] The availability of this saying is bolstered by its presence in both Matthew and Luke within the Sermon on the Mount/Plain. Not only would this memorable sermon have been likely known by early Jesus followers, but we have argued for Peter's reference to these verses already (1:6-9, 17; 2:11-12, 18-21; 3:9, 14) and we will note his reference to them again (3:16; 5:7).

Table 8.1: 1 Peter 3:9a and Luke 6:27-30; Matthew 5:39-44

1 Peter 3:9a	Luke 6:27-30	Matthew 5:39-44
μὴ ἀποδιδόντες κακὸν <u>ἀντὶ</u> κακοῦ ἢ λοιδορίαν ἀντὶ λοιδορίας, τοὐναντίον δὲ <u>εὐλογοῦντες</u>	Ἀλλ' ὑμῖν λέγω τοῖς ἀκούουσιν· ἀγαπᾶτε τοὺς ἐχθροὺς ὑμῶν, καλῶς ποιεῖτε τοῖς μισοῦσιν ὑμᾶς, 28 <u>εὐλογεῖτε</u> τοὺς καταρωμένους ὑμᾶς, προσεύχεσθε περὶ τῶν ἐπηρεαζόντων ὑμᾶς. 29 τῷ τύπτοντί σε ἐπὶ τὴν σιαγόνα πάρεχε καὶ τὴν ἄλλην, καὶ ἀπὸ τοῦ αἴροντός σου τὸ ἱμάτιον καὶ τὸν χιτῶνα μὴ κωλύσῃς. 30 Παντὶ αἰτοῦντί σε δίδου, καὶ ἀπὸ τοῦ αἴροντος τὰ σὰ μὴ ἀπαίτει.	ἐγὼ δὲ λέγω ὑμῖν μὴ <u>ἀντιστῆναι</u> τῷ πονηρῷ· ἀλλ' ὅστις σε ῥαπίζει εἰς τὴν δεξιὰν σιαγόνα [σου], στρέψον αὐτῷ καὶ τὴν ἄλλην· 40 καὶ τῷ θέλοντί σοι κριθῆναι καὶ τὸν χιτῶνά σου λαβεῖν, ἄφες αὐτῷ καὶ τὸ ἱμάτιον· 41 καὶ ὅστις σε ἀγγαρεύσει μίλιον ἕν, ὕπαγε μετ' αὐτοῦ δύο. 42 τῷ αἰτοῦντί σε δός, καὶ τὸν θέλοντα ἀπὸ σοῦ δανίσασθαι μὴ ἀποστραφῇς. 43 Ἠκούσατε ὅτι ἐρρέθη· ἀγαπήσεις τὸν πλησίον σου καὶ μισήσεις τὸν ἐχθρόν σου. 44 ἐγὼ δὲ λέγω ὑμῖν· ἀγαπᾶτε τοὺς ἐχθροὺς ὑμῶν καὶ προσεύχεσθε ὑπὲρ τῶν διωκόντων ὑμᾶς.

The differences between the Gospel accounts along with the way this tradition is handled in the NT has led some to believe the tradition is heavily redacted. For instance, in his commentary on this passage, Best argues that the present saying as recorded in Peter's epistle probably comes "from the common instruction of the church rather than directly from the words of Jesus." His justification for this claim is that "In the epistles the thought is nowhere ascribed to Jesus."[12] But if the standard for legitimate JT is direct attribution in the epistles, surely we know very little of what Jesus taught, for much of what Jesus taught lacks direct epistolary attribution. Such considerations lead Piper to call Best's conclusion "totally unwarranted."[13]

---

11. Along with the commentators noted in the footnotes below, see also Schelkle, *Die Petrusbriefe*, 93; Grudem, *First Epistle of Peter*, 155; Stibbs, *First Epistle General of Peter*, 130; Brown, "Synoptic Parallels," 34; Spicq, "Ia Petri et Le Témoignage," 42.

12. Best, *1 Peter*, 129.

13. Piper, "Hope," 223n47.

Best is right, however, to note the diversity of the tradition as it has been handed down. Piper carefully walks through the differences between the Lukan and Matthean recording of the sayings with an eye towards answering which elements of the sayings are redacted by the composers of the Gospels.[14] He reveals that there is no unanimity among scholars in this regard. Some see Matthew's contribution as more original, while others see Luke's as more original. It is significant to note that Peter's text includes elements unique to both Gospel passages. In agreement with Matthew, Peter says the readers are not to repay evil for evil (κακὸν ἀντὶ κακοῦ; see also ἀνθίστημι in Matt 5:39).[15] In agreement with Luke, Peter calls his readers to bless (εὐλογέω) those who abuse the readers. This is the same word Luke uses in 6:28 when he records Jesus' words, "bless (εὐλογέω) those who curse you." Taken together, this suggests that Peter knew a tradition that includes elements from both Gospel passages.[16]

In light of the striking similarities between 1P 3:8–9 and Romans 12:10–16, some have suggested that Peter's text reflects Romans, not the JT. For instance, Foster boldly declares that this passage "most certainly depends upon Romans 12, so we need not go back of Paul for the doctrine taught in 1 Pt 3:9."[17] Indeed, if Peter knew the book of Romans, this is one of the chief passages to evidence that knowledge.[18]

While there are noticeable similarities, the limited lexical similarity and the lack of mirrored structure lead to significant doubt that Peter is dependent on Romans in this passage.[19] As some scholars have argued, the best explanation for both the similarities and differences is that both Peter and Paul are reflecting a shared tradition, though each express that tradition differently for his own epistolary purposes.[20] In light of this conclusion, Maier appropriately asks, if we acknowledge "that there was a common

---

14. Piper, "Hope," 221n34.

15. Piper agrees that "Jesus' word in all likelihood shaped the tradition behind 1 Peter 3:9. The ἀντι-principle was forbidden by him in Matt 5:39a (μὴ ἀντιστῆναι τῷ πονηρῷ)" (Piper, "Hope," 220–21). Metzner likewise notes this connection, while also suggesting a few other, less persuasive connections (Metzner, *Rezeption*, 285, 75–89).

16. Moo notes that Paul does something similar in Romans: "Paul seems to combine these two forms of Jesus' saying from the 'Sermon on the Mount/Plain' suggesting perhaps that he quotes here a pre-Synoptic form" (Moo, *Epistle to the Romans*, 781).

17. Foster, *Literary Relations*, 493. See also Beare, *First Epistle of Peter*, 160.

18. Achtemeier, *1 Peter*, 16; Michaels, *1 Peter*, 174; Elliott, *1 Peter*, 602.

19. Achtemeier, *1 Peter*, 221. See also Piper, who says, "the imprecise similarities amid wide divergences make any kind of literary dependence improbable" (Piper, "Hope," 219).

20. Jobes, *1 Peter*, 215. Cf. Achtemeier, *1 Peter*, 221; Elliott, *1 Peter*, 602; Feldmeier, *First Letter of Peter*, 186; Michaels, *1 Peter*, 174.

Christian catechetical tradition, is not it obvious to assume their common origin from the *verba Christi*?"[21]

The agreement between 1P and the Gospel passages has been touched on above but needs to be addressed once more. While we noted some lexical similarities, they are not exceedingly strong. The primary agreement is structural and ideological, which Metzner details in relation to 1P and Matthew 5: "A negative statement (renunciation of retaliation) is followed by a positive statement (love or blessing), with an attached promise (Mt: divine sonship, 1P: inheritance of blessing)."[22] Luke follows this same pattern, though in a different order with the love command, a call for the rejection of retaliation, and the promise of reward (divine sonship and unspecified rewards).

Despite the above agreements, many see the connection between 1P and the Gospel passages as indirect.[23] According to this perspective, these ideas are distinctive of Jesus' call to his disciples and when mentioned would certainly have drawn the readers to consider both the action and words of Jesus. Nevertheless, one cannot draw the line back to any particular Gospel saying.

However, it seems that the consideration of agreement with Romans 12 has led interpreters too quickly away from the evidence that Peter is echoing a particular tradition very similar to that recorded in Luke's Gospel. As has been noted above, Peter has an affinity for the traditions recorded in this section of Luke's Sermon on the Plain. It is for this reason that Gundry was willing to admit the influence of Romans on Peter's text, but he was not willing to forego the reliance Peter seemed to have on a tradition similar to that recorded in Luke 6.[24] Accordingly, Gundry appears correct to see this as a case where a remembrance of the Lord's teaching that has been influenced by the catechetical tradition.[25]

If Peter was reflecting these words of Christ, how would his readers have heard such an echo? We will develop three areas of significance.

21. Translated from, "Wieder zugegeben, daß eine gemein-christliche katechetische Tradition bestand - ist es dann nicht naheliegend, ihre gemeinsame Herkunft von verba Christi anzunehmen?" (Maier, "Jesustradition," 92).

22. Translated from, "An eine negative Aussage (Vergeltungsverzicht) schließt sich eine positive Aussage (Liebes- bzw. Segensgebot) an, die mit einer Verheißung (Mt: Gottessohnschaft; 1. Petr: Segenserbschaft) verbunden isu" (Metzner, *Rezeption*, 285–86).

23. "Both Romans 12:14 and 1 Peter 3:9 are free adaptations of Jesus' word which had been taken up (albeit not word for word) into the paraenetic tradition" (Piper, "Hope," 221).

24. Gundry, "'Verba Christi' in I Peter," 342.

25. Gundry, "Further Verba," 226.

First, the echo clarifies what Peter means by responding with "blessing" (εὐλογέω). In Greek literature, to proclaim a blessing (εὐλογέω) meant to speak well of someone. Elliott explains how such a reading could make sense in the Petrine context: "By such a tactic one ignores the insult as a challenge, thereby extricating oneself from the socially destructive cycle of challenge-retaliation, and shifts the subject from shame to honor, from defamation to praise."[26] But the echo of Jesus' words suggests another sense. In accordance with the way the word is used in the LXX and, more importantly, by Jesus, Peter speaks of blessing as "ask[ing] for bestowal of special favor, especially of calling down God's gracious power."[27] Those who hear the echo of Jesus' words recognize that Peter's command to bless includes praying for them (cf. Luke 6:28b; Matt 5:44).[28]

By calling on God to bless those who persecute them, Peter's readers are further reminded of the evangelistic thrust of their actions. While they refuse to retaliate, they join prayer with their gracious response in order to draw others to see the love of God displayed through their works. In so doing, they follow the steps of Jesus, who when he endured unjust suffering was willing to pray, "Father forgive them" (Luke 23:34).

The second element of significance is that when Peter calls his readers to non-retaliation and blessing, he does so with the authority of Jesus. In other words, as Peter calls the readers to such action, they are by Peter's call reminded that the Lord himself asked this of them. Further, such remembrance—especially so close to 2:22–25—would draw the reader's attention to the way Jesus accomplished these commands in his own life. Thus, both the command and example of Jesus provide strong incentive to fulfill Peter's call. As Jobes has rightly noted, "It has sometimes been debated whether Jesus' atoning sacrifice or his teachings are at the heart of Christianity. This passage eloquently demonstrates that the two cannot be separated."[29]

That the allusion to the words of Jesus helps resolve a difficult exegetical issue is the third area of significance. It has long been recognized that there is ambiguity in 2:9. Peter says, "It is for this that you were called," but it is not clear whether the demonstrative pronoun (οὗτος; "this") refers to what precedes or what follows. If it refers to what precedes, the sense is, "It is to blessing and non-retaliation that you were called so that you may

---

26. Elliott does not ultimately take this position, but instead takes the word in its LXX sense (see below; Elliott, *1 Peter*, 608).

27. Bauer et al., BDAG, s.v. "εὐλογέω," 408. Cf. Selwyn, *First Epistle of St. Peter*, 190.

28. Michaels, *1 Peter*, 178.

29. Jobes, *1 Peter*, 217.

receive a blessing."³⁰ If this reading is accurate, the inheritance of eternal life is related to the reader's conformity to such a call.³¹ If it refers to what follows, the sense is, "It is for an inherited blessing you were called."³² This second reading confirms the divine election of the readers and calls them to respond graciously to others because of the gift of grace they received.

According to Elliott, the second view—that the pronoun referred to what follows—is accepted by "a majority of the commentators."³³ Nevertheless, it appears that Piper's article on the topic has created a noticeable shift in opinion.³⁴ As Elliott himself recognizes, Piper's article, "convincingly refutes" the arguments from the other side.³⁵ Since the publication of that article, nearly all of the major commentaries have embraced the view that the pronoun refers to what precedes.³⁶

It is not possible to provide all of the exegetical evidence offered by Piper and others in defense of the position that the pronoun refers to what precedes.³⁷ What we can do, however, is supplement the case by reference to the words of Jesus echoed in the text. First, others have noted that both 2:21 and 4:6 have the same demonstrative pronoun which could refer to what precedes or follows. Unfortunately, one refers to what precedes (2:21) and the other to what follows (4:6). Nevertheless, because 2:21 shares the verbal form of 3:9 (εἰς τοῦτο γὰρ ἐκλήθητε [2:21]; compared to ὅτι εἰς τοῦτο ἐκλήθητε [3:9]) and matches the text in content (both reference the right

30. The following is representative of those taking this position: Marshall, *1 Peter*, 109; Best, *1 Peter*, 130; Michaels, *1 Peter*, 178–79; Elliott, *1 Peter*, 609–10; Piper, "Hope"; Achtemeier, *1 Peter*, 224; Jobes, *1 Peter*, 219.

31. That the inheritance is eternal life is confirmed by the citation of Psalm 34 and the overall context.

32. The following is representative of those taking this position: Kelly, *Peter and Jude*, 137; Goppelt, *Commentary on I Peter*, 234n15; Davids, *First Epistle of Peter*, 127; Selwyn, *First Epistle of St. Peter*, 190.

33. Elliott, *1 Peter*, 609.

34. Piper, "Hope."

35. Elliott, *1 Peter*, 609n218.

36. A notable exception is Davids, who recognizes that the arguments in the article "are persuasive," yet is convinced that they are "not as persuasive as those on the other side" (Davids, *First Epistle of Peter*, 127n6).

37. In summary, the following can be marshalled in its favor. First, Peter uses the same pronoun in a similar way in 2:21, sharing both form and content. And while he uses the same pronoun to refer to what follows in 4:6, the context and form are quite different. Second, the context of the supporting Psalm strongly supports this reading. Piper calls the Psalm the "decisive factor" (Piper, "Hope," 226). Third, while some may see the reading as opposite Peter's theology of grace, Elliott and others show that such a thought is "consistent with future, teleological motivations of conduct occurring elsewhere in the letter" (Elliott, *1 Peter*, 610).

response to suffering), many have found it a more helpful parallel than 4:6, which matches in neither form nor content. We can add to that evidence by noting that while 2:21 also references the words of Jesus (just as we are arguing for in 3:9), 4:6 does not.[38] More importantly, we argued that 1P 2:21 was alluding to Luke 6:32–35, the very context we are arguing Peter is also alluding to here. Thus, the similarity in terminology and content between 2:21 and 3:9 appears to be related to the underlying allusion to the words of Jesus.

The position that the pronoun refers to what precedes is usually criticized on the basis that it appears to contradict Peter's theology of election and grace.[39] Nevertheless, the second reason to hold the preceding-referent view is that such a view matches the teaching of Jesus. In the words of Elliott, "In contrast to Paul, who generally grounds imperatives on a prior experience of grace, our author varies references to a present experience of grace as a basis for conduct with references to a future outcome. The latter is close to Israelite thought, including *the perspective of Jesus*."[40] In sum, Peter appears to be picking up the theme from the teaching of Jesus. The followers of Jesus must act rightly in order to obtain the final, eschatological reward.

It is important to note, however, the following phrase in Luke's text: "and you will be sons of God." Stein clarifies that since this section of the Gospel addresses believers, "the verb 'will be' should not be understood as 'will become' but rather 'will show yourselves to be.'"[41] Consequently, we find here an unresolved tension between the divine sonship conferred upon believers and the requisite acts that secure/confirm that sonship.

Thus, just as Jesus includes commands that must be obeyed in order to experience the reward, so Peter, mirroring his Lord, also includes commands that must be obeyed in order for the reward to be given. And just as Jesus' commands are given to those who are already considered children of God, so Peter's are as well. Both Jesus and Peter can call on the listeners to obey these commands because they are already the children of God and therefore have been given the grace to live as children of God, reflecting

---

38. The appendix, which considers scholar's opinions on the presence of echoes and allusions to Jesus' teaching in 1P, contains no proposed parallels to 4:6.

39. This is likely what is meant by Davids's assertion that the following-referent view fits better the "general theological milieu of 1 Peter" (Davids, *First Epistle of Peter*, 127).

40. Emphasis added. Elliott, *1 Peter*, 610. See also Marshall and Vahrenhorst, who argue for a similar view of Jesus' teaching (Marshall, *Luke*, 264; Vahrenhorst, *Erste Brief Des Petrus*, 144). In the same light, Michaels summarizes Luke 6:37b–38 and connects it to 1P 3:9: "'forgive, and you will be forgiven; give, and it will be given you. . . . with the measure that you measure, it will be measured to you in return'; similarly here, the thought is, 'Bless, and you will be blessed'" (Michaels, *1 Peter*, 178–79).

41. Stein, *Luke*, 209.

their Father's character. We find here the delicate balance present elsewhere in the NT; the believer must exhibit certain characteristics in order to obtain the eschatological inheritance, nevertheless those characteristics are born out of the previous grace of God that gave them new life.[42] It is for this reason that the reward is called an inheritance (κληρονομέω) in 1P, for "an inheritance is never earned; it is received as a gift."[43]

In conclusion, hearing the allusion to the words of Jesus would naturally lead the hearers to connect the pronoun to what preceded. They would recognize that just as Jesus called them to live out their Sonship by reflecting the character of the Father, so Peter does likewise. Such commands do not call grace into question; rather they call the reader to confirm his experience of the grace that brought him life by being obedient. Those who have been made the children of God will act as the children of God, and thus the call for them to act as such will be heard.

1 PETER 3:13-17

Verse 13 introduces an inference from the preceding verses.[44] The sense is as follows: "since the eyes of the Lord are on the righteous, who can cause lasting harm to those who do good?"[45] Verse 14 comments on what appears to be an exception to God's verdict of blessing, for sometimes people do suffer for doing good. Nevertheless, Peter calls on the readers to recognize that they are, in fact, blessed when persecuted for doing good. And, instead of responding in fear to those who oppress them, Peter calls his readers to fear the Lord over all others.[46] Finally, through fearing the Lord and rejecting

---

42. Schreiner argues for this position, noting also that in the NT "good works are often introduced as evidence that one is truly redeemed (Rom 2:6-10, 27-29; 1 Cor 6:9-11; 2 Cor 5:10; Gal 5:19-21; 2 Pet 1:5-11; 1 John 2:3-6; Rev 20:11-15)" (Schreiner, *1, 2 Peter*, 165).

43. Best, *1 Peter*, 130. Cf. Kistemaker, *Exposition of the Epistles of Peter*, 128-29; Jobes, *1 Peter*, 219.

44. This can be seen from both the copulative (καὶ) that begins the sentence and the cognates ποιοῦντας κακά (the one doing evil; v. 12) and κακώσων (the one harming you; v. 13).

45. It is possible to take the third-class conditional as indicating a reality that is likely not to happen. Nevertheless, it is best to interpret it here in reference to a general statement of fact that stresses the permanent harm to the believer. This is supported by the future participle, the reference to shame for the unbeliever, and the fact that his readers are already experiencing suffering for doing good.

46. Peter is alluding to Isaiah 8:12-13, and this confirms that "sanctifying" (ἁγιάζω) the Lord means to fear Him, for Isaiah 8:13 parallels "sanctify the Lord" with "let him be your fear and let him be your dread."

the fear of men, they should be prepared to give an answer to any who ask them about their hope. Peter indicates that they must answer with gentleness and respect,[47] maintaining a good conscience knowing that those who do evil against them will be put to shame.[48] But even if the unbeliever is not persuaded by such a persecution-induced testimony, Peter states that it is better to suffer for doing good than for doing evil. Peter concludes by noting that suffering for doing good is sometimes God's will for his people.

The importance of this paragraph in 1P can be seen in the striking parallels with 2:18–25 and the density of central themes presented here:[49] Christians suffer for doing good; experience undeserved verbal abuse; actively avoid suffering for doing evil; are secure in Christ; are blessed when they suffer; and have a living hope.[50] A new theme is present here, however, and this theme explains why this passage has frequently been used in Christian apologetics.[51] Here, for the first time, Peter introduces the importance of the believer's words. Up to this point, Peter has solely emphasized the evangelistic thrust of the believer's actions. Now, Peter enjoins actions with words to bring about the shame of the opponent.

While Peter clearly alludes to Isaiah 8:12–13 in these verses, much of this paragraph is also informed by the teaching of Jesus. We will argue for the following parallels:[52] 3:14 and Matthew 5:10; Luke 6:22; 3:14 and Matthew 10:26–28; 3:16 and Luke 6:28; and 3:13–17 and Luke 21:12–19.

1 Peter 3:14 and Matthew 5:10; Luke 6:22

This is one of the most commonly identified reflections of dominical teaching in all of 1P.[53] The verse clearly reflects the wording of Isaiah 8:12–13 in

---

47. There is some debate concerning how to translate φόβος. Is it fear directed towards God? (Michaels, *1 Peter*, 189). Or is it respect towards men? (Jobes, *1 Peter*, 231). Since the gentleness is directed towards men, it is likely that the text speaks of respect towards men as well.

48. It is not clear whether Peter is speaking of an eschatological shame, leading to condemnation or a temporal shame, with the possibility of repentance. The use of shame language, especially in relation to the Psalm 34 (the face of the Lord is against those who do evil) suggests eschatological judgment (Schreiner, *1, 2 Peter*, 177–78; Elliott, *1 Peter*, 633). But the parallel with 2:11–12 suggests that such verbal response and gracious action can lead to a temporal shame that may further lead to repentance.

49. Achtemeier, *1 Peter*, 228–29.

50. Achtemeier, *1 Peter*, 229.

51. Miller, "Use of 1 Peter 3:13–17," 193–209.

52. See the appendix for a list of other proposed parallels.

53. Cranfield notes that Peter "doubtless had in mind the saying of Christ recorded in Matthew 5:10" (Cranfield, *First Epistle of Peter*, 81). Selwyn adds that Peter's text is

the latter portion, but also clearly reflects the wording of Jesus in Matthew 5:10 in its earlier portion.

Table 8.2: 1 Peter 3:14 and Matthew 5:10; Luke 6:22

1 Peter 3:14	Matthew 5:10	Luke 6:22
ἀλλ' εἰ καὶ πάσχοιτε διὰ <u>δικαιοσύνην</u>, <u>μακάριοι</u>. τὸν δὲ φόβον αὐτῶν μὴ φοβηθῆτε μηδὲ ταραχθῆτε	<u>μακάριοι</u> οἱ δεδιωγμένοι ἕνεκεν <u>δικαιοσύνης</u>, ὅτι αὐτῶν ἐστιν ἡ βασιλεία τῶν οὐρανῶν.	<u>μακάριοί</u> ἐστε ὅταν μισήσωσιν ὑμᾶς οἱ ἄνθρωποι καὶ ὅταν ἀφορίσωσιν ὑμᾶς καὶ ὀνειδίσωσιν καὶ ἐκβάλωσιν τὸ ὄνομα ὑμῶν ὡς πονηρὸν ἕνεκα τοῦ υἱοῦ τοῦ ἀνθρώπου.

We addressed the availability of this saying when we examined the echo of this same text in 1:6. There we noted that this tradition is undoubtedly influenced by OT and inter-testamental factors but is picked up by Peter because of its prominence in the words of Jesus. In his detailed study of the μακάριος (blessed) passages, Millauer notes not only that both 1P and Matthew derive this teaching from Jesus,[54] but that it is "beyond doubt" that 1P and Matthew are in the same tradition; nevertheless, he rejects the idea that 1P knew the tradition in the literary form of Matthew's Gospel.[55] In this, he follows Nauck, who likewise rejects the direct use of Matthew's text, primarily on lexical grounds.[56] Though literary reliance cannot be definitively rejected, it is more likely that Peter knew a tradition similar to the one recorded in Matthew.[57]

The agreement between the passages is both lexical and ideological. Lexically, both passages share the relatively rare μακάριος ("blessed") and relate the term to δικαιοσύνη ("righteousness"). The relation of the terms leads us to the primary ideological parallel. In both cases, one is the recipient of blessing for being persecuted for righteousness. While the idea that

---

"no doubt based on the *verbum Christi* in Matt 5:10" (Selwyn, *The First Epistle of St. Peter*, 192). Along with the sources noted below, see Kelly, *Peter and Jude*, 140; Marshall, *1 Peter*, 114; Senior and Harrington, *1 Peter, Jude, and 2 Peter*, 94; Vinson et al., *1 & 2 Peter, Jude*, 165–66; Witherington, *Letters and Homilies for Hellenized Christians*, 178; Powers, *1 & 2 Peter, Jude*, 116; Hiebert, *First Peter*, 210; Watson and Callan, *First and Second Peter*, 85; Stibbs, *First Epistle General of Peter*, 134; Feuillet, "Quelques Reflexions," 243; Vahrenhorst, *Erste Brief Des Petrus*, 147; Gourbillon and Buit, *Première Épitre de Saint Pierre*, 78.

54. Millauer, *Leiden Als Gnade*, 165.

55. Millauer, *Leiden Als Gnade*, 146.

56. Nauck, "Freude Im Leiden," 70.

57. Brown, "Synoptic Parallels," 30; Gundry, "'Verba Christi' in I Peter," 342; Best, *1 Peter*, 109; Vahrenhorst, *Erste Brief Des Petrus*, 147. Contra Metzner, *Rezeption*.

there is a blessing for those who suffer is not unique, the connection between blessing (μακάριος) and righteousness (δικαιοσύνη) is only expressed in these passages. Indeed, Metzner notes that this combination "has no parallel in the rest of the Jewish, Hellenistic, and early Christian literature."[58]

The two significant lexical divergences should be explained.[59] First, Matthew uses διώκω to speak of persecution, while Peter uses πάσχω. This change in verb form is sufficiently explained by Peter's preference for πάσχω.[60] The second difference concerns the preposition used (διά [1P 3:14]; ἕνεκα [Matt 5:10]), which Metzner rightly calls "irrelevant."[61] The preposition used in Matthew (ἕνεκα) is relatively rare in the NT (twenty-six occurrences) and occurs nowhere else in 1P, while Peter's choice of preposition (διά) occurs often in the NT (667 occurrences) and is used eighteen times in 1P. In line with Peter's evident freedom to use his sources with modification elsewhere, the shift in preposition is unremarkable.

That Peter is reflecting these words of Jesus can be further defended by observing the pattern of Peter's JT references. Elsewhere, Peter references texts within the Sermon on the Mount/Plain (1:17; 2:11–12, 18–21; 3:9, 14; 4:13–14; 5:7). More importantly, two other times Peter echoes or alludes to this same passage (1:6; 4:13). Finally, while scholarly opinion should be subject to the evidence, it is significant that nearly all scholars agree that Peter is reflecting the words of Jesus here.

Having discussed the availability of the Gospel saying and the agreement between the passages, we can now consider what significance such an echo has in 1P.[62] First, the echo clarifies the meaning of verse 13. Commentators disagree whether the verse indicates that (a) generally people will not

---

58. Translated from, "Ist in der übrigen jüdischen, hellenistischen und christlichen Literatur ohne Parallele" (Metzner, *Rezeption*, 283).

59. The following paragraph assumes that Peter and Matthew had access to a similar tradition. It is possible Matthew modified the tradition in line with his own purposes. It is also possible Peter changed the tradition in line with his own preferences. That we argue for something closer to the latter is because the differences between Matthew and 1P here are more easily explained by 1P's lexical and stylistic preferences.

60. Metzner, *Rezeption*, 289.

61. Metzner, *Rezeption*, 284.

62. While Peter echoes the tradition found in Matt 5:10, it is likely 5:11–12 would also be recalled by the citation of 5:10. This can be defended by the following considerations. First, Peter's citation in 4:14 suggests that he also knew 5:11 (see the comments on that passage below). Second, 5:11 clarifies that one type of persecution Jesus' followers will experience is that people will "utter all kinds of evil against you falsely." This fits nicely with 3:16, which indicates that believers will be spoken against (καταλαλέω). Finally, it is likely that the traditions of 5:10–12 all belong together in the tradition.

harm those who do good,⁶³ or that (b) no *ultimate* harm will come to those who do good.⁶⁴ The echo of Jesus' words strengthens the case for the second reading. Jesus said that his followers will suffer persecution, and that such suffering actually evidences their blessing, confirming their inheritance of the kingdom. Thus, by echoing the words of Jesus, Peter is saying, "Now who can harm you if you zealously pursue right living? But even if you experience suffering, such suffering actually confirms your blessing of an eternal inheritance." Reading the latter portion of the verse in connection with Jesus' words implies that the harm is an eschatological harm.⁶⁵

Such a reading follows nicely from the preceding quotation of Psalm 34. Jobes, who has extensively studied the relationship between this Psalm and 1P, has argued that in 1P the Psalm is understood to speak of the blessing as the fullness of spiritual life, including eternal life.⁶⁶ Now, in verse 14, Peter clarifies that suffering, rather than bringing God's blessing into question, actually confirms one's reception of blessedness, especially eternal blessedness. Further support comes from the possible echo of Jesus' statement in Matthew 10:28: "Do not fear those who kill the body but cannot kill the soul; rather fear him who can destroy both soul and body in hell." If Peter modified the LXX quote in order to match Matthew 10:26–28 (see below), then Matthew 10:28 supports a "enduring harm" reading of verse 13.

While this echo encourages readers to recognize that their enemies cannot *ultimately* harm them, the passage likely also reminded them that their enemies have the power to cause great temporal suffering. Hearing the echo, the readers would be reminded that by their suffering, they are walking the same path the prophets of Israel walked (Matt 5:12). And, unfortunately, the prophets were mocked, beaten, and even killed. Nevertheless, Jesus encouraged his followers to view such suffering from an eschatological viewpoint, and Peter's readers would also be directed that way as well. Instead of focusing on the suffering being experienced, Jesus' and Peter's audiences were drawn to consider that their reward is "great in heaven." The adjective notes that the reward is worth the sacrifice, and the prepositional phrase indicates that this reward is reserved for them in an eternal place where moth, rust, and thief are absent (Matt 6:19–20).

---

63. Davids, *First Epistle of Peter*, 130. Cf. Marshall, *1 Peter*, 113.

64. Achtemeier, *1 Peter*, 229; Elliott, *1 Peter*, 620.

65. Further, it is possible Peter is echoing the words of Jesus from Luke 21:18–19 (see below): "But not a hair of your head will perish. By your endurance you will gain your souls." While we must wait for the argumentation below, it can be stated here that if Peter is echoing this passage, then the harm is clearly eschatological.

66. Jobes, *1 Peter*, 223–24. Cf. Goppelt, *Commentary on I Peter*, 236–37.

1 Peter 3:14 and Matthew 10:26-28

While nearly all commentators have noted a connection between Matthew 5:10 and 1P 3:14, only a few have suggested a connection with Matthew 10:26-28.[67] Nevertheless, there are good reasons to argue that Peter is also echoing this passage.

Table 8.3: 1 Peter 3:14 and Matthew 10:26-28

1 Peter 3:14	Matthew 10:26-28
ἀλλ᾽ εἰ καὶ πάσχοιτε διὰ δικαιοσύνην, μακάριοι. τὸν δὲ φόβον αὐτῶν <u>*μὴ φοβηθῆτε*</u> μηδὲ ταραχθῆτε	<u>*Μὴ*</u> οὖν <u>*φοβηθῆτε*</u> αὐτούς· οὐδὲν γάρ ἐστιν κεκαλυμμένον ὃ οὐκ ἀποκαλυφθήσεται καὶ κρυπτὸν ὃ οὐ γνωσθήσεται. 27 ὃ λέγω ὑμῖν ἐν τῇ σκοτίᾳ εἴπατε ἐν τῷ φωτί, καὶ ὃ εἰς τὸ οὖς ἀκούετε κηρύξατε ἐπὶ τῶν δωμάτων. 28 Καὶ μὴ φοβεῖσθε ἀπὸ τῶν ἀποκτεννόντων τὸ σῶμα, τὴν δὲ ψυχὴν μὴ δυναμένων ἀποκτεῖναι· φοβεῖσθε δὲ μᾶλλον τὸν δυνάμενον καὶ ψυχὴν καὶ σῶμα ἀπολέσαι ἐν γεέννῃ.

While Luke records this broad tradition (12:2-7), he does not have the important phrase, μὴ οὖν φοβηθῆτε, which leads us to believe Peter is citing from a tradition closer to that later recorded by Matthew (see below). The content of this dominical teaching would have been important to the early church undergoing persecution, and therefore would likely have been known by Peter's audience.

The connection between 1P 3:14 and this passage comes by way of Matthew 10:26a: "do not fear them" (μὴ οὖν φοβηθῆτε αὐτούς). This line is strikingly close to 1P's "do not fear them" (φόβον αὐτῶν μὴ φοβηθῆτε). While it is clear that Peter is quoting from Isaiah 8:12, which in the LXX reads, "do not fear the fear of it" (φόβον αὐτοῦ οὐ μὴ φοβηθῆτε), some explanation must be given for what appears to be Peter's modification of the LXX text from the singular (αὐτοῦ) to plural (αὐτῶν).[68] In the Isaian context, the Lord tells Isaiah not to fear *what the people fear*, but Peter's modification has the sense, "do not fear them."[69] Why make this change? Davids explains, "By making it plural Peter refers it to the enemies of the

---

67. E.g., Davids, *First Epistle of Peter*, 130-31; McKnight, *1 Peter*, 213.

68. That Peter is following a text close to the LXX is evident by the stark similarities. See the comparison in Carson, "1 Peter," 1039.

69. There is some debate concerning how to interpret the genitive. We have taken it as an objective genitive, as have others (Elliott, *1 Peter*, 624; Michaels, *1 Peter*, 186-87).

Christians. Christians are not to fear their persecutors; instead, *following Matt. 10:28*, they are to take a longer-range perspective and fear God."[70]

If Peter intended to echo Matthew 10:28, why didn't he simply change the wording to match that passage? Selwyn suggests that it is because Peter is also seeking to faithfully reflect Isaiah.[71] Michaels notes that if Peter had made this change "the similarity of his thought to that of certain synoptic passages (e.g., Mt 10:26-33) might have been more obvious."[72] Nevertheless, when the following points are considered, Peter's reflection of the words of Jesus appears likely. First, the dominical teaching explains the change from the LXX rendering. Second, the context of Matthew 10:26 fits 1P 3:13-17 quite nicely. Matthew 10 concerns the persecution of believers and specifically mentions that since Jesus has been verbally maligned, followers of him should expect the same treatment (vv. 24-25). The text gives hope that though such persecution persists, God cares for his own and will protect them from eternal harm (vv. 28-31).[73] Such a context is precisely what Peter is referencing in 3:13-17.

There are three elements of significance that should be mention in regard to this echo. Each of them flows from one of the reasons given in the echo for not fearing people. First, one reason Peter's readers should not fear the opponents is because everything will one day be made public. In the words of Jesus, "have no fear of them; for nothing is covered up that will not be uncovered, and nothing secret that will not become known" (10:26). In the final analysis, all will be made evident and what really matters will be exposed. It is likely Peter's readers were being falsely accused (2:12; 3:16), and this may lead to temporal shame before others in society. Peter calls them, by means of the echo of Jesus' words, to remember that all will be made clear. Their righteous acts will be revealed to be righteous, and the false claims of others will be revealed to be false. In the end, they will be honored, while their accusers will be shamed (3:17). It is for this reason that Peter reminds them to respond with gentleness and reverence while maintaining a good conscience. The final analysis will reveal right from wrong, and they must remain on the right side.

Second, by means of echoing these words of Jesus, Peter calls his readers to endurance and perseverance. We have mentioned before that Peter

---

70. Davids, *First Epistle of Peter*, 130-31. Emphasis added.
71. Selwyn, *First Epistle of St. Peter*, 192.
72. Michaels, *1 Peter*, 187.
73. If the textual reading that excludes "do not be intimidated" (μηδὲ ταραχθῆτε) is original, the case for an echo here would be strengthened. The absence of this phrase has some support ($\mathfrak{P}$72 B L Jerome) and the presence of the addition here is easily explained (i.e., to complete the LXX quotation) (Michaels, *1 Peter*, 183).

does not directly address apostasy, but instead seeks to curtail it by encouraging faithfulness. Here the words of Jesus bring to the fore the importance of a right response to persecution. Those who endure persecution, fear the Lord and gain the kingdom of heaven. But the alternative is also true, those who buckle under persecution show that they do not fear the Lord and do not inherit the blessing. Instead of gaining the eternal honor Jesus promised to those who fear and obey Him, they will receive the shame of those who will experience disgrace and rejection.

Finally, Jesus indicates that his followers should fear the Lord because they are "of more value than many sparrows." These words would certainly give comfort to those who hear the echo. The comparison between birds and Jesus followers shows that since God knows the death of a single, relatively worthless sparrow, he also knows the experiences of his beloved saints. The thought that each individual hair is known by God gives comfort to those who might ask, *does God care*? Further, the passage emphasizes God's sovereignty even over the death of a sparrow, indicating that he is sovereign over the lives of his people. Such sovereignty is likely echoed by Peter's statement, "if suffering should be God's will" (3:17). Thus, the Lord knows their suffering, and he cares for them in the midst of it. Such considerations provide encouragement to persevere in the face of suffering.

1 Peter 3:16 and Luke 6:28

When 1P 3:16 describes the type of abuse endured by the followers of Jesus, it appears to reflect a tradition like that recorded in Luke 6:28. We have already discussed the availability of this teaching and the fact that this section of the text is a favorite of Peter's (1:6; 2:3, 18–21; 3:9).

Table 8.4: 1 Peter 3:16 and Luke 6:28

1 Peter 3:16	Luke 6:28
ἀλλὰ μετὰ πραΰτητος καὶ φόβου, συνείδησιν ἔχοντες ἀγαθήν, ἵνα ἐν ᾧ καταλαλεῖσθε καταισχυνθῶσιν οἱ <u>ἐπηρεάζοντες</u> ὑμῶν τὴν ἀγαθὴν ἐν Χριστῷ ἀναστροφήν	εὐλογεῖτε τοὺς καταρωμένους ὑμᾶς, προσεύχεσθε περὶ τῶν <u>ἐπηρε- αζόντων ὑμᾶς</u>.

The lexical case for an echo is strong in that only in these two places in the NT does ἐπηρεάζω (revile) appear.[74] Further, both 1P 3:16 and Luke 6:28 use the accusative object with the verb, while the dative is the normal

---

74. Elliott, *1 Peter*, 630.

use.⁷⁵ And though 3:16 does not reference blessing (εὐλογεω), the idea is invoked in the immediate context (1P 3:9). Added to the lexical and grammatical evidence, the contexts of both passages are quite similar, with both addressing verbal abuse.

Given the strong lexical and contextual connections, what is the significance of this echo? A primary significance is a call to pray for the persecutors. Accordingly, this echo gives some credibility to the view that Peter intended a shaming *before* the day of judgment, leaving room for repentance and salvation. That is, since Peter reminds his readers by means of the echo that they should pray for their persecutors, he probably also holds out hope that the abusers will repent. Of course, we argued that this was the sense of 2:12, a clear parallel to this passage. There, Peter suggested that those who persecuted believers may possibly glorify God on the day of judgment. Nevertheless, it is likely that Peter is emphasizing the judgment here, even as he was emphasizing the possibility of repentance in 2:12. Both texts contain both hope and the possibility of judgment. Those who see—by means of the conduct and words of believers—the truth may presently be shamed and repent, leading them to glorify God on the day of judgment. But if they fail to accept this truth, they will experience a more devastating shame in the final judgment.

1 Peter 3:13–17 and Luke 21:12–19

The final dominical echo we will explore in these verses is from Luke 21:12–19. This one has not been widely considered in previous scholarly literature.⁷⁶ Nevertheless, just as Hays argued that echoes of the OT would be much more easily discerned by the original recipients of Paul's letters, so it will be maintained that echoes of Jesus' teaching would also likewise be discerned more easily by the original recipients of Peter's epistle. While the case is certainly not indubitable, there are reasons to believe this tradition is being echoed here.

Table 8.5: 1 Peter 3:13–15 and Luke 21:12–19

1 Peter 3:13–15	Luke 21:12–19

---

75. Michaels suggests that this means Peter knew the JT in Greek (Michaels, *1 Peter*, 190).

76. Though see Michaels, *1 Peter*, 184.

Καὶ τίς ὁ κακώσων ὑμᾶς, ἐὰν τοῦ ἀγαθοῦ ζηλωταὶ γένησθε; 14 ἀλλ' εἰ καὶ πάσχοιτε διὰ δικαιοσύνην, μακάριοι. τὸν δὲ φόβον αὐτῶν μὴ φοβηθῆτε μηδὲ ταραχθῆτε, 15 κύριον δὲ τὸν Χριστὸν ἁγιάσατε <u>ἐν ταῖς καρδίαις ὑμῶν</u>, ἕτοιμοι ἀεὶ πρὸς <u>ἀπολογίαν</u> παντὶ τῷ αἰτοῦντι ὑμᾶς λόγον περὶ τῆς ἐν ὑμῖν ἐλπίδος,	Πρὸ δὲ τούτων πάντων ἐπιβαλοῦσιν ἐφ' ὑμᾶς τὰς χεῖρας αὐτῶν καὶ διώξουσιν, παραδιδόντες εἰς τὰς συναγωγὰς καὶ φυλακάς, ἀπαγομένους ἐπὶ βασιλεῖς καὶ ἡγεμόνας ἕνεκεν τοῦ ὀνόματός μου· 13 ἀποβήσεται ὑμῖν εἰς μαρτύριον. 14 θέτε οὖν <u>ἐν ταῖς καρδίαις ὑμῶν</u> μὴ προμελετᾶν <u>ἀπολογηθῆναι</u>· 15 ἐγὼ γὰρ δώσω ὑμῖν στόμα καὶ σοφίαν ᾗ οὐ δυνήσονται ἀντιστῆναι ἢ ἀντειπεῖν ἅπαντες οἱ ἀντικείμενοι ὑμῖν. 16 παραδοθήσεσθε δὲ καὶ ὑπὸ γονέων καὶ ἀδελφῶν καὶ συγγενῶν καὶ φίλων, καὶ θανατώσουσιν ἐξ ὑμῶν, 17 καὶ ἔσεσθε μισούμενοι ὑπὸ πάντων διὰ τὸ ὄνομά μου. 18 καὶ θρὶξ ἐκ τῆς κεφαλῆς ὑμῶν οὐ μὴ ἀπόληται. 19 ἐν τῇ ὑπομονῇ ὑμῶν κτήσασθε τὰς ψυχὰς ὑμῶν.

The availability of this tradition is supported by its presence within the Olivet Discourse, which is recorded in all three Gospels (Mark 13:3–13; Matt 24:3–14; Luke 21:12–19). The similarities between 1P and this text, however, are found chiefly in the Olivet Discourse as expressed in Luke's Gospel. As elsewhere, a literary explanation is not necessary and is difficult to sustain in light of the presence of shared oral tradition in the early church.

The similarities are both lexical and ideological. On the lexical side, both passages speak of making a defense (ἀπολογέομαι [Luke 21:14]; ἀπολογία [1P 3:15]) and share the precise phrase "in your hearts" (ἐν ταῖς καρδίαις ὑμῶν).[77] In regard to the former, the echo of the JT provides an answer to what appears to be an odd word choice in regard to 1P; namely, if 1P concerns non-formal verbal abuse and not formal governmental persecution, why does Peter use a term strongly associated with the courtroom (ἀπολογία)?[78] Peter's word choice is designed to connect Peter's words to the words of Jesus, which provides rich resonance as we will see below.

The second lexical similarity is precise in verbiage but does not appear to be parallel in conception. As noted above, both have the exact phrase "in your hearts" (ἐν ταῖς καρδίαις ὑμῶν); nevertheless, Peter tells his readers to sanctify the Lord in their hearts, while Jesus tells his listeners to decide in their hearts not to prepare a defense in advance. It will be argued below that

77. On the basis of these lexical similarities, Davids says, "the situation presupposed in v 15 parallels Jesus' instructions to his disciples in the eschatological setting of Luke 21:14–15" (Davids, *First Epistle of Peter*, 184).

78. Beare, for example, argues that Peter's use of ἀπολογία, especially in connection with αἰτεῖν λόγον ("to require an accounting"), "can only apply to judicial interrogation" (Beare, *First Epistle of Peter*, 164). While others have shown that ἀπολογία *can* be used in a non-judicial sense, (e.g., Elliott, *1 Peter*, 627; Achtemeier, *1 Peter*, 233) the judicial sense is certainly primary. An explanation like the one above has the advantage of explaining why Peter chose to use a word in its rare sense.

the differences and similarities are intentional; in other words, Peter uses the same phrase to remind the reader of Jesus' words, yet by his alteration of the citation, he applies the teaching of Jesus to his audience's situation.

The ideological parallels are evident, though some differences must be explained. Both texts speak of persecution, the necessity of a verbal defense, and divine protection from enemies. More specifically, 1P is speaking about verbal abuse by individuals and not organized persecution by the government, while the Lukan context speaks of being brought before human rulers.[79] Nonetheless, it appears Peter is drawing inference from a specific situation to a more general situation. More problematic, however, is that 1P encourages the believers to be *ready* (ἕτοιμος) to make a defense, presumably preparing for such an event, while Jesus told his followers "not to prepare your defense in advance" (μὴ προμελετᾶν ἀπολογηθῆναι; Luke 21:14).

One possible response—and one that some Lukan commentators have embraced without regard to 1P—is that Jesus was commanding his disciples not to memorize a speech or prepare with exact precision the words that would be used. If so, this would not prevent thinking about what one should say; rather, it gives place for the Spirit to guide the actual defense.[80] Given this interpretation, Peter's reflection likewise emphasizes that his readers should be prepared in such a way that they are dependent on the Spirit's guidance.

On the other hand, if we assume that Peter expected his readers to recognize the allusion, there is another way to resolve this tension. First Peter indicates that the followers of Jesus are required to sanctify the Lord in their hearts, which, as we noted above, is equivalent to fearing the Lord. How is this to be accomplished? Peter answers in 3:15 by the plural adjective, ἕτοιμοι, which requires an elided equative, whether participle (ὄντες) or imperative (ἔστε).[81] If imperative, as the NRSV translation takes it, then Peter is making a further command: "Always be ready." If participial, however, the import of the dependent clause must be examined. Achtemeier argues that it is a participle of means, indicating the way one sanctifies the Lord: "by being prepared."[82] But, in light of the echo of Jesus, it is also possible that this is an adverbial participle of result: "with the result that you are prepared." On this reading, Peter is telling his audience to prepare to make a defense *by sanctifying the Lord* in their hearts. When the time of

---

79. Elliott, *1 Peter*, 627.
80. Marshall, *Gospel of Luke*, 768; Stein, *Luke*, 517.
81. Dubis, *1 Peter*, 111; Forbes, *Exegetical Guide*, 116.
82. Achtemeier, *1 Peter*, 233n34.

questioning comes, they may rely on the Spirit to aid them in their response. Given this interpretation, the activity in the heart is similar in both texts, for by sanctifying the Lord, the readers are trusting in the Lord to aid them.[83]

There are numerous layers of significance. First, Jesus indicates that the way of safety is by means of divine power ("not a hair of your head will perish") accomplished through the endurance of the believer ("by your endurance you will gain your souls"). Again, we see the intricate balance of human and divine; the believer must endure to be saved, yet God promises the protection of his people. This allusion reminds Peter's readers that what is at stake is nothing less than their souls. Further, this allusion confirms the veiled way in which 1P encourages the perseverance of the saints; without directly mentioning the prospect of judgment, such a prospect is nevertheless clearly present.

Second, Jesus promises his disciples that he will "give [them] words and a wisdom that none of [their] opponents will be able to withstand or contradict" (Luke 21:15). Thus, when Peter, alluding to these words of Jesus, indicates that his readers should offer a reason (λόγος) for the hope they have, his readers should take comfort that the Lord will not leave them helpless. Such confidence is not in their own ability to respond, but in the promise of God that when they sanctify the Lord, the Spirit will aid them.

Third, the allusion to this passage reminds the readers that, just as Jesus indicated, persecution will come upon the followers of Jesus. Indeed, the allusion shows that greater suffering than they are experiencing was foretold by Jesus (prison, government persecution, death). Since Jesus promised divine protection and guidance in such extreme cases, it is implied that he also offers protection and guidance in their cases of suffering. And since those who endure grater suffering will be able to endure, surely they will also be able to endure.

1 PETER 3:18-22

This section of 1P is widely recognized as the most difficult passage in the epistle.[84] The difficulty can be attributed to various factors. First, these verses touch on numerous and important theological issues, increasing the

---

83. While either of the two options provided here indicate how Peter and Jesus could be in harmony, the first proposal appears more likely to the present writer. Nevertheless, the second option is exegetically possible and has the advantage that it correlates the "in your heart" statements.

84. Luther candidly admitted, "This is a strange text, and a more obscure passage, perhaps, than any other in the New Testament, for I do not certainly know what St. Peter means" (Luther, *Epistles of St. Peter*, 188).

potential tension between theological positions and exegetical readings.[85] Second, the passage is terse, suggesting that the author assumed his audience's knowledge of much of the subject matter,[86] a knowledge, at least partly, lost to history.[87] Third, there are grammatical, textual, and lexical ambiguities in the text.[88] Fourth, and most important for our purposes, the passage is clearly dependent on prior tradition.[89]

Before discussing the role of prior tradition, it will be helpful to provide a brief summary of the passage. While there are widely differing interpretations of what Peter is specifically saying,[90] there is general unanimity concerning Peter's overall point. 3:18 begins with ὅτι (for/because), which connects these verses back to the entirety of 3:13–17. Verses 18 and 22 provide the broad outline, from which 19–21 include the details. The broad outline is that Jesus suffered vicariously, died physically, rose triumphantly, and ascended regally. The specific details of what Peter speaks of in verses 19–21 appears to occur between the resurrection and the ascension.

Commentators agree that the broad outline provides confidence to Peter's readers that *it is better* to suffer for doing good than for doing evil. This is not only because unjust suffering can, according to God's plan, lead to blessing (as with Jesus), but also because Jesus has secured their victory through his death, resurrection, and victorious ascent to the right hand of the Father, where he can exercise his power and authority over all things.

---

85. Chad Pierce notes that the verses touch on many aspects of theology, leading to a tendency for works to be "primarily written to counteract the various theological claims which resulted from a specific exegesis of these verses rather than being concerned with an independent, focused study of the particular passage itself" (Pierce, "Spirits and the Proclamation of Christ, 1–2).

86. E.g., Maier, "Jesustradition," 109.

87. Watson's exposition of this passage concludes that "this tradition is so unusual that its plain meaning was either lost to interpreters or purposely ignored, for the plain meaning was not recovered until recently." He believes 1 Enoch unlocks much of the lost history, allowing modern interpreters to see once more the text's plain meaning (Watson, "Early Jesus Tradition," 155; cf. Westfall, "Relationship between the Resurrection," 106–35).

88. Jobes, *1 Peter*, 327.

89. Shimada lists ten indicators that traditional material is being used in these verses. While some are debatable, the cumulative weight is persuasive (Shimada, "Formulary Material," 307–8).

90. Pierce indicates the following three major positions on the meaning of verses 19–21: "1) Christ's proclamation to human souls between his death and resurrection, 2) the proclamation of the pre-existent Christ through the person of Noah, and 3) Christ's proclamation to fallen angels or giants" (Pierce, "Spirits and the Proclamation of Christ," 2).

Various attempts have been made to discern the traditions that reside behind this text. It is not necessary here to develop such proposals at length; instead, we will follow Jeremias, who, after detailing the views of Windisch, Cullman, and Bultmann, concluded that the only thing *certain* is that "in verses 18 and 22 older christological traditions are used."[91] In other words, the competing theories combined with the sparse background data prevent firm conclusions concerning whether a broader tradition is being used in 1P. Nevertheless, in light of the continuity in thought and content between verses 18 and 22 with other JT, it is quite clear that Peter is using tradition in these verses. In the words of Watson, "1 Peter 3:18 and 22 stand firmly in the Jesus tradition as it was being transmitted and developed by early Christianity."[92]

Goppelt notes that this section of 1P is unique in that it reflects the second article of the Apostles Creed more than any other NT passage.[93] In line with this observation, Achtemeier concludes that though this text is based on prior tradition, it is the unique formulation of Peter. He points particularly to verse 22: "The elements combined in this verse—ascension, exaltation, subjugation—occur frequently in various combinations in the NT; this particular combination, however, is unique, and shows the extent to which the author was independent in his use and combination of such traditions."[94]

As was made clear in consideration of the other two short catechisms concerning Jesus in 1P (1:18-21; 2:21-25), part of the challenge is determining what particular traditions 1P is referencing. In other words, much of the material present here has been passed down in various traditions, and it is possible Peter is not thinking of any one particular tradition but is rather combining the ideas of the early tradition to form this terse summary. For this reason, Watson, in an article on the use of the JT in this passage, does not dwell on any one saying of Jesus.[95]

---

91. Translated from, "Sicher ist nur, daß in V. 18 u. 22 ältere chrietologische Formeln verwendet sind" (Jeremias, "Zwischen Karfreitag und Ostern," 196; cf. Cranfield, "Interpretation," 369).

92. Watson, "Early Jesus Tradition," 155.

93. Goppelt, *Commentary on I Peter*, 247.

94. Achtemeier, *1 Peter*, 273.

95. "This pericope draws from the interconnected sources of early Christian tradition regarding Christ's teachings, redemptive sufferings, resurrection and exaltation.... Many common elements of the early Jesus tradition are found here." Watson, "Early Jesus Tradition," 152.

If we are to find particular traditions being echoed here, it is likely we would find them in verses 18 and 22 for the reasons noted above.[96] In reference to verse 18, there are no verbal clues that a particular JT is being referenced; instead, the broad NT theme concerning the substitutionary sacrifice of Jesus is being referenced (Rom 8:3; 1 Cor 15:3; 1 Thess 5:10; 1 John 2:2; 4:10), and while this tradition likely derives from Jesus (e.g., Mark 10:45), there is nothing in this text to suggest that Peter is drawing his readers to consider any particular saying. Further, Michaels is right to note that reference to the death and resurrection of Jesus "is so common in the NT (even though the vocabulary used here is untypical) that there is no way to trace the origin of such a simple formula with confidence."[97]

Much the same can be said concerning the sayings of Jesus and verse 22. While the ascension and present session are not as prevalent in NT literature as the traditions concerning Jesus' death and resurrection, they are not unique elements either. As Watson notes, "Christ's exercise of power at God's right hand is central to early Christian tradition (Mk 12:35-37 || Mt. 22:41-46 || Lk. 20:41-44; Mk 14:62 || Mt. 26:64; Mk 16:19; Lk. 22:69)."[98] Likely, this was based on the early church belief, sourced in dominical teaching (Mark 14:62; Matt 26:64; Luke 22:69), that Jesus was fulfilling LXX Psalm 109:1.[99]

That Peter is not developing LXX Psalm 109 directly is suggested by the lexical differences between the texts.[100] Significantly, all three Gospel passages which record Jesus' testimony before the Jewish council (Mark 14:62; Matt 26:64; Luke 22:69) use the LXX Psalm form, which includes the plural ἐκ δεξιῶν (at the right hand) and includes a verb for sit (κάθημαι). Peter, using the singular ἐν δεξιᾷ (at the right hand) follows the way the Psalm is used in Pauline literature and Hebrews (Rom 8:34; Eph 1:20; Col 3:1; Heb 1:3; 8:1; 10:12; 12:2), while the lack of a verb for "sit" matches Romans 8:34.

---

96. It is possible that Peter is reflecting the words of Jesus in 3:20 in reference to the few (ὀλίγος) who were saved (Matt 7:14; Luke 13:23). Nevertheless, this reflection is certainly not clear. Likewise, while Peter mentions the "days of Noah" (ἐν ἡμέραις Νῶε) in a way that "suggests some literary connection" with Matt 24:37-38 (αἱ ἡμέραι τοῦ Νῶε) and Luke 17:26 (ἐν ταῖς ἡμέραις Νῶε), Foster is right that the connections are too sparse to make a case (Foster, *Literary Relations*, 493-94).

97. Michaels, *1 Peter*, 198.

98. Watson, "Early Jesus Tradition," 154-55.

99. Shimada, "Formulary Material," 395; Achtemeier, *1 Peter*, 273.

100. Michaels, *1 Peter*, 218-19. Achtemeier further explains, "Allusions to this tradition take two forms, the one of which retains the ἐκ δεξιῶν of the psalm, the other of which employs the comparable phrase ἐν δεξιᾷ. It is this latter tradition that our author follows, thus indicating his dependence on tradition rather than on the psalm directly" (Achtemeier, *1 Peter*, 273).

These divergences from the Gospel tradition and similarity with other NT tradition suggest that Peter is here reflecting church tradition.

Nevertheless, it is quite possible Peter intended the reference to Jesus at the right hand of God to bring Jesus' testimony before the Jewish council to the minds of the readers.[101] That the tradition was available can be defended by its presence in all three Synoptics within a central scene of the passion narrative (Mark 14:62; Matt 26:64; Luke 22:69).

Table 8.6: 1 Peter 3:22 and Mark 14:62; Matthew 26:64; Luke 22:69

1 Peter 3:22	Mark 14:62	Matthew 26:64	Luke 22:69
ὅς ἐστιν <u>ἐν δεξιᾷ</u> τοῦ θεοῦ πορευθεὶς εἰς <u>οὐρανὸν</u> ὑποταγέντων αὐτῷ ἀγγέλων καὶ ἐξουσιῶν καὶ δυνάμεων	ὁ δὲ Ἰησοῦς εἶπεν· ἐγώ εἰμι, καὶ ὄψεσθε τὸν υἱὸν τοῦ ἀνθρώπου <u>ἐκ δεξιῶν</u> καθήμενον τῆς δυνάμεως καὶ ἐρχόμενον μετὰ τῶν νεφελῶν τοῦ <u>οὐρανοῦ</u>.	λέγει αὐτῷ ὁ Ἰησοῦς· σὺ εἶπας. πλὴν λέγω ὑμῖν· ἀπ' ἄρτι ὄψεσθε τὸν υἱὸν τοῦ ἀνθρώπου καθήμενον <u>ἐκ δεξιῶν</u> τῆς δυνάμεως καὶ ἐρχόμενον ἐπὶ τῶν νεφελῶν τοῦ <u>οὐρανοῦ</u>.	ἀπὸ τοῦ νῦν δὲ ἔσται ὁ υἱὸς τοῦ ἀνθρώπου καθήμενος <u>ἐκ δεξιῶν</u> τῆς δυνάμεως τοῦ θεοῦ.

We have already addressed the similarity of ἐν δεξιᾷ and ἐκ δεξιῶν above. Added to this, Mark and Matthew agree with 1P concerning the location to which Jesus has gone—heaven (οὐρανοῦ). The Gospels indicate Jesus will *come from* heaven, while Peter indicates Jesus has *gone to* heaven. Nevertheless, the second is necessary for the first to occur. Further, the movement of Jesus after resurrection to the place of proclamation (v. 19) necessitated Peter mentioning the movement of Jesus to the right hand (v. 22). While Peter indicates that Jesus went to the right hand of *God* (τοῦ θεοῦ), Mark and Matthew indicate the right hand of *Power* (τῆς δυνάμεως). Luke's Gospel, however, shows that the latter is likely circumlocution in place of "the power of God" (τῆς δυνάμεως τοῦ θεοῦ).

Ideologically, both passages are political in nature. In 1P, Jesus ascends to the highest position of power and authority, and this is precisely what the Jewish Council recognized Jesus to be saying when he quoted LXX Psalm 109:1. Accordingly, "angels, authorities, and powers made subject to him" is parallel to "seated at the right hand of the Power."

---

101. The difference between ἐκ δεξιῶν and ἐν δεξιᾷ is minor and would not prevent the listener from hearing the echo of the Gospel narrative. Further, it is possible that some retellings of the Gospel narrative would conform to the form used more frequently in epistolary material.

If we are correct to say that Peter's original readers, steeped in the traditions of Jesus' teaching, would have recognized this echo, what significance would the echo have? First, it would not be missed that Jesus was facing unjust suffering before the highest Jewish court when he made this statement. He had confidence in the midst of the suffering that God's promises were true and would come to pass. In like manner, Peter is calling the readers to endure unjust suffering (perhaps even politically motivated suffering; see below), trusting in the promise of God that it is better to suffer for doing good than for doing evil. In the case of Jesus, the promise has now come to fulfilment, and thus the reader may have confidence that God's other promises will likewise come to pass. If Williams is right in his recent arguments concerning the nature of persecution in 1P,[102] then there was a political motivation to the persecution. Knowing that Jesus boldly stood before the highest Jewish court while trusting his Father and then was abundantly rewarded for his faithfulness would surely provide encouragement to Peter's readers to maintain steadfastly in the face of similar challenges.

Second, in the JT, Jesus merged LXX Psalm 109 with Daniel 7:13, which indicated that the Son of Man would come with the clouds of heaven to establish an everlasting kingdom. Hearing the echo, it is likely Peter's readers would be drawn to consider the future coming of Jesus to establish a permanent kingdom for the elect-exiles. It is possible Peter did not explicitly mention the return of Jesus because he wanted to encourage his readers that Jesus has present power, even before returning. Nevertheless, the connection with this Gospel narrative reminds the readers that Jesus will return in power. Such a consideration gives teeth to the claim that it is better to suffer for doing good than for doing evil and fits well with the future-oriented hope of the epistle. The present life circumstances are not permanent, and the reader's exilic status will not be forever. Instead, the one who has ascended to receive all power will descend and exercise his power. In that day, suffering will cease, and faithfulness will be rewarded.

1 PETER 4:1–6

These verses begin with a resumptive "since" (οὖν), which connects the admonition to the detailed victory-through-suffering of 3:18–22.[103] Having

---

102. Williams, "Suffering from a Critical Oversight," 275–92; Williams, *Persecution in 1 Peter*.

103. "Since" (οὖν) connects the present context back to 3:18 directly, but since 3:18 and 4:1 are best seen as an inclusio, the entirety of 3:18–22 is in view (Achtemeier, *1 Peter*, 277).

already called his readers to follow the steps of Jesus in suffering (2:21), here Peter focuses on the necessity of mimicking Jesus' attitude in suffering. If they do this, Peter assures them that they will be able to successfully avoid the life of sin that once consumed them. Indeed, Peter argues that they have already spent enough time captive to human desires, but now their new birth provides opportunity for them to live according to the will of God.

Verse 4 helps to understand the challenging statement of verse 1 that "whoever has suffered in the flesh has finished with sin." It does so by revealing that suffering is induced by righteous living and the faithful endurance of such suffering indicates that one has definitively stepped out from the previous life of sin and into a life of obedience. It is in this way that believers imitate the resolve of Jesus, for he likewise chose obedience though it led to great suffering. In the words of Jobes, "those who suffer unjustly because of their faith in Christ have demonstrated that they are willing to be through, or done, with sin by choosing obedience, even if it means suffering."[104]

Peter's description of unbelievers in this section centers on three activities: they are surprised by the actions of believers; they consequently blaspheme; and they will give an account to God, their judge. Verse 5 indicates that God judges both the living and the dead, which indicates that those who reject the Gospel and satiate the lusts of the flesh will not escape judgment through death. But verse 6 clarifies that Peter's point in mentioning it concerns believers chiefly.[105] They may experience rejection and ridicule in this life "according to human standards," but they will be vindicated "according to God's standard" resulting in life in the Spirit.[106] Thus believers have hope beyond this life, so that even if they continuously suffer until death, God has power over death. The "gentile" viewpoint appears victorious presently, but the judge will set all straight.

Few proposed parallels to Jesus' words have been offered in the history of scholarship in relation to these verses. Spicq highlights a potential ideological connection between 4:1 and Mark 8:34–35, where Jesus calls those who would be his disciples to deny themselves, take up their cross, and follow him. The broader context of Mark 8:34–38, which concerns the final

---

104. Jobes, *1 Peter*, 265.

105. For an exegetical case against the view that verse 6 indicates a post-partem opportunity at salvation, see Dalton, *Christ's Proclamation to the Spirits*, 263–77; Achtemeier, *1 Peter*, 286–91.

106. "According to human standards" and "according to God's standard" is based on Elliott's translation (Elliott, *1 Peter*, 711). That Peter speaks of the Spirit and not the spirit is defended in the work of Dalton, who notes that the contrast here is "between the sphere of the merely human and the sphere of the divine, a new order brought about by the presence and activity of God's Spirit" (Dalton, *Christ's Proclamation to the Spirits*, 276).

judgment and the proclamation of life to those who avoid the adulterous and sinful generation, may give some evidence for a parallel. Nevertheless, despite the general similarity between the passages, there is no clear verbal cue that would lead Peter's readers to consider this Gospel saying.

Selwyn, more confidently, asserts that in 4:4, "The *verba Christi* in Matt. 12:31-6 may well have been in St. Peter's mind."[107] The connection between these passages is partly verbal and partly ideological. Verbally, both speak of blasphemy (βλασφημέω; 1P 4:4; Matt 12:31) and the consequent giving account (λόγος; 1P 4:5; Matt 12:36) for it.[108] On the ideological side, in both cases "the blasphemy consisted in calling good evil and evil good."[109] Further, both speak of the possibility of vindication or condemnation and the decision between the two is revealed by the words one speaks.

Despite some suggestive connections, there are considerable challenges to maintaining an allusion or even an echo here. First, the Matthean passage chiefly concerns blasphemy against the Spirit, something entirely lacking in 1P. Second, neither the verbal nor the ideological similarity is unique. Further, while Selwyn accurately notes that the blasphemy in both passages consists in calling evil good and good evil, such is the essence of blasphemy. Finally, no substantial significance is found between the passages, indicating that Peter was likely not reflecting the tradition.

As for 4:5, Selwyn notes that the idea of the living and the dead giving an account to God is broadly based on the sayings Jesus as preserved throughout the Gospels (Mark 8:38; 13:33-37; Matt 25:31-46; Luke 12:35-46; 13:24-30; 21:34-36).[110] Nevertheless, the verbiage does not isolate any particular saying.

In sum, 4:1-6 clearly aligns with the teaching of Jesus, but there are no clear allusions or echoes to the teaching of Jesus as preserved in the Gospels.

1 PETER 4:7-11

First Peter 4:7-11, which serves as the conclusion to the body middle, repeats many of the themes from the opening of the body middle in 2:11-12, forming an inclusio.[111] While 4:1-6 chiefly concerned the relationship to those outside the assembly, these verses turn the attention to duties and

---

107. Selwyn, *First Epistle of St. Peter*, 213.

108. Elliott includes 1P 3:14 with Matt 12:36 on his short list of "affinities with specific dominical sayings" (Elliott, *1 Peter*, 24).

109. Selwyn, *First Epistle of St. Peter*, 213.

110. Selwyn, *First Epistle of St. Peter*, 213.

111. Jobes, *1 Peter*, 274-75; Achtemeier, *1 Peter*, 292.

responsibilities followers of Jesus have to one another. More specific advice will be given later to certain segments of the congregation, but here Peter provides instruction that pertains to the entirety of the Jesus-followers.

Verse seven begins with a statement concerning the nearness of the end, which informs the rest of the admonitions.[112] In light of the coming eschatological fulfillment of God's plan, how should these believers live? These verses contain only two commands, which are likely a hendiadys: "be sane and clear-headed."[113] Such contemplated seriousness is necessary in light of the coming judgment and is foundational for the prayer life of the believer.

Following these imperatives, Peter includes a series of three admonitions that carry imperatival force.[114] First and most importantly (πρὸ πάντων; "above all") believers are to have constant love for one another, for this "covers a multitude of sins." Second, they are to show hospitality to one another without grumbling. Finally, they are to serve one another by using their God-given gifts for the sake of one another. Doing so, Peter indicates, will result in glory to God through Jesus Christ. Verse 11 ends with a doxology, which formally closes the body middle.[115]

Numerous parallels to the words of Jesus have been proposed in this section of Peter's epistle.[116] A chief difficulty, however, concerns the similarity between this passage and Romans 12–13, 1 Thessalonians 5:1–10, and James 5:7–20.[117] Since there is overlap of theme and vocabulary, it is likely that each author is reflecting a shared tradition, which is ultimately grounded in the words of Jesus.

1 Peter 4:7–8 and Jesus' Eschatological Teaching

While Peter's emphasis on clear-headed and sane prayer is likely derivative of the Gospel traditions concerning the necessity of staying awake

---

112. With Sisti, it seems best to read the nearness of the end to refer to the incoming of the new epoch whose inauguration indicates that the final consummation has come closer (Sisti, "Vita Cristiana," 125.

113. This is Davids's translation (Davids, *First Epistle of Peter*, 155).

114. Michaels indicates that the participles and adjective take on the force of the opening imperatives (Michaels, *1 Peter*, 246–51).

115. The presence of a doxology does not indicate the end of the letter; rather doxologies are often present at the close of sections of letters in the NT (Rom 11:36; Gal 1:5; Eph 3:21; Phil 4:20), as it is here.

116. See the appendix for a full list of proposed parallels.

117. We cannot develop all of the similarities and differences here. For a good summary, see Goppelt, *Commentary on I Peter*, 293–94.

and remaining watchful in prayer (Mark 14:38; Matt 24:42; 25:13; 26:41), the difference in terminology and core ideas prevents a clear correlation of the passages. As for terminology, the Gospel contexts consistently use γρηγορέω (stay awake), while Peter uses σωφρονέω (be sensible) and νήφω (be sober). In regard to ideological similarity, Selwyn suggests the following distinction: "in 1 Pet. 4:7 it is self-discipline and not wakefulness which is connected with prayer, as means to end."[118] On the other hand, it is also possible Peter is expressing the same thought in language more appropriate to his Hellenized audience.

First Peter 4:7 has also been frequently connected to the Olivet Discourse in Luke 21:31-36 (Mark 13:29-37; Matt 24-25).[119] Gundry makes an argument for a relationship between the passages, noting the following three parallels: (1) Both speak about the nearness (ἐγγύς in Luke 21:31; ἐγγίζω in 1P 4:7) of the eschatological consummation of God's plan for this age. (2) "Peter's exhortations to be of sound mind (σωφρονήσατε) and sober (νήψατε) echo the same exhortation in expanded form in Luke 23:34."[120] (3) Both passages lead the disciple to a prepared state *for the sake of prayer*.[121]

Added to Gundry's list are the following two points. First, the connection between sobriety and prayer is significant, for only these passages correlate the two.[122] Second, the significance of the Olivet Discourse and the fact that Peter was one of the disciples whose question was the cause of the teaching (Mark 13:3) likewise leans in favor of an intertextual reference.[123]

While Gundry makes a case for Luke 21 being *a source* for Peter's thought, the similarities are not sufficient. First, while the concept of eschatological nearness is shared between the passages, the idea is common, and the form of the word is different between the passages (verb in 1P and adverb in Luke). Second, it is not clear that Luke's text is an "expanded form" of Peter's imperatives. True, νήφω can be used in reference to avoiding drunkenness, but Peter's use of the word does not suggest that is his meaning here.[124] Further, Peter lacks any notion of the cares of this life, something figuring prominently in Luke. Finally, while Gundry is right to

---

118. Selwyn, *First Epistle of St. Peter*, 381.

119. Selwyn, *First Epistle of St. Peter*, 110.

120. Gundry, "'Verba Christi' in I Peter," 343.

121. Gundry, "'Verba Christi' in I Peter," 343.

122. Gundry, "Further Verba," 225.

123. As suggested elsewhere in this work, the increased likelihood of a tradition associated with Peter being referenced does not require Peter to be the author. If someone were writing in Peter's name, it is likely the author would focus on those sayings and teachings historically associated with the apostle.

124. Michaels, *1 Peter*, 246.

see a similarity between the passages in regard to the focus on prayer in an eschatological context, such a focus is not unique to the Olivet Discourse (e.g., Mark 14:38; Matt 26:41).

Maier concludes that while Gundry has rightly recognized some similarities between Luke 21 and 1P 4:7–11, one cannot limit the connections to those passages. Instead, Maier highlights that Peter's words are best seen as a developed representation of numerous *dominical logia* (including Matt 3:2; 4:17; 10:7; 13:49ff; 24:3, 42ff; 26:41; 28:20; Luke 21:31ff).[125] Likewise, Wong concludes that "significant elements are spread over a large swatch of text" and thus, "it remains less certain that intentional allusion to a specific text is present."[126]

Despite not being able to indicate a single *particular* teaching of Jesus, it does seem likely that Peter's readers would have recognized the voice of their Lord in Peter's admonition. Thus, Peter's terminology is likely influenced by his desire to communicate that his teachings are in line with what their common Lord taught. Further, in nearly all the passages stressing eschatology and prayer, Jesus connects attention to prayer as the means of successful escape from falling and potential eschatological judgment (Mark 13:32–37; 14:38; Matt 24:42; 25:13; 26:41; Luke 21:34). It is likely, then, that Peter's readers are once more reminded of the danger of apostasy—not by direct reference to such a danger, but by the admonition to do all to avoid that end.

As for 4:8, Peter's admonition to "above all" (πρὸ πάντων) pursue love for one another may reflect the love command of John 13:34 and 15:12, but the lack of explicit verbal connections renders this unlikely.[127] On the other hand, 4:8 may contain a *dominical logion* when it reflects the words, "love covers a multitude of sins," but if so it is an agrapha.[128] Clearly, the phrase reflects Proverbs 10:12, but it does not follow the LXX, which is Peter's clear preference. Further, the verbiage is quite similar to the way James 5:20 reads.[129] The primary reason to believe this is an agrapha comes from the *Didascalia Apostolorum*,[130] which explicitly states that the Lord said these

---

125. Maier, "Jesustradition," 92–93. Cf. Achtemeier, *1 Peter*, 293.

126. Wong, "Use of Jesus' Sayings," 212.

127. Contra Gundry, "'Verba Christi' in I Peter," 340; Foster, *Literary Relations*, 531.

128. The term *agrapha* refers to sayings of Jesus that are not recorded in the four Gospels.

129. James indicates that the love of a brother "will cover a multitude of sins" (καλύψει πλῆθος ἁμαρτιῶν). This is quite similar to Peter's language of "covering a multitude of sins" (καλύπτει πλῆθος ἁμαρτιῶν).

130. "For the Lord hath said that love shall cover a multitude of sins" (Gibson, *The Didascalia Apostolorum*, 2.3). On the other hand, the later revision of the *Didascalia*

words. Support is found in Clement of Alexandria,[131] who also appears to indicate these words were stated by Jesus.[132]

But even if more evidence could be cited in favor of this agrapha, the fact that it is unrecorded in the Gospels produces problems for the purposes of this thesis. Perhaps Peter is echoing a known tradition concerning the words of Jesus, and it is possible he is using it for a specific rhetorical end. Nevertheless, since we have no access to the context of that teaching, it is impossible to make meaningful connections.

1 Peter 4:10 and Luke 12:42-48

In the debate between Gundry and Best, it was Best who first suggested an allusion to Luke 12:42-48 in 1P 4:10.[133] In response to Best, Gundry indicated that while he initially missed this allusion, he finds it compelling.[134] Others have likewise found Luke 12 to be a primary source for Peter's exhortation.[135]

(the *Constitutiones Apostolorum*, 2.3) substitutes John 13:35 for the saying.

131. Clement of Alexandria, *The Instructor (Paedagogus)*, 3.12.
132. Cf. Resch, *Agrapha*, 310-11; Spicq, "Prière," 22n1.
133. Best, *1 Peter*, 104.
134. Gundry, "Further Verba," 225.
135. Michaels, *1 Peter*, 249; Selwyn, *First Epistle of St. Peter*, 218; Maier, "Jesustradition," 101; Spicq, "Prière," 24; Michel, *Theological Dictionary of the NT*, s.v. "Οἰκονόμος," 151; Goppelt, *Commentary on I Peter*, 301.

Table 8.7: 1 Peter 4:10 and Luke 12:42-48

1 Peter 4:10	Luke 12:42-48
ἕκαστος καθὼς ἔλαβεν χάρισμα εἰς ἑαυτοὺς αὐτὸ διακονοῦντες ὡς καλοὶ <u>οἰκονόμοι</u> ποικίλης χάριτος θεοῦ.	καὶ εἶπεν ὁ κύριος· τίς ἄρα ἐστὶν ὁ πιστὸς <u>οἰκονόμος</u> ὁ φρόνιμος, ὃν καταστήσει ὁ κύριος ἐπὶ τῆς θεραπείας αὐτοῦ τοῦ διδόναι ἐν καιρῷ [τὸ] σιτομέτριον; 43 μακάριος ὁ δοῦλος ἐκεῖνος, ὃν ἐλθὼν ὁ κύριος αὐτοῦ εὑρήσει ποιοῦντα οὕτως. 44 ἀληθῶς λέγω ὑμῖν ὅτι ἐπὶ πᾶσιν τοῖς ὑπάρχουσιν αὐτοῦ καταστήσει αὐτόν. 45 ἐὰν δὲ εἴπῃ ὁ δοῦλος ἐκεῖνος ἐν τῇ καρδίᾳ αὐτοῦ· χρονίζει ὁ κύριός μου ἔρχεσθαι, καὶ ἄρξηται τύπτειν τοὺς παῖδας καὶ τὰς παιδίσκας, ἐσθίειν τε καὶ πίνειν καὶ μεθύσκεσθαι, 46 ἥξει ὁ κύριος τοῦ δούλου ἐκείνου ἐν ἡμέρᾳ ᾗ οὐ προσδοκᾷ καὶ ἐν ὥρᾳ ᾗ οὐ γινώσκει, καὶ διχοτομήσει αὐτὸν καὶ τὸ μέρος αὐτοῦ μετὰ τῶν ἀπίστων θήσει. 47 Ἐκεῖνος δὲ ὁ δοῦλος ὁ γνοὺς τὸ θέλημα τοῦ κυρίου αὐτοῦ καὶ μὴ ἑτοιμάσας ἢ ποιήσας πρὸς τὸ θέλημα αὐτοῦ δαρήσεται πολλάς· 48 ὁ δὲ μὴ γνούς, ποιήσας δὲ ἄξια πληγῶν δαρήσεται ὀλίγας. παντὶ δὲ ἐδόθη πολύ, πολὺ ζητηθήσεται παρ' αὐτοῦ, καὶ ᾧ παρέθεντο πολύ, περισσότερον αἰτήσουσιν αὐτόν.

Michel is likely right in his conjecture that "under the influence of the parabolic material in the Synoptic Gospels οἰκονόμος came to have a place in the common legacy of primitive Christian proclamation."[136] And since οἰκονόμος only occurs in Luke's Gospel (12:42; 16:1-8),[137] a tradition like that in Luke's Gospel was likely known in the early church.[138] Pauline literature evidences use of the term in relation to personal responsibility, often within God's house (1 Cor 4:1-2; 9:17; Eph 3:2; Col 1:25; 1 Tm 1:4; Titus 1:7), an application of the Gospel teaching which is consistent with its use in 1P.

The agreement between 1P and Luke 12 rests chiefly on the lexical commonality of the word οἰκονόμος, which is rare in NT literature. Such a connection is strengthened by the substantial ideological parallels. First, both occur in eschatological contexts. That Luke is eschatological is evident by its focus on the return of the Master (12:43). That 1P is eschatological is confirmed by the opening clause in 4:7: "the end of all things is near."

---

136. Michel, "Οἰκονόμος," 151.

137. The related terms, οἰκονομέω and οἰκονομία, also only occur in Luke's Gospel (16:2-4).

138. In addition, this tradition is also reflected in Matt 24:45-51, though Matthew has δοῦλος ("slave") in the place of οἰκονόμος ("steward"). Best asserts that since δοῦλος is less apt, Luke must have modified Jesus' word to make it more fitting. But it is also possible that Matthew changed the word to conform to the more common term (Best, "I Peter and the Gospel Tradition," 104; cf. Gundry, "Further Verba," 224-25).

Second, both passages refer to the proper distribution and use of resources given by a Master in a household.[139]

In addition to the commonalities noted above, Michaels notes the specific focus on Peter in the Lukan context: "The usage in 1 Peter is of particular interest in light of the question attributed to Peter himself in Luke 12:41 ("Lord, are you addressing this parable to us or to everyone?")."[140] As noted before, the specific focus on Peter within the context of the particular Gospel teaching increases the likelihood that such a teaching would be referenced and that it would be caught by the audience.

This is best classified as an echo, for while the recognition of the intertextual reference gives color and significance to the meaning of the passage, it is not necessary to understand Peter's overall meaning. Numerous elements of significance are evident at the intersection of these passages. First, the Gospel context recalls and reinforces the eschatological emphasis of 4:7. The readers are to be good stewards because the Lord is going to return and call them to account.

Second, by echoing the words of Jesus, Peter brings before his readers the reality of divine reward and divine censure. On the one hand, those who are found faithful in the task God has given by divine gifting are called faithful and wise and will be outrageously (i.e., out of proportion) rewarded for their labor (12:44). On the other hand, Peter indirectly brings the threat of eternal censure before his readers. In the Gospel passage, Jesus stressed that those who know God's will and are given a task by God will be judged in accordance with their knowledge. Peter implicitly includes all of his readers in the camp of those with great knowledge. It is for this reason that Peter indicates the end is near; he wants the readers to be ready for the return of the Lord. They must not say to themselves, as the steward in the parable says, "My master is delayed in coming" (12:45). Instead, alongside a constant expectation of the coming of the Lord (1P 1:13), Peter encourages his readers to serve the community by means of exercising their gifts for the benefit of one another. If they do not, Peter holds out the prospect that they will be "cut in pieces" and "put with the unfaithful" (12:46). Once more, a *dominical logion* is used to encourage faithfulness to Jesus by warning of the danger that exists for those who do not remain faithful.

---

139. In the words of Best, both passages "depict the Christian as a servant in the house of God supervising the use of God's gifts for others" (Best, "I Peter and the Gospel Tradition," 104).

140. Michaels, *1 Peter*, 249.

CONCLUSION TO 1 PETER 3:8—4:11

We have made the case that Peter has frequently reflected the teaching of Jesus in the second half of the body middle. While some echoes were too faint to be firmly established, we have made the case for seven reflections, consisting of two allusions and five echoes.

Table 8.8: Intertextual Resonances to *Dominical Logia* in 1 Peter 3:8—4:11

1P Reference	Gospel Reference	Type of Reference
3:9	Luke 6:27–30 (Matt 5:39–44)	Allusion
3:14	Matt 5:10 (Luke 6:22)	Echo
3:14	Matt 10:26–28	Echo
3:16	Luke 6:28	Echo
3:13–17	Luke 21:12–19	Allusion
3:22	Mark 14:62 (Matt 26:64; Luke 22:69)	Echo
4:10	Luke 12:42–48	Echo

As Peter turns from specific admonitions to certain groups within the church to admonitions that pertain to all of the congregation, he invokes the nearness of the eschatological end, a theme borrowed from the teaching of Jesus. He specifically reflects the teaching of Jesus in 3:9 that believers ought to forego retaliation and repay with blessing (Luke 6:27–30; Matt 5:39–44).

Further consideration of the suffering of his readers leads him to other teachings of Jesus. First, he indicates that suffering guarantees blessing (3:14), a theme directly from Jesus (Matt 5:10; Luke 6:22). Second, he indicates that though it is natural to fear, the readers ought only to fear the Lord (3:14). Such a conclusion is based both on the testimony of the OT (Isa 8:12–13) as well as that of Jesus (Matt 10:26–28). Third, by echoing Jesus' distinctive description of the type of suffering his disciples will endure (3:16; Luke 6:28), Peter indicates that believers ought to pray for their persecutors with the hope they will be brought to repentance. Finally, Peter encourages those enduring persecution by reflecting the teaching of Jesus that those who endure persecution will be aided in their verbal defense by the Spirit (Luke 21:12–19).

While the next sections of 1P (3:18–22 and 4:1–6) are widely recognized to be reflective of the JT, there are few direct reflections of Jesus' sayings. We did, however, make the case for Peter's reflection of Jesus' defense before the Sanhedrin (Mark 14:62; Matt 26:64; Luke 22:69), which would have encouraged the readers in recognizing that Jesus' ascension is connected to his second coming, which the readers are to be prepared for.

The final section of the body middle (4:7–11) offered many potential reflections of Jesus' words. We focused on one likely reference: 4:10 and Luke 12:42–48. In that text, Jesus speaks of the necessity of being a good steward and the associated rewards. Further, Jesus warned about stewards who failed in their duties (believing the owner not to be returning). By echoing this passage, Peter likewise warns and encourages the readers towards faithfulness to their God-appointed tasks.

As with the first half of the body middle, Peter's reflections on the words of Jesus do not fall into a discernible pattern. Instead, Peter seems to mine the depths of the JT in order to reinforce his various points by means of recalling Jesus' teaching and bringing it to bear on his audience.

9

First Peter 4:12—5:14

PETER COMPLETES THE EPISTLE with a body closing (4:12—5:11) and an epistolary conclusion (5:12-14).[1] The body closing consists of three logical sections. The first (4:12-19) and third (5:6-11) focus on the suffering of believers and the proper response to that suffering, while the second (5:1-5) gives admonition to the Jesus-followers concerning relationships and duties within the body. This chapter will examine each of these sections along with the epistolary conclusion for the influence of Jesus' words on the letter.

1 PETER 4:12-19

The body closing begins with two commands concerning the proper emotional response to suffering. On the one hand, Peter indicates that his readers are *not* to be surprised by suffering (μὴ ξενίζεσθε; 4:12). On the other hand, they are to rejoice in suffering (χαίρω; 4:13). Taken together, Peter is indicating that his readers should expect suffering and to rejoice when they suffer. The cause for rejoicing is that suffering leads to gladness and excessive joy at the return of Jesus (4:13).

Verses 14-16 contains two conditional clauses concerning suffering for the faith.[2] Verse 14 indicates that if any are reviled for the name of Christ,

---

1. Peter signals the beginning of the body conclusion with a vocative followed by a command (Ἀγαπητοί, μὴ ξενίζεσθε; 4:12), and he concludes the body with a doxology (5:11). The recurrence of words concerning suffering indicate that this continues to be a major theme (4:13, 15, 19; 5:1, 9, 10; Green, *1 Peter*, 148).

2. On the basis of dominical teaching, Elliott notes that these conditionals may be

they are blessed, for the Spirit of God rests on them. Verse 16 indicates that if any suffers as a Christian, they are to not consider it a disgrace, but should instead use the opportunity to glorify God. The prior verses suggest that the two potential realities should be expected, and that suffering will be experienced by all. Verse 15 once more warns, however, that not all suffering is for the faith; instead, some may suffer for evildoing, and Peter admonishes his readers to avoid such causes of suffering.

Verses 17–19 provide reason to rejoice in suffering for righteousness and to avoid suffering for wrongdoing—the judgment will begin at God's household. Those who suffer for righteousness have grounds for expecting that God's verdict will be positive. By use of rhetorical questions, Peter indicates that those who disobey the gospel and live ungodly lives have no hope at the final judgment. Therefore, though righteousness leads to suffering, such suffering can be endured, for it is according to God's sovereign will and provides hope of God's gracious intention at the final judgment.

The following two parallels to Jesus' words will be examined: 4:13–14 and Matthew 5:10–12; Luke 6:22–23; 4:14; and Luke 12:10–12; Mark 13:11; Matthew 10:20.[3]

1 Peter 4:13–14 and Matthew 5:10–12; Luke 6:22–23

An intertextual relationship between 4:13–14 and Jesus' words in the Sermon on the Mount/Plain (Matt 5:10–12; Luke 6:22–23) is suggested by many scholars: Brox speaks of the "astonishing parallelism" that exists between the passages;[4] Kelly indicates that Peter's words "doubtless" derive from "our Lord's own promise in Mt. 5:11; Lk 6:22";[5] and Beare asserts that Peter is "clearly appealing to the well-known saying of Jesus in Matthew 5:11."[6]

---

intended to be read temporally: "Since this verse, along with terms in v 13 (*chairete, agalliōmenoi*), is close to the dominical saying reworked in Matt 5:11–12/Luke 6:22–23, the force of *ei* may be less conditional ('if') than temporal ('when,' as *hotan* in Matthew and Luke)" (Elliott, *1 Peter*, 778).

3. Other parallels which have been proposed are noted in the appendix. One notable proposed parallel is between 4:19 and Luke 23:46. A few scholars have suggested a reliance on the dominical teaching here, most notably Spicq and Gundry (Spicq, "Ia Petri et Le Témoignage," 53; Gundry, "'Verba Christi' in I Peter," 343–44). Despite some limited textual (παρατίθημι) and ideological similarity (entrusting the spirit/soul), the evidence is not strong enough to indicate a connection (Maier, "Jesustradition," 93).

4. Translated from, "erstaunlich parallele" (Brox, *Erste Petrusbrief*, 215).

5. Kelly, *Peter and Jude*, 186.

6. Beare, *First Epistle of Peter*, 191. Along with the resources cited below, see also Brown, "Synoptic Parallels," 30; Harink, *1 & 2 Peter*, 115; Feldmeier, *First Letter of Peter*, 225; Schreiner, *1, 2 Peter*, 220; Vahrenhorst, *Erste Brief Des Petrus*, 180; Davids, *First*

Table 9.1: 1 Peter 4:13-14 and Matthew 5:10-12; Luke 6:22-23

1 Peter 4:13-14	Matthew 5:10-12	Luke 6:22-23
ἀλλὰ καθὸ κοινωνεῖτε τοῖς τοῦ Χριστοῦ παθήμασιν, <u>χαίρετε</u>, ἵνα καὶ ἐν τῇ ἀποκαλύψει τῆς δόξης αὐτοῦ <u>χαρῆτε ἀγαλλιώμενοι</u>. 14 εἰ <u>ὀνειδίζεσθε ἐν ὀνόματι Χριστοῦ, μακάριοι</u>, ὅτι τὸ τῆς δόξης καὶ τὸ τοῦ θεοῦ πνεῦμα ἐφ' ὑμᾶς ἀναπαύεται.	μακάριοι οἱ δεδιωγμένοι ἕνεκεν δικαιοσύνης, ὅτι αὐτῶν ἐστιν ἡ βασιλεία τῶν οὐρανῶν. 11 <u>μακάριοί</u> ἐστε ὅταν <u>ὀνειδίσωσιν</u> ὑμᾶς καὶ διώξωσιν καὶ εἴπωσιν πᾶν πονηρὸν καθ' ὑμῶν [ψευδόμενοι] <u>ἕνεκεν ἐμοῦ</u>. 12 <u>χαίρετε</u> καὶ <u>ἀγαλλιᾶσθε</u>, ὅτι ὁ μισθὸς ὑμῶν πολὺς ἐν τοῖς οὐρανοῖς· οὕτως γὰρ ἐδίωξαν τοὺς προφήτας τοὺς πρὸ ὑμῶν.	<u>μακάριοί</u> ἐστε ὅταν μισήσωσιν ὑμᾶς οἱ ἄνθρωποι καὶ ὅταν ἀφορίσωσιν ὑμᾶς καὶ <u>ὀνειδίσωσιν</u> καὶ ἐκβάλωσιν τὸ ὄνομα ὑμῶν ὡς πονηρὸν <u>ἕνεκα τοῦ υἱοῦ τοῦ ἀνθρώπου</u>· 23 χάρητε ἐν ἐκείνῃ τῇ ἡμέρᾳ καὶ σκιρτήσατε, ἰδοὺ γὰρ ὁ μισθὸς ὑμῶν πολὺς ἐν τῷ οὐρανῷ· κατὰ τὰ αὐτὰ γὰρ ἐποίουν τοῖς προφήταις οἱ πατέρες αὐτῶν.

The availability of this tradition has been touched on in reference to 1P 1:6 and 3:14. In both of those passages, we argued for an intertextual reference to Jesus' famous sermon, portions of which appear to have been clearly known by Peter in some form. While we cannot repeat all of the argumentation presented earlier, we agree with Gundry that "The manifestness of the verbum Christi in 1P 3:14 establishes that the same verbum Christi lies behind 1P 4:13f."[7] Indeed, we will also argue the opposite; the manifestness of the verbum Christi in 1P 4:13-14 establishes that Peter knew and used the same tradition in 3:14 as well as 1:6.[8]

The agreement is strongly verbal but includes ideological parallels as well. On the verbal side, Matthew and Luke agree with 1P in the use of the following significant words: χαίρω (rejoice), ὀνειδίζω (revile), μακάριοί (blessed). Further, Matthew (not Luke) shares ἀγαλλιάω (exult) with 1P. Each of these words deserves comment. First, while χαίρω is not a rare word in the NT (seventy-four occurrences), it appears in persecution contexts only here, in Colossians 1:24, and in dominical teaching (Matt 5:11; Luke

---

Epistle of Peter, 167; Green, *1 Peter*, 156; Maier, "Jesustradition," 101-2.

7. Gundry, "'Verba Christi' in I Peter," 343n1.

8. Though Peter reflects this same tradition in three places, each use is distinct. First Peter 3:14 chiefly reflects 5:10, while 4:13-14 chiefly reflects 5:11. As for 1:6, Michaels notes that the "principal difference" between that text and 4:13-14 "is that instead of urging present faithfulness for the sake of future joy, he is now weighing present joy in the face of trials against the far greater joy to come" (Michaels, *1 Peter*, 262). In light of the use of this tradition in 1P, Beare concludes, "These words of our Lord must have been known to the writer in almost the very form in which they have been transmitted to us" (Beare, *First Epistle of Peter*, 191).

6:23).[9] On the other hand, ὀνειδίζω and ἀγαλλιάω are rare verbs (nine and eleven occurrences respectively) and strongly suggest a connection between these passages. More significantly, ὀνειδίζω is only used in this way in these two passages in the NT.[10] Finally, while μακάριοί is not a rare word (fifty occurrences), it is strongly associated with Jesus in the Sermon on the Mount/Plain and its use in a suffering context is distinct.

Despite the lexical similarities, Peter's grammatical structure is unique. It appears that Peter has taken the saying and adapted it to his context, retaining the vocabulary of the saying, while making the grammar of the saying more amenable to his purposes.[11] Thus, while it seems clear that Peter follows a tradition closer to Matthew than Luke,[12] the differences in grammar hinder the conclusion that Peter knew Matthew's Gospel in written form.[13]

Ideologically, the shared, rare emphasis on being blessed (μακάριοί) in spite of being reviled (ὀνειδίζω) indicates a connection.[14] Further, that the readers are not only called to consider themselves blessed but also to rejoice (χαίρω) with excessive joy (ἀγαλλιάω) signals a distinct connection. And that this passage reflects Matthew 5:10a (Blessed are those who are persecuted for righteousness' sake) may not be evident on the surface, but Peter's emphasis in 4:15 on avoiding suffering for doing evil is an equivalent formulation. In other words, Jesus' words encourage *only* those suffering for righteousness, while Peter's epistle encourages the avoidance of suffering for unrighteousness; these are two sides of the same coin.

Peter's "for the name of Christ" (ἐν ὀνόματι Χριστοῦ) is ideologically equivalent to Matthew's "on account of me" (ἕνεκεν ἐμοῦ). And while Michaels is right to note that reflection of something like the Matthean phrase is difficult to prove, the cumulative weight of the other lexical and ideological similarities leans heavily in its favor.[15] Finally, both passages speak

---

9. Elliott, *1 Peter*, 776.

10. Goppelt, *Commentary on I Peter*, 322.

11. See Metzner for details (Metzner, *Rezeption*, 34–48).

12. The use of χαίρω with ἀγαλλιάω strongly suggests this. On the other hand, Michaels rightly indicates that Luke's Gospel matches 1P better when it references a future rejoicing ("Rejoice in that day . . ."), which aligns with Peter's emphasis on rejoicing "when his glory is revealed" (Michaels, *1 Peter*, 262). Accordingly, it is possible Peter knew traditions in both Luke's and Matthew's form. With Matthew he indicates there is present joy, but with Luke he emphasizes the future joy.

13. Nauck, "Freude Im Leiden," 70.

14. Wong, "Use of Jesus' Sayings," 214.

15. Michaels, *1 Peter*, 264. Cf. Elliott, *1 Peter*, 780–81.

of heavenly rewards. This is obvious in reference to the Gospels (Matt 5:10; Luke 6:23) but is implied in reference to Peter's epistle.[16]

Having argued for this echo, it is time to consider what significance the echo has to Peter's epistle. First, the echo clarifies why the reader should not be surprised at suffering; namely, Jesus predicted that this would happen. Second, the reader who hears the echo would recognize that Peter is defining "persecution for righteousness sake" as "sharing Christ's sufferings." In other words, Jesus evidenced what a life of righteousness looked like and he suffered for it. Now, those who follow him in a life of righteousness will share in his sufferings.

The most significant resonance, however, is the substitution Peter makes in the teaching. While Jesus used the example of the prophets ("in the same way they persecuted the prophets who were before you" [Matt 5:10]), Peter uses the example of Jesus ("sharing Christ's sufferings"; 1P 4:13). Peter essentially says, if following the example of the prophets was commendable, consider how commendable following the Son of God is. Indeed, in the Gospels, following the footsteps of the prophets gave one confidence that he was eligible for the heavenly reward. In a similar way, sharing in the sufferings of Jesus is cause for rejoicing as well, for if one endures such suffering, the joy will be multiplied when Jesus comes. Therefore, while Peter does not explicitly mention heavenly rewards, the parallelism of concept indicates that this is Peter's meaning here. If experiencing persecution like the prophets leads one to rejoice and be glad for a future, heavenly reward, then experiencing persecution like Jesus more abundantly leads one to rejoicing and gladness, for when he comes, he will reward his servants.[17]

Peter follows the makarism with ὅτι ("because") just as Jesus frequently does in the Gospels (Matt 5:3–10; Luke 6:20–21). Yet what Peter follows the makarism with—"you are blessed, *because the spirit of glory, which is the Spirit of God, is resting on you*"—is not evidently coordinate with the Gospel beatitudes. The next proposed parallel will help us understand why Peter used these words.

---

16. Gundry, "'Verba Christi' in I Peter," 343.

17. Therefore, Wong appears mistaken in his claim that "the reason for rejoicing in 4:13a *is not reward* . . . but identification with Christ and a greater eschatological exultation," for reward and identification with Christ are not incompatible, and the exultation is likely due, at least in part, to the reward (Wong, "Use of Jesus' Sayings," 215; emphasis added).

1 Peter 4:14 and Luke 12:10-12; Mark 13:11; Matthew 10:20

The last proposed parallel we examined was one of the most commonly noted parallels in all of 1P. We turn now to one of the least common, yet one that deserves serious consideration. Only a few have explicitly suggested this parallel, though many others have noted the similarity of theme.[18] We will argue that there is reason to believe Peter was reflecting this dominical tradition.

Table 9.2: 1 Peter 4:14 and Luke 12:11-12; Mark 13:11; Matthew 10:20

1 Peter 4:14	Luke 12:10-12	Mark 13:11	Matthew 10:20
εἰ ὀνειδίζεσθε ἐν ὀνόματι Χριστοῦ, μακάριοι, ὅτι τὸ τῆς δόξης καὶ τὸ τοῦ θεοῦ πνεῦμα ἐφ᾽ ὑμᾶς ἀναπαύεται.	Καὶ πᾶς ὃς ἐρεῖ λόγον εἰς τὸν υἱὸν τοῦ ἀνθρώπου, ἀφεθήσεται αὐτῷ· τῷ δὲ εἰς τὸ ἅγιον πνεῦμα βλασφημήσαντι οὐκ ἀφεθήσεται. 11 Ὅταν δὲ εἰσφέρωσιν ὑμᾶς ἐπὶ τὰς συναγωγὰς καὶ τὰς ἀρχὰς καὶ τὰς ἐξουσίας, μὴ μεριμνήσητε πῶς ἢ τί ἀπολογήσησθε ἢ τί εἴπητε· 12 τὸ γὰρ ἅγιον πνεῦμα διδάξει ὑμᾶς ἐν αὐτῇ τῇ ὥρᾳ ἃ δεῖ εἰπεῖν.	καὶ ὅταν ἄγωσιν ὑμᾶς παραδιδόντες, μὴ προμεριμνᾶτε τί λαλήσητε, ἀλλ᾽ ὃ ἐὰν δοθῇ ὑμῖν ἐν ἐκείνῃ τῇ ὥρᾳ τοῦτο λαλεῖτε· οὐ γάρ ἐστε ὑμεῖς οἱ λαλοῦντες ἀλλὰ τὸ πνεῦμα τὸ ἅγιον.	οὐ γὰρ ὑμεῖς ἐστε οἱ λαλοῦντες ἀλλὰ τὸ πνεῦμα τοῦ πατρὸς ὑμῶν τὸ λαλοῦν ἐν ὑμῖν.

There are significant textual and grammatical ambiguities in this text.[19] As for the grammar, it is best to understand the apparent dual reference concerning the Spirit (τῆς δόξης καὶ τὸ τοῦ θεοῦ πνεῦμα; "the Spirit of glory *and* the Spirit of God") as a hendiadys: "the divine Spirit of glory."[20] As for the textual variants, there are four considered in the UBS 5th edition, though each is rated "A." We will examine one of the textual variants below.

It is likely that Peter is here reflecting LXX Isaiah 11:2a: καὶ ἀναπαύσεται ἐπ᾽ αὐτὸν πνεῦμα τοῦ θεοῦ ("And the spirit of God shall rest

---

18. E.g., Elliott, *1 Peter*, 782n589; Achtemeier, *1 Peter*, 305n12; Davids, *First Epistle of Peter*, 167-68; Green, *1 Peter*, 156; Michaels, *1 Peter*, 259, 264; Kelly, *Peter and Jude*, 187.

19. Kelly notes the difficulty: "the Greek is bafflingly difficult to construe, and it is possible that the original text (copyists very soon began altering it) is lost" (Kelly, *Peter and Jude*, 187).

20. Elliott, *1 Peter*, 782.

on him").²¹ Nevertheless, it appears that Peter derives the idea from Jesus' words. Michaels argues this way as well when he notes that "The language is Isaiah's, even though the thought (like that of the beatitude itself) is probably derived from the Gospel tradition (cf., e.g., Luke 12:11–12; Mark 13:11; Mt 10:20)."²² He further develops the same thought:

> To interpret this clause, it is helpful to distinguish between thought and actual terminology. The Gospel tradition amply attests Jesus' promise that "the Holy Spirit" (Mark 13:11; Luke 12:12) or "the Spirit of your Father" (Matt 10:20) will stand by his disciples and tell them what to say when they are arrested or questioned by the authorities. It is hard not to assume that Peter had these traditions in mind.²³

The obvious challenge to seeing an echo of the JT here is the lack of explicit verbal agreement. Nevertheless, there are, as Michaels notes, suggestive ideological agreements.²⁴

Another defense of this echo is based on a textual variant which is present at end of verse 14 in the majority of Greek manuscripts: κατὰ μὲν αὐτοὺς βλασφημεῖται κατὰ δὲ ὑμᾶς δοξάζεται (blasphemed indeed by them, but glorified by you).²⁵ Peter Rodgers and Ramsay Michaels have offered a defense of the originality of this reading.²⁶ First, its absence can be explained by *homoeoteleuton* (note the similar endings of ἀναπαύεται and δοξάζεται). Second, and following from the first, the line is approximately

---

21. This line matches 1P well (τοῦ θεοῦ πνεῦμα ἐφ᾽ ὑμᾶς ἀναπαύεται), and the use of ἀναπαύσεται, a relatively rare word (twelve NT occurrences) strengthens the connection, for it is only in this use in the NT that the word has the sense "to rest upon" (Wong, "Use of Jesus' Sayings," 102).

22. Michaels, *1 Peter*, 259.

23. Michaels, *1 Peter*, 264.

24. Peter's allusion to the LXX Isaiah may provide evidence for a dominical connection. Why is Peter drawn to Isaiah 11:2, which addresses the Spirit coming to "the root of Jesse"? The connection is likely that since Peter's readers share in the sufferings of Christ (4:13), they may also share in the same Spirit as the Messiah. This Spirit is a "spirit of wisdom and understanding, a spirit of counsel and might, a spirit of knowledge and fear of the Lord," who will "fill him" with a "fear of God." This combination—fearing God and having a spirit of knowledge—are two elements stressed in 1P 3:14–16, a passage which likewise reflects this same beatitude. Perhaps, then, Peter reflects Isaiah 11:2 because it reinforces the dominical teaching that the Spirit of God gives to those who righteously suffer the Spirit of wisdom to respond.

25. The variant is supported by the following: Ψ, K, L, P, 1799, 2412, Lat 64, 65, 91, 95, Vg (pc), Cy, Au, Cops, Syrh. On the other hand, some significant witnesses lack the phrase: P72 ℵ A B (Rodgers, "Longer Reading," 93; Michaels, *1 Peter*, 257).

26. Rodgers, "Longer Reading"; Michaels, *1 Peter*, 265–66.

one line-length, making it more likely to suffer from *homoeoteleuton*. Third, the line is in agreement with Petrine style.[27]

If the variant is genuine, there is further evidence for a dominical reference, for as noted above, Luke 12:10 references the blasphemy of the Spirit directly before encouraging those who remain faithful that the Spirit will aid them in their defense. Nevertheless, even if the variant is not original, we must ask why it was inserted in the text. Davids suggests that it is transferred by a scribe from 4:14.[28] But if so, why would the scribe insert that text here? Perhaps the scribe saw a connection between Peter's reference to the resting of the Spirit and Jesus' promise of the Spirit in a context that warned of the blasphemy of the Spirit (Luke 12:10–12), just as we are suggesting here.

The significance of this echo can now be considered. Hearing this echo, one realizes that Peter does not leave the missionary mindset even in the midst of the most suffering-centric passage in the book. It may initially appear that Peter is no longer interested in engaging outsiders but is simply helping his readers through times of suffering. But when this text is read in light of the Psalm and Jesus words, the reader is drawn back to 3:14–16 and is reminded that the Spirit they have been given is able to defend them and perhaps even bring repentance to those who persecute them. They must be prepared to give an answer, for they have been given the Spirit who aids in giving a defense. In the words of Davids, "This experience of the Spirit of God [in 1P 4:14] is what Jesus promised in Matthew 10:19–20."[29]

1 PETER 5:1–5

This section of 1P follows the pattern Peter used earlier in 2:18—3:12: instruction is given to a first group (2:18), followed by instruction to subsequent group(s) (connected by ὁμοίως ["likewise"]; 3:1, 7), culminating in instruction to all (3:8–9) before concluding with an OT quotation (3:10–12).[30] In this case, Peter addresses the "elders" (5:1–4), the "younger" (5:5a), and then all (5:5b) and concludes with a quotation of LXX Proverbs 3:34.[31]

There is significant debate concerning the identity of the "elders" and "younger." On one hand, it is clear from the passage that the "elders"

---

27. Particulalry the use of μέν . . . δέ to indicate contrast (cf. 1:20; 2:4; 3:18; 4:6; Michaels, *1 Peter*, 265).

28. Davids, *First Epistle of Peter*, 168n11.

29. Davids, *First Epistle of Peter*, 167–68.

30. Achtemeier, *1 Peter*, 321.

31. The similar pattern may suggest that this is an extension of the household codes. For such an argument, see Elliott, *1 Peter*, 812.

(πρεσβύτερος) have authority in the church. On the other hand, the apparent contrast with "younger" (νεώτερος) seems to be in relation to age. This will be discussed below in relation to the proposed parallels. For now, it is enough to say that Peter seems to consider age and authority together, presumably because the two often correlate.

After identifying himself as a fellow-elder, a fellow-witness, and a fellow-partaker in the coming glory,[32] Peter admonishes the elders to care for the flock by willingly and eagerly exercising oversight and to provide an example for others to follow. On the other hand, they must avoid using their position to abuse the flock by fleecing them financially or ruling over them tyrannically. If they do this, Peter assures them that they will receive an unfading crown of glory from the chief-shepherd.

Peter's admonition to the younger is much shorter; he simply tells them to accept the authority of the elders (5:5a). And while his admonition to all is developed more fully in vv. 6–11, his initial instruction is likewise short—act humbly in regard to one another (5b). He concludes this section with an OT reference which provides a stable foundation for all three admonitions: God opposes the proud but gives grace to the humble (Prov 3:34).

Many have recognized the signs of traditional material in this section of the epistle.[33] Even the title "fellow-elder" suggests the author would appeal to such tradition, for it represents Peter passing on shepherding advice to other shepherds.[34] The present challenge is sorting out which traditions are being used, and discerning whether Peter is explicitly drawing attention to any dominical traditions in particular. While other parallels have been proposed,[35] we will examine the following three: (1) 5:2–4 and John

---

32. Peter governs both initial descriptors with one article, suggesting that the prefix on the first may govern both (ὁ συμπρεσβύτερος καὶ μάρτυς; fellow-elder and fellow-witness) (Jobes, *1 Peter*, 301).

33. Elliott indicates that "the literary structure of 5:2–3 with its triadic arrangement, parallelism and antithetic form" suggests the use of prior tradition (Elliott, "Ministry and Church Order," 372). Nevertheless, it does not appear that Peter merely copied a prior source. Instead, this is a creative blend in line with the style of the rest of the letter (Achtemeier, *1 Peter*, 326; Elliott, *1 Peter*, 811).

34. Achtemeier notes, such a designation "serves the purpose of a contemporary application of the traditions associated with Peter as one of the apostolic leaders of the earliest Christian community to the leaders of the persecuted Christian communities of Asia Minor" (Achtemeier, *1 Peter*, 323).

35. Though some have suggested various shepherd/sheep passages as influencing Peter's text (e.g., Matt 9:36; 18:12–13; 25:32; Mark 14:27; Luke 12:32; John 10:11–18), it does not appear Peter is seeking to draw attention to any of those texts in particular, even if he does derive the overall metaphor from the richness of Jesus' words on the topic.

21:15-17; (2) 5:2-4 and Luke 22:25-30; Mark 10:42-45; Matthew 20:25-28; and (3) 5:5 and John 13:1-17.

1 Peter 5:2-4 and John 21:15-17

One of the more memorable events concerning Peter is his lake-side meeting with Jesus. It is therefore not surprising that numerous scholars have suggested that episode as a source for the present text.[36]

Table 9.3: 1 Peter 5:2-4 and John 21:15-17

1 Peter 5:2-4	John 21:15-17
<u>ποιμάνατε</u> τὸ ἐν ὑμῖν ποίμνιον τοῦ θεοῦ ἐπισκοποῦντες μὴ ἀναγκαστῶς ἀλλ' ἑκουσίως κατὰ θεόν, μηδὲ αἰσχροκερδῶς ἀλλὰ προθύμως, 3 μηδ' ὡς κατακυριεύοντες τῶν κλήρων ἀλλὰ τύποι γινόμενοι τοῦ ποιμνίου· 4 καὶ φανερωθέντος τοῦ ἀρχιποίμενος κομιεῖσθε τὸν ἀμαράντινον τῆς δόξης στέφανον.	Ὅτε οὖν ἠρίστησαν λέγει τῷ Σίμωνι Πέτρῳ ὁ Ἰησοῦς· Σίμων Ἰωάννου, ἀγαπᾷς με πλέον τούτων; λέγει αὐτῷ· ναὶ κύριε, σὺ οἶδας ὅτι φιλῶ σε. λέγει αὐτῷ· βόσκε τὰ ἀρνία μου. 16 λέγει αὐτῷ πάλιν δεύτερον· Σίμων Ἰωάννου, ἀγαπᾷς με; λέγει αὐτῷ· ναὶ κύριε, σὺ οἶδας ὅτι φιλῶ σε. λέγει αὐτῷ· <u>ποίμαινε</u> τὰ πρόβατά μου. 17 λέγει αὐτῷ τὸ τρίτον· Σίμων Ἰωάννου, φιλεῖς με; ἐλυπήθη ὁ Πέτρος ὅτι εἶπεν αὐτῷ τὸ τρίτον· φιλεῖς με; καὶ λέγει αὐτῷ· κύριε, πάντα σὺ οἶδας, σὺ γινώσκεις ὅτι φιλῶ σε. λέγει αὐτῷ [ὁ Ἰησοῦς]· βόσκε τὰ πρόβατά μου.

While the agreement between these passages is based chiefly on ideological and contextual factors,[37] there is one notable lexical agreement.[38] The relatively rare shared term verb ποιμαίνω (shepherd; eleven occurrences in the NT) is used as an imperative in only these two passages. Further, outside these passages only one other verse (Acts 20:28) uses the word positively in

---

36. In addition to the sources below, see also Bigg, *Epistles of St. Peter*, 188; Foster, *Literary Relations*, 529; Michaels, *1 Peter*, 282, 286-87; Gundry, "'Verba Christi' in I Peter," 346.

37. Tenney overstates the case when he says that Peter's words are "almost a verbatim repetition" of Jesus' words (Tenney, "Possible Parallels," 375).

38. Another lexical agreement is argued for by Elliott. He believes John 21:18, where Jesus speaks about Peter when he was younger (νέος), is meaningfully connected to the "younger" of the flock, for Peter uses νέος to reference them as well. As for John 21, Elliott sees in it a contrast between Peter's impetuousness in youth and the difference in his later maturity (Elliott, "Ministry and Church Order," 383). But, as Carson argues, the likely contrast is not between the impetuousness of youth and the maturity of age, but rather the freedom to do what one wants and the contrast with losing control of one's life even to the point of death (Carson, *Gospel according to John*, 679-80).

reference to a leader of God's people guiding the followers of Jesus.[39] Thus, it is likely, when this lexical agreement is combined with the ideological agreements noted below, Peter's readers would have been drawn to this tradition.

Elliott indicates that there are "striking parallels" between these passages, and lists nine of them:[40] (1) Peter is in both; (2) there is a shepherd/sheep analogy in both; (3) both have clothing metaphors (John 21:18; 1P 5:5); (4) both speak of discipleship; 5) both refer to the Lord's return (21:22; 5:4); (6) a common glory/glorification motif is in both (21:19; 5:1, 4); (7) both speak of authority and rank; (8) both have connections with John 13;[41] (9) and both have connections with Mark 10:25-45 and parallels. While Elliott's parallels are not of equal value,[42] he has made a helpful cumulative case for a connection between these passages.

The strongest argument for an echo to the tradition recorded in John 21, however, remains that—granted the audience knew the tradition—Peter's audience could not help but recall such a significant event. Nor could an author, whether Peter or one writing in his name, write without an awareness of the event. Further, the present text suggests the presence of tradition. Throughout 1P, the author has not drawn attention to himself, yet he does so here (συμ-πρεσβύτερος). The best explanation is that he is drawing his readers to consider the intersection of his words and his life.

What is the significance of this passage when considered in light of Jesus' encounter with Peter? First, there is rich import to the chain of testimony which began with Jesus was passed to Peter and is now being handed down to these elders. As Selwyn notes, the command to shepherd the flock "would come with special force from one who had received Christ's last charge to do this very thing."[43] Further, that Peter is a fellow-sharer in the glory that is to be revealed suggests that much of the reward promised to him is likewise promised to these shepherds.

Second, the echo helps us make sense of the connection between 4:19 and 5:1. Interpreters have expressed puzzlement over the apparent abrupt

---

39. Additionally, Jude 12 references false teachers who are described as ποιμαίνοντες (feeding themselves).

40. Elliott, "Ministry and Church Order," 383-84.

41. "In John both sections concern the 'beloved disciple,' and both have to do with meal settings. 1 Pt 5,1-5 is related to Jn 13 through their mutual coincidence with Luke 22,24ff. which also involves a meal or eucharistic setting" (Elliott, "Ministry and Church Order," 384).

42. Notably, the third and sixth are suspect since the clothing metaphor and the glory theme are handled differently in the two texts.

43. Selwyn, *First Epistle of St. Peter*, 31.

shift from suffering to the exhortation of the elders.⁴⁴ John 21 may provide an explanation. Directly following the restoration of Peter, Jesus speaks of the suffering Peter would endure for the sake of Jesus (vv. 18–19). By drawing the reader to this life episode, Peter reveals that as he anticipates the coming "suffering according to God's will," he too "entrusts himself to a faithful creator while doing good." In 5:1, Peter indicates that he is a fellow-witness, which Davids rightly suggests "is indicating that not only does he talk about Christ's sufferings, but as in 4:13, that he also identifies with them as a result of his witness."⁴⁵ Thus, the connection between 4:19 and 5:1 is personal. Peter encourages the elders—those who are most likely to endure suffering—on the basis that he is a fellow-elder and a fellow-sufferer with them.

A third significance comes from Jesus' three-fold question to Peter: Do you love me? Only after affirming that he loved Jesus did Jesus call Peter to shepherd the flock. Likewise, then, the motivation for other elders in the service of God must be love for the Lord. Perhaps this is at the root of Peter's commands to shepherd willingly and eagerly, for those who serve out of love for the Lord will not do so out of compulsion or for improper gain; rather, they do it because the Lord desires it of them ("as God would have you do it"; κατὰ θεόν).

1 Peter 5:2–4 and Luke 22:25–30; Mark 10:42–45; Matthew 20:25–28

In his instruction to the elders, Peter indicates that they are not to "lord it over" those in their charge. This line, along with a number of other similarities with Luke 22:25–30 (Mark 10:42–45; Matt 20:25–28) suggest to many that Peter is deliberately reflecting the teaching of the Lord here.⁴⁶

---

44. The textual variant οὖν was present at the beginning of the verse in NA27 but was dropped in NA28. Whether the connective is present or absent, however, the connection between the passages is challenging (Spicq, *Épîtres de Saint Pierre*, 162).

45. Davids, *First Epistle of Peter*, 177.

46. Along with those noted in the comments below, see also Brox, *Erste Petrusbrief*, 230; Jobes, *1 Peter*, 305; Spicq, "Ia Petri et Le Témoignage," 45.

Table 9.4: 1 Peter 5:2-4 and Luke 22:25-30; Mark 10:42-45; Matthew 20:25-28

1 Peter 5:2-4	Luke 22:25-30	Mark 10:42-45	Matthew 20:25-28
ποιμάνατε τὸ ἐν ὑμῖν ποίμνιον τοῦ θεοῦ ἐπισκοποῦντες μὴ ἀναγκαστῶς ἀλλ' ἑκουσίως κατὰ θεόν, μηδὲ αἰσχροκερδῶς ἀλλὰ προθύμως, 3 μηδ' ὡς κατακυριεύοντες τῶν κλήρων ἀλλὰ τύποι γινόμενοι τοῦ ποιμνίου· 4 καὶ φανερωθέντος τοῦ ἀρχιποίμενος κομιεῖσθε τὸν ἀμαράντινον τῆς δόξης στέφανον.	ὁ δὲ εἶπεν αὐτοῖς· οἱ βασιλεῖς τῶν ἐθνῶν κυριεύουσιν αὐτῶν καὶ οἱ ἐξουσιάζοντες αὐτῶν εὐεργέται καλοῦνται. 26 ὑμεῖς δὲ οὐχ οὕτως, ἀλλ' ὁ μείζων ἐν ὑμῖν γινέσθω ὡς ὁ νεώτερος καὶ ὁ ἡγούμενος ὡς ὁ διακονῶν. 27 τίς γὰρ μείζων, ὁ ἀνακείμενος ἢ ὁ διακονῶν; οὐχὶ ὁ ἀνακείμενος; ἐγὼ δὲ ἐν μέσῳ ὑμῶν εἰμι ὡς ὁ διακονῶν. 28 Ὑμεῖς δέ ἐστε οἱ διαμεμενηκότες μετ' ἐμοῦ ἐν τοῖς πειρασμοῖς μου· 29 κἀγὼ διατίθεμαι ὑμῖν καθὼς διέθετό μοι ὁ πατήρ μου βασιλείαν, 30 ἵνα ἔσθητε καὶ πίνητε ἐπὶ τῆς τραπέζης μου ἐν τῇ βασιλείᾳ μου, καὶ καθήσεσθε ἐπὶ θρόνων τὰς δώδεκα φυλὰς κρίνοντες τοῦ Ἰσραήλ.	καὶ προσκαλεσάμενος αὐτοὺς ὁ Ἰησοῦς λέγει αὐτοῖς· οἴδατε ὅτι οἱ δοκοῦντες ἄρχειν τῶν ἐθνῶν κατακυριεύουσιν αὐτῶν καὶ οἱ μεγάλοι αὐτῶν κατεξουσιάζουσιν αὐτῶν. 43 οὐχ οὕτως δέ ἐστιν ἐν ὑμῖν, ἀλλ' ὃς ἂν θέλῃ μέγας γενέσθαι ἐν ὑμῖν ἔσται ὑμῶν διάκονος, 44 καὶ ὃς ἂν θέλῃ ἐν ὑμῖν εἶναι πρῶτος ἔσται πάντων δοῦλος· 45 καὶ γὰρ ὁ υἱὸς τοῦ ἀνθρώπου οὐκ ἦλθεν διακονηθῆναι ἀλλὰ διακονῆσαι καὶ δοῦναι τὴν ψυχὴν αὐτοῦ λύτρον ἀντὶ πολλῶν	25 ὁ δὲ Ἰησοῦς προσκαλεσάμενος αὐτοὺς εἶπεν· οἴδατε ὅτι οἱ ἄρχοντες τῶν ἐθνῶν κατακυριεύουσιν αὐτῶν καὶ οἱ μεγάλοι κατεξουσιάζουσιν αὐτῶν. 26 οὐχ οὕτως ἔσται ἐν ὑμῖν, ἀλλ' ὃς ἐὰν θέλῃ ἐν ὑμῖν μέγας γενέσθαι ἔσται ὑμῶν διάκονος, 27 καὶ ὃς ἂν θέλῃ ἐν ὑμῖν εἶναι πρῶτος ἔσται ὑμῶν δοῦλος· 28 ὥσπερ ὁ υἱὸς τοῦ ἀνθρώπου οὐκ ἦλθεν διακονηθῆναι ἀλλὰ διακονῆσαι καὶ δοῦναι τὴν ψυχὴν αὐτοῦ λύτρον ἀντὶ πολλῶν.

A chief difficulty in tracing the influence of Jesus' words on this text is the diversity of traditions in the Gospels.[47] For instance, it is clear that there is a division between the saying as presented in Matthew and Mark with that as presented in Luke. In regard to the temporal placement of the saying, Matthew/Mark have it in the midst of Jesus' Judean ministry following a question from James and John about rank in the kingdom. In the Lukan account, the teaching is part of the passion narrative.

In regard to the content of the saying, there is both agreement and difference. First, the verb describing how the Gentiles lead is different between the accounts (Matt/Mark: κατακυριεύω; Luke: κυριεύω). Second, the contrasting illustrations are different. In Matthew/Mark, Jesus says those who wish to be great (μέγας) must be servants (διάκονος), and those who

---

47. See Elliott, "Ministry and Church Order," 374-75.

wish to be first (πρῶτος) must be a slave (δοῦλος) to all. On the other hand, Luke indicates that the greatest (μέγας) must be like the youngest (νέος), and the leaders (ἡγέομαι) like those who serve (διακονέω). Third, while both passages give Jesus as an example, they conclude differently. In Matthew/Mark, Jesus concludes the teaching with a reference to his sacrificial death. In Luke, Jesus provides an analogy of his service (Jesus is a Master who serves his servants at the table) and concludes with a declaration of the future reward to the disciples.

It is not expressly clear which tradition Peter is reflecting here. As Elliott notes, "Despite the divergences between Mk-Mt and Lk, 1 Pt 5,1 ff. has affinities with both—and exactly there where they differ!"[48] In agreement with Matthew/Mark, Peter uses κατακυριεύω, which only occurs once outside this tradition (Acts 19:16), where it is used in an entirely different sense.[49] In agreement with Luke, Peter speaks of the νεώτερος. Further, Luke's conclusion concerning the return of the Lord with rewards is similar to Peter's encouragement concerning the coming of the Chief Shepherd.[50]

Davids concludes that the affinity and difference with both versions of the saying indicates that Peter is reflecting this tradition, though not directly from any written Gospel.[51] Elliott agrees. After noting that this text in 1P and the Jesus saying are "close in language (κατακυριεύω, Mk 10:42/ Mt 20:25; . . . νεώτερος, Lk 22:26), form (contrast between negative and positive), and point (model of conduct: Jesus)," Elliott concludes that the similarities are due not to literary dependence but to the traditions tracing back to Jesus.[52]

While we cannot be dogmatic, in light of the agreements above, it appears that Peter knew a tradition that included the compound κατακυριεύω like Matthew/Mark, yet also included the ending which is attested in Luke's Gospel. Accordingly, we will consider resonances between 1P and these elements of the saying, though we will not appeal to the broader context (e.g., the Last Supper in Luke or the question by James and John in Matthew/ Mark).[53]

---

48. Elliott, "Ministry and Church Order," 375.

49. Acts 19:6 speaks of a demonic spirit which physically overpowered (κατακυριεύω) the seven sons of Sceva.

50. This similarity further reinforces the fact that Peter likely knew a tradition that precisely matches none of the Synoptics but includes elements from all of them (Elliott, "Ministry and Church Order," 386).

51. Davids, *First Epistle of Peter*, 180n118.

52. Elliott, *1 Peter*, 830.

53. Gundry argues that whether one considers the setting of the saying as following the question of James and John (as in Matt/Mark) or at the last supper (as in Luke),

Two exegetical issues are clarified when we recognize the dominical reference. First, Achtemeier draws attention to the fact that Peter uses the particle ὡς in two primary ways throughout the epistle, and it is possible that either is used here.[54] It can be translated "like" or "as" and would in this instance be translated as, "do not shepherd as lording over those in your charge." It can alternatively be translated "in the manner of" or "functioning as" and would in this instance be translated as "do not shepherd by functioning like those who lord it over their underlings."[55] The dominical reference gives preference to the latter, for in Jesus' teaching, he warns not to be like the world's leaders.[56] This reading is further confirmed in that it allows the particle to govern the two participles in the same way.

Elliott has drawn attention to a second exegetical issue that he claims is partially resolved by means of the reflection of dominical teaching—the identity of the "young" (νεώτερος). For Elliott, one key to understanding Peter's use of this word is the use of the word in Luke, which poetically parallels "one who serves" with νεώτερος.[57] He concludes that, in early church teaching, the νεώτερος were "designated members of the community who were differentiated from and subordinate to the elders."[58] While Elliott goes further and suggests more speculatively that these individuals were newly baptized members, such a position goes beyond the evidence of 1P.[59] It is enough here to recognize that just as Jesus used the word to reference those without power and authority (i.e., those who were not leaders),[60] so Peter does likewise. Such a reading is in line with the observations of Vahrenhorst, who notes that it is "probable that 1P thinks of all church members who have no leading function."[61]

Peter's presence in the tradition is significant and gives further credibility to the conclusion that the tradition is referenced here (Gundry, "'Verba Christi' in I Peter," 346).

54. Achtemeier, *1 Peter*, 327.
55. This is Achtemeier's translation (Achtemeier, *1 Peter*, 320).
56. Achtemeier, *1 Peter*, 327n95. Contra, Michaels, *1 Peter*, 285.
57. Elliott, "Ministry and Church Order," 376.
58. Elliott, "Ministry and Church Order," 377.
59. Elliott, "Ministry and Church Order," 379, 385. For a critique of Elliott, see Brox, *Erste Petrusbrief*, 233.
60. Stein notes that the νεώτερος in Luke represent "people who possess the least claim for 'ruling over' others" (Stein, *Luke*, 549; cf. Green, *Gospel of Luke*, 769).
61. He continues, "They would then be—regardless of their actual age—called νεώτεροι, because this is the logical counter-concept to πρεσβύτεροι" (translated from, "Es ist demnach wahrscheinlich, dass der 1Petr in der Tat an alle Gemeindeglieder denkt, die keine Leitungsfunktion innehaben. Sie würden dann - unabhängig von ihrem tatsächlichen Lebensalter - *neōteroi* genannt, weil dies der logische Gegenbegriff zu *presbyteroi* ist" [Vahrenhorst, *Erste Brief Des Petrus*, 192]).

Outside of its exegetical assistance, the allusion has a significant rhetorical effect. Peter commands the elders not to be domineering in leadership but to set an example. Why does Peter speak of being an example? Perhaps he assumes his readers will recall the dominical teaching and connect the dots. Jesus indicates that the type of leadership they are to exercise is servant-leadership: the "greatest" do not consider themselves better than those they lead, and when they have a position of authority, they exercise it through service. In both lines of tradition, Jesus offers himself as the example to follow.[62] Thus, when Peter calls the elders not to lead domineeringly and to alternatively be an example, they would recognize immediately that they are to model Jesus. Such a reading is reinforced when Jesus is referred to as the Chief-Shepherd (ἀρχιποίμην; 4:4), for how should the shepherds act except how their leader acts? In sum, when Peter says the under-shepherds must "be an example," such a command brings to light the full-scope of Jesus' self-sacrificial way of life and provides the paradigm for successful leadership.[63]

1 Peter 5:5 and John 13:1–17

Jesus' self-imposed humiliation of washing his disciples' feet (John 13:1–17) is a memorable tradition, and many scholars have suggested that it served as a source for Peter's epistle.[64] But the similarity between the account recorded in John 13 and 1P 5:5 is not based on lexical similarity. Indeed, Peter's word choice (ἐγκομβόομαι) is peculiar, and has been the source of some speculation.[65] It has been defined as "to put or tie something on oneself,"[66] but the word never occurs in the LXX or the Apostolic Fathers and only occurs here in the NT. Achtemeier notes that ἐγκομβόομαι likely refers to "a garment or

---

62. The Matthew/Mark tradition emphasizes Jesus' self-sacrifice even to the point of death. The Lukan text, while not directly connecting to Jesus' sacrificial service, nevertheless expresses the humility of the Son of God to serve those who should logically serve Him.

63. For this reason, Michaels says, "Peter's emphasis on servanthood is wholly consistent with the teaching attributed to Jesus in Mark 10:42–45//Matt 20:25–28//Luke 22:25–27, especially when account is taken of his appeal to Jesus as example in 2:21–23" (Michaels, *1 Peter*, 285).

64. In addition to the sources noted below, see Kelly, *Peter and Jude*, 206; Gundry, "'Verba Christi' in I Peter," 345; Best, *1 Peter*, 172; Spicq, "Ia Petri et Le Témoignage," 45; Cranfield, *First Epistle of Peter*, 117; Witherington, *Letters and Homilies for Hellenized Christians*, 232; Tenney, "Possible Parallels," 376.

65. Harris argued that it referred to religious clothing, but his position has not been widely accepted (Harris, "Religious Meaning," 131–39).

66. Bauer et al., BDAG, s.v. "ἐγκομβόομαι," 274.

apron a slave tied over other garments in order to perform certain menial tasks."[67] Similarly, Elliott concludes that "the verb denotes the binding of an apron, as done by slaves in performance of their domestic duties, including washing the feet of guests."[68]

According to these descriptions, the word provides an apt metaphor for Jesus' action in tying up his garments in order to wash the disciple's feet (John 13:1-17).[69] But Peter's text certainly does not reflect the wording of John's text (and therefore there is no table for comparison),[70] leading some to reject the allusion.[71]

Nevertheless, recognizing an allusion to the teaching of Jesus does not require a direct lexical connection with John's Gospel. As Davids notes, "If Peter the apostle is the author (even in the sense that his thought stands behind the work of Silvanus), and John 13:1-17. refers to a historical incident, Peter might well remember it and thus refer to it in complete independence of the Fourth Gospel."[72] Of course, as we have argued throughout the thesis, anyone writing in Peter's name would likely seek to connect the important events of Peter's life to this letter as well.

The following ideological agreements suggest a common tradition behind Peter's text and the Johannine tradition.[73] First, both speak of putting on a servant's garment in humility.[74] Second, both passages address something all members of the community are to model. Third, both contexts speak explicitly about Jesus.[75] Fourth, 1P 5:3 alludes to following the

67. Achtemeier, *1 Peter*, 333.
68. Elliott, *1 Peter*, 846.
69. "By his choice of metaphor, Peter is no doubt reflecting on the scene in the Upper Room" (Hillyer, *1 and 2 Peter, Jude*, 144).
70. Michaels notes that Peter knows the metaphor used by John, for Peter used it in 1:13. Therefore, it is quite likely that Peter's knowledge of this event does not come through John's Gospel (Michaels, *1 Peter*, 290).
71. Achtemeier, *1 Peter*, 333.
72. Davids, *First Epistle of Peter*, 185n36.
73. Elliott, who assumes a Petrine tradition behind the epistle, notes its presence here: "The prominent role of Peter in this scene (vv 6-11) along with the accent on humility in this Petrine letter (see also 3:8) and its call for emulating the example of Jesus the servant Lord (2:21-23; 3:18; 4:1) suggest that a stress on mutual humility grounded in Jesus' humility (see also Mark 10:35-45 par.; and 1 Pet 5:3) was one of the several features of the tradition associated with Peter in the early Church" (Elliott, *1 Peter*, 846).
74. This point is complicated by the lack of lexical data we have on ἐγκομβόομαι. Nevertheless, as the commentators above have noted, it seems best to understand the word in this way. Jesus literally takes a towel, while Peter uses a metaphor. Nevertheless, the metaphor is based on Jesus' historical action.
75. One of the hints that an allusion is present is the explicit mentioning of Jesus in the narrow context.

example of Jesus (see above), and the tradition recorded by John indicates that Jesus drew attention to himself as an example to follow (13:14).[76] Fifth, both passages address the reversal of roles of master and servant.[77]

These agreements suggest that while Peter did not have John's Gospel as a guide, Peter knew this tradition in some form and alludes to it. As elsewhere, the allusion to the words of Jesus are significant. The use of this tradition reinforces the necessity of the community to act in humility to one another, for if Jesus did this, how could they do any less for one another? Consequently, Jesus provides the example, not only for the shepherds (5:3), but also for all of the sheep. In the words of Jesus, if he their Lord and teacher has done these things, then they ought to do the same for one another. Further, it is possible that Peter knew a tradition similar to John 13, which included Jesus' statement, "If you know these things, you are blessed (μακάριος) if you do them" (13:17). We have already noted Peter's appreciation for this dominical term (e.g., 1:6, 8, 10), and it is possible that Peter is once more reflecting on what a blessed life looks like.

1 PETER 5:6-11

These verses are the conclusion to the body and consist of what initially appear to be loosely related exhortation. There are four commands given which are accompanied with a reason given for obedience: (1) be humble so that you may be exalted; (2) cast your care on God because you know he cares for you;[78] (3) be actively watchful because the enemy prowls like a lion seeking someone to devour; and (4) resist the enemy for you know the same trials are being experienced by Christians throughout the world. After these commands, Peter concludes with an encouragement concerning the shortness of the trials they face, the goodness of the God who has called

---

76. The fourth and fifth points appear to confirm Elliott's assessment that "1 Pt 5,1–5 is related to Jn 13 through their mutual coincidence with Lk 22,24ff" (Elliott, "Ministry and Church Order," 384). Interestingly, Jeremias argues that Luke's text is a development of the tradition of foot washing (Jeremias, "Lössegeld Für Viele," 225).

77. In John, Jesus says, "servants are not greater than their master" (15:20). In 1P 5:3 Peter echoes the teaching of Jesus from Luke 22:26 (see above): "For who is greater, the one who is at the table or the one who serves? Is it not the one at the table? But I am among you as one who serves." In John, Jesus reverses the roles through service, and in Luke Jesus speaks about his activity in reversing the role through service.

78. As Elliott notes, "cast" (ἐπιρίψαντες) appears to be another imperatival participle (Elliott, 1 Peter, 851). That it is participial is likely explained by its close connection to the prior imperative (ταπεινώθητε).

them, and the blessedness of God's promise to "restore, support, strengthen, and establish" them. The body appropriately closes with a short doxology.

While the exhortations of this section may at first appear uniquely fitted for the challenging situation of Peter's audience, the similarity between this passage and James 4:6–10 suggests that Peter is echoing early church tradition (see the comparison chart below). Indeed, Kelly notes that the correspondences between these passages are "remarkable."[79]

Despite the substantial similarities, it is clear that Peter and James have used the material differently.[80] While both start with the same LXX quotation, the other similarities are not in order, nor are they stated in precisely the same way. Further, the overall message of each passage is different: Peter's immediate concern is believers who are enduring trials of faith, while James' immediate concern is believers in their relation with one another. On the basis of such differences, Achtemeier concludes that "If there was a common tradition, . . . it was either very loose in form, or one or the other of the authors has taken great liberty with it."[81] Others have also found a common tradition a possibility,[82] and Davids specifies that "the common tradition in James and 1 Peter is an application of Jesus' saying by the church."[83]

Since we are not able to recover traditions now lost (if there were such traditions), it seems best to proceed with the assumption that even if Peter and James are referencing a shared tradition that is derivative of the JT, the reliance of that tradition on the words of Jesus would be recognized by those who heard the tradition.[84] Accordingly, we will examine the following dominical teachings and their influence on 1P: 5:6 and Matthew 23:12; Luke 14:11 (cf. 18:14); 5:7 and Matthew 6:25–34; Luke 12:22–31; 5:8–9a and Luke 22:31–32.[85]

---

79. Kelly, *Peter and Jude*, 207. Three similarities stand out: both have a verbatim quotation of LXX Prov 3:34; both speak of humility leading to exaltation; and both speak of resisting the devil.

80. For more developed consideration of the intersection of the passages, see Elliott, *1 Peter*, 849n731; Metzner, *Rezeption*, 95–99.

81. Achtemeier, *1 Peter*, 337.

82. Michaels, *1 Peter*, 294. See also Schreiner, *1, 2 Peter*, 240.

83. Davids, *First Epistle of Peter*, 187n3.

84. Marshall notes that the links with the teaching of Jesus in this passage suggest that "Christian teaching in this area was built up on the basis of the tradition of his sayings" (Marshall, *1 Peter*, 168n1).

85. Other potential parallels are listed in the appendix. One notable proposed parallel is made by Metzner in regard to the temptation of Jesus (particularly Matt 4:1–11), but while the parallel is suggestive, it falls short of the ideological and lexical standard in this study (Metzner, *Die Rezeption*, 99–103).

1 Peter 5:6 and Matthew 23:12; Luke 14:11 (cf. Luke 18:14)

Michaels expresses surprise that Gundry did not identify this as one of the examples of Peter reflecting the words of the Lord.[86] And while a number of commentators have made the suggestion,[87] a developed defense of the echo has not yet been made. Thus, we will seek to fill that gap by making the argument that Peter is reflecting these words of Jesus.

Table 9.5: 1 Peter 5:6 and Matthew 23:12; Luke 14:11 (cf. 18:14)

1 Peter 5:6	Matthew 23:12	Luke 14:11	Luke 18:14
<u>Ταπεινώθητε</u> οὖν ὑπὸ τὴν κραταιὰν χεῖρα τοῦ θεοῦ, ἵνα ὑμᾶς <u>ὑψώσῃ</u> ἐν καιρῷ	ὅστις δὲ <u>ὑψώσει</u> ἑαυτὸν <u>ταπεινωθήσεται</u> καὶ ὅστις <u>ταπεινώσει</u> ἑαυτὸν <u>ὑψωθήσεται</u>.	ὅτι πᾶς ὁ ὑψῶν ἑαυτὸν <u>ταπεινωθήσεται</u>, καὶ ὁ <u>ταπεινῶν</u> ἑαυτὸν <u>ὑψωθήσεται</u>.	λέγω ὑμῖν, κατέβη οὗτος δεδικαιωμένος εἰς τὸν οἶκον αὐτοῦ παρ' ἐκεῖνον· ὅτι πᾶς ὁ ὑψῶν ἑαυτὸν <u>ταπεινωθήσεται</u>, ὁ δὲ <u>ταπεινῶν</u> ἑαυτὸν <u>ὑψωθήσεται</u>.

The agreement between the verses is both lexical and ideological. Lexically, both share the same contrasting terms, ταπεινόω and ὑψόω. Both terms occur less than twenty times in the NT, and they occur together in only six texts (Matt 23:12; Luke 14:11; 18:14; 2 Cor 11:7; Jas 4:10; 1P 5:6). And while the mood of the verbs differs, the change from the divine passive to the imperative actually points to dependence on this dominical teaching.[88] That is, Peter's command for humility is based upon Jesus' proclamation that those who humble themselves will be exalted.

The ideological similarities are evident, yet the theme of humility leading to exaltation is not unique to Jesus. Best cites Selwyn's comment that the idea is "thoroughly Hebraic"[89] and concludes, "there is no necessary dependence on the words of Jesus."[90] In an earlier article, Best noted that 1P links "the saying directly to an OT text; the authority for it is found in the OT and not in the words of Jesus."[91]

But granting that Peter has explicitly referenced LXX Proverbs 3:34, Peter's application departs from the language of the Proverb and matches

---

86. Michaels, *1 Peter*, 295–96.

87. Marshall, *1 Peter*, 168n1; Powers, *1, 2 Peter and Jude*, 149; Selwyn, *First Epistle of St. Peter*, 235; Davids, *First Epistle of Peter*, 187n3; Spicq, "Ia Petri et Le Témoignage," 44; Goppelt, *Commentary on I Peter*, 357–58; Hiebert, *First Peter*, 294.

88. Goppelt, *Commentary on I Peter*, 357–58n5.

89. Selwyn, *First Epistle of St. Peter*, 235.

90. Best, *1 Peter*, 173.

91. Best, "I Peter and the Gospel Tradition," 107. Cf. Michaels, *1 Peter*, 295–96.

precisely the language of Jesus' teaching. Thus, even if the idea is "thoroughly Hebraic," the way it is fashioned is distinctively dominical. Accordingly, in agreement with Schreiner, "there is no reason to doubt that Peter recalled the teaching of his Lord here."[92] Indeed, we will argue for two other dominical echoes in this same short paraenetic section, which will strengthen the case for this echo.[93]

That this saying is reflected in three substantially different contexts in the life of Jesus suggests that it is a saying Jesus was remembered to have spoken in various contexts. Accordingly, it is impossible to determine which, if any in particular, Peter is drawing attention to.[94] Nevertheless, each illustrates the saying by providing an example.[95] The influence of this saying on the Petrine context is chiefly to draw the reader to consider Jesus. This happens in two ways. First, the teaching is doubly reinforced by being given in both the OT Scriptures and from Jesus. Peter could have simply quoted the OT or alluded to Jesus, but by doing both, Peter asserts that this teaching is consistent with God's working in the past and remains important to God's people today.

The second way the teaching points to Jesus is by connecting the teaching of Jesus to the life of Jesus. Achtemeier notes that "The author draws here on a commonplace in biblical thought, the contrast between lowliness and exaltation, a contrast that, because it characterized both *a number of sayings of Jesus as well as his life, particularly his death and subsequent resurrection*, became normative for Christians."[96] Just as Jesus did not lord it over those in his charge (5:3), and just as Jesus clothed himself with a servant's towel to serve (5:5), so he is the chief example of the humbling that leads to exaltation. Indeed, these prior acts presaged the ultimate humility (the cross), which resulted in the highest exaltation (3:22). Thus, in this way also, Jesus left an example so that the readers "should follow in his steps" (2:21).

---

92. Schreiner, *1, 2 Peter*, 239.

93. That Matthew has this saying directly following instruction concerning leadership ("The greatest among you will be your servant"; 23:11) further reinforces the case for this echo. It also may suggest that Peter knew the tradition in a form similar to the Matthean form.

94. That Matthew's Gospel contains a phrase ("The greatest among you will be your servant") which is also present in the context of a tradition Peter echoed in 5:3 may suggest a tradition closer to that of Matthew.

95. Matthew provides a negative example in regard to the Scribes and Pharisees (23:1–12), while Luke provides a positive example of a repentant tax-collector (18:9–14). Luke also presents Jesus' reflection on choosing a seat at a feast (14:7–11), which provides both a negative and positive example of the saying.

96. Achtemeier, *1 Peter*, 338. Emphasis added.

1 Peter 5:7 and Matthew 6:25-34; Luke 12:22-31

Peter's second command—cast your anxiety on the Lord—is closely related to the first command,[97] and many have found it to likewise reflect Jesus' words.[98] Selwyn thinks that Peter's admonition is "no doubt" based upon Jesus' teaching.[99] And Cranfield, likewise, believes there is "no doubt the memory of Christ's teaching was in Peter's mind."[100]

Table 9.6: 1 Peter 5:7 and Matthew 6:31-33; Luke 12:22, 29-31

1 Peter 5:7	Matthew 6:31-33	Luke 12:22, 29-31
πᾶσαν τὴν <u>μέριμναν</u> ὑμῶν ἐπιρίψαντες ἐπ' αὐτόν, ὅτι αὐτῷ μέλει περὶ ὑμῶν.	Μὴ οὖν <u>μεριμνήσητε</u> λέγοντες· τί φάγωμεν; ἤ· τί πίωμεν; ἤ· τί περιβαλώμεθα; 32 πάντα γὰρ ταῦτα τὰ ἔθνη ἐπιζητοῦσιν· οἶδεν γὰρ ὁ πατὴρ ὑμῶν ὁ οὐράνιος ὅτι χρῄζετε τούτων ἁπάντων. 33 ζητεῖτε δὲ πρῶτον τὴν βασιλείαν [τοῦ θεοῦ] καὶ τὴν δικαιοσύνην αὐτοῦ, καὶ ταῦτα πάντα προστεθήσεται ὑμῖν.	διὰ τοῦτο λέγω ὑμῖν· μὴ <u>μεριμνᾶτε</u> τῇ ψυχῇ τί φάγητε, μηδὲ τῷ σώματι τί ἐνδύσησθε. ... καὶ ὑμεῖς μὴ ζητεῖτε τί φάγητε καὶ τί πίητε καὶ μὴ μετεωρίζεσθε· 30 ταῦτα γὰρ πάντα τὰ ἔθνη τοῦ κόσμου ἐπιζητοῦσιν, ὑμῶν δὲ ὁ πατὴρ οἶδεν ὅτι χρῄζετε τούτων. 31 πλὴν ζητεῖτε τὴν βασιλείαν αὐτοῦ, καὶ ταῦτα προστεθήσεται ὑμῖν.

This teaching is found within the Sermon on the Mount, a tradition Peter has shown to reflect elsewhere. Further, McKnight speaks of the "picturesque words of Jesus" in this teaching,[101] rightly implying that this is a type of teaching that is likely to be remembered, valued, and passed on in the early church. The agreement between the passages is both lexical and ideological, though leaning to the latter. The sole lexical agreement is the shared root μεριμ-.[102] And though Peter uses the noun form (μέριμνα), while Jesus uses the verb form (μεριμνάω), the commonality would likely not be missed.

In light of the above, Green is wrong to say that "linguistic parallels are practically nonexistent." Nevertheless, we agree with him when he notes

---

97. The participle borrows the imperatival force of the prior command.

98. E.g., Goppelt, *Commentary on I Peter*, 356; Green, *1 Peter*, 179; McKnight, *1 Peter*, 277; Senior and Harrington, *1 Peter, Jude, and 2 Peter*, 150; Metzner, *Rezeption*, 105; Spicq, "Ia Petri et Le Témoignage," 43; Maier, "Jesustradition," 102.

99. Selwyn, *First Epistle of St. Peter*, 236.

100. Cranfield, *First Epistle of Peter*, 118.

101. McKnight, *1 Peter*, 277.

102. That the passages have only this lexical commonality makes Selwyn's comment concerning Peter's "striking exactness to the teaching of Christ in the Sermon on the Mount" an overstatement (Selwyn, *First Epistle of St. Peter*, 78).

that "conceptually there are numerous points of contact."[103] First both passages speak about the incongruity of Jesus-followers being anxious. Second, both make the distinctive point that the anxiety is resolved by the recognition that God cares for his followers.[104]

A challenge to seeing a dominical reference here, however, is the fact that Peter appears to be referencing an OT text.[105] Achtemeier, for instance, notes that Peter's reflection on the words of Jesus questionable because of the similarity to LXX Psalm 54:23.[106] It should be noted, though, that the similarity to the LXX is not exact (as Peter shows he is capable of elsewhere—e.g., 5:5). The word order is different, and Peter makes the referent θεός (God; from 5:6), whereas the LXX has κύριος (Lord). Further, 5:7b does not derive from the LXX passage, but is almost certainly sourced in the teaching of Jesus. It is for this reason that numerous commentators have noted that while there is lexical similarity to the OT passage, the ideological core of the passage derives from the teaching of Jesus.[107]

It is possible that Jesus' teachings concerning the cares of this life were considered together by those who repeatedly heard Jesus teaching. If so, the memorable element of the Sermon on the Mount/Plain may have been combined with three other important texts. First, Luke 12:11 (cf. Matt 10:19; Luke 21:14), a passage we argued Peter reflected in 3:13–17 and 4:14, says, "When they bring you before the synagogues, the rulers, and the authorities, do not worry (μεριμνάω) about how you are to defend yourselves or what you are to say." There are clear connections to Jesus' teaching here,[108]

---

103. Green, *1 Peter*, 179.

104. Davids notes that Jesus "makes precisely the same point" as Peter in regard to God's care for his disciples (Davids, *First Epistle of Peter*, 188).

105. Though some commentators have drawn attention to Wisdom 12:13 as a potential source for the latter half of verse 7, the similarities are not particularly strong (Achtemeier, *1 Peter*, 340n57).

106. Achtemeier, *1 Peter*, 337. See also Boring, who says, "While the thought is similar to that of the Sermon on the Mount, once again 1 Peter's teaching is not based on a saying of Jesus but on a biblical text: Ps 55:22" (Boring, *1 Peter*, 175).

107. Consider the following: "Yet if the language is close to LXX Psalm 54, the intent of the saying of Jesus is surely to be found here as well" (Achtemeier, *1 Peter*, 340). "The participial phrase derives straight from Ps. 55:22.... The passage recalls, and probably depends on, the community's remembrance of our Lord's advice (Mt. 6:25–34)" (Kelly, *Peter and Jude*, 208). "The actual form of the expression of the first half comes from Ps 55:22... but no doubt the memory of Christ's teaching was in Peter's mind" (Cranfield, *First Epistle of Peter*, 118). "The author seems to borrow the language of this exquisite verse from the Septuagint version of Ps 54:23, yet the spirit of the passage also resonates with the sayings of Jesus in Matt 6:25–34" (Senior and Harrington, *1 Peter, Jude, and 2 Peter*, 150; cf. Metzner, *Die Rezeption*, 105).

108. Michaels, *1 Peter*, 296.

and such an encouragement fits Peter's larger purposes throughout the text (3:15; 4:14). Best, likewise, after noting that "it is not directly stated what anxieties the writer has in mind," indicates that these words of Jesus may provide a clue to Peter's meaning.[109] Consequently, casting one's care on the Lord is equivalent to sanctifying the Lord (3:15), for both indicate how one may avoid fearing others by submitting to God.

The other two μεριμ- texts occur in Luke's Gospel. Luke 8:14, speaking about the parable of the soils, which we argued Peter reflects in 1:23—2:3, notes that some seeds will be "choked by the cares (μέριμνα)" of life.[110] Likewise, Luke 21:34, which occurs in an eschatological context, warns about the cares of this life (μέριμνα) which may lead one to lack preparedness (Luke 21:34). The proposed parallel is made more likely in light of the next verse in 1P (5:7), which commands watchfulness and warns of the enemy who seeks to bring ultimate destruction.

If Peter intended to bring the full force of Jesus' μεριμ- teaching on the readers, the impact is significant. First, the full range of worldly cares are covered by Jesus' teaching. Of course, in the Sermon on the Mount, Jesus indicated that his disciples need not worry about the basic essentials of life (food and clothing), for the Father knows and takes care of his own. But the context of 1P suggests that this is not the only meaning of Peter's words here. Indeed, the other μεριμ- texts indicate that the anxieties of this life can lead them away from God. Consequently, the readers must pay attention to their hearts, lest their anxieties drive them away from the Father who cares for them.

This latter point is likely the reason the LXX Psalm is referenced.[111] The verse from the Psalm reads, "Cast your care on the Lord, and he will continually sustain you; he will never give shaking to him who is righteous."[112] The Psalm speaks of the voice of an enemy which brings great fear (v. 4-5), though it holds out hope that when God hears the righteous man's prayer, God will humble (ταπείνωσις) the enemies (vv. 17-21). Verse 23 is

---

109. Best, *1 Peter*, 173. Achtemeier, however, finds Best's connection "speculative" and "fanciful" concluding that "our author dealt with that problem in 3:15, and there is nothing in this context to give reason to think that problem is being revisited" (Achtemeier, *1 Peter*, 339n54). Such a negative conclusion overlooks the impact of Jesus teaching in the early church and the power of the μεριμ- word group to evoke that teaching. Further, Peter explicitly noted that a source of fear for the readers may be such a situation (3:14), and here he offers a resolution to that fear.

110. Davids also draws attention to this passage (Davids, *First Epistle of Peter*, 187).

111. See also Wong, "Use of Jesus' Sayings," 128-29.

112. This translation evidences elements of both the *Lexham English Septuagint* and the *New English Translation of the Septuagint*.

the pinnacle of the Psalm, where the author encourages the readers to cast their care on the Lord who will sustain them and never allow them to be moved.[113]

How do the words of Jesus and this Psalm interrelate? It seems that Peter is reflecting the warnings of Jesus that the cares of this world may lead the readers away from God. Jesus, however, indicates that his followers ought not to carry their own burden of care, but should trust in the One who cares for them. By means of casting their anxieties on the Lord, the readers will preserve their own souls, for the Lord will never let those who trust in him be moved. On the other hand, those who nurture their anxieties and refuse to transfer them to the Lord should be forewarned that they may become spiritually drowsy, lacking in watchfulness and prove themselves to be among the seeds that do not mature to fruitfulness. Once more, then, Peter appears to be warning of apostasy by means of a positive admonition to endurance.

1 Peter 5:8–9a and Luke 22:31–32

Having argued that Peter's first two commands in this section are reflective of the words of Jesus, it might come as no surprise that we will also argue that the third command is sourced out of Jesus' words. This command, consisting of two imperatives that are asyndetically linked (νήψατε and γρηγορήσατε),[114] heavily invests the saying with eschatological import. The same two words are used together in an eschatological setting in 1 Thessalonians 5:6 and, in the words of Elliott, "belong to early Christian hortatory tradition linked with the teaching of Jesus concerning the dangers of the end time and the vigilance required."[115] Having signaled the appeal to

---

113. The LXX uses σάλος, which can refer to a large wave or an earthquake. In either case, the LXX makes picturesque the idea in the Hebrew that one will not be moved.

114. The relatively rare word γρηγορέω (twenty-two occurrences in the NT) is not significant in the LXX nor in other known literature (Silva, *New International Dictionary*, s.v. "γρηγορέω," 1:609). But it has a heavy presence in Jesus' teaching. Therefore, its use here would likely signal the presence of Jesus' teaching. Numerous Gospel passages use the term (e.g., Matt 24:42, 43; 25:13; 26:38, 40, 41: Mark 13:34–37; 14:34–38; Luke 12:37), so it is difficult to absolutely determine which is being referenced. Nevertheless, since 5:8 echoes Luke 22:31–32 (see below), Mark 14:38 and Matthew 26:40–41 are likely candidates. This is because those Gospel passages are paralleled in Luke 22:39–46. Nevertheless, Luke does not have the key word γρηγορέω, which may suggest that Peter knew a tradition like Luke's Gospel that also contained γρηγορέω and the narrative concerning Satan's plan to make Peter fall.

115. Elliott, *1 Peter*, 853.

JT by the use of these introductory words, Peter next appeals to one of the more memorable events in the Gospel narratives concerning himself—Jesus' warning concerning Satan's intention for Peter.[116]

Table 9.7: 1 Peter 5:8–9a and Luke 22:31–32

1 Peter 5:8–9a	Luke 22:31–32
νήψατε, γρηγορήσατε. ὁ ἀντίδικος ὑμῶν διάβολος ὡς λέων ὠρυόμενος περιπατεῖ ζητῶν τινα καταπιεῖν ᾧ ἀντίστητε στερεοὶ τῇ *πίστει*	Σίμων Σίμων, ἰδοὺ ὁ σατανᾶς ἐξῃτήσατο ὑμᾶς τοῦ σινιάσαι ὡς τὸν σῖτον· 32 ἐγὼ δὲ ἐδεήθην περὶ σοῦ ἵνα μὴ ἐκλίπῃ ἡ *πίστις* σου· καὶ σύ ποτε ἐπιστρέψας στήρισον τοὺς ἀδελφούς σου.

Peter has shown knowledge of many of the traditions in this Lukan text block already (3:22; 5:2–4). Here, the similarities are not lexical, as though Peter knew Luke's Gospel, but they are strongly ideological, suggesting that Peter knew a tradition very much like the one presented in Luke's Gospel. *Both passages are connected to Peter and speak of Satan seeking to destroy Christians, the necessity of faith and prayer to persevere, and Peter's role in strengthening other disciples.* Each element of this succinct sentence can be helpfully developed.

First, the significance of Petrine tradition should not be overlooked. The Lukan context highlights Peter as the one Satan is seeking to destroy. And since, as Vinson rightly notes, "First Peter's readers have heard these stories, or other versions of them, read aloud in worship,"[117] it is natural to connect Peter's warning to Peter's own experience. When added to the distinctive elements the passages have in common, it is hard to imagine an early church audience would not be drawn back to consider this tradition when reading a letter associated with Peter.

Second, both passages speak of Satan. The difference in the name for the chief enemy (διάβολος in 1P and σατανᾶς in Luke) is insignificant. First, the two names are semantically equivalent.[118] Second, Silva shows that "Luke clearly prefers this name in material unique to him (Lk 10:18; 13:1; 22:3, 31)."[119] Consequently, it is possible that some traditions included διάβολος while others had σατανᾶς, and that the tradition handed down in Luke's

---

116. The following scholars have found a reflection on this memorable event likely in the epistle: Seesemann, "Πειράζω," 31–32; Vinson et al., *1 & 2 Peter, Jude*, 239; Gundry, "'Verba Christi' in I Peter," 344; Selwyn, *First Epistle of St. Peter*, 381; Cranfield, *First Epistle of Peter*, 119.

117. Vinson et al., *1 & 2 Peter, Jude*, 239. Cf. Davids, *First Epistle of Peter*, 189n11.

118. Silva, *New International Dictionary*, s.v. "διαβάλλω," 1:692.

119. Silva, *New International Dictionary*, s.v. "σατάν," 4:266.

Gospel is given with the terminology preferred by Luke. The difference in the precise term, however, should not mask the significance of this ideological parallel.[120]

A third ideological parallel is the conception that the Devil/Satan is seeking to destroy believers. Of course, the referent switches from an individual to a group, but such a shift is anticipated in the original tradition, for Peter is told to strengthen the brethren after he is restored, and Jesus' initial warning to Peter is given in the plural, indicating that Satan sought to destroy all of the disciples. A major challenge is present here, however. Best asks, if Peter knew this tradition, why is there a change of metaphor?[121] In 1P, the chief enemy is imagined as a roaring lion, while in the Gospel context the enemy is imagined as one who sifts wheat. There are two potential reasons Peter may have shifted the metaphor. First, his recent analogy of his readers as a flock encourages the image of the enemy as a ravenous lion.[122]

It is also possible that Peter is seeking to reflect the OT as well as the JT, a combination he has shown himself adept at making throughout this epistle but especially in this section. If so, Peter may be reflecting the image of the enemy in Job walking around the earth (Job 1:7).[123] Alternatively, Jesus may be reflecting LXX Psalm 21:14, which describes a lion which roars (ὠρύομαι; the same participle as used in 1P) and snatches away.[124] In the end, though the shift in metaphor must be considered, the congruity of the two passages in reference to an enemy who seeks to destroy is distinctive and significant.

Fourth, there is parallel between these passages in reference to what is necessary to persevere in light of the enemy's attack. First, both passages explicitly bring to the fore the significance of faith for endurance (πίστις; 1P 5:9; Luke 22:32). Second, both speak to the efficacy of prayer. Luke speaks of the Lord's prayer on behalf of Peter, but only a few verses later (Luke 22:40), Luke indicates that Jesus encouraged Peter to pray that he would not come into the time of trial, a likely reference back to the warning about

---

120. Wong notes that since there are few references to Satan in the Gospels, this passage would have likely been brought to mind (Wong, "Use of Jesus' Sayings," 218).

121. Best, "I Peter and the Gospel Tradition," 107.

122. Amos 3:12a shows the compatibility of the sheep and lion metaphor: "As the shepherd rescues from the mouth of the lion" (Elliott, *1 Peter*, 857).

123. This may be further defended by the observation that Jesus may use ἐξαιτέω as an allusion to Job (Stählin, "Ἐξαιτέω," 1:194). Accordingly, Peter may be picking up the reference and extending it in light of the sheep metaphor earlier.

124. Elliott notes that "This psalm figured prominently in the theological formulations of Christ's passion" (Elliott, *1 Peter*, 857; cf. Kelly, *Peter and Jude*, 210).

the enemy.¹²⁵ Significantly, Mark 14:32-42 and Matthew 26:36-46, parallel passages to Luke 22:39-46, include the word γρηγορέω in reference to the disciples watching and praying. This is the same word Peter uses here, suggesting that Peter also has prayer in mind. Additionally, Peter couples γρηγορέω with νήφω, a word he used in relation to prayer earlier (4:7; discipline yourselves for the sake of your prayers).¹²⁶

Finally, both passages speak to the role of Peter in strengthening the brothers. In Luke's Gospel, Jesus commands Peter to strengthen (στηρίζω; 22:32) the brothers after he is restored. First Peter directly applies this by means of the author commending the readers to steadfast (στερεός; 5:9) faith.¹²⁷ Considered alone, such a similarity is weak, but when added to above connections, it becomes more persuasive.¹²⁸

Having detailed the agreement between the passages, we may now turn to consider the significance. First, it is possible that some among Peter's readers have failed in living out their faith. Perhaps some have even spoken against the Lord in order to escape persecution. For these, Peter's admonition is particularly effective, for Peter stands as evidence that one can fall and be restored. Peter now is watchful in prayer and is standing fast in faith while resisting the devil. Likewise, Peter's readers can be restored to fruitfulness in God's service.

Second, it is clear from the Gospel context that a primary reason Peter persevered was the effective prayer of Jesus on his behalf. This echo gives hope to Peter's readers that they too are the recipients of Jesus' prayer (see also John 17 and Jesus' extended pre-Garden of Gethsemane prayer for believer's past and present).

---

125. Bock, *Luke 9:51—24:53*, 1757.

126. Gundry suggests that Peter may have known a tradition that substituted προσεύχεσθε for νήφω (Gundry, "Further Verba," 220-21).

127. Gundry draws attention to this parallel: "I Peter's admonition to be στερεοί in faith goes back to Jesus' command, στήρισον τους αδελφούς σου, στερεοί being an adjective drawn from στηρίζω" (Gundry, "'Verba Christi' in I Peter," 344).

128. Meier, who is generally favorable towards echoes and allusions to the words of Jesus in 1P notes of this parallel, "As appealing as it may seem to associate the στερεόι of 1 Peter 5.9 with Lk 22.32: στηρίζειν, it is better to remain cautious at this point also" (translated from, "So reizvoll es anmutet, das stereoi von 1.Petr 5,9 mit Lk 22,32: sterizein zu verbinden, bleibt man besser auch an diesem Punkt vorsichtig" [Maier, "Jesustradition," 96]).

1 PETER 5:12-14

These verses are the epistolary closing of 1P. Along with noting the letter-carrier and sending greetings, Peter includes a final statement that encapsulates his purpose in writing, which is "to testify that this is the true grace of God" and to encourage the believers to "Stand fast in it." While some have suggested dominical reflections, none are persuasive.[129]

CONCLUSION TO 1 PETER 4:12—5:14

We have found in this final section of 1P eight intertextual references to the words of Jesus, consisting of six echoes and two allusions.

Table 9.8: Intertextual Resonances to *Dominical Logia* in 1 Peter 4:12—5:14

1P Reference	Gospel Reference	Type of Reference
4:13-14	Matt 5:10-12; Luke 6:22-23	Echo
4:14	Luke 12:10-12 (Mark 13:11; Matt 10:20)	Echo
5:2-4	John 21:15-17	Echo
5:2-4	Luke 22:25-30 (Mark 10:42-45; Matt 20:25-28)	Allusion
5:5	John 13:1-17	Allusion
5:6	Matt 23:12 & Luke 14:11 (cf. 18:14)	Echo
5:7	Matt 6:25-34 (Luke 12:22-31)	Echo
5:8-9a	Luke 22:31-32	Echo

It is unsurprising that Peter concludes the epistle with a distinct focus on suffering and that he does so by echoing and alluding to the JT. These are two elements we have found consistently throughout the letter. As Peter returns to the theme of suffering, he reminds the readers for a third time (1:6; 3:14; 4:13-14) that Jesus indicated the righteous sufferers are blessed and will be rewarded (Matt 5:10-12). One distinct blessing was first promised to the Messiah in the OT (Isa 11:2), but through echoing the words of Jesus (Luke 12:10-12), Peter shows that the blessing is also available to all suffering Christians. This is the blessing of the Spirit (1P 4:14), who aids the believer in times of trial, specifically giving words of wisdom and insight.

As Peter turns to consider the responsibilities believers have towards one another, he does not depart from echoing the words of Jesus. First, Peter echoes the lake-side tradition concerning Jesus' reinstatement of Peter to a

---

129. See the appendix for the full listing.

shepherding type of ministry (John 21:15-17). In like manner, Peter calls the elders of the Anatolian communities to shepherd as Jesus has indicated. One clear command from Jesus concerned how they ought to lead (Luke 22:25-30)—not by lording over others but by being an example. Peter concludes the section by echoing the tradition of Jesus' footwashing (John 13:1-17), which masterfully exemplified the servant role each believer ought to model. If Jesus, who was the unique Son of God, served his disciples, how then ought they to treat one another?

The final section of the body closing appropriately returns to the theme of suffering, and once more Peter reflects the words of Jesus. First, while Peter is clearly reflecting Proverbs 3:34 in 1P 5:5-6, distinctive textual agreement with the JT indicates that Peter reflects these words because they were emphasized by Jesus (Matt 23:12). In regard to the readers, Peter is reminding them that future exaltation requires present humility. And according to Jesus, casting one's anxieties on the heavenly Father is one way that such humility should be expressed among the assembly. Jesus indicated that his disciples need not worry about the essentials of life (Matt 6:25-34), nor should they allow their anxieties to lead them away from the Father who loves them (Luke 8:14; 21:34). Finally, Peter makes one final appeal to a tradition concerning himself. Jesus indicated that Satan sought to destroy Peter (Luke 22:31-32), and now Peter warns his readers that Satan is likewise seeking to destroy them (5:8-9a). By echoing this tradition, Peter indicates that watchfulness in prayer is the effective means of perseverance.

As with previous sections, there is no discernible pattern to Peter's reflections; rather, it appears that Peter cites the words of Jesus as they intersect with the themes he is seeking to express. Within this section, this leads to a focus on dominical teachings concerning suffering and service.

10

Summary and Conclusions

THIS STUDY HAS ARGUED for the presence and significance of dominical teaching throughout the text of 1P. We have discerned 34 intertextual reflections, consisting of 26 echoes and 8 allusions. The collation of detailed arguments for each of these intertextual resonances in one place, along with the consideration of the rhetorical impact of each provides a contribution to both JT and 1P scholarship. This concluding chapter will seek to add to that contribution by considering the larger picture and addressing important questions in light of the detailed study we have done above.

Since each chapter concluded with a summary of the use of Jesus' words in that chapter, we will not repeat that information here. Instead, we will provide a detailed table of the findings, which will help us as we address some of the implications of the study.

TABLES OF RESEARCH

The following tables provide in summary form what has been argued extensively above. The first table (9.1) provides a comprehensive view of the use of Jesus' words in 1P, while the second table (9.2) focuses on the distribution of references to Gospel traditions in 1 Peter.

SUMMARY AND CONCLUSIONS 227

Table 10.1: Comprehensive Table on the Use of Jesus' Words in 1 Peter

1P Reference	Gospel Reference	Type of Reference	Key Agreement(s)	Degree of Confidence	Closest to Gospel	Combined with OT	Significance	Text Block	Peter's Involvement
1:2	Mark 14:23; Matt 26:28; Luke 22:20b	Echo	Blood (αἷμα) of Jesus; New Covenant	Likely	–	Exodus 24*	Identity	–	Spoken to the Disciples at the Last Supper
1:2	Matt 28:28–30	Echo	Trinitarian Formula; Baptism; Obedience	Possible	Matthew	–	Identity	–	Jesus' Great Commission to the Disciples
1:3	John 3:3–7	Allusion	Born Again Concept	Likely	John	–	Identity	–	–
1:4	Luke 12:33; Matt 6:20	Echo	Imperishable, Secure Heavenly Reward; Temporal Worldly Goods	Likely	–	–	Identity; Reward	Matt SOM; Luke 12	Spoken to the Disciples
1:6	Matt 5:10–12; Luke 6:22–23	Echo	Rejoicing in Suffering; Blessed (μακάριος)	Very Likely	Matthew	–	Blessing (μακάριος); Reward; Suffering; Rejoicing	Matt SOM; Luke 6	Spoken to the Disciples
1:8	John 20:29	Echo	Not Seeing (ὁράω and εἶδον), yet Believing in the Risen Christ; Joy	Likely	John	–	Rejoicing; Blessing (μακάριος)	–	Spoken to the Disciples

1P Reference	Gospel Reference	Type of Reference	Key Agreement(s)	Degree of Confidence	Closest to Gospel	Combined with OT	Significance	Text Block	Peter's Involvement
1:10	Matt 13:16–17; Luke 20:23–24	Echo	Prophets Desired to Know what the Readers Know	Possible	–	–	Blessing (μακάριος); Identity; Rejoicing	Matt 13; Luke 20	Spoken in response to the Disciples' question
1:11	Luke 24:25–27	Echo	Suffering (πάθημα) to Glory (δόξα); Χριστός Alone	Possible	Luke	–	Suffering; Eschatology	–	–
1:13	Luke 12:35, 45	Echo	Girding (ζωσάμενοι) the Loins (ὀσφὺς) of the Mind with Eschatological Expectation; Grammatical Sequence and Structure	Likely	Luke	Exod 2:1.1*	Perseverance; Eschatology; Blessing (μακάριος)	Luke 12	Peter asked the Question that Occasioned the Saying (12:41)
1:17	Matt 6:9 and Luke 11:2	Echo	Calling on the Father (πάτερ) in Prayer	Likely	–	–	Perseverance; Imitation	Matt SOM	Luke—Based on the Disciples' request; Matthew—Spoken to the Disciples
1:18	Mark 10:45 and Matt 20:28	Echo	Ransomed (λυτρόω; λύτρον) by Jesus	Likely	–	Isa 52:3*	Community Building; Identity; Imitation	Mark 10; Matt 20	Spoken to the Disciples

SUMMARY AND CONCLUSIONS 229

1P Reference	Gospel Reference	Type of Reference	Key Agreement(s)	Degree of Confidence	Closest to Gospel	Combined with OT	Significance	Text Block	Peter's Involvement
1:22	John 13:34–35; 15:12	Echo	"love one another" (ἀγαπᾶτε ἀλλήλους)	Likely	John	–	Community Building; Imitation	–	Spoken to the Disciples; Peter is Directly mentioned in the Close Context (13:36)
1:23–25	Parable of the Sower (Matt 13:1–23; Luke 8:4–15; Mark 4:3–20)	Allusion	Word of God (λόγος τοῦ θεοῦ) as Seed (σπορά/σπόρος) Bringing New Life	Very Likely	–	Isa 40:6–8	Perseverance; Identity; Community Building	Matt 13	Spoken to the Disciples
2:3	Luke 6:35	Echo	The Lord is kind (χρηστός); Love for Others; Children of God	Possible	Luke (not in Mt)	LXX Ps 33:9	Identity; Community Building; Reward; Imitation	Luke 6	Spoken to the Disciples

1P Reference	Gospel Reference	Type of Reference	Key Agreement(s)	Degree of Confidence	Closest to Gospel	Combined with OT	Significance	Text Block	Peter's Involvement
2:4–8	Mark 12:10, 11; Matt 21:42, 43; Luke 20:17, 18	Echo	Stone Rejected by Men, Approved by God; Building Process	Very Likely	—	Isa 8:14; 28:16; LXX Ps 117:22*	Identity; Perseverance	Luke 20	Parable spoken to Crowds, but Peter is elsewhere called the "Rock"
2:12	Matt 5:14–16	Allusion	Believers Showing Good (καλός) Works (ἔργον) Leading Others to Give God Glory (δοξάζω)	Very Likely	Matthew+ (not in Lk)	—	Evangelism; Eschatology	Matt SOM	Spoken to the Disciples
2:13–17	Matt 17:25–27 (cf. Matt 22:21)	Echo	Believers as Free (ἐλεύθερος) in Regard to Civil Authority, yet Subordinate for the sake of Testimony	Very Likely	Matthew	—	Evangelism; Imitation	—	The Account is Specifically Connected to Peter
2:18–21	Luke 6:32–35	Echo	Unique Lexical Similarities: Good Works (ἀγαθοποιέω) and Creditable (χάρις); Rhetorical Question	Very likely	Luke+ (not in Mt)	—	Reward; Identity; Imitation	Luke 6	Spoken to the Disciples
2:25	John 10:11–18	Echo	Jesus as the Shepherd (ποιμήν) and Guardian	Likely	John	Isa 53*	Identity	—	—

SUMMARY AND CONCLUSIONS   231

1P Reference	Gospel Reference	Type of Reference	Key Agreement(s)	Degree of Confidence	Closest to Gospel	Combined with OT	Significance	Text Block	Peter's Involvement
3:9	Luke 6:27–30; Matt 5:39–44	Allusion	When Persecuted, do not Retaliate but Bless (εὐλογέω), and you will Receive a Reward	Very Likely	Both Matthew and Luke	–	Reward; Persecution; Evangelism; Imitation	Luke 6; Matt SOM	Spoken to the Disciples
3:14a	Matt 5:10; Luke 6:22	Echo	Suffering for Righteousness (δικαιοσύνη) Resulting in Blessing (μακάριος)	Very likely	Matthew+ (δικαιοσύνη not in Lk)	–	Blessing (μακάριος); Reward; Persecution; Imitation	Luke 6; Matt SOM	Spoken to the Disciples
3:14b	Matt 10:26–28	Echo	The Command do not "Fear Them"	Possible	Matthew (Luke missing phrase)	Isa 8:12–13	Perseverance; Eschatology	Matt 10	Spoken to the Disciples
3:16	Luke 6:28	Echo	When Reviled (ἐπηρεάζω), Bless	Possible	Luke+	–	Persecution; Blessing; Evangelism; Imitation	Luke 6	Spoken to the Disciples
3:13–17	Luke 21:12–19	Allusion	Believers must Give a Defense (ἀπολογία) when Persecuted, and they must Trust the Lord for the Response	Possible	Luke (not like Matt/Mark traditions)	–	Perseverance; Evangelism	–	Spoken to the Disciples
3:22	Mark 14:62; Matt 26:64; Luke 22:69	Echo	Jesus Seated at the Right Hand (ἐν δεξιᾷ; ἐκ δεξιῶν) of God	Likely	–	LXX Ps 109:1*; Dan 7:13	Perseverance; Eschatology	–	Spoken to the Disciples (Answering their Question)
									–

1P Reference	Gospel Reference	Type of Reference	Key Agreement(s)	Degree of Confidence	Closest to Gospel	Combined with OT	Significance	Text Block	Peter's Involvement
4:10	Luke 12:42–48	Echo	Stewards (οἰκονόμος) of God must use their Resources Rightly	Likely	Luke + (Matt 24 has slave)	–	Perseverance; Reward; Eschatology	Luke 12	Given in Answer to Peter's Question
4:13–14	Matt 5:10–12; Luke 6:22–23	Echo	Key Words: χαίρω (Rejoice), ὀνειδίζω (Revile), μακάριοι (Blessed), and ἀγαλλιάω (Exult)	Very likely	Matthew+ (Luke missing ἀγαλλιάω)	?	Blessing (μακάριος); Rejoicing; Persecution; Reward; Imitation	Matt SOM; Luke 6	Spoken to the Disciples
4:14	Luke 12:10–12; Mark 13:11; Matt 10:20	Echo	The Spirit is Given to Those who are Persecuted	Possible	–	LXX Isa 11:2a	Blessing; Reward	Luke 12; Matt 10	Peter, with James and John, Asked Jesus Privately (Mark 13:3)
5:2–4	John 21:15–17	Echo	Command (involving Peter) to Tend the Flock (ποιμαίνω)	Very Likely	John	–	Reward; Suffering	–	Peter Directly Involved
5:2–4	Luke 22:25–30; Mark 10:42–45; Matt 20:25–28	Allusion	Leaders of God's People are not to Lord Over (κατακυριεύω) but should be an Example	Very Likely	Evidences both Matt/Mark and Luke streams	–	Reward; Imitation	Luke 22; Mark 10; Matt 20	Spoken to the Disciples

SUMMARY AND CONCLUSIONS 233

1P Reference	Gospel Reference	Type of Reference	Key Agreement(s)	Degree of Confidence	Closest to Gospel	Combined with OT	Significance	Text Block	Peter's Involvement
5:5	John 13:1–17	Allusion	Clothing Oneself in Humility in Service to One Another	Very Likely	John	–	Imitation; Community Building	~	Peter Directly Involved
5:6	Matt 23:12 & Luke 14:11 (cf. 18:14)	Echo	Humble Yourselves (ταπεινόω) so that God may Exalt (ὑψόω) You	Very likely	–	LXX Prov 3:34*	Imitation	Luke 18	–
5:7	Matt 6:25–34; Luke 12:22–31	Echo	Followers of Jesus should not be Anxious (μέριμνα; μεριμνάω), but should Trust the Lord	Likely	–	LXX Ps 54:23	Perseverance	Luke 12; Matt SOM	Spoken to the Disciples
5:8–9a	Luke 22:31–32	Echo	Satan Seeking to Destroy Christians; the Necessity of Faith and Prayer to Persevere; Peter's Role in Strengthening other Disciples.	Very Likely	Luke	Job 1:7*; LXX Ps 21:14	Eschatology; Perseverance	Luke 22	Peter Directly involved

+: Indicates distinctive verbal similarity
*: Indicates that the OT reference is also reflected by Jesus

Table 10.2: Distribution of References to Gospel Traditions in 1 Peter

Chapter	Mark	Matthew	Luke	John
1				
2				
3				1
4	1			
5		5		
6		3	7	
7				
8			1	
9				
10	2	2		1
11			1	
12	1		5	
13	1	2		2
14	2		1	
15				1
16				
17		1		
18			1	
19				
20		2	2	1
21		1	1	1
22		2	3	
23		1		
24			1	
25				
26		2		
27				
28		1		
TOTAL	7	22	23	7

IMPLICATIONS OF THE RESEARCH

The first chapter of this work surveyed the history of scholarship in regard to the JT in 1P. Two issues—authorship and Gospel affinity—were consistently raised in prior literature, and since we have examined the whole text of 1P in regard to Jesus' words, it would be helpful to revisit those topics. After discussing them, we will summarize our findings as it relates to two issues not as frequently discussed in previous literature: the relationship between the dominical teachings and the OT and the rhetorical uses of Jesus' words in 1P.

Authorship

As revealed in the survey of scholarship, it was once thought that the use of Jesus' words in 1P would provide evidence for the authorship of the letter. Indeed, some have used these dominical reflections as proof of genuine Petrine authorship, while others have argued that they evidence pseudonymous authorship. Our findings are unable to resolve the stalemate within scholarship. While it does appear that many of the traditions reflected in 1P emphasize Peter (see Table 9.1), such a finding is not surprising. First, it is not surprising because the prominence of Peter in Gospel literature almost naturally leads to this situation. Second, even if there is an intentional focus on sayings and scenes involving Peter, it is always possible that a pseudonymous author recognized this and focused on those portions of the JT to add credibility to the letter. Consequently, the dominical echoes may tell us much about what the author thought and believed, but they cannot tell us who the author was.

Gospel Affinity

Another controversial element has been the source of 1 Peter's reflections. Did Peter know one of the canonical Gospels, either in its present form or even in a preliminary form? As noted in the history of research, Best believed Peter knew elements of Luke's Gospel (portions of chapter 6 and 12). Metzner, on the other hand, argued for Peter's knowledge of the Gospel of Matthew. Other scholars have shown a preference for Matthean (Selwyn, Wong) or Lukan (Gundry) influence.

In regard to the present study, it may be best to start with the other two Gospels before we address Matthew and Luke. First, no lexical connection to John's Gospel clearly indicates Peter's literary knowledge of that Gospel. Nevertheless, we identified seven ideological parallels, and a few notable lexical similarities (1P 1:8 [John 20:29]; 1P 5:2 [John 21:16]). Accordingly, though 1P gives no clear evidence of literary knowledge of the Gospel of John, its echoes of traditions which are also recorded in John's

Gospel suggest that these traditions were known outside the Johannine communities.

First Peter likewise shows no definitive lexical links to Mark's Gospel. And while we suggested that seven Markan passages show some lexical or ideological similarity to 1P, it is important to note that no text is echoed or alluded to from Mark's Gospel that could not also have come from Matthew or Luke. Gundry's explanation for this lack of agreement—i.e., Mark's Gospel is narratival—is true, yet in these seven areas where Mark's Gospel does record a saying that Peter reflected, it is notable that none show distinct similarity with Mark's Gospel. Thus, despite whatever historical relationship may have existed between the authors of the works,[1] little distinctive agreement is evident.

As for Matthew's Gospel, Peter shows evidence of knowing traditions similar to the Matthean form of a tradition in twenty-two instances. The predominance of references occurs in the Sermon on the Mount (1:4, 6, 17; 2:12; 3:9, 14; 4:13–14; 5:7). Nevertheless, none of the references appeal to traditions in Matthew 7. Outside of the Sermon material, the references are fairly evenly spread throughout the epistle. The references with a Matthew+ in the table above are notable (2:12; 3:14; 4:13–14), for they are passages where 1P shows clear lexical connections with Matthew's Gospel. Such evidence is far from showing lexical dependence, but it does suggest that Peter knew a tradition in a similar form as that distinctively recorded by Matthew.

The use of Luke's Gospel is quite similar to Matthew's Gospel in that 1P frequently reflects traditions similar to that Gospel (twenty-three instances) and these instances are concentrated in certain text blocks. Luke 6, the Sermon on the Plain, has seven references (1:6; 2:3, 18–21; 3:9, 14, 16; 4:13–14), while Luke 12 has five (1:4, 13; 4:10, 14; 5:7). The remaining eleven references are fairly evenly scattered throughout the Gospel. As with Matthew, a few passages in Luke's Gospel show distinctive lexical or grammatical agreement to 1P (1:13; 2:18–21; 3:16; 4:10), which indicate that Peter knew a tradition similar to that distinctively recorded in Luke.

An interesting finding concerning Gospel affinity is revealed when we consider the Sermon on the Mount/Plain texts together. As noted above, Peter often reflects these texts, but he does so in such a way that it appears he knows traditions very similar to Luke's Sermon on the Plain *and* Matthew's

---

1. France notes that "The tradition of the early church ... affirms consistently that [Mark's] gospel was written by Mark in Rome *as a record of Peter's teaching*" (France, *Gospel of Mark*, 38; emphasis added). Accordingly, the lack of similarity between the Gospel and the epistle is unexpected for those who maintain the historical teaching of the church concerning both the authorship of this epistle and Peter's connection to the author of the Gospel of Mark.

Sermon on the Mount. For instance, 2:12, 3:14, and 4:13-14 distinctively reveal Peter's knowledge of a tradition very much like Matthew's Sermon on the Mount. Importantly, each of these references comes from the same tradition block: Matthew 5:10-16. On the other hand, 2:3 and 2:18-21, and 3:16 distinctively reveal Peter's knowledge of a tradition very much like Luke's Sermon on the Plain. These passages are also limited to one tradition block: Luke 6:27-36. When added to the fact that there are a few passages that appear to show Peter's knowledge of a tradition that included elements present in *both* Matthew and Luke (3:9; 5:2-4), the above considerations suggest that Peter did not know Matthew or Luke's Gospel, but instead reflects traditions common to both.

In conclusion, while there are a few striking lexical similarities with the canonical Gospels, these are too few and sporadic to suggest they reveal the literary knowledge of the Gospels by Peter. Such similarities are adequately and better explained by the existence of oral tradition. Consequently, 1P should not be seen as reflective of a particular tradition strand, but rather as a witness to early JT.

Peter's Rhetorical Use of Jesus' Words

We noted at the beginning of this study that one deficiency in scholarship on the use of the JT in 1P was attention to Peter's rhetorical use of Jesus' words. This lack has been due, in large part, to the debate over where Peter references Jesus' words. Having sought to answer that question, we can give attention to this deficiency. Of course, it is not possible to repeat all that has been said in the preceding chapters. Instead, we will seek to organize the uses of the sayings in regard to the themes Peter applies them towards. The following table summarizes the themes and locations of Peter's rhetorical uses of Jesus' words.

Table 10.3: Themes of Peter's Dominical Reflections

Theme	Dominical Reflections	# of References
Imitation	1:17, 18, 22; 2:3, 13-17, 18-21; 3:9, 14a, 16; 4:13-14; 5:2-4, 5, 6	13
Reward	1:4, 6; 2:3, 18-21; 3:9, 14a; 4:10, 13, 14; 5:2-4 (x2)	11
Perseverance	1:13, 17, 23-25; 2:4-8; 3:13-17, 14b, 22; 4:10; 5:7, 8-9a	10

Theme	Dominical Reflections	# of References
Identity	1:2, 3, 4, 10, 18; 2:3, 4–8, 18–21, 25	9
Blessing	1:6, 8, 10, 13; 3:14a, 16; 4:13, 14	8
Persecution/ Suffering	1:6, 11; 3:9, 14a, 16; 4:13–14; 5:2–4	7
Eschatology	1:11, 13; 2:12; 3:14b, 22; 4:10; 5:8–9a	7
Community Building	1:18, 22, 23–25; 2:3, 5:5	5
Evangelism	2:12, 13–17; 3:9, 13–17, 16	5
Rejoicing	1:6, 8, 10; 4:13–14	4

The most common theme to the dominical reflections concerns imitation of Jesus. In some instances, the imitation is directly indicated within the source text (1:17, 22; 2:3; 5:2–4, 5), while elsewhere it is stated by Peter's text (2:21; 4:13–14). It is also sometimes the unspoken result of the intersection of Peter's text and the JT (1:18; 2:3, 13–17; 5:6). These finding suggest that imitation of Jesus, only explicitly mentioned in 2:21, is nevertheless a theme present throughout 1P. Jesus is the prime example of a faithful life, and Peter frequently uses Jesus' words to highlight that fact.

Heavenly rewards are mentioned explicitly (and in a dominical reflection) near the beginning of 1P (1:4). A consideration of the use of Jesus' words shows that Peter never fully leaves the topic. This is not surprising in light of some of the other themes of 1P. Since Peter believes the readers are children of God, they have a heavenly inheritance. And since Peter believes righteous sufferers will be rewarded (1:6), it is not surprising that he echoes traditions surrounding the future heavenly rewards awaiting his persecuted readers. Indeed, Peter encourages faithfulness by means of echoing Jesus' promise of future reward (2:3, 18–21; 3:9; 4:10, 13–14; 5:2–4).

That perseverance is mentioned so frequently within these passages may be initially surprising. But we have argued throughout this thesis that Peter exhibts a "rhetorical strategy of suppression," meaning Peter "stresses notions antithetical to defection as he attempts to move the mind of his readers away from scandal and defection to hope, sobriety, and steadfastness."[2] One chief way he does this is through citing traditions concerning the words of Jesus that either directly encourage perseverance (1:13, 23–25; 3:22), address the means of perseverance (1:17, 3:13–17; 5:7, 8–9a), or provide warnings about the danger of missing salvation (2:2, 4–8; 4:10). Accordingly, 1P

---

2. Martin, *Metaphor and Composition*, 275. See also Thurén, *Argument and Theology in 1 Peter*, 224.

fits nicely within the non-Pauline literature of the NT in calling believers to persevere in the faith.

Many scholars have recognized the importance of identity in 1P, and the present study reinforces that the theme is important. Peter is obviously burdened to communicate that these readers are a new people, and he uses Jesus' sayings to reinforce that point. Many of the references are concentrated at the beginning of the letter, with reference to the New Covenant (1:2) and the new birth (1:3), along with its accompanying inheritance (1:4). These readers are told they are members of a privileged class, who have come to know what Jesus indicated the prophets desired to know (1:10). And they are no longer, as their ancestors, bound to a futile way of life, for they have been ransomed (1:18). Peter trusts that as needy children (2:2), they long for the milk of the One they have found gracious (2:3). The central passage of identity, however, occurs in 2:4–8, where Peter reflects the words of Jesus concerning himself as the stone. The readers are those who have obeyed and thus are built upon the stone, as against those who have rejected the Word, have been disobedient, and stumble over the stone. In sum, Peter uses the reflection on Jesus' words to reinforce the distinctive identity of these disciples.

Peter is also concerned to stress that, despite appearances, his readers are blessed. This blessing is part of the eschatological hope that will result in rewards (4:13–14), but it is not only that. Through reflection on the words of Jesus, Peter stresses that the readers are *presently* blessed. It is for this reason, Peter speaks of their present rejoicing in trial (1:6) and rejoicing in the absence of sight of the Lord (1:8). Both of these references are significant in that they are sourced out of dominical references in which Jesus calls the readers blessed (μακάριος). Jesus further calls them blessed in regard to their knowledge (1:10), for which prophets longed to know and angels longed to observe. Having echoed three passages in which Jesus identifies Peter's readers as blessed, Peter then echoes the promise of eschatological blessing for those who wait expectantly for the Lord's return (1:13). Peter returns to the theme of blessedness twice more (3:14–16; 4:13–14) with specific regard for the blessedness of those who suffer for righteousness. On the whole, the reflection of JT shows that Peter's readers are blessed now and should expect future blessing.

A focus on suffering and persecution may be one of the least surprising themes, for 1P is known for its focus on these challenges. This emphasis is closely related to many of the prior themes. In regard to imitation, 2:12 (a dominical reflection) explicitly notes that the readers are to follow in the steps of Jesus, the Righteous Sufferer. Just as Jesus suffered and entered his glory, so the readers should follow (1:11). In regard to reward, suffering and persecution are the gateways to blessedness (1:6; 3:9, 14a; 4:13–14). Further, it is because of their identity that they are persecuted, and it is due to the pressure of the persecution that they must persevere.

A few other themes are evident from the dominical reflections as well, and these are connected to the prior themes. First, Peter seeks to encourage acts which build community, particularly acts of love. Accordingly, he encourages believers to imitate Jesus (1:18; 2:3; 5:5) and echoes the direct teaching of Jesus that the disciples ought to love one another (1:22). Second, Peter frequently refers by means of Jesus' words to the coming eschatological fulfilment of God's plan. It is then that the faithful will be rewarded (1:13; 4:10), the king will have full reign (3:22), all will be revealed (3:14), and those who were once persecutors may offer glory to God (2:12).

The final theme we will consider is evangelism. As with the prior themes, this is also related to the others. Peter foresees that just as the suffering of Jesus was redemptive, so the suffering of believers may be as well (2:12; 3:13–17), though in a different fashion. Jesus was sacrificed for the sins of many, but the gracious response of God's people towards those who speak evil of believers is able to point others to the sacrifice of Jesus, where forgiveness is found (3:13–17). For this reason, Peter encourages obedience in the civil sphere (2:13–17). Importantly, Peter's central thoughts about the evangelistic power of good works is clearly sourced out of the words of his Lord (2:12; Matt 5:14–16).

In sum, the major themes of the letter are reinforced by reference to the words of Jesus. This suggests that Peter considered these dominical teachings as foundational to his message and motivational for his readers.

SUGGESTIONS FOR FUTURE RESEARCH

Due to the limited scope of this study, many associated questions had to be passed over. One area that deserves further research concerns the impact JT in epistolary material may have on the broader discussion of the historical Jesus. Scholars are now giving more attention to this relatively untapped resource for understanding what the early church though about Jesus. The present study has provided a basis for further work in this area, and it is hoped other epistolary material will receive a similar treatment, leading to conclusions that may impact broader Jesus scholarship.

Related to the last point, many interesting relationships between JT cited in 1P and the same JT cited in other epistolary works are rich in potential fruit for research. A future study may take the echoes and allusions to the JT in 1P and compare them with the JT echoed or alluded to in, e.g.,

Pauline literature or the letter of James. Such a comparison will aid in understanding how the early church used the JT and could give further insight into what Peter was doing with the Lord's words.

Perhaps the most interesting avenue of future research concerns how Peter merged the use of JT with OT traditions. Indeed, in thirteen of the dominical traditions, Peter also reflects an OT text. It will be helpful to briefly consider the intersection of these sources of authority.

Sometimes Peter echoes an OT tradition chiefly because Jesus echoed that same tradition (e.g., 1:2, 13, 18; 2:4–8, 25; 3:22; 5:6). For example, Peter's extensive consideration of the stone passages of the OT (2:4–8) is due to Jesus' own consideration of those passages (Mark 12:10, 11; Matt 21:42, 43; Luke 20:17, 18). In these cases, Peter seems to be building on the foundation of Jesus' interpretation of OT Scripture. For instance, when Peter reflects the preparatory metaphor of the Gospels (gird up the loins of the mind; 1:13), Jesus himself is reflecting the Exodus event (Luke 12:34, 45). Peter seems to capitalize on both, for he desires the eschatological perspective from Jesus' teaching, yet he embraces the Exodus motif from the OT reference.

At other times, the traditions are set next to one another so that they are complementary. For instance, Peter cites Isaiah 40:1–3 and then subsequently reflects Jesus' parable of the soils (1P 1:23—2:3). By placing these next to one another, Peter shows the continuity between these sources of authority. Just as the OT indicated that the Word was seed, so Jesus did.[3] Peter then capitalizes on the intersection of these two, showing that they agree on the importance of the Word and its effects.

Peter's most interesting use of combined tradition is when he finds connections between OT texts and the tradition of Jesus' words that aid his rhetorical purposes. For instance, one of Peter's favorite dominical traditions, Luke 6:27–36 has an interesting lexical connection to one of Peter's favorite OT texts, LXX Psalm 33. Both of these passages use the rare term χρηστός (kind/good), which would have been pronounced the same as χριστός. It is quite unlikely that Jesus was echoing LXX Psalm 33, yet as Peter considers these two favorite traditions, he sees the connection and uses it to effect in his epistle. Those aware of his traditions see that the Lord being χρηστός has rich meaning. In line with the Psalm, it is a metaphor of taste, yet that is supplemented with the Gospel context, which indicates that the metaphor finds its realization in the kindness of the Lord, who shows love even to those who are enemies.

---

3. It is, of course, possible that Jesus was echoing Isaiah 40, and if so, Peter is once more referencing the OT through Jesus.

A second example is found in 1P 3:14b. Peter has invoked the wording of Isaiah 8:12–13, yet his modification of the text suggests he is also reflecting the language of Matthew 10:26–28. By combining these passages, Peter leverages the contextual weight of each. First, by means of the OT reference, he shows that the modern readers are in the same situation as the faithful of old, and by that reminder he calls them to endurance. By the Gospel reflection, he encourages them that all will be revealed in the final day. Both passages together, however, argue that only the Lord should be feared, and by combining the passages Peter emphasizes this point.

While other examples of this final use could be mentioned here (e.g., 1P 4:14 and LXX Isa 11:2a; 5:7 and LXX Ps 54:3), we will address only one more here. Peter's reflection on Jesus' warning concerning Satan has been challenged as a reflection of dominical tradition because the image is significantly altered (from sifting wheat to a ravenous lion). But it is likely that Peter is once more combining his traditions. From the JT he recalls the stark warning concerning Satan, and yet from Job he gets the concept of one roaming the earth (1:7). This latter concept is clearly not harmonious with sifting wheat, but it is harmonious with the popular conception of a roaming lion. Thus, it is likely Peter is combining these two traditions with cultural ideas to create an appropriate analogy for the sake of his readers.

In sum, Peter creatively weaves OT tradition with JT in order to develop his points. He shows a willingness to modify the precise language of both in order to merge them. Further, by their seamless combination, he appears to show that they are of equal authority for the life of his readers.

Because of the breadth of this study, it was not possible to fully develop the interesting interplay between the OT and the JT in 1P. Significant questions remain to be fully answered: Is this study right to imply that Peter's references suggest equal authority between the two? Does Peter show a preference for modifying JT or OT tradition, and what is the significance? What is the rhetorical purpose of doubling traditions, and is there a pattern to such doubling? Unfortunately, these questions must simply be posed here, but the field of research is white for harvest.

Appendix

Proposed Parallels

THE FOLLOWING TABLE (A.1) provides a comprehensive guide for where various scholars have suggested the presence of dominical teaching. The guide is necessarily limited by the ambiguity of the lists provided in each scholarly work. Sometimes a scholar will distinguish what he believes are likely parallels from unlikely, while at other times they are listed together. Nevertheless, the following table should prove helpful to those seeking to do further work in this area. After the table, a comprehensive list of parallels by each author is presented. Table A.2 derives from the first table and includes only references mentioned by more than one scholar. Finally, table A.3 provides a distribution of the multiple proposed parallels within the Gospels.

Table A.1 All Proposed Gospel Parallels

	Mark	Matthew	Luke	John
1:1				7:35b
1:2	7:4	28:19		
1:3	10:14, 15	19:28		3:3, 5, 7; 20:3–8
1:4	12:7	5:5; 6:20; 21:38; 25:34	12:33; 20:14	
1:5	8:38		12:35–37	10:28–30
1:6		5:10–12	6:22, 23; 24:12	16:17–21; 20:29
1:7			17:26–35	20:29
1:8		5:11, 12	6:22, 23	20:29, 31

APPENDIX

	Mark	Matthew	Luke	John
1:9	8:36–38		21:19	20:29, 31
1:10		11:13; 13:17	10:24, 25; 24:25–27	
1:11		13:17	10:24; 24:25–27, 44	12:41; 14:16–17; 15:26; 16:13
1:12		5:12; 13:17	15:10; 24:12, 25–27	14:16–17; 15:26; 16:13; 20:5
1:13	8:38; 13:5, 6	24:4	12:35, 37, 45; 17:30; 21:8, 34	
1:14				
1:15		5:48		
1:16		5:48		
1:17		6:9; 10:28; 22:16	11:2; 12:4, 5, 35–37	
1:18	7:3; 8:37; 10:45	15:26; 20:28		1:29
1:19				1:29, 36
1:20		25:34		17:24
1:21			24:26	12:44; 14:1, 6
1:22				3:3, 5; 13:15, 34–35; 15:3, 12; 17:19
1:23	4:14	13:18–23	8:12–15	1:13; 3:3, 7; 13:15; 15:12
1:24				
1:25		5:18		1:1
2:1		24:29	21:34	
2:2	10:15	18:2–3; 19:14; 24:29	18:17; 21:34	3:3, 7
2:3		5:45; 20:1–16	6:35	
2:4	12:10, 11	11:28; 16:18; 21:42, 43	20:17–18	6:37; 7:37
2:5	3:31–35; 12:10–11	16:18		1:42
2:6	12:10–11	21:42–43		
2:7	12:10–11	5:16; 21:42–43	20:12, 17–18	
2:8	12:10–11	16:23; 21:42–43	20:17–18	

PROPOSED PARALLELS 245

	Mark	Matthew	Luke	John
2:9	4:21; 13:20–27	5:13–16; 22:14	16:8; 11:35–36; 18:7	8:12; 12:35, 46
2:10				
2:11	13:14–18			
2:12	4:21	5:13–16; 21:42	19:44	
2:13	12:17; 13:9–13	5:14–16; 38–42; 17:25–27; 22:21	20:26	
2:14	13:9–13	5:14–16; 17:25–27		
2:15	1:25; 4:39	5:14–16; 17:25–27		
2:16		5:14–16; 17:25–27		
2:17	12:17	5:14–16; 17:25–27; 22:21	20:26	
2:18			6:27–36	
2:19	10:29–30, 33–34; 13:10–13	5:10, 34–39, 46, 47	6:26–28, 32–35	
2:20	10:29–30, 33–34; 13:10–13; 14:65	5:10, 39, 44, 46, 47	6:32–35	
2:21	8:34; 10:29–30, 33–34; 13:10–13	5:46, 47; 10:38	6:32, 33; 9:23	13:5, 15
2:22				8:46
2:23	14:61; 15:5	9:36; 27:14	15:4; 23:46	8:48–50
2:24	15:15	27:26	12:32	1:29, 36; 10:11, 14; 21:15–17
2:25	6:34; 14:27	9:36; 18:12, 13	12:32; 15:4	10:2–18, 26, 27; 21:15–17
3:1		5:5, 16; 7:21–27		
3:2		5:5, 16; 7:21–27		
3:3		5:5		
3:4	14:3	5:1–9; 6:4–6; 11:29; 12:34–36; 15:18, 19		
3:5				
3:6				
3:7				
3:8		5:44	6:28	13:1–17
3:9	10:17	5:10, 38–44	6:22, 27–30	

APPENDIX

	Mark	Matthew	Luke	John
3:10		5:44	6:28	10:10
3:11		5:44	6:28	
3:12		5:44	6:28	9:31
3:13	13:13	5:16; 7:21–27	10:19; 21:18	
3:14		5:10; 10:26–28	6:22, 23	14:27
3:15	1:14; 13:9–10		6:28; 12:11	
3:16		5:16, 44	6:28; 12:11	
3:17		5:10–12	6:22	
3:18			23:46	13:15
3:19				
3:20		7:14; 22:14; 24:37–38	13:23; 17:26	
3:21				3:5, 6
3:22	3:27	16:18	11:21, 22	
4:1	8:34–35			13:15
4:2				
4:3				
4:4		12:31–36		
4:5	8:38; 13:33–37	12:36; 25:31	12:35–46; 13:24–30; 16:2; 21:34–36	5:22
4:6				
4:7	13:29, 33, 35; 14:38	24:42; 25:13; 26:41	12:37; 21:31, 34, 36	
4:8	12:30–33	5:7	7:47	13:15, 34–35; 15:12
4:9		25:35		
4:10	13:34	24:45	12:42–48	
4:11	8:29, 13:11	5:16		13:31–32; 14:13; 15:8; 17:1, 4
4:12		5:11–12; 26:41		
4:13	13:9–13	5:10–12, 39, 44; 10:24, 25; 26:41	6:22–23, 28	13:16; 15:20; 20:29
4:14	3:28–30; 9:41; 13:11, 13;	5:10–12; 6:28; 10:19–20, 22; 12:31–32; 26:41	6:22–23, 28; 12:11–12; 21:17	

	Mark	Matthew	Luke	John
4:15		5:11–12; 26:41		
4:16		5:11–12; 26:41		
4:17	1:14; 3:31–35		23:31	
4:18	13:19–20	24:22		
4:19		6:25–27	23:46	
5:1	10:37	19:28	22:28–30; 24:47, 48	15:27
5:2	10:35–47; 14:27	26:31	12:32	10:11, 14, 16; 21:15–17
5:3	10:42–45; 15:24	20:25–28	12:32; 22:24–30	13:4–17
5:4	10:42–45	9:36; 18:12, 13; 19:28; 20:25–28; 25:32	12:32; 22:25–30	10:11–18; 13:4–17; 21:15–17
5:5	10:42–45	20:25–28	22:25–30	13:1–17
5:6		4:1–11; 23:12	1:52; 14:11; 18:14	
5:7	12:14	4:1–11; 6:25–34	12:22–31	
5:8	13:14, 33, 35, 37; 14:38	4:1–11; 5:25, 26, 38–42; 24:42; 25:13; 26:40–41	12:58; 22:31–32	
5:9	14:38	4:1–11; 5:38–42, 7:25; 26:40–41	22:31–32	
5:10		7:25	6:48	
5:11				
5:12				
5:13	2:19			3:29
5:14			24:36	20:19, 21, 26

PARALLELS ORGANIZED BY AUTHOR

1. Ernst Scharfe: 1:3 (John 3:3ff): 1:8 (John 20:29); 1:10ff (Luke 10:24); 1:13 (Luke 12:35); 1:25 (Matt 5:18); 2:12 (Matt 5:16); 2:17 (Matt 22:21); 2:19 (Matt 5:10); 2:20 (Matt 5:10); 3:9 (Matt 5:44; Luke 6:27-28); 4:14 (Matt 5:11–12); 4:15 (Matt 5:11–12); 5:2 (John 21:15ff); 5:7 (Matt 6:31, 32); 5:8 (Mark 14:38).[1]

---

1 Scharfe, *Petrinische Strömung*, 140-41. He notes other echoes, which he classifies

2. Charles Bigg: 1:3 (John 3:3); 1:10 (Luke 10:24, 25); 1:11 (Luke 24:26); 1:13 (Luke 12:35); 1:17 (Luke 11:2); 1:19 (John 1:29); 1:21 (Luke 24:26); 1:23 (Luke 8:12; John 1:13); 2:7 (Luke 20:17, 18); 2:12 (Matt 5:16); 2:25 (John 10:11); 3:9 (Luke 6:28); 3:14 (Matt 5:10); 4:10 (Luke 12:42); 5:2 (John 21:16).[2]

3. H. D. M. Spence: 1:6 (Matt 5:12; Luke 24:12); 1:12 (Matt 5:12; Luke 24:12); 1:19 (John 1:29); 1:20 (Matt 25:34); 1:22 (John 15:12); 2:5 (John 1:42); 2:7 (Mark 12:10; Matt 21:42; Luke 20:17); 2:8 (Matt 16:23); 2:12 (Luke 19:44); 2:15 (Mark 1:25; 4:39); 2:19 (Matt 5:39; Luke 6:32); 2:21 (John 13:15); 2:25 (Matt 9:36; 18:12-13; John 10:11-18); 3:9 (Matt 5:39); 3:14 (Matt 5:10); 3:20 (Matt 24:37-38; Luke 13:23); 4:10 (Luke 12:42); 4:11 (Matt 5:16); 4:13 (Matt 5:12); 4:14 (Matt 5:10); 4:19 (Luke 23:46); 5:2 (John 21:16); 5:3 (Matt 20:25); 5:4 (Matt 9:36; 18:12-13; John 10:11-18); 5:7 (Matt 6:25, 28); 5:8 (Matt 5:25); 5:9 (Matt 7:25).[3]

4. F. H. Chase: 1:3 (John 3:3); 1:4 (Matt 5:5; 6:20; 25:34); 1:6 (Matt 5:12; John 20:29); 1:8 (Matt 5:12; John 20:29); 1:10 (Luke 10:24); 1:11 (Luke 24:26, 44); 1:13 (Luke 12:35; 21:34); 1:17 (Matt 6:9; Luke 11:2); 1:19 (John 1:29, 36); 1:22 (John 13:34ff; 15:12); 1:23 (John 3:3); 2:2 (Matt 18:2ff; 19:14; Luke 18:17); 2:4 (Matt 11:28; John 6:37; 7:37); 2:5 (Matt 16:18); 2:7 (Matt 21:42); 2:9 (John 8:12; 12:46); 2:12 (Matt 5:16); 2:13 (Matt 22:21); 2:17 (Matt 22:21); 2:21 (Matt 10:38); 2:23 (Matt 9:36; Luke 15:4; 23:46); 2:24 (John 1:29, 36); 2:25 (John 10:11, 14, 16); 3:9 (Luke 6:28); 3:13 (Luke 10:19; 21:18); 3:14 (Matt 5:10; Matt 10:26ff); 3:15 (Luke 6:28); 3:16 (Matt 5:16); 4:7 (Matt 24:42; 25:13; 26:41; Luke 12:37; 21:34); 4:13 (Matt 5:12; John 20:29); 4:14 (Matt 5:11); 4:19 (Matt 6:25ff; Luke 23:46); 5:1 (Matt 19:28; Luke 22:28ff; 24:47); 5:2 (John 21:16, 17); 5:3 (Matt 20:25ff); 5:4 (John 21:16, 17); 5:6 (Matt 23:12); 5:8 (Matt 24:42).[4]

5. Ora Delmer Foster: 1:1 (John 7:35b); 1:3 (John 3:3); 1:4 (Matt 25:34); 1:5 (John 10:28ff); 1:6 (Matt 5:11,12; Luke 6:22,23); 1:8 (Matt 5:11,12; Luke 6:22,23; John 20:29, 31); 1:9 (John 20:29, 31); 1:10 (Matt 13:17; Luke 10:24); 1:11 (Luke 24:26; John 12:41); 1:13 (Luke 12:35; 17:30);

---

as too weak to be confirmed: 1:6 (John 16:20); 2:2 (Matt 18:3); 2:21 (John 13:5); 5:6 (Matt 23:12; Luke 14:11). Notably, all but the first were suggested by other commentators. Thus, only 1:6 (John 16:20) is not represented in the chart. Scharfe's proposed analogy is certainly between 2:19-20 with Matt 5:10, though his text suggests 4:19-20.

2 Bigg, *Epistles of St. Peter*, 23.

3 Spence, *1 Peter*, ii-iii. While the *Pulpit Commentary* indicated a parallel between 1P 2:21 and John 3:15, the parallel is certainly 13:15.

4 Chase, "Peter, First Epistle," 787-88.

PROPOSED PARALLELS 249

1:17 (Matt 6:9; Luke 11:2); 1:18 (Mark 7:3; 10:45; Matt 15:26; 20:28; John 1:29); 1:19 (John 1:29); 1:21 (John 12:44); 1:22a (John 15:3); 1:22b (John 13:34); 1:23 (Mark 4:14; Matt 13:18; Luke 8:12ff; John 1:13); 1:25 (John 1:1); 2:2 (Mark 10:15; Matt 18:2; Luke 18:17); 2:5 (Matt 16:18); 2:7 (Mark 12:10; Matt 21:42; Luke 20:12); 2:12 (Matt 5:16; Luke 19:44); 2:13 (Mark 12:17; Matt 22:21; Luke 20:26); 2:17 (Mark 12:17; Matt 22:21; Luke 20:26); 2:21 (Mark 8:34; Matt 10:38; Luke 9:23; John 13:15); 2:22 (John 8:46); 2:23 (Mark 14:61; 15:5; Matt 27:14; Luke 23:46; John 8:48-50); 2:24 (Mark 15:15; Matt 27:26); 2:25 (Mark 6:34; Matt 9:36; Luke 15:4); 3:9 (Matt 5:39; Luke 6:29); 3:12 (John 9:31); 3:14 (Matt 5:10; 10:26; John 14:27); 3:20 (Matt 24:37, 38; Luke 17:26); 3:21 (John 3:5, 6); 4:5 (Luke 16:2; John 5:22); 4:7 (Mark 13:33; Matt 24:42; Luke 12:37); 4:8 (Luke 7:47; John 15:12); 4:10 (Matt 24:45; Luke 12:42); 4:11 (John 14:13); 4:19 (Luke 23:46); 5:1 (Luke 24:48; John 15:27); 5:2 (21:15ff); 5:3 (Mark 10:42; Matt 20:25; Luke 22:24); 5:4 (John 10:11ff); 5:6 (Matt 23:12; Luke 14:11); 5:8 (Matt 5:25; Luke 12:58); 5:10 (Matt 7:25; Luke 6:48).[5]

6. Edward Gordon Selwyn: 1:2 (Matt 28:19); 1:3 (Mark 10:14-15; Matt 19:28); 1:8 (John 20:29); 1:12 (Luke 15:10); 1:18 (Mark 10:45; Matt 20:28); 2:1 (Matt 24:29; Luke 21:34); 2:2 (Matt 24:29; Luke 21:34); 2:4 (Matt 11:28); 2:6 (Matt 21:42); 2:7 (Matt 21:42); 2:9 (Mark 13:20, 22, 27; Matt 5:14-16; 22:14; Luke 18:7; John 8:12, 12:35, 46); 2:12 (Matt 5:16); 2:13-17 (Matt 5:14-16); 2:16 (Matt 17:26); 2:19 (Matt 5:34-38; Luke 6:32-34); 2:20 (Mark 14:65; Matt 5:39); 2:25 (Mark 6:34; 14:27; John 10:2, 11ff); 3:4 (Matt 5:1-9; 6:4, 6; 11:29; 12:34-36; 15:18-19); 3:8-12 (Matt 5:44; Luke 6:28); 3:10 (John 10:10); 3:13 (Mark 13:13); 3:14 (Matt 5:10); 3:20 (Matt 7:14; 22:14; 24:37-38; Luke 13:23; 17:26); 3:22 (Mark 3:27; Matt 16:18; Luke 11:21, 22); 4:4 (Matt 12:31-36); 4:5 (Mark 8:38; Matt 13:33-37; 25:31; Luke 12:35-46; 13:24-30; 21:34-36); 4:7 (Mark 13:33, 35; Matt 26:41); 4:8 (Mark 12:30-33; Luke 7:47; John 13:34ff.); 4:9 (Matt 25:35); 4:10 (Luke 12:42ff.); 4:13 (Matt 10:24-25; John 13:16; 15:20); 4:14 (Mark 9:41; 13:13; Matt 5:11; 10:22; Luke 21:17); 4:18 (Mark 13:19, 20); 5:3 (Mark 10:42ff.); 5:6 (Matt 23:12; Luke 1:52; 14:11; 18:14); 5:7 (Matt 6:25-32; Luke 12:22-31); 5:8

---

[5] All of Foster's proposed parallels are included here, though in many of them he concludes that the evidence is less than convincing (Foster, *Literary Relations*, 492-535). While the author has a parallel between 2:12 and Luke 10:44, the reference is clearly Luke 19:44.

(Mark 13:33, 35); 5:13 (Mark 2:19; John 3:29); 5:14 (Luke 24:36; John 20:19, 21, 26).[6]

7. Johannes A. E. van Dodewaard: 1:2 (Mark 7:4); 1:4 (Mark 12:7); 1:18 (Mark 10:45); 2:7 (Mark 12:10); 2:15 (Mark 1:25; 4:39); 2:25 (Mark 6:34); 3:4 (Mark 14:3); 3:9 (Mark 10:17); 4:17 (Mark 1:14); 5:3 (Mark 10:42; 15:24); 5:7 (Mark 12:14).[7]

8. Johannes Schattenmann: 2:11 (Mark 13:14–18); 2:13–14 (Mark 13:9–13); 4:7 (Mark 13:29); 4:10ff. (Mark 13:34); 4:11 (Mark 13:11); 5:8 (Mark 13:14, 37).[8]

9. Alan Marshall Stibbs: 1:16 (Matt 5:48); 1:17 (Matt 22:16); 1:18 (Mark 10:45); 1:22 (John 15:12); 2:4 (Matt 21:42ff); 2:19 (Matt 5:39; Luke 6:32); 3:9 (Matt 5:39); 3:14 (Matt 5:10); 3:16 (Matt 5:44; Luke 6:28); 3:20 (Matt 24:37ff); 4:11 (Matt 5:16); 4:13 (Matt 5:10ff); 4:18 (Matt 24:22); 5:3 (Matt 20:25); 5:7 (Matt 6:25ff).[9]

10. John Pairman Brown: 2:9 (Mark 4:21; Matt 5:13–16); 2:12 (Mark 4:21; Matt 5:13–16); 2:13 (Matt 5:38–42); 2:20 (Matt 5:44); 3:9 (Matt 5:44); 3:14 (Matt 5:10); 3:15 (Mark 1:14; 13:9–10; Luke 12:11); 4:13 (Matt 5:11–12); 4:14 (Matt 5:11–12); 5:8 (Matt 5:38–42); 5:9 (Matt 5:38–42).[10]

11. Ceslas Spicq: 1:5 (Mark 8:38; Luke 12:35–37); 1:8 (John 20:29); 1:11 (John 12:41; 14:16–17; 15:26; 16:13); 1:12 (John 14:16–17; 15:26; 16:13; 20:5); 1:13 (Mark 8:38; Luke 12:35–37); 1:17 (Matt 10:28; Luke 12:4–5, 35–37); 1:18 (Mark 8:37; 10:45); 1:19 (John 1:29, 36); 1:20 (John 17:24); 1:22 (John 13:15; 17:19); 1:23 (John 3:3–7; 13:15);

12. A. Feuillet: 1:3 (John 3:3, 7); 1:4 (Luke 12:33); 1:6 (John 16:17–21); 1:7, 8 (John 20:29); 1:10–12 (Luke 24:25); 1:13 (Luke 12:35); 1:20 (John 17:24); 1:21 (John 14:1, 6); 2:4 (Mark 12:10; Matt 16:18); 2:12 (Matt 5:16); 2:16 (Matt 17:26–27); 2:19–20 (Luke 6:26–27, 32–35); 2:25 (John 10:2–18; 21:15–17); 3:14 (Matt 5:10); 4:7 (Luke 21:31, 34,

---

6 Selwyn, *First Epistle of St. Peter*. These parallels were mined from throughout Selwyn's commentary. The proposed parallel between 3:18–4:6 and John 5:19–29 was not included in the chart, for its connection was too broad, thus inclusion would have substantially affected the overall presentation.

7 His parallels are based on words strongly connected to 1P and Mark (Dodewaard, "Sprachliche Übereinstimmung," 236).

8 Schattenmann, "Little Apocalypse."

9 Stibbs, *First Epistle General of Peter*, 35n1. He notes that "these may not all, of course, be conscious reminiscences."

10 Brown, "Synoptic Parallels."

36); 4:19 (Luke 23:46); 5:2 (John 21:15–17); 5:4 (John 21:15–17); 5:3–5 (Luke 22:25–30); 5:5 (John 13:1–17); 5:8–9 (Luke 22:31).[11]

13. Ernest Best 1:4 (Luke 12:33); 1:13 (Luke 12:35); 2:12 (Matt 5:16); 2:19ff (Luke 6:32ff); 3:14 (Matt 5:10); 3:16 (Luke 6:28); 4:10ff. (Luke 12:42); 4:14 (Luke 6:22); 5:2–4 (Luke 12:32).[12]

14. Gundry: 1:3 (John 3:3, 7); 1:4 (Luke 12:33); 1:8 (John 20:29); 1:10, (Luke 24:25); 1:11 (Luke 24:25); 1:12 (Luke 24:25); 1:13 (Luke 12:35, 45); 1:21 (John 14:1, 6); 1:22 (John 13:34ff, 15:12); 1:23 (John 3:3, 7); 2:2 (John 3:3, 7); 2:4 (Mark 12:10; Matt 21:42); 2:7 (Mark 12:10; Matt 21:42); 2:9 (Matt 5:16); 2:12 (Matt 5:16); 2:13–17 (Matt 17:26ff); 2:18 (Luke 6:27ff); 2:24 (Luke 12:32; John 10:11, 14; 21:15–17); 2:25 (Luke 12:32; John 10:11,14; 21:15–17); 3:8 (John 13:1–17); 3:9 (Matt 5:39, 44; Luke 6:27ff;); 3:14 (Matt 5:10; Luke 6:22); 4:7 (Mark 14:38; Luke 21:31, 34, 36;); 4:8 (John 13:34ff, 15:12); 4:19 (Luke 23:46); 5:2 (Luke 12:32; John 10:11,14; 21:15–17); 5:3–5 (Mark 10:42–45; Matt 20:25–28; Luke 22:25–30); 5:4 (Luke 12:32; John 10:11, 14; 21:15–17); 5:8 (Mark 14:38; Luke 22:31).[13]

15. Merrill Chaplin Tenney: 1:3 (John 20:3–8); 1:8 (John 20:29); 1:19 (John 1:29, 36); 1:22 (John 15:12); 1:23 (John 15:12); 2:25 (John 10:2–16, 26, 27); 4:11 (John 17:1, 4); 5:2 (John 10:16); 5:5 (John 13:1–17).[14]

16. Karl Hermann Schelkle: 1:10ff (Matt 11:13; 13:17); 1:17 (Matt 6:9); 2:7 (Matt 5:16; 21:42); 2:12 (Matt 5:16; 21:42) 3:9 (Matt 5:10, 39, 44); 4:13 (Matt 5:10, 39, 44); 5:8 (Matt 5:25–26, 41).[15]

17. Norbert Brox: 1:4 (Luke 12:33); 1:8 (John 20:29); 1:22 (John 13:34ff); 2:12 (Matt 5:16); 2:19ff (Luke 6:32–35); 3:9 (Luke 6:27ff); 4:14 (Matt 5:11ff); 5:3–5 (Luke 22:25–30; Mark 10:42–45); 5:8ff (Mark 14:38).[16]

18. Gerhard Maier: 1:3 (John 3:3); 1:4 (Luke 12:33); 1:7 (Luke 17:26ff); 1:8 (John 20:29); 1:9 (Mark 8:36ff; Luke 21:19); 1:10 (Luke 24:25–27); 1:11 (Luke 24:25–27); 1:12 (Luke 24:25–27); 1:13 (Luke 12:35); 1:15 (Matt 5:48); 1:22 (John 13:34; 15:12); 1:23 (Matt 13:18ff; John 3:3ff); 2:2 (John 3:3ff); 2:3 (Matt 5:45, 20:1ff; Luke 6:35); 2:4ff (Mark 12:10); 2:9

---

11 Feuillet highlights what he calls the "most remarkable references" (translated from "des références les plus remarquables" [Feuillet, "Quelques Reflexions," 241–47, 242]).

12 Best, "1P and the Gospel Tradition," 105–6.

13 Gundry, "'Verba Christi' in I Peter"; Gundry, "Further Verba."

14 Tenney, "Possible Parallels."

15. Schelkle, *Die Petrusbriefe*, 6.

16. Brox, "Erste Petrusbrief."

(Matt 5:14, 16; Luke 16:8, 11:35ff); 2:13–17 (Matt 17:25ff); 2:19ff (Matt 5:10ff; Luke 6:28, 33); 3:4 (Matt 5:5); 3:9 (Luke 6:27ff); 4:7ff (Mark 14:38; Luke 21:31ff); 4:8 (John 13:34; 15:12); 4:10 (Luke 12:42ff); 4:12–16 (Matt 5:11–12; 26:41); 4:19 (Luke 23:46); 5:1 (Luke 24:48); 5:3–5 (Mark 10:42–45; Luke 22:25–30; John 13:4ff); 5:7 (Matt 6:25ff); 5:8ff (Mark 14:38; Luke 22:31ff).[17]

19. D. Edmond Hiebert: 1:13 (Luke 12:35); 2:12 (Matt 5:16); 3:9, 14, 17 (Matt 5:10–12; Luke 6:22); 4:10 (Luke 12:42); 4:14 (Matt 5:10–12; Luke 6:22).[18]

20. C. G. Wilkes: 1:4 (Mark 12:7; Matt 6:20; 21:38; Luke 12:33b; 20:14); 1:6 (Matt 5:10–12; Luke 6:22, 23a); 1:13 (Mark 13:5, 6; Matt 24:4; Luke 21:8); 1:18 (Mark 10:45; Matt 20:28); 2:4 (Mark 12:10, 11; Matt 21:42, 43; Luke 20:17–18); 2:6–8 (Mark 12:10, 11; Matt 21:42, 43; Luke 20:17–18); 2:12 (Matt 5:16; Luke 19:44); 2:19–21 (Mark 13:10–13; 10:29–30, 33–34; Matt 5:46–47; Luke 6:32–33); 2:25 (Mark 6:34; Matt 9:36); 3:14 (Matt 5:10–12; Luke 6:22, 23a); 3:18 (Luke 23:46); 4:7 (Mark 13:29; Matt 26:41; Luke 21:34, 36); 4:13 (Matt 5:10–12; Luke 6:22, 23a); 4:14 (Matt 5:10–12; Luke 6:22, 23a); 5:2 (Mark 14:27; Matt 26:31; Luke 12:32); 5:4 (Matt 25:32; John 10:11–18); 5:8 (Mark 13:33, 35, 37; Matt 25:13).[19]

21. Simon Kistemaker: 1:8 (John 20:29); 1:22 (John 13:34–35); 2:12 (Matt 5:6); 3:9 (Luke 6:27–28); 4:7 (Luke 21:31, 34, 36); 5:8–9 (Luke 22:31–32).[20]

22. J. Ramsey Michaels: 1:3 (John 3:3, 5); 1:4 (Luke 12:33); 1:8 (Matt 5:12); 1:13 (Luke 12:35); 1:22 (John 3:3, 5); 2:12 (Matt 5:16); 2:19 (Luke 6:32–34); 2:20 (Luke 6:32–34); 3:9 (Luke 6:28); 3:14 (Matt 5:10, Luke 6:22); 3:15 (Luke 12:11); 3:16 (Luke 6:28; 12:11); 4:10 (Luke 12:42); 4:13 (Matt 5:12); 4:14 (Mark 3:28–30; 13:11; Matt 5:11; 10:19–20; 12:31–32; Luke 12:11–12); 5:7 (Luke 12:22).[21]

23. I. Howard Marshall: 1:4 (Luke 12:33); 1:13 (Luke 12:35); 1:18 (Mark 10:45); 3:14 (Matt 5:10).[22]

---

17. Maier, "Jesustradition."
18. Hiebert, *First Peter*, 3n14.
19. Wilkes, "Synoptic Tradition."
20. Kistemaker, *Exposition of the Epistles of Peter*, 12.
21. Michaels, *1 Peter*, xli–xlii.
22. Marshall, *1 Peter*, 20.

PROPOSED PARALLELS   253

24. Norman Hillyer: 1:10–12 (Luke 24:25–27); 1:16 (Matt 5:48); 1:17 (Matt 22:16); 1:18 (Mark 10:45); 1:22 (John 15:12); 3:9 (Matt 5:39); 3:14 (Matt 5:10); 4:11 (Matt 5:16); 4:13 (Matt 5:10); 5:3 (Matt 20:26); 5:7 (Matt 6:25–34).[23]

25. Paul J. Achtemeier: 1:3 (John 3:3); 1:4 (Matt 5:5; 6:20; 25:34; Luke 12:33); 1:6 (Matt 5:12); 1:8 (John 20:29); 1:10 (Luke 10:24); 1:11 (Luke 24:26, 44); 1:13 (Luke 12:35; 21:34); 1:17 (Matt 6:9; Luke 11:2); 1:19 (John 1:29, 36); 1:22 (John 13:34–35; 15:12); 1:23 (John 3:3); 2:2 (Matt 18:2–3; 19:14; Luke 18:17); 2:4 (Matt 11:28); 2:5 (Matt 16:18); 2:7 (Matt 21:42); 2:9 (John 8:12; 12:46); 2:12 (Matt 5:16); 2:13 (Matt 22:21); 2:17 (Matt 22:21); 2:19–20 (Luke 6:32–35); 2:21 (Matt 10:38); 2:23 (Luke 23:46); 2:25 (Matt 9:36; Luke 15:4; John 10:11, 14, 16); 3:9 (Luke 6:27–28); 3:13 (Luke 10:19; 21:18); 3:14 (Matt 5:10; 10:26–28); 3:16 (Luke 6:28); 4:7 (Matt 24:42; 25:13; 26:41; Luke 12:37; 21:34); 4:14 (Matt 5:11–12); 4:19 (Matt 6:25–27); 5:1 (Matt 19:28; Luke 22:28–30; 24:47); 5:2 (John 21:16, 17); 5:3–5 (Mark 10:42–45; Luke 22:25–30); 5:3 (Matt 20:25–26); 5:4 (John 21:16, 17); 5:6 (Matt 23:12); 5:8–9 (Mark 14:38).[24]

26. Scot McKnight: 1:13 (Luke 12:35); 1:17 (Luke 11:2); 2:12 (Matt 5:16); 3:9 (Luke 6:28); 3:14 (Matt 5:10).[25]

27. Rainer Metzner: 1:15 (Matt 5:38–48); 2:12 (Matt 5:16); 3:9 (Matt 5:38–48); 3:14 (Matt 5:10); 4:13 (Matt 5:11ff); 5:6–9 (Matt 4:1–11).[26]

28. John H. Elliott: 1:10–12 (Matt 13:17; Luke 24:26); 1:13 (Luke 12:35); 1:17 (Matt 6:9; Luke 11:2); 1:18 (Mark 10:45); 1:19–21, 2:21–25, 3:18 (Mark 14–16 par.); 2:4–8 (Mark 12:1–12 par.); 2:5 (Mark 3:31–35 par.); 2:12 (Matt 5:16); 2:18–3:7, 5:2–5a (Mark 10:2–45 par.); 2:19–20 (Luke 6:27–36); 3:9 (Matt 5:38–42; Luke 6:29–30); 3:14 (Matt 5:10); 4:5 (Matt 12:36); 4:13 (Mark 13:9–13; Matt 5:10–11; Luke 6:22–23, 28); 4:14 (Matt 5:10–11;Luke 6:22–23, 28); 4:17 (Mark 3:31–35 par.); 5:1 (Mark 10:37); 5:2–5 (Mark 10:35–45 par.); 5:4 (Mark 10:37; Matt 19:28); 5:6 (Luke 14:11); 5:7 (Matt 6:25–34); 5:8 (Mark 13:33, 37).[27]

23. Hillyer, *1 and 2 Peter, Jude*, 1.

24. Achtemeier, *1 Peter*, 10n97. After listing this vast number of parallels, he indicates that "only a handful have any persuasive power." He lists the following as members of that elect group: 3:14; 4:14 (Matt 5:10); 2:12b (Matt 5:11–12); 1:4 (Matt 25:34); 1:11 (Luke 24:26–27). Though Achtemeier suggests a parallel between 1:4 and Luke 12:23, it is clear he meant 12:33. Likewise, the parallel is between 4:7 and Luke 12:37, not 12:27.

25. McKnight, *1 Peter*, 28.

26. Metzner, *Rezeption*.

27. Elliott, *1 Peter*, 24–25; Elliott, "Ministry and Church Order," 386. Elliott suggests

29. Daniel Powers: 1:3 (John 3:3, 7); 1:4 (Luke 12:33); 1:8 (John 20:29); 1:21 (John 14:1, 6); 1:22 (John 13:34-35; 15:12); 2:2 (John 3:3, 7); 2:4, 7 (Mark 12:10; Matt 21:42); 2:12 (Matt 5:16); 2:13-17 (Matt 17:26-27); 2:25 (John 10:11, 14); 3:14 (Matt 5:10); 5:2, 4 (John 10:11, 14); 5:8-9 (Mark 14:38; Matt 26:40-41).[28]

Table A.2: Parallels Proposed by more than One Scholar

	Mark	Matthew	Luke	John
1:3				3:3, 5, 7
1:4	12:7	5:5; 6:20; 25:34	12:33	
1:6		5:10-12		20:29
1:8		5:12		20:29
1:9			21:19	
1:10		13:17	10:24, 25; 24:25-27	
1:11		13:17	24:25-27, 44	
1:12		13:17	24:25-27	
1:13			12:35, 37; 21:34	
1:15		5:48		
1:16		5:48		
1:17		6:9; 10:28; 22:16	11:2	
1:18	10:45	20:28		
1:19				1:29, 36
1:21				14:1, 6
1:22				13:34-35; 15:12
1:23				3:3, 7
2:2		18:2-3; 19:14	18:17	3:3, 7
2:4	12:10, 11	11:28; 21:42, 43		
2:5		16:18		
2:6	12:10-11	21:42-43		
2:7	12:10-11	21:42-43	20:17, 18	

some other, larger connections, which have not been considered in the chart; e.g., 2:18-3:7, 5:2-5a (Mark 10:2-45 par., domestic instruction for the household of God); 1 Pet 1:19-21, 2:21-25, 3:18 (Mark 14-16 par.).

28. Powers, *1 and 2 Peter*, 27-28.

PROPOSED PARALLELS 255

	Mark	Matthew	Luke	John
2:8	12:10-11			
2:9		5:13-16		8:12; 12:46
2:12		5:13-16; 21:42	19:44	
2:13		17:25-27; 22:21		
2:14		17:25-27		
2:15	1:25; 4:39	17:25-27		
2:16		17:25-27		
2:17		17:25-27; 22:21		
2:19		5:10, 34-39	6:28, 32-35	
2:20			6:32-35	
2:21		10:38		
2:23			23:46	
2:24				
2:25	6:34	9:36		10:2-18
3:4		5:1-9		
3:9		5:10, 38-44	6:27-30	
3:13			10:19; 21:18	
3:14		5:10; 10:26-28	6:22, 23	
3:15			12:11	
3:16			6:28	
3:20		24:37-38	13:23; 17:26	
4:7	13:29; 14:38	24:42; 25:13; 26:41	12:37; 21:31, 34, 36	
4:8				13:34ff; 15:12
4:10			12:42ff	
4:11		5:16		17:1, 4
4:13		5:10-12	6:22-23	
4:14	13:11, 13	5:10-12	6:22-23	
4:15		5:11-12		
4:18		24:22		
4:19		6:25-27	23:46	
5:1		19:28	22:28-30; 24:47, 48	

	Mark	Matthew	Luke	John
5:2			12:32	10:11, 14, 16; 21:15–17
5:3	10:42–45	20:25–28	22:25–30	
5:4	10:42–45		12:32; 22:25–30	10:11–18; 21:15–17
5:5	10:42–45		22:25–30	13:1–17
5:6		23:12	14:11	
5:7		6:25–34	12:22–31	
5:8	13:33, 35, 37; 14:38	5:25, 26, 38–42;	22:31–32	
5:9	14:38			

Table A.3: Distribution of the Multiple Proposed Parallels within the Gospels

Chapter	Mark	Matthew	Luke	John
1	1			2
2				
3				3
4	1			
5		16		
6	1	4	8	
7				
8				1
9		1		
10	2	3	2	2
11		1	1	
12	2		6	1
13	3	1	1	3
14	2		1	2
15				2
16		1		
17		1		1
18		1	1	
19		2	1	
20		2	1	1
21		3	4	1

Chapter	Mark	Matthew	Luke	John
22		3	3	
23		1	2	
24		3	3	
25		2		
26		1		

Bibliography

Abernathy, David. *An Exegetical Summary of 1 Peter*. 2nd ed. Dallas: SIL International, 2008.
Achtemeier, Paul J. *1 Peter*. Hermeneia. Minneapolis: Fortress, 1996.
———. "Suffering Servant and Suffering Christ in 1 Peter." In *The Future of Christology: Essays in Honor of Leander E. Keck*, edited by Abraham J. Malherbe and Wayne A. Meeks, 176–88. Minneapolis: Fortress, 1993.
Agnew, Francis H. "1 Peter 1:2—An Alternative Translation." *Catholic Biblical Quarterly* 45 (1983) 68–73.
Aland, Barbara, et al. *Nestle-Aland—Novum Testamentum Graece*. 28th rev. ed. Stuttgart: Deutsche Bibelgesellschaft, 2012.
Albl, Martin C. *And Scripture Cannot Be Broken: The Form and Function of the Early Christian Testimonia Collections*. Supplements to Novum Testamentum 96. Boston: Brill, 1999.
Alfaro, María Jesús Martínez. "Intertextuality: Origins and Development of the Concept." *Atlantis* 18 (1996) 268–85.
Allison, Dale C. *Constructing Jesus: Memory, Imagination, and History*. Grand Rapids: Baker, 2013.
———. *The Intertextual Jesus: Scripture in Q*. Harrisburg, PA: Trinity, 2000.
———. "The Pauline Epistles and the Synoptic Gospels: The Pattern of the Parallels." *New Testament Studies* 28 (1982) 1–32.
Alter, Robert. *The Pleasures of Reading in an Ideological Age*. New York: Norton, 1996.
Bailey, Kenneth E. "Informal Controlled Oral Tradition and the Synoptic Gospels." *Asia Journal of Theology* 5 (1991) 34–54.
———. "Informal Controlled Oral Tradition and the Synoptic Gospels." *Themelios* 20 (1995) 4–11.
———. "Middle Eastern Oral Tradition and the Synoptic Gospels." *Expository Times* 106 (1995) 363–67.
Balz, Horst, and Wolfgang Schrage. *Die "Katholischen" Briefe: die Briefe des Jakobus, Petrus, Johannes und Judas*. Göttingen: Vandenhoeck & Ruprecht, 1980.
Barnard, Leslie William. "The Testimonium concerning the Stone in the New Testament and in the Epistle of Barnabas." In vol. 3 of *Studia Evangelica*, edited by F. L. Cross, 306–13. Texte und Untersuchungen zur Geschichte der altchristlichen Literatur 88. Berlin: Akademie Verlag, 1964.

Barrett, C. K. "The Background of Mark 10:45." In *New Testament Essays: Studies in Memory of Thomas Walter Manson, 1893–1958*, edited by A. J. B. Higgins, 1–18. Manchester: Manchester University Press, 1959.

Barth, Gerhard. "1 Petrus 1, 3–9: Exegese, Meditation und Predigt." *Estudios teológicos* 6 (1966) 148–60.

Batten, Alicia J. "The Jesus Tradition and the Letter of James." *Review & Expositor* 108 (2011) 381–90.

Batten, Alicia J., and John S. Kloppenborg. *James, 1 & 2 Peter, and Early Jesus Traditions*. New York: Bloomsbury, 2014.

Bauckham, Richard. "For Whom Were the Gospels Written?" In *The Gospels for All Christians: Rethinking the Gospel Audiences*, edited by Richard Bauckham, 9–48. Grand Rapids: Eerdmans, 1998.

———. *James: Wisdom of James, Disciple of Jesus the Sage*. New Testament Readings. New York: Routledge, 1999.

———. *Jesus and the Eyewitnesses: The Gospels as Eyewitness Testimony*. 2nd ed. Grand Rapids: Eerdmans, 2017.

———. "The Study of Gospel Traditions outside the Canonical Gospels: Problems and Prospects." In *The Jesus Tradition outside the Gospels*, edited by David Wenham, 369–403. Gospel Perspectives 5. Sheffield: JSOT, 1985.

———, ed. *The Gospels for All Christians: Rethinking the Gospel Audiences*. Grand Rapids: Eerdmans, 1998.

Bauer, Walter, et al. *A Greek-English Lexicon of the New Testament and Other Early Christian Literature*. 3rd ed. Chicago: University of Chicago Press, 2000.

Beale, G. K. *Handbook on the New Testament Use of the Old Testament: Exegesis and Interpretation*. Grand Rapids: Baker, 2012.

———. *John's Use of the Old Testament in Revelation*. Journal for the Study of the New Testament Supplement Series 166. Sheffield: Sheffield Academic, 1998.

Beale, G. K., and D. A. Carson, eds. *Commentary on the New Testament Use of the Old Testament*. Grand Rapids: Baker, 2007.

Beare, Francis Wright. *The First Epistle of Peter*. 3rd ed. Oxford: Blackwell, 1970.

Beasley-Murray, George Raymond. "John 3:3, 5: Baptism, Spirit, and the Kingdom." *Expository Times* 97 (1986) 167–70.

Beetham, Christopher A. *Echoes of Scripture in the Letter of Paul to the Colossians*. Biblical Interpretation Series 96. Boston: Brill, 2008.

Belleville, Linda L. "'Born of Water and Spirit': John 3:5." *Trinity Journal* 1 (1980) 125–41.

Ben-Porat, Ziva. "The Poetics of Literary Allusion." *PTL: A Journal for Descriptive Poetics and Theory of Literature* 1 (1976) 105–28.

Best, Ernest. *1 Peter*. New Century Bible Commentary. Grand Rapids: Eerdmans, 1982.

———. "I Peter and the Gospel Tradition." *New Testament Studies* 16 (1970) 95–113.

———. "I Peter II 4–10: A Reconsideration." *Novum Testamentum* 11 (1969) 270–93.

Bieder, Werner. *Grund und Kraft der Mission nach dem 1. Petrusbrief*. Zürich: Verlag der evangelischen Buchhandlung, 1938.

Bigg, Charles. *A Critical and Exegetical Commentary on the Epistles of St. Peter and St. Jude*. 2nd ed. International Critical Commentary. New York: T. & T. Clark, 1902.

Bird, Michael F. *The Gospel of the Lord: How the Early Church Wrote the Story of Jesus*. Grand Rapids: Eerdmans, 2014.

Black, Matthew. "The Christological Use of the OT in the NT." *New Testament Studies* 18 (1971) 1–14.
Blomberg, Craig. *Matthew*. New American Commentary. Nashville: B&H, 1992.
Bock, Darrell L. *Luke 1:1—9:50*. Baker Exegetical Commentary on the New Testament. Grand Rapids: Baker, 1994.
———. *Luke 9:51—24:53*. Baker Exegetical Commentary on the New Testament. Grand Rapids: Baker, 1996.
Boismard, M. E. "Une Liturgie Baptismale Dans La Prima Petri (1)." *Revue Biblique* 64 (1957) 161–83.
———. "Une Liturgie Baptismale Dans La Prima Petri (2)." *Revue Biblique* 63 (1956) 182–208.
Boring, M. Eugene. *1 Peter*. Abingdon New Testament Commentaries. Nashville: Abingdon, 1999.
———. "First Peter in Recent Study." *Word & World* 24 (2004) 358–67.
Bovon, François. "Foi Chretienne et Religion Populaire dans la Premiere Epitre Pierre." In *Révélations et écritures: Nouveau Testament et littérature apocryphe chrétienne*, 95–112. Genève: Labor et Fides, 1993.
Brandt, Wilhelm. "Wandel Als Zeugnis Nach Dem 1. Petrusbrief." In *Verbum Dei Manet in Aeternum. Eine Festschrift Für O. Schmitz Zu Seinem 70. Geburtstag*, edited by W. Förster, 10–25. Wittenberg: Luther-Verlag, 1953.
Braumann, Georg. "Zum Traditionsgeschichtlichen Problem Der Seligpreisungen Mt 5:3–12." *Novum Testamentum* 4 (1960) 253–60.
Bray, Gerald Lewis, and Thomas C. Oden, eds. *James, 1–2 Peter, 1–3 John, Jude*. Ancient Christian Commentary on Scripture 11. Downers Grove, IL: InterVarsity, 2000.
Bromiley, Geoffrey W. "Baptism." In *Evangelical Dictionary of Theology*, edited by Daniel J. Treier and Walter A. Elwell. Grand Rapids: Baker, 2017.
Brown, John Pairman. "Synoptic Parallels in the Epistles and Form-History." *New Testament Studies* 10 (1963) 27–48.
Brown, Raymond E., ed. *The Gospel according to John*. Anchor Bible 29. Garden City, NY: Doubleday, 1966.
———. *The Sensus Plenior of Sacred Scripture*. Baltimore: St. Mary's University, 1955.
Brox, Norbert. *Der Erste Petrusbrief*. 4th ed. Evangelisch-Katholischer Kommentar zum Neuen Testament 21. Zürich: Benzinger, 1993.
———. "Der Erste Petrusbrief in der literarischen Tradition des Urchristentums." *Kairos: Zeitschrift für Religionswissenschaft und Theologie* 20 (1978) 183–92.
Bruce, F. F. *The Epistle to the Hebrews*. New International Commentary on the New Testament. Grand Rapids: Eerdmans, 2012.
———. "Paul and 'the Powers That Be.'" *Bulletin of the John Rylands Library* 66 (1984) 78–96.
Bultmann, Rudolf Karl. *The Gospel of John*. Philadelphia: Westminster, 1971.
———. *The History of the Synoptic Tradition*. Rev. ed. Peabody, MA: Hendrickson, 1963.
Calvin, John. *Commentaries on the Catholic Epistles*. Translated by John Owen. Bellingham, WA: Logos, 2010.
Capes, David B. "Jesus Tradition in Paul." In *The Routledge Encyclopedia of the Historical Jesus*, edited by Craig A. Evans. New York: Routledge, 2008.
Carrington, Philip. *The Primitive Christian Catechism: A Study in the Epistles*. Cambridge: Cambridge University Press, 2014.

Carson, D. A. "1 Peter." In *Commentary on the New Testament Use of the Old Testament*, edited by G. K. Beale and D. A. Carson, 1015–46. Grand Rapids: Baker, 2007.

———. *The Gospel according to John*. Pillar New Testament Commentary. Grand Rapids: Eerdmans, 1991.

Casurella, Anthony. *Bibliography of Literature on First Peter*. New Testament Tools and Studies 23. New York: Brill, 1996.

Charles, Robert Henry, ed. *The Apocrypha and Pseudepigrapha of the Old Testament*. Oxford: Clarendon, 1913.

Chase, F. H. "Peter, First Epistle." In *Dictionary of the Bible*, edited by James Hastings. New York: T. & T. Clark, 1909.

Chester, Andrew, and Ralph P. Martin. *The Theology of the Letters of James, Peter, and Jude*. Cambridge: Cambridge University Press, 1994.

Chin, Moses. "A Heavenly Home for the Homeless: Aliens and Strangers in 1 Peter." *Tyndale Bulletin* 42 (1991) 96–112.

Clement of Alexandria. *The Instructor (Paedagogus)*. In vol. 2 of *The Ante-Nicene Fathers: Translations of the Writings of the Fathers down to A.D. 325*, edited by Alexander Roberts and James Donaldson. Buffalo, NY: Christian Literature, 1885.

Clerck, Paul de. "Baptism." In *Encyclopedia of Christian Theology*, edited by Jean-Yves Lacoste. New York: Routledge, 2004.

Clowney, Edmund P. *The Message of 1 Peter: The Way of the Cross*. Bible Speaks Today. Downers Grove, IL: InterVarsity, 1988.

Conzelmann, Hans. *The Theology of St. Luke*. Philadelphia: Fortress, 1982.

Cothenet, Edouard. "La Première Epître de Pierre, L'Epître de Jacques." In *Le ministère et les ministères selon le Nouveau Testament*, edited by Paul Bony and Jean Delorme, 138–54. Coll. Parole de Dieu. Paris: Seuil, 1974.

Craddock, Fred B. *First and Second Peter and Jude*. Louisville: Westminster John Knox, 1995.

Cranfield, Charles E. B. *The First Epistle of Peter*. London: SCM, 1950.

———. "Interpretation of 1 Peter 3:19 and 4:6." *Expository Times* 69 (1958) 369–72.

Crossan, John Dominic. "The Parable of the Wicked Husbandmen." *Journal of Biblical Literature* 90 (1971) 451–65.

Crossley, James G. *The Date of Mark's Gospel: Insight from the Law in Earliest Christianity*. New York: Bloomsbury, 2004.

Cullmann, Oscar. *The Earliest Christian Confessions*. London: Lutterworth, 1949.

Dalton, William J. *Christ's Proclamation to the Spirits: A Study of 1 Peter 3:18–4:6*. Rome: Pontifical Biblical Institute, 1965.

Das, A. Andrew. *Paul and the Stories of Israel: Grand Thematic Narratives in Galatians*. Minneapolis: Fortress, 2016.

Davids, Peter H. "Exalted Lord and Suffering Servant: The Response to Jesus in James and 1 Peter." In *The Earliest Perceptions of Jesus in Context: Essays in Honor of John Nolland*, edited by Aaron White et al., 253–67. New York: Bloomsbury, 2018.

———. *The First Epistle of Peter*. 2nd ed. Grand Rapids: Eerdmans, 1990.

———. "The Gospels and Jewish Tradition: Twenty Years after Gerhardsson." In *Studies of History and Tradition in the Four Gospels*, edited by R. T. France and David Wenham, 75–99. Gospel Perspectives 1. Sheffield: JSOT, 1983.

———. "James and Jesus." In *The Jesus Tradition outside the Gospels*, edited by David Wenham, 63–84. Gospel Perspectives 5. Sheffield: JSOT, 1984.

———. "Review: Die Rezeption Des Matthäusevangeliums Im 1. Petrusbrief." *Catholic Biblical Quarterly* 59 (1997) 387–89.

———. "What Glasses Are You Wearing? Reading Hebrew Narratives through Second Temple Lenses." *Journal of the Evangelical Theological Society* 55 (2012) 763–71.

Delling, Gerhard. "Der Bezug Der Christlichen Existenz Auf Das Heilshandeln Gottes Nach Dem Ersten Petrusbrief." In *Neues Testament Und Christliche Existenz (Festschrift H. Braun)*, edited by Luise Schottroff and Hans Dieter Betz, 95–113. Tübingen: Mohr Siebeck, 1973.

Deppe, Dean B. "The Sayings of Jesus in the Paraenesis of James." PhD diss., Vrije Universiteit Te Amsterdam, 1990.

Derico, T. M. *Oral Tradition and Synoptic Verbal Agreement: Evaluating the Empirical Evidence for Literary Dependence*. Eugene, OR: Pickwick, 2016.

Deterding, Paul E. "Exodus Motifs in First Peter." *Concordia Journal* 7 (1981) 58–65.

Dibelius, Martin. *From Tradition to Gospel*. Edited by William Barclay. Translated by Bertram Lee Woolf. Cambridge: Clarke, 1971.

Dodd, C. H. *Historical Tradition in the Fourth Gospel*. Cambridge: Cambridge University Press, 1963.

———. *The Parables of the Kingdom*. London: Nisbet, 1935.

———. "The Primitive Catechism and the Sayings of Jesus." In *New Testament Essays: Studies in Memory of T. W. Manson*, edited by A. J. B. Higgins, 106–18. Manchester: Manchester University Press, 1959.

Dodewaard, Johannes A. E. van. "Die Sprachliche Übereinstimmung Zwischen Markus-Paulus und Markus-Petrus, Pt 1." *Biblica* 30 (1949) 91–108.

———. "Die Sprachliche Übereinstimmung Zwischen Markus-Paulus und Markus-Petrus, Pt 2." *Biblica* 30 (1949) 218–38.

Dubis, Mark. *1 Peter: A Handbook on the Greek Text*. Waco, TX: Baylor University Press, 2010.

Dungan, David L. *The Sayings of Jesus in the Churches of Paul: The Use of the Synoptic Tradition in the Regulation of Early Church Life*. Philadelphia: Fortress, 1971.

Dunn, James D. G. *Christology in the Making: A New Testament Inquiry into the Origins of the Doctrine of the Incarnation*. Grand Rapids: Eerdmans, 1996.

———. *Jesus Remembered*. Christianity in the Making 1. Grand Rapids: Eerdmans, 2003.

———. "Jesus Tradition in Paul." In *Studying the Historical Jesus: Evaluations of the State of Current Research*, edited by Bruce David Chilton and Craig Alan Evans, 155–78. Boston: Brill, 1998.

———. *The Oral Gospel Tradition*. Grand Rapids: Eerdmans, 2013.

Edwards, James R. *The Gospel according to Luke*. Pillar New Testament Commentary. Grand Rapids: Eerdmans, 2015.

———. *The Gospel according to Mark*. Pillar New Testament Commentary. Grand Rapids: Eerdmans, 2002.

Ellingworth, Paul. *The Epistle to the Hebrews*. New International Greek Testament Commentary. Grand Rapids: Eerdmans, 1993.

Elliott, John H. *1 Peter*. Anchor Yale Bible 37B. New Haven: Yale University Press, 2001.

———. *The Elect and the Holy: An Exegetical Examination of I Peter 2:4–10 and the Phrase "Basileion Hierateuma."* Supplements to Novum Testamentum 12. Eugene, OR: Wipf & Stock, 2005.

———. *A Home for the Homeless: A Social-Scientific Criticism of 1 Peter, Its Situation and Strategy*. Eugene, OR: Wipf & Stock, 2005.

———. "Ministry and Church Order in the NT: A Traditio-Historical Analysis (1 Pt 5:1–5 and Parallels)." *Catholic Biblical Quarterly* 32 (1970) 367–91.

———. "The Rehabilitation of an Exegetical Step-Child: 1 Peter in Recent Research." *Journal of Biblical Literature* 95 (1976) 243–54.

———. "Review: Die Rezeption Des Matthäusevangeliums Im 1. Petrusbrief." *Journal of Biblical Literature* 116 (1997) 379–82.

———. "The Roman Provenance of 1 Peter and the Gospel of Mark. A Response to David Dungan.'" In *Colloquy on New Testament Studies: A Time for Reappraisal and Fresh Approaches*, edited by Bruce Corley, 181–94. Macon, GA: Mercer University Press, 1983.

Eslinger, Lyle M. "Hosea 12,5a and Genesis 32,29: A Study in Inner Biblical Exegesis." *Journal for the Study of the Old Testament* 5 (1980) 91–99.

———. "Inner-Biblical Exegesis and Inner-Biblical Allusion: The Question of Category." *Vetus Testamentum* 42 (1992) 47–58.

Feldmeier, Reinhard. *The First Letter of Peter*. Waco, TX: Baylor University Press, 2008.

Felix, Minucius. "The Octavius of Minucius Felix." In vol. 4 of *The Ante-Nicene Fathers: Translations of the Writings of the Fathers down to A.D. 325*, edited by Alexander Roberts and James Donaldson. Buffalo, NY: Christian Literature, 1885.

Feuillet, A. "Quelques Reflexions Sur Le Quatrième Évangile à Propos d'un Livre Récent, l'apôtre Pierre, Garant de La Tradition Évangélique." *Bulletin du Comité des études* 57/58 (1969) 235–47.

Fishbane, Michael. *Biblical Interpretation in Ancient Israel*. Oxford: Oxford University Press, 1985.

Flender, Helmut. *St. Luke: Theologian of Redemptive History*. London: SPCK, 1967.

Forbes, Greg. *Exegetical Guide to the Greek New Testament: 1 Peter*. Nashville: B&H, 2014.

Foster, Ora Delmer. *The Literary Relations of "The First Epistle of Peter" with Their Bearing on Date and Place of Authorship*. New Haven: Yale University Press, 1913.

France, R. T. *The Gospel of Mark*. New International Greek Testament Commentary. Grand Rapids: Eerdmans, 2002.

———. *The Gospel of Matthew*. New International Commentary on the New Testament. Grand Rapids: Eerdmans, 2007.

———. "The Servant of the Lord in the Teaching of Jesus." *Tyndale Bulletin* 19 (1968) 26–52.

Francis, J. "'Like Newborn Babes'—the Image of the Child in 1 Peter 2:2–3." In *Papers on Paul and Other New Testament Authors*, edited by E. A. Livingstone, 111–17. Journal for the Study of the New Testament Supplement Series 3. Sheffield: JSOT, 1980.

Frankemölle, Hubert. *1 Petrusbrief, 2 Petrusbrief, und Judasbrief: Die Neue Echter-Bibel, Kommentar zum Neuen Testament mit Einheitsübersetzung*. Würzburg: Echter, 1990.

Fronmüller, G. F. C. *The Epistles General of Peter*. Edited by John Peter Lange. Translated by J. Isidor Mombert and Philip Schaff. Commentary on the Holy Scriptures. New York: Scribner, 1867.

Furnish, Victor Paul. "Elect Sojourners in Christ: An Approach to the Theology of I Peter." *Perkins Journal* 28 (1975) 1–11.

———. *The Love Command in the New Testament*. Nashville: Abingdon, 1972.
Gamble, Harry Y. *Books and Readers in the Early Church: A History of Early Christian Texts*. New Haven: Yale University Press, 1995.
Garcia del Moral, Antonio. "Critica Textual de I Ptr. 4.14." *Estudios Biblicos* 20 (1961) 45–77.
Garner, Richard. *From Homer to Tragedy: The Art of Allusion in Greek Poetry*. New York: Routledge, 2015.
Gerhardsson, Birger. *Memory and Manuscript with Tradition and Transmission in Early Christianity*. Translated by Eric J. Sharpe. Rev. ed. Grand Rapids: Eerdmans, 1998.
———. *The Reliability of the Gospel Tradition*. Grand Rapids: Baker, 2001.
Gibson, Margaret Dunlop. *The Didascalia Apostolorum in English*. Cambridge: Cambridge University Press, 2011.
Giesen, Heinz. "Der Gott Israels als der Vater unseres Herrn Jesus Christus im ersten Petrusbrief." In *Der Gott Israels im Zeugnis des Neuen Testaments*, 130–61. Quaestiones disputatae 201. Freiburg: Herder, 2003.
Gleaves, G. Scott, and Rodney Eugene Cloud. *Did Jesus Speak Greek?: The Emerging Evidence of Greek Dominance in First-Century Palestine*. Eugene, OR: Pickwick, 2015.
Glenny, W. Edward. "The Hermeneutics of the Use of the Old Testament in 1 Peter." ThD diss., Dallas Theological Seminary, 1987.
———. "The Israelite Imagery of 1 Peter 2." In *Dispensationalism, Israel and the Church: The Search for Definition*, edited by Craig A. Blaising and Darrell L. Bock, 156–87. Grand Rapids: Zondervan, 1992.
Goldstein, Horst. "Die Politischen Paränese in 1 Petr Und Röm 13." *Bibel und Leben* 14 (1973) 88–104.
Goppelt, Leonhard. *A Commentary on I Peter*. Edited by Ferdinand Hahn. Translated by John E. Alsup. Grand Rapids: Eerdmans, 1993.
———. *Theology of the New Testament*. 2 vols. Grand Rapids: Eerdmans, 2009.
Gourbillon, J. G., and F. M. du Buit. *Première Épitre de Saint Pierre*. Evangile 50. Paris: Evangile, 1963.
Greaux, Eric James. "'To the Elect Exiles of the Dispersion . . . from Babylon': The Function of the Old Testament in 1 Peter." PhD diss., Duke University, 2003.
Green, Gene L. "The Use of the Old Testament for Christian Ethics in 1 Peter." *Tyndale Bulletin* 41 (1990) 276–89.
Green, Joel B. *1 Peter*. Two Horizons New Testament Commentary. Grand Rapids: Eerdmans, 2007.
———. *The Gospel of Luke*. New International Commentary on the New Testament. Grand Rapids: Eerdmans, 1997.
Greever, Joshua Matthew. "New Covenant in Ephesians." PhD diss., The Southern Baptist Theological Seminary, 2014.
Grudem, Wayne A. "Christ Preaching through Noah: 1 Peter 3:19–20 in the Light of Dominant Themes in Jewish Literature." *Trinity Journal* 7 (1986) 3–31.
———. *The First Epistle of Peter*. Tyndale New Testament Commentaries. Grand Rapids: Eerdmans, 1988.
Gundry, Robert H. "Further Verba on 'Verba Christi' in First Peter." *Biblica* 55 (1974) 211–32.
———. *Mark: A Commentary on His Apology for the Cross*. Grand Rapids: Eerdmans, 1993.

———. *A Survey of the New Testament*. 5th ed. Grand Rapids: Zondervan, 2012.
———. "'Verba Christi' in I Peter: Their Implications concerning the Authorship of I Peter and the Authenticity of the Gospel Tradition." *New Testament Studies* 13 (1967) 336–50.
Gustave, Thils. *L'Enseignement de Saint Pierre*. Paris: Lecoffre, 1943.
Hagner, Donald A. "The Sayings of Jesus in the Apostolic Fathers and Justin Martyr." In *The Jesus Tradition outside the Gospels*, edited by David Wenham, 233–68. Gospel Perspectives 5. Sheffield: JSOT, 1980.
Hall, Randy. "For to This You Have Been Called: The Cross and Suffering in 1 Peter." *Restoration Quarterly* 19 (1976) 137–47.
Hamlyn, D. W. "Unconscious Intentions." *Philosophy* 46 (1971) 12–22.
Harink, Douglas Karel. *1 & 2 Peter*. Brazos Theological Commentary on the Bible. Grand Rapids: Brazos, 2009.
Harmon, William. "Allusion." *A Handbook to Literature*. Upper Saddle River, NJ: Prentice Hall, 2000.
Harnack, Adolf von. *Geschichte der Altchristlichen Litteratur bis Eusebius*. Leipzig: Hinrich, 1897.
———. *The Sayings of Jesus*. Translated by John Richard Wilkinson. New Testament Studies 2. London: Putnam, 1908.
Harris, James Rendel. *Testimonies*. Vol. 2. Cambridge: Cambridge University Press, 1920.
———. "The Religious Meaning of 1 Peter V 5." *The Expositor* 8 (1919) 131–39.
Harrison, Everett Falconer. "Exegetical Studies in 1 Peter." *Bibliotheca Sacra* 97 (1940) 325–34.
Harrison, Paul V., and Robert E. Picirilli. *James, 1, 2 Peter, Jude*. Nashville: Randall, 1992.
Hartin, Patrick J. "James and the Jesus Tradition: Some Theological Reflections and Implications." In *The Catholic Epistles and Apostolic Tradition: A New Perspective on James and Jude*, edited by Karl-Wilhelm Niebuhr and Robert W. Wall, 55–70. Waco, TX: Baylor University Press, 2009.
———. *James and the "Q" Sayings of Jesus*. New York: Bloomsbury, 2015.
Hays, Richard B. *The Conversion of the Imagination: Paul as Interpreter of Israel's Scripture*. Grand Rapids: Eerdmans, 2005.
———. *Echoes of Scripture in the Gospels*. Waco, TX: Baylor University Press, 2016.
———. *Echoes of Scripture in the Letters of Paul*. New Haven: Yale University Press, 1993.
———. "On the Rebound: A Response to Critiques of Echoes of Scripture in the Letters of Paul." In *Paul and the Scriptures of Israel*, edited by Craig A. Evans and James A. Sanders, 70–97. Sheffield: JSOT, 1993.
Helm, David R. *1 and 2 Peter and Jude: Sharing Christ's Sufferings*. Edited by R. Kent Hughes. Preaching the Word. Wheaton, IL: Crossway, 2008.
Helyer, Larry R. *The Life and Witness of Peter*. Downers Grove, IL: InterVarsity, 2012.
Hengel, Martin. *Between Jesus and Paul: Studies in the Earliest History of Christianity*. Eugene, OR: Wipf & Stock, 2003.
———. *Saint Peter: The Underestimated Apostle*. Translated by Thomas Trapp. Grand Rapids: Eerdmans, 2010.
Hiebert, D. Edmond. *First Peter*. Chicago: Moody, 1984.

---. "Living in the Light of Christ's Return: An Exposition of 1 Peter 4:7–11." *Bibliotheca Sacra* 139 (1982) 243–54.
Hiestermann, Heinz Arnold. "Paul's Use of the Synoptic Jesus Tradition." PhD diss., University of Pretoria, 2016.
Hill, David. *The Gospel of Matthew*. New Century Bible Commentary. Grand Rapids: Eerdmans, 1981.
Hillyer, Norman. *1 and 2 Peter, Jude*. New International Biblical Commentary. Peabody, MA: Hendrickson, 1992.
---. "'Rock-Stone' Imagery in I Peter." *Tyndale Bulletin* 22 (1971) 58–81.
Himes, Paul A. *Foreknowledge and Social Identity in 1 Peter*. Eugene, OR: Wipf & Stock, 2014.
---. *Lexham Bible Guide: 1 Peter*. Edited by Douglas Magnum. Lexham Bible Guides. Bellingham, WA: Lexham, 2017.
Hirsch, E. D. *Validity in Interpretation*. New Haven: Yale University Press, 1967.
Hoffman, Yair. "The Technique of Quotation and Citation as an Interpretive Device." In *Creative Biblical Exegesis: Christian and Jewish Hermeneutics through the Centuries*, edited by Henning Graf Reventlow and Benjamin Uffenheimer, 71–80. Sheffield: JSOT, 1988.
Hollander, John. *The Figure of Echo: A Mode of Allusion in Milton and After*. Berkeley: University of California Press, 1984.
Hooker, Morna D. *Jesus and the Servant: The Influence of the Servant Concept of Deutero-Isaiah in the New Testament*. Eugene, OR: Wipf & Stock, 2010.
Horrell, David G. *1 Peter*. New Testament Guides. New York: T. & T. Clark, 2008.
---. "Jesus Remembered in 1 Peter? Early Jesus Traditions, Isaiah 53, and 1 Peter 2:21–25." In *James, 1 & 2 Peter, and Early Jesus Traditions*, edited by Alicia J. Batten and John S. Kloppenborg, 151–65. Library of New Testament Studies. London: T. & T. Clark, 2014.
---. "The Image of Jesus in 1 Peter and its Paradigmatic Significance: Sociological and Psychological Correlations." In *Jesus—Gestalt und Gestaltungen: Rezeptionen des Galiläers in Wissenschaft, Kirche und Gesellschaft*, edited by Petra von Gemünden et al., 299–316. Novum Testamentum et Orbis Antiquus 100. Göttingen: Vandenhoeck und Ruprecht, 2013.
Hort, Fenton John Anthony. *The First Epistle of St. Peter: 1:1—2:17*. London: Macmillan, 1898.
Hunter, Archibald M., and Elmer G. Homrighausen. *The First Epistle of Peter*. The Interpreter's Bible. New York: Abingdon, 1957.
Hunzinger, Claus-Hunno. "Ραντίζω." In *Theological Dictionary of the New Testament*, edited by Gerhard Kittel et al. Grand Rapids: Eerdmans, 1964.
Irwin, William. "What Is an Allusion?" *Journal of Aesthetics & Art Criticism* 59 (2001) 287–97.
Iser, Wolfgang. *The Act of Reading: A Theory of Aesthetic Response*. Baltimore: Johns Hopkins University Press, 1978.
Jeremias, Joachim. "Das Lössegeld Für Viele (Mk. 10,45)." In *Abba: Studien Zur Neutestamentlichen Theologie und Zeitgeschichte*, 249–64. Göttingen: Vandenhoeck & Ruprecht, 1966.
---. *New Testament Theology*. Translated by John Bowden. New York: Scribner, 1971.

———. *The Parables of Jesus*. Translated by S. H. Hooke. 2nd ed. New York: Scribner, 1972.

———. "Zwischen Karfreitag und Ostern: Descensus und Ascensus in Der Karfreitagstheologie Des Neuen Testamentes." *Zeitschrift für die neutestamentliche Wissenschaft und die Kunde der älteren Kirche* 42 (1949) 194–201.

Jewett, Robert. *Romans*. 2nd ed. Hermeneia. Minneapolis: Fortress, 2006.

Jobes, Karen H. *1 Peter*. Baker Exegetical Commentaries. Grand Rapids: Baker, 2005.

———. "'Got Milk?': A Petrine Metaphor in 1 Peter 2.1–3 Revisited." *Leaven* 20.3 (2012) 121–26.

———. "Got Milk? Septuagint Psalm 33 and the Interpretation of 1 Peter 2:1–3." *Westminster Theological Journal* 63 (2002) 1–14.

———. "'O Taste and See': Septuagint Psalm 33 in 1 Peter." *Stone-Campbell Journal* 18.2 (2015) 241–51.

Juhl, Peter D. *Interpretation: An Essay in the Philosophy of Literary Criticism*. Princeton Legacy Library. Princeton: Princeton University Press, 2014.

Jülicher, Adolf. *Die Gleichnisreden Jesu*. Freiburg: Mohr Siebeck, 1899.

———. *An Introduction to the New Testament*. Translated by Janet Penrose Ward. London: Smith, Elder, & co., 1904.

Karnetzki, Manfred. "Die Galiläische Redaktion Im Markusevangelium." *Zeitschrift für die neutestamentliche Wissenschaft und die Kunde der älteren Kirche* 52 (1961) 238–72.

Kelly, J. N. D. *A Commentary on the Epistles of Peter and of Jude*. Black's New Testament Commentaries. London: A. & C. Black, 1969.

Kendall, R. T. "The Literary and Theological Function of 1 Peter 1:3–12." In *Perspectives on First Peter*, edited by Charles H. Talbert, 103–20. Eugene, OR: Wipf & Stock, 2010.

Kim, Seyoon. "Sayings of Jesus." In *Dictionary of Paul and His Letters*, edited by Gerald F. Hawthorne et al. Downers Grove, IL: InterVarsity, 1993.

Kirk, Gordon E. "Endurance in Suffering in 1 Peter." *Bibliotheca Sacra* 138 (1981) 46–56.

Kistemaker, Simon. *Exposition of the Epistles of Peter and of the Epistle of Jude*. Baker New Testament Commentary. Grand Rapids: Baker, 1987.

Kittel, Gisela. "Der geschichtliche Ort des Jakobusbriefes." *Zeitschrift für die Neutestamentliche Wissenschaft und die Kunde der älteren Kirche* 41 (1942) 71–105.

Kline, Leslie. "Ethics for the End Time: An Exegesis of I Peter 4:7–11." *Restoration Quarterly* 7 (1963) 113–23.

Kloppenborg, John S. "The Emulation of the Jesus Tradition in the Letter of James." In *Reading James with New Eyes*, edited by Robert L. Webb and John S. Kloppenborg, 121–50. Library of New Testament Studies 342. New York: T. & T. Clark, 2007.

———. "The Reception of the Jesus Tradition in James." In *The Catholic Epistles and Apostolic Tradition*, edited by Karl-Wilhelm Niebuhr and Robert W. Wall, 71–100. Waco, TX: Baylor University Press, 2009.

Knoch, Otto. *Der Erste und Zweite Petrusbrief; Der Judasbrief*. Regensburg: Verlag Friedrich Pustet, 1990.

Knopf, Rudolf. *Die Briefe Petri und Judä*. Göttingen: Vandenhoeck & Ruprecht, 1912.

Koester, Helmut. *Ancient Christian Gospels: Their History and Development*. Philadelphia: SCM, 1990.

Kokot, Mirosław. "Znaczenie 'Nasienia Niezniszczalnego' w 1 P 1,23." *Collectanea Theologica* 44 (1974) 35–44.
Kristeva, Julia. "Word, Dialogue, and Novel." In *The Kristeva Reader*, edited by Toril Moi, 34–61. Oxford: Blackwell, 1996.
Kümmel, Werner Georg. *Introduction to the New Testament*. Translated by Howard Clark Kee. Rev. ed. Nashville: Abingdon, 1975.
Kynes, Will. *My Psalm Has Turned into Weeping: Job's Dialogue with the Psalms*. Berlin: de Gruyter, 2012.
Lea, Thomas D. "How Peter Learned the Old Testament." *Southwestern Journal of Theology* 22 (1980) 96–102.
Leaney, A. R. C. *The Letters of Peter and Jude*. Cambridge Bible Commentary. Cambridge: Cambridge University Press, 1967.
———. "Lucan Text of the Lord's Prayer (Luke 11:2–4)." *Novum Testamentum* 1 (1956) 103–11
Lecomte, Pierre. "Aimer La Vie: I Pierre 3/10." *Etudes Théologiques* 56 (1981) 288–93.
Leonard, Jeffery M. "Identifying Inner-Biblical Allusions: Psalm 78 as a Test Case." *Journal of Biblical Literature* 127 (2008) 241–65.
Lewis, C. S. "The Literary Impact of the Authorised Version." In *Selected Literary Essays*, edited by Walter Hooper, 126–45. Cambridge: Cambridge University Press, 2013.
Liebengood, Kelly D. *The Eschatology of 1 Peter: Considering the Influence of Zechariah 9–14*. Cambridge: Cambridge University Press, 2014.
Lindars, Barnabas. *New Testament Apologetic*. Philadelphia: Westminster, 1961.
Lohse, Eduard. "Paränese und Kerygma Im 1. Petrusbrief." *Zeitschrift für die Neutestamentliche Wissenschaft und die Kunde der Älteren Kirche* 45 (1954) 68–89.
Longenecker, Richard N. *The Epistle to the Romans*. New International Greek Testament Commentary. Grand Rapids: Eerdmans, 2016.
Love, Julian Price. "The First Epistle of Peter." *Interpretation* 8 (1954) 63–87.
Lövestam, Evald. *Spiritual Wakefulness in the New Testament*. Lund: Gleerup, 1963.
Luther, Martin. *The Epistles of St. Peter and St. Jude*. Translated by E. H. Gillett. New York: Randolph, 1859.
Luz, Ulrich. *Matthew 1–7*. Translated by James E. Crouch. Rev. ed. Hermeneia. Minneapolis: Fortress, 2007.
Maier, Gerhard. "Jesustradition Im 1. Petrusbrief?" In *The Jesus Tradition outside the Gospels*, edited by David Wenham, 85–128. Gospel Perspectives 5. Sheffield: JSOT, 1980.
Manson, Thomas Walter. *The Teaching of Jesus: Studies of Its Form and Content*. Cambridge: Cambridge University Press, 1955.
Margot, J. C. *Les Épîtres de Pierre. Commentaire*. Genève: Labor & Fides, 1960.
Marshall, I. Howard. *1 Peter*. IVP New Testament Commentary. Downers Grove, IL: InterVarsity, 1991.
———. *The Gospel of Luke*. New International Greek Testament Commentary. Grand Rapids: Eerdmans, 1978.
Martin, Troy W. *Metaphor and Composition in 1 Peter*. Society of Biblical Literature Dissertation Series 131. Atlanta: Society of Biblical Literature, 1992.
Mayor, Joseph B. "Reminiscences of the Parable of the Sower Contained in the Epistle of St. James." *The Expositor Eighth Series* 4 (1912) 407–14.
McCabe, Robert. "The Meaning of 'Born of Water and the Spirit' in John 3:5." *Detroit Baptist Seminary Journal* 4 (1999) 85–107.

McCartney, Dan G. "Λογικός in 1 Peter 2, 2." *Zeitschrift für die Neutestamentliche Wissenschaft und die Kunde der älteren Kirche* 82 (1991) 128–32.

———. "The Use of the Old Testament the First Epistle of Peter." PhD diss., Westminster Theological Seminary, 1989.

McKnight, Scot. *1 Peter*. NIV Application Commentary. Grand Rapids: Zondervan, 1996.

Metzner, Rainer. *Die Rezeption des Matthäusevangeliums im 1. Petrusbrief: Studien zum traditionsgeschichtlichen und theologischen Einfluss des 1. Evangeliums auf den 1. Petrusbrief.* Tübingen: Mohr Siebeck, 1995.

Meyer, F. B. *Tried by Fire: Expositions of the First Epistle of Peter.* Grand Rapids: Zondervan, 1950.

Michaels, J. Ramsey. *1 Peter*. Word Biblical Commentary 49. Waco, TX: Nelson, 1988.

Michel, Otto. "Οἰκονόμος." In *Theological Dictionary of the New Testament*, edited by Gerhard Kittel et al. Grand Rapids: Eerdmans, 1964.

Millauer, Helmut. *Leiden Als Gnade: Eine Traditionsgeschichtliche Untersuchung Zur Leidenstheologie Des Ersten Petrusbriefes.* Bern: Lang, 1976.

Miller, Timothy E. "The Use of 1 Peter 3:13–17 for Christian Apologetics." *Bibliotheca Sacra* 174 (2017) 193–209.

Milligan, George. *St. Paul's Epistles to the Thessalonians.* London: Macmillan, 1908.

Miner, Earl. "Allusion." In *The Princeton Handbook of Poetic Terms*, edited by Alex Preminger et al. Princeton: Princeton University Press, 2014.

Moo, Douglas J. *The Epistle to the Romans.* New International Commentary on the New Testament. Grand Rapids: Eerdmans, 1996.

Morris, Leon. *The Gospel according to Matthew.* Pillar New Testament Commentary. Grand Rapids: Eerdmans, 1992.

Moule, C. F. D. "The Nature and Purpose of I Peter." *New Testament Studies* 3 (1956) 1–11.

———. "Some Reflections on the 'Stone' Testimonia in Relation to the Name Peter." *New Testament Studies* 2 (1956) 56–58.

———. "The Use of Parables and Sayings as Illustrative Material in Early Christian Catechesis." *Journal of Theological Studies* 3 (1952) 75–79.

Moyise, Steve. "Isaiah in 1 Peter." In *Isaiah in the New Testament: The New Testament and the Scriptures of Israel*, edited by Maarten J. J. Menken, 175–88. New York: T. & T. Clark, 2005.

Nauck, Wolfgang. "Freude Im Leiden: Zum Problem Einer Urchristlichen Verfolgungstradition." *Zeitschrift für die neutestamentliche Wissenschaft* 46 (1955) 68–80.

———. "Probleme Des Frühchristlichen Amtsverständnisses (I Ptr 5 2f.)." *Zeitschrift Für die Neutestamentliche Wissenschaft* 48 (1957) 200–220.

Neugebauer, F. "Zur Deutung Und Bedeutung Des 1. Petrusbriefes." *New Testament Studies* 26 (1979) 61–86.

Neusner, Jacob. "The Use of the Later Rabbinic Evidence for the Study of First-Century Pharisaism." In *Approaches to Ancient Judaism*, edited by William Scott Green, 215–28. Missoula, MT: Scholars, 1978.

Nolland, John. *The Gospel of Matthew.* New International Greek Testament Commentary. Grand Rapids: Eerdmans, 2005.

O'Brien, Kelli S. *The Use of Scripture in the Markan Passion Narrative.* New York: Bloomsbury, 2010.

Osborne, Thomas P. "Guidelines for Christian Suffering: A Source-Critical and Theological Study of 1 Peter 2,21–25." *Biblica* 64 (1983) 381–408.

———. "L'utilisation Des Citations de l'Ancien Testament Dans La Première Épître de Pierre." *Revue Théologique de Louvain* 12 (1981) 64–77.

Oss, Douglas A. "The Interpretation of the 'Stone' Passages by Peter and Paul: A Comparative Study." *Journal of the Evangelical Theological Society* 32.2 (1989) 181–200.

Page, Sydney H. T. "Obedience and Blood-Sprinkling in 1 Peter 1:2." *Westminster Theological Journal* 72 (2010) 291–98.

Parker, Brent E. "The Church as the Renewed Israel in Christ: A Study of 1 Peter 2:4-10." *Southern Baptist Journal of Theology* 21 (2017) 41–52.

Paulien, Jon. "Criteria and the Assessment of Allusions." In *Studies in the Book of Revelation*, edited by Steve Moyise, 113–30. New York: T. & T. Clark, 2002.

———. *The Deep Things of God*. Hagerstown, MD: Review and Herald, 2004.

———. "Elusive Allusions: The Problematic Use of the Old Testament in Revelation." *Bulletin of Biblical Research* 33 (1988) 37–53.

Perdelwitz, Richard. *Die Mysterienreligion und Das Problem Des 1. Petrusbriefes*. Religionsversuche und Vorarbeiten 11. Giessen: Töpelmann, 1911.

Perkins, Pheme. *First and Second Peter, James, and Jude*. Interpretation. Louisville: Westminster John Knox, 1995.

Perri, Carmela. "On Alluding." *Poetics* 7 (1978) 289–307.

Pierce, Chad. "Spirits and the Proclamation of Christ: 1 Peter 3:18–22 in Its Tradition-Historical and Literary Context." PhD diss., Durham University, 2009.

Pietersma, Albert, and Benjamin Wright, eds. "Ezekiel." In *The New English Translation of the Septuagint*, translated by J. Noel Hubler and J. Noel Hubler. Oxford: Oxford University Press, 2014.

Piper, John. "Hope as the Motivation of Love: 1 Peter 3:9–12." *New Testament Studies* 26 (1980) 212–30.

———. *Love Your Enemies: Jesus' Love Command in the Synoptic Gospels and the Early Christian Paraenesis*. Wheaton, IL: Crossway, 2012.

Porter, Stanley E. "Allusions and Echoes." In *As It Is Written: Studying Paul's Use of Scripture*, edited by Stanley E. Porter and Christopher D. Stanley, 29–40. Society of Biblical Literature Symposium Series 50. Atlanta: Society of Biblical Literature, 2008.

———. "Did Jesus Ever Teach in Greek?" *Tyndale Bulletin* 44 (1993) 199–235.

———. "Further Comments on the Use of the Old Testament in the New Testament." In *The Intertextuality of the Epistles: Explorations of Theory and Practice*, edited by T. L. Brodie et al., 98–110. New Testament Monographs 16. Sheffield: Sheffield Phoenix, 2006.

———. "The Use of the Old Testament in the New Testament: A Brief Comment on Method and Terminology." In *Early Christian Interpretation of the Scriptures of Israel*, edited by Craig A. Evans and James A. Sanders, 79–96. Library of New Testament Studies 148. Sheffield: Sheffield Academic, 1997.

Powers, Daniel. *1 & 2 Peter, Jude*. New Beacon Bible Commentary. Kansas City, MI: Beacon Hill, 2010.

Prasad, Jacob. *Foundations of the Christian Way of Life according to 1 Peter 1, 13–25: An Exegetico-Theological Study*. Rome: Gregorian Biblical BookShop, 2000.

Pryor, John W. "First Peter and the New Covenant (1)." *Reformed Theological Review* 45 (1986) 1–4.

———. "First Peter and the New Covenant (2)." *Reformed Theological Review* 45 (1986) 44–51.

Quintilian. *Institutio Oratoria*. Translated by Harold Edgeworth Butler. Medford, MA: Harvard University Press, 1921.

Reicke, Bo Ivar, ed. *The Epistles of James, Peter, and Jude*. Anchor Bible 37. Garden City, NY: Doubleday, 1964.

Rensburg, Fika J. van "The Outline of 1 Peter: A Reconsideration." *Ekklesiastikos Pharos* 74 (1992) 26–41.

Resch, Alfred. *Agrapha: Aussercanonische Schriftfragmente*. Leipzig: Hinrich, 1906.

———. *Der Paulinismus und Die Logia Jesus*. Leipzig: Hinrich, 1904.

Riesenfeld, Harald. *The Gospel Tradition: Essays*. Philadelphia: Fortress, 1970.

Riesner, Rainer. "Back to the Historical Jesus through Paul and His School (the Ransom Logion—Mark 10.45; Matthew 20.28)." *Journal for the Study of the Historical Jesus* 1 (2003) 171–99.

Rodgers, Peter R. "The Longer Reading of 1 Peter 4:14." *Catholic Biblical Quarterly* 43 (1981) 93–95.

Ross, Stephanie. "Art and Allusion." *Journal of Aesthetics and Art Criticism* 40 (1981) 59–70.

Ruppert, Lothar. *Der leidende Gerechte und seine Feinde: Eine Wortfelduntersuchung*. Würzburg: Echter, 1973.

———. *Jesus als der leidende Gerechte?: Der Weg Jesu im Lichte eines alt- und zwischentestamentlichen Motivs*. Stuttgart: KBW, 1972.

Russell, Ronald. "Eschatology and Ethics in I Peter." *Evangelical Quarterly* 47 (1975) 78–84.

Sandmel, Samuel. "Parallelomania." *Journal of Biblical Literature* 81 (1962) 1–13.

Scharfe, Ernst. *Die petrinische Strömung der neutestamentlichen Literatur: Untersuchungen über die schriftstellerische Eigentümlichkeit des ersten Petrusbriefs, des Marcusevangeliums und der petrinischen Reden der Apostelgeschichte*. Berlin: Reuther & Reichard, 1893.

———. "Die schriftstellerische Originalität des ersten Petrusbriefs." *Theologische Studien und Kritiken* 62 (1889) 633–69.

Scharlemann, Martin H. "'He Descended into Hell': An Interpretation of 1 Peter 3:18–20." *Concordia Theological Monthly* 27 (1956) 81–94.

Schattenmann, Johannes. "Little Apocalypse of the Synoptics and the First Epistle of Peter." *Theology Today* 11 (1954) 193–98.

Schelkle, Karl Hermann. *Die Petrusbriefe, Der Judasbrief*. 2nd ed. Herders Theologischer Kommentar zum Neuen Testament. Freiburg: Herder, 1976.

Schiwy, Günther. *Die Katholischen Briefe*. Der Christ in der Welt. Aschaffenburg: Pattloch, 1973.

Schlosser, Jacques. "Ancien Testament et Christologie Dans La Prima Petri.'" In *Études Sur La Première Lettre de Pierre*, edited by Charles Perrot, 65–96. Lectio Divina 102. Paris: Éd. du Cerf, 1980.

Schmidt, Karl Matthias. *Mahnung und Erinnerung im Maskenspiel: Epistolographie, Rhetorik und Narrativik der pseudepigraphen Petrusbriefe*. Herders Biblische Studien 38. Freiburg: Herder, 2003.

Schrage, Wolfgang. *Das Verhältnis des Thomas-Evangeliums zur synoptischen Tradition und zu den koptischen Evangelienübersetzungen. Zugleich ein Beitrag zur gnostischen Synoptikerdeutung.* ZNTW 29. Berlin: Töpelmann, 1964.

Schreiner, Thomas R. *1, 2 Peter, Jude.* New American Commentary. Nashville: B&H, 2003.

Schreiner, Thomas R., and Shawn D. Wright, eds. *Believer's Baptism: Sign of the New Covenant in Christ.* NAC Studies in Bible & Theology. Nashville: B&H, 2006.

Schultz, Richard L. *The Search for Quotation: Verbal Parallels in the Prophets.* Journal for the Study of the Old Testament Supplement Series 180. Sheffield: Sheffield, 1999.

Schürmann, Heinz. *Jesu Abschiedsrede Lk 22, 21–38.* Münster: Aschendorff, 1977.

Schutter, William L. *Hermeneutic and Composition in I Peter.* Tübingen: Mohr Siebeck, 1989.

Seeberg, Alfred. *Der Katechismus Der Urchristenheit.* Theologische Bücherei 26. Leipzig: Kaiser, 1966.

Seesemann, Heinrich. "Πειράζω." In *Theological Dictionary of the New Testament*, edited by Gerhard Kittel et al. Grand Rapids: Eerdmans, 1964.

Seland, Torrey. "Resident Aliens in Mission: Missional Practices in the Emerging Church of 1 Peter." *Bulletin for Biblical Research* 19 (2009) 565–89.

Selwyn, Edward Gordon. *The First Epistle of St. Peter.* London: Macmillan, 1946.

———. "Unsolved New Testament Problems: The Problem of the Authorship of I Peter." *Expository Times* 59 (1948) 256–58.

Senior, Donald, and Daniel J. Harrington. *1 Peter, Jude, and 2 Peter.* Sacra Pagina. Collegeville, MN: Liturgical, 2003.

Shimada, K. "The Formulary Material in First Peter. A Study according to the Method of Traditionsgeschichte." PhD diss., Union Theological Seminary, 1966.

Silva, Moisés, ed. *New International Dictionary of New Testament Theology and Exegesis.* Grand Rapids: Zondervan, 2014.

Sisti, A. "La Vita Cristiana Nell'attesa Della Parusia (1 Piet. 4,7–11)." *Bibbia E Oriente* 7 (1965) 123–28.

Snodgrass, Klyne R. "I Peter II. 1–10: Its Formation and Literary Affinities." *New Testament Studies* 24 (1977) 97–106.

———. "The Parable of the Wicked Husbandmen: Is the Gospel of Thomas Version the Original?" *New Testament Studies* 21 (1974) 142–44.

Soden, Hermann von. *Hand-commentar zum Neuen Testament.* Freiburg: Mohr Siebeck, 1893.

Sommer, Benjamin D. "Exegesis, Allusion, and Intertextuality in the Hebrew Bible: A Response to Lyle Eslinger." *Vetus Testamentum* 46.4 (1996) 479–89.

———. *A Prophet Reads Scripture: Allusion in Isaiah 40–66.* Stanford: Stanford University Press, 1998.

Spence, H. D. M. *1 Peter.* Edited by Joseph S. Excell. Pulpit Commentary. New York: Funk & Wagnalls, 1909.

Spicq, Ceslas. "La Ia Petri et Le Témoignage Évangélique de Saint Pierre." *Studia Theologica—Nordic Journal of Theology* 20 (1966) 37–61.

———. *Les Épîtres de Saint Pierre.* Sources bibliques. Paris: Gabalda, 1966.

———. "Prière, Charité, Justice . . . et Fin Des Temps (I Pet 4:7–11)." *Assemblées du Seigneur* 50 (1966) 15–29.

Stählin, Gustav. "Ἐξαιτέω." In *Theological Dictionary of the New Testament*, edited by Gerhard Kittel et al. Grand Rapids: Eerdmans, 1964.

Stanley, Christopher D. *Arguing with Scripture: The Rhetoric of Quotations in the Letters of Paul*. New York: T. & T. Clark, 2004.

———. *Paul and the Language of Scripture: Citation Technique in the Pauline Epistles and Contemporary Literature*. Cambridge: Cambridge University Press, 1992.

Stanton, Graham. "Jesus Traditions." In *Dictionary of the Later New Testament & Its Developments*, edited by Peter H. Davids and Ralph P. Martin. Downers Grove, IL: InterVarsity, 1997.

Stead, Michael R. *The Intertextuality of Zechariah 1–8*. New York: Bloomsbury, 2009.

Stein, Robert H. *Luke*. New American Commentary. Nashville: B&H, 1992.

Stendahl, Krister. *The School of St. Matthew and Its Use of the Old Testament*. Philadelphia: Fortress, 1968.

Stewart, Robert B., et al. *Memories of Jesus: A Critical Appraisal of James D. G. Dunn's Jesus Remembered*. Nashville: B&H, 2010.

Stibbs, Alan Marshall. *The First Epistle General of Peter*. Tyndale New Testament Commentaries. Grand Rapids: Eerdmans, 1959.

Strecker, Georg. "Μακάριος." In *Exegetical Dictionary of the New Testament*, edited by Horst Balz and Gerhard Schneider. Grand Rapids: Eerdmans, 1990.

Streeter, Burnett Hillman. *The Primitive Church: Studied with Special Reference to the Origins of the Christian Ministry*. New York: Macmillan, 1929.

Strobel, August. *Untersuchungen zum eschatologischen Verzögerungsproblem: auf Grund der spätjüdischurchristlichen Geschichte von Habakkuk 2:2 FF*. Boston: Brill, 1961.

Stuhlmacher, Peter. *Biblische Theologie Des Neuen Testaments. I. Grundlegung Von Paulus Zu Jesus*. 2nd ed. Göttingen: Vandenhoeck & Ruprecht, 1997.

———. "Jesus Tradition Im Römerbrief, Eine Skizze." *Theologische Beiträge* 14 (1983) 240–50.

Talbert, Charles H., ed. *Perspectives on First Peter*. Eugene, OR: Wipf & Stock, 2010.

Tenney, Merrill C. "Some Possible Parallels between 1 Peter and John." In *New Dimensions in New Testament Study*, edited by Richard N. Longenecker and Merrill C. Tenney, 370–77. Grand Rapids: Zondervan, 1974.

Thils, Gustave. *L'Enseignement de saint Pierre*. Paris: Gabalda, 1943.

Thompson, Michael. *Clothed with Christ: The Example and Teaching of Jesus in Romans 12.1–15.13*. Library of New Testament Studies 59. Sheffield: JSOT, 1991.

———. "The Holy Internet: Communication between Churches in the First Christian Generation." In *The Gospels for All Christians: Rethinking the Gospel Audiences*, edited by Richard Bauckham, 49–70. Grand Rapids: Eerdmans, 1998.

Thurén, Lauri. *Argument and Theology in 1 Peter: The Origins of Christian Paraenesis*. Journal for the Study of the New Testament Supplement Series 114. Sheffield: JSOT, 1995.

Tite, Philip L. "Nurslings, Milk, and Moral Development in the Greco-Roman Context: A Reappraisal of the Paraenetic Utilization of Metaphor 1 Peter 2.1–3." *Journal for the Study of the New Testament* 31.4 (2009) 371–400.

Trench, Richard Chenevix. *Synonyms of the New Testament*. 7th ed. London: Macmillan, 1871.

Unnik, W. C. van. "Christianity according to 1 Peter." In vol. 2 of *Sparsa Collecta*, 111–22. Novum Testamentum 30. Boston: Brill, 1980.

———. "A Parallel to I Peter II 14 and 20." In vol. 2 of *Sparsa Collecta* 106–10. Novum Testamentum 30. Boston: Brill, 1980.

———. "The Redemption in I Peter I 18-19 and the Problem of the First Epistle of Peter." In vol. 2 of *Sparsa Collecta* 3-82. Novum Testamentum 30. Boston: Brill, 1980.

———. "The Teaching of Good Works in I Peter." *New Testament Studies* 1 (1954) 92-110.

Vahrenhorst, Martin. *Der Erste Brief Des Petrus*. Theologischer Kommentar Zum Neuen Testament. Stuttgart: Kohlhammer, 2015.

Vanhoozer, Kevin J. *Is There a Meaning in This Text? The Bible, the Reader, and the Morality of Literary Knowledge*. Grand Rapids: Zondervan, 2009.

Villiers, J. L. de. "Joy in Suffering in 1 Peter." *Neotestamentica* 9 (1975) 64-86.

Vinson, Richard Bolling, et al. *1 & 2 Peter, Jude*. Smyth & Helwys Bible Commentary. Macon, GA: Smyth & Helwys, 2010.

Vlach, Michael J. *Has the Church Replaced Israel? A Theological Evaluation*. Nashville: B&H, 2010.

Vögtle, Anton. *Die Tugend- und Lasterkataloge im Neuen Testament exegetisch, religions- und formgeschichtlich untersucht*. Münster: Aschendorff, 1936.

Wachob, W. H. *The Voice of Jesus in the Social Rhetoric of James*. Society for New Testament Studies Monograph Series 106. Cambridge: Cambridge University Press, 2000.

Wachob, W. H., and L. T. Johnson. "The Sayings of Jesus in the Letter of James." In *Authenticating the Words of Jesus*, edited by Bruce Chilton and Craig A. Evans, 431-50. Boston: Brill, 2002.

Wagner, J. Ross. *Heralds of the Good News: Isaiah and Paul in Concert in the Letter to the Romans*. Boston: Brill, 2003.

Wallace, Daniel B. *Greek Grammar beyond the Basics*. Grand Rapids: Zondervan, 1996.

Walter, Nikolaus. "Paul and the Early Christian Jesus-Tradition." In *Paul and Jesus*, edited by A. J. M. Wedderburn, 51-80. Sheffield: Sheffield, 1989.

Waltner, Erland, and Charles, J. Daryl. *1-2 Peter, Jude*. Scottdale, PA: Herald, 1999.

Wand, J. W. C. *The General Epistles of St. Peter and St. Jude*. Westminster Commentaries. London: Methuen, 1934.

Watson, Duane F. "Early Jesus Tradition in 1 Peter 3:18-22." In *James, 1 & 2 Peter, and Early Jesus Traditions*, edited by Alicia J. Batten and John S. Kloppenborg, 123-50. Library of New Testament Studies. London: T. & T. Clark, 2014.

———. "The Prophets of 1 Peter 1:10-12." *Restoration Quarterly* 31 (1989) 1-12.

Watson, Duane F., and Terrance Callan. *First and Second Peter*. Paideia. Grand Rapids: Baker, 2012.

Watts, Rikki E. "Jesus' Death, Isaiah 53, and Mark 10:45: A Crux Revisited." In *Jesus and the Suffering Servant: Isaiah 53 and Christian Origins*, edited by William H. Bellinger Jr. and William R. Farmer, 125-51. Eugene, OR: Wipf & Stock, 2009.

Wedderburn, A. J. M. "Paul and Jesus: The Problem of Continuity." *Scottish Journal of Theology* 38 (1985) 189-203.

———. "Paul and Jesus: Similarity and Continuity." *New Testament Studies* 34 (1988) 161-82.

Wellum, Stephen J. "Baptism and the Relationship Between the Covenants." In *Believer's Baptism: Sign of the New Covenant in Christ*, edited by Thomas R. Schreiner and Shawn D. Wright, 97-161. NAC Studies in Bible & Theology. Nashville: B&H, 2006.

Wenham, David. "Paul's Use of the Jesus Tradition: Three Samples." In *The Jesus Tradition outside the Gospels*, edited by David Wenham, 7–38. Gospel Perspectives 5. Sheffield: JSOT, 1980.

Westfall, Cynthia Long "The Relationship between the Resurrection, the Proclamation to the Spirits in Prison, and Baptismal Regeneration: 1 Peter 3:19–22." In *Resurrection*, edited by S. E. Porter et al., 106–35. Sheffield: Sheffield Academic, 1999.

Weyde, Karl William. "Inner-Biblical Interpretation: Methodological Reflections on the Relationship between Texts in the Hebrew Bible." *Svensk exegetisk årsbok* 70 (2005) 287–300.

Wibbing, S. *Die Tugend- und Lasterkataloge im Neuen Testament und ihre Traditionsgeschichte unter besonderer Berücksichtigung der Qumran-Texte*. Beihefte für die Neutestam 25. Berlin: Töpelmann, 1959.

Wilkes, C. G. "The Synoptic Tradition in 1 Peter: An Investigation into Its Forms and Development." PhD diss., Southwestern Baptist Theological Seminary, 1985.

Williams, Jocelyn A. "A Case Study in Intertextuality: The Place of Isaiah in the 'Stone' Sayings of 1 Peter 2." *The Reformed Theological Review* 66.1 (2007) 37–55.

Williams, Travis B. *Good Works in 1 Peter: Negotiating Social Conflict and Christian Identity in the Greco-Roman World*. Tübingen: Mohr Siebeck, 2014.

———. "Intertextuality and Methodological Bias: Prolegomena to the Evaluation of Source Materials in I Peter." *Journal for the Study of the New Testament* 39 (2016) 169–87.

———. *Persecution in 1 Peter: Differentiating and Contextualizing Early Christian Suffering*. Boston: Brill, 2012.

———. "Suffering from a Critical Oversight: The Persecutions of 1 Peter within Modern Scholarship." *Currents in Biblical Research* 10 (2012) 275–92.

Wimsatt, W. K., and M. C. Beardsley. "The Intentional Fallacy." *The Sewanee Review* 54.3 (1946) 468–88.

Windisch, Hans. *Die Katholischen Briefe*. Vol. 15. 3rd ed. Handbuch zum Neuen Testament. Tübingen: Mohr Siebeck, 1951.

Witherington, Ben, III. *Letters and Homilies for Hellenized Christians: A Socio-Rhetorical Commentary on 1–2 Peter*. Vol. 2. Downers Grove, IL: InterVarsity, 2007.

Woan, Susan Ann. "The Psalms in 1 Peter." In *The Psalms in the New Testament*, edited by Steve Moyise and Maarten J. J. Menken, 213–30. New York: T. & T. Clark, 2004.

———. "The Use of the Old Testament in 1 Peter, with Especial Focus on the Role of Psalm 34." PhD diss., University of Exeter, 2008.

Won, Hyun Chul. "The Date of Mark's Gospel: A Perspective on Its Eschatological Expectation." PhD diss., University of Birmingham, 2009.

Wong, Theron K. "The Use of Jesus' Sayings in 1 Peter." PhD diss., Dallas Theological Seminary, 2008.

Young, Brad H. *Meet the Rabbis: Rabbinic Thought and the Teachings of Jesus*. Grand Rapids: Baker, 2007.

Young, Stephen E. *Jesus Tradition in the Apostolic Fathers: Their Explicit Appeals to the Words of Jesus in Light of Orality Studies*. Wissenschaftliche Untersuchungen zum Neuen Testament 311. Tübingen: Mohr Siebeck, 2011.

www.ingramcontent.com/pod-product-compliance
Lightning Source LLC
Chambersburg PA
CBHW071240230426
43668CB00011B/1521